D0930467

REAL ESTATE FINANCE

SECOND EDITION

PHILLIP T KOLBE
GAYLON E. GREER | HENRY G. RUDNER III

President: Mehul Patel
Vice President of Product Development & Publishing: Evan M. Butterfield
Editorial Director: Kate DeVivo
Development Editor: Liz Austin
Director of Production: Daniel Frey
Production Editor: Caitlin Ostrow
Production Artist: Virginia Byrne
Creative Director: Lucy Jenkins
Director of Product Management: Melissa Kleeman

Published by Dearborn™ Real Estate Education
30 South Wacker Drive
Chicago, Illinois 60606-7481
(312) 836-4400
www.dearbornRE.com

The Library of Congress has cataloged the first edition as follows:

Kolbe, Phillip T.
   Real estate finance / Phillip T. Kolbe, Gaylon E. Greer, Henry G. Rudner III—1st ed.
      p. cm.
   Includes bibliographical references and index.
   ISBN 0-7931-6593-8
   1. Mortgage loans. 2. Mortgage banks. 3. Real property—Finance. 4. Housing—Finance. 5. Real estate business. I. Greer, Gaylon E. II. Rudner, Henry G. III. Title.
HG2040.K65 2003
332.7'2—dc21   2003010223

Second edition ISBN-13: 978-1-4277-6760-8
Second edition ISBN-10:   1-4277-6760-2

Dedication

To our beautiful brides whose love and understanding were felt and appreciated during the many hours of writing and rewriting.

CONTENTS

PART ONE

The Real Estate Lending Environment

v

C H A P T E R 5

Capital Costs and the Incentive to Borrow—Leverage   102

C H A P T E R 6

Sources and Uses of Real Estate Credit   122

C H A P T E R 7

Government's Role in Mortgage Markets   152

PART TWO

The Borrowing and Lending Decisions   171

CHAPTER 8

Alternative Financing Methods and Products   172

CHAPTER 9

Calculating Mortgage Values and Yields   194

CHAPTER 10

Residential Borrowing and Lending Decisions   210

Observe constantly that all things take place by change, and accustom thyself to consider that the nature of the Universe loves nothing so much as to change the things which are and to make new things like them.

Marcus Aurelius Antoninus. (121–180). *The Meditations of Marcus Aurelius.* The Harvard Classics. 1909–1914. Reprinted by permission of Bartleby.com, Inc.

Is yet another book about real estate finance really necessary? Existing books run the gamut from the "no-money-down, get-rich-quick" genre to academic treatments of the mathematics and theory of finance. Yet, as one studies the financing of real estate, its dynamic nature becomes increasingly clear. Real estate investors in general and the financial market in particular have learned to pay close attention to change The debt and equity markets are constantly changing and evolving to accommodate the needs of borrowers, lenders, and equity investors. Over the years congressional tinkering with federal tax laws, inflation, the S&L debacle, the subprime mortgage crisis, and, of course, the Federal Reserve have at one time or another all rocked or attempted to right the real estate finance boat. Sometimes it seemed that capsize was imminent but, as always, the markets adapted to change and moved on.

This text is divided into three sections, grouped by the nature of the content.

▌PART ONE: THE REAL ESTATE LENDING ENVIRONMENT

This part has two objectives:

1. Introduce the nature of real estate borrowing and lending, provide a historical framework that will help readers understand the current environment and the events that led to it, and introduce the organization and content of the text. This is accomplished in Chapter 1: The Borrowing and Lending Kaleidoscope.

2. Explain the organizational structure of the mortgage lending market, introduce the major players and what motivates them, and show the economic and government forces that influence the cost and availability of mortgage loans. This is accomplished in Chapters 2 through 7: Credit Instruments, Credit Procedures, Interest Rate Determinants,

Capital Costs and the Incentive to Borrow—Leverage, Sources and Uses of Real Estate Credit, and Government's Role in Mortgage Markets.

PART TWO: THE BORROWING AND LENDING DECISIONS

This section explains the "nuts-and-bolts" of borrowing and lending. It presents analysis of alternative financing, mortgage yields and values, and the key decisions on loans, and addresses the issue of problem loans. This is accomplished in Chapters 8 through 11: Alternative Financing Methods and Products, Calculating Mortgage Values and Yields, Residential Borrowing and Lending Decisions, and Problem Loans and Foreclosures.

PART THREE: CONSTRUCTION AND COMMERCIAL FINANCING

Having set the stage by presenting the economic and legal environment and the borrowing and lending decisions of residential mortgages, the narrative proceeds to the logical next step of explaining contruction and commercial financing. This is covered in Chapters 12 through 16: Development and Construction Financing, Developing and Analyzing the Income Property Operating Statement, Traditional Approaches to Measuring Property Value, Complex Property Valuation Problems, and Real Estate Value from the Borrower's Perspective.

ORGANIZATION

- Each chapter opens with a Learning Objectives section that clearly describes the information students will acquire.
- The key terms discussed in each chapter appear in boldface for emphasis. These terms are defined in the end-of-book Glossary.
- A variety of tables and illustrative diagrams are provided throughout the text to clarify the concepts under discussion.
- To help students review their understanding of the primary concepts, each chapter ends with a Summary.
- Insightful Review Questions, Discussion Questions, and Problems are provided at the end of each chapter.
- Though the chapters cover the topics in some depth, they cannot exhaust the topics covered. Many of the chapters could be expanded into a book of their own. For the students who wish to delve deeper into a particular topic, each chapter contains a Recommended Reading list.

Multiple Uses

While developing this text, the authors recognized that there may be many uses for the book. While the principal use may be for undergraduate real estate finance classes, the authors realized that instructors follow many teaching paths. The book is organized in such a way as to give instructors different options in the sequencing of chapters. The Instructor's Manual provides several alternative paths and provides suggestions for using the book. Many schools offer only one course that combines real estate finance and investments. Budgetary constraints prohibit the use of two texts. Commercial real estate is integrated fully into the text, and the analysis of commercial real estate in the final section of this text provides much of the material needed by professors who teach the dual course. Furthermore, Dearborn Real Estate Education offers a discounted package of *Real Estate Finance* and *Investment Analyses for Real Estate Decisions* for students in the dual course.

Many practitioners have asked the authors for a book that can be utilized for those new employees who need an understanding of real estate finance. The authors incorporated these requests into this text and kept these users in mind during its development.

INSTRUCTOR SUPPORT

For instructors, we have developed an extensive package of support materials that can be accessed and downloaded (with password) from the publisher's Web site at *www.dearbornre.com*. These support materials include:

- Detailed lecture notes, including Chapter Purpose, Learning Objectives, and a Lecture Outline, in Microsoft PowerPoint and PDF format for each chapter
- Suggested answers to the end-of-chapter Review Questions, Discussion Questions, and Problems
- A vast multiple-choice test bank for creating customized assignments and examinations

In addition, the test-building software Microtest® is available to instructors by contacting your sales representative.

FINANCIAL TEMPLATE CD-ROM

Included in the back of the book is a Financial Template CD-ROM that can be used to help solve end-of-chapter questions and problems, as well as add further insight and illustration for certain topics within the text. When material is available on the CD-ROM, the following icon will appear in the margin:

■ ACKNOWLEDGMENTS

We sincerely thank all of the people who provided comments and suggestions that have provided guidance and suggestions in creating this text. This edition of *Real Estate Finance* was reviewed by Dr. Karen Eilers Lahey, University of Akron, and Richard J. Madden, Wind Point Presentations, Inc. The first edition was reviewed by Mark A. Sunderman, University of Wyoming; Abdullah Yavas, Pennsylvania State University; and Emily Norman Zietz, Middle Tennessee State University.

The authors would also like to thank Keith Schmitt, John Farley, Anna Thasdottir, Kevin Hallquist, Mustafa Kayali, Matthew Powell, Brian Jones, and Holliday Jones, all of whom were critical to our success. All of the recommendations and reactions from our students are also greatly appreciated.

Phillip T. Kolbe, PhD, is the Director of Graduate Studies in Real Estate at the University of Memphis, one of the few schools in the country to offer a master's degree in real estate. He has taught for more than 30 years, starting at the University of Arizona while he was the president of a real estate research corporation and CEO of a real estate market research firm. Kolbe has twice received the University of Memphis's Distinguished Teaching Award and was the first recipient of the Thomas W. Briggs Foundation Excellence in Teaching Award. In total, he has received ten teaching awards during his academic career. He serves as a consultant to a wide variety of real estate companies and has published numerous articles and several books on real estate and investing. Kolbe also teaches companies "Executive Leadership Lessons from General Ulysses S. Grant," where he portrays the Civil War general.

Gaylon E. Greer, MAI, PhD, is a real estate consultant, writer, and educator. He holds the MAI designation from the Appraisal Institute, is a Certified General Appraiser in Tennessee, and has served on that state's appraiser regulatory commission. Greer has written several books related to real estate, contributes regularly to professional journals, and is active in the American Real Estate Society and other professional organizations. Greer lectures to investors and professional practitioners on a nationwide basis. He recently resigned from the Morris S. Fogelman Chair of Excellence in Real Estate at the University of Memphis to devote full time to writing and consulting.

Henry G. Rudner III, CCIM, is the CEO of AmPro Industries. He was the Senior Director, Dispositions for Storage USA, the second largest company in the self-storage industry. He has more than 30 years of real-world experience in real estate, ranging from acquisition to zoning, commercial real estate brokerage to development. In addition to experience developing, acquiring, and selling self-storage properties, Rudner has done numerous hotel, retail, and retirement housing transactions. He holds the Certified Commercial Investment Member (CCIM) designation. His articles have been published in *Real Estate Review* and the *Commercial Investment Real Estate Journal*.

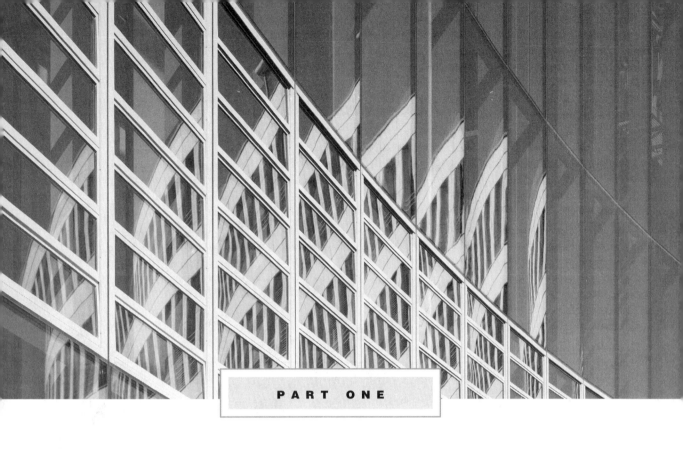

PART ONE

The Real Estate Lending Environment

Financial markets have gone through tremendous change and have been transformed by those transitions. Students of real estate finance must understand the historical framework of borrowing and lending in order to comprehend the current status in the industry. Part One introduces the nature of real estate borrowing and lending, as well as the organization and content of the book. It also illustrates the government and economic forces that influence the cost and availability of mortgage loan funds and examines the influences of the federal government in the mortgage market. Furthermore, it explains the organizational structure of the real estate lending market and the major players in it.

The Borrowing and Lending Kaleidoscope

After studying this chapter, you should understand the relationship between real estate finance and real estate investment and see how changes in the legal and institutional environment have altered the nature of real estate investment and finance decisions. You should also understand how various chapters in the book relate to and build upon each other.

An artificial dichotomy splits real estate studies into **finance,** which usually means borrowing and lending, and **investments.** Yet real estate lending is as much an investment as the **buying** of real estate itself. Moreover, real estate sellers often advance funds to buyers—a practice that makes them as much lenders as are commercial banks and other lending institutions. This inherent unity of lending and financing requires that practitioners and researchers approach the topic in terms of a common denominator; they need an analytical approach that is universally applicable.

Underlying all financial and investment decision making is that fact that money has time value. Because money earns interest, a dollar to be received in a year has a smaller value than a dollar-in-hand today. Failure to thoroughly understand this simple concept will render much of the material in this text utterly incomprehensible. Accordingly, a detailed discussion of the concept of compounding interest and its inverse, discounting, may be found in Appendix B: Mathematics of Compounding and Discounting. Appendix C: Compounding and Discounting with Financial Calculators illustrates the use of these calculators to work out today's common financial problems. Any student not thoroughly comfortable with these concepts should review those sections of the appendixes.

▌ THROUGH THE KALEIDOSCOPE, LIGHTLY

To casual observers, real estate capital markets are suggestive of the symmetrical color patterns seen through the viewing end of a kaleidoscope. Everything seems ordered and clear. There are lenders and there are borrowers, and the latter group mixes borrowed funds with personal resources to acquire title to real estate.

Closer examination, however, gives a different impression, more like looking through the *other* end of the kaleidoscope, where the random bits of colored glass are a jumble and the view obscured. From this perspective, patterns are less discernable. Borrowers, lenders, and equity investors are mixed together almost randomly. Indeed, borrowers are seen as intermittent lenders, and lenders are constant borrowers, and all are investors motivated by a return on investment (yield). Yet one thing is clear: interest paid by a borrower is return of *and on* invested capital to a lender; one is dependent on the other in the exchange.

With changing market conditions and personal fortunes, investors sometimes shift operational emphasis from borrowing to lending, then from lending to equity investing, and quickly back again. These institutional realities often confuse the traditional practice of compartmentalizing real estate market participants. Investing and financing decisions are inextricably linked, and lending is as much an investment decision as is acquiring title to real estate. To divide real estate studies into separate finance and investment compartments is to risk omitting vital pieces of the pattern.

Finding order in this seeming hodgepodge of the marketplace requires that common themes be identified. Indeed, there is a unifying factor that drives all rational financial decisions: the relationship between fund costs, investment yield expectations, and perceived risk. On this foundation, subsequent chapters build a framework that helps us to understand how real estate capital markets function and how various activities and institutions fit into the grand design. Interest is the cost of borrowed money. Because credit far exceeds equity funds channeled into real estate, borrowing costs are critical factors determining the supply side of the real estate supply and demand equation.

The real estate lending environment is further examined in the next chapters of the first part of this book. The functions of notes and mortgages and the key provisions of common mortgage instruments are described in Chapter 2, followed by the explanation of the credit procedures for approving loans in Chapter 3. Chapter 4 explains how interest rates are determined in our economy. Chapter 5 analyzes borrowing and investing incentives in terms of the difference between the cost of funds and the expected return on assets. Chapter 6 explains how capital is accumulated and channeled through financial intermediaries into various real estate ventures. Since the severe economic depression of the 1930s, the federal government has played a large—sometimes a dominant—role in real estate finance. Its influence on investment and ownership decisions has been pervasive. Chapter 7 details one extensive dimension of that role: the government's influence on mortgage markets.

Institutional borrowing and lending decisions are the focus of the second part of this book. Alternative financing methods are examined in Chapter 8. Chapter 9 demonstrates the calculations of market value and yield of a mortgage. Chapter 10 is devoted to the owner-occupied-residence loan. Chapter 11 explains what happens when things go wrong in the lending and repayment process, as they all too often do.

The final part of the book analyzes construction and commercial financing. The unique financing required for development and construction is the focus of Chapter 12. Chapter 13 introduces analysis of commercial loans with the development of the operating statement for income property. The traditional approaches to measuring property value are examined in Chapter 14, and complex property valuation problems are explained in Chapter 15. The final chapter is dedicated to the analysis of real estate value from the borrower's perspective.

THE MANY FACES OF REAL ESTATE INVESTING

Real estate market participants face a daunting array of alternatives. They can speculate in real estate futures—either to hedge a position or to satisfy a primordial instinct to gamble—by buying and selling options on property. Investors who prefer fixed-income assets can buy mortgage-backed promissory notes or acquire buildings that are under long-term leases to financially secure tenants. Desire for liquidity can be appeased by investing in securitized real estate assets, such as shares in real estate investment trusts (REITs) or pass-through mortgage loan certificates. *Securitization* is simply the process of converting assets into financial instruments.

Figure 1.1 organizes alternatives according to the degree of involvement in operations and the nature of claims. **Passive** investors simply put money at risk and hope for the best. They have no control over operations and therefore are unable to influence the course of events. **Active** investors, in contrast, make decisions (hiring and firing employees, setting policies, and approving major expenditures, for example) that significantly influence a venture's fortunes.

FIGURE 1.1 | Variety in Real Estate Investment Opportunities

	Debt	Equity
Active	Mortgage Origination: • Construction • Take Out • Junior Lien Secondary Mortgage Market	Direct Investment: • Apartment Building • Offices • Warehouses • Shopping Centers • Industrial Parks • Other
Passive	Pass-through Securities Real Estate Investment Trusts Real Estate Mortgage Investment Conduits	Limited Partnerships Real Estate Investment Trusts Real Estate Corporations

Those who take a debt position lend money—either directly or indirectly—and expect to recover their principal with interest. Equity investors acquire an actual ownership interest in real estate assets. The ownership may be direct—title may be in their own names—or may be represented by an interest in an entity that holds title. The lower left quadrant of Figure 1.1 illustrates some of the alternatives available to investors who take a passive position in real estate–related credit instruments. They can buy securities that represent a participatory interest in a package of mortgage-secured promissory notes or that represent an ownership interest in a company that makes loans or acquires promissory notes in the secondary mortgage market. The specific assets listed in this quadrant (pass-through securities, real estate investment trust shares, and real estate mortgage investment conduits) are explored in later chapters.

Moving clockwise around Figure 1.1, we next consider active investment in real estate–related debt. Investors who elect this sector either originate mortgage-secured loans or buy mortgage-secured notes in the secondary mortgage market. These positions are, as we have seen, investments in every sense of the term.

Active investment in real estate equities, depicted in the upper right quadrant of Figure 1.1, implies direct ownership of real property, with operational control either directly or through hired management. Yields depend not only on how much one pays for assets but also on one's cost of capital and the mix of equity and borrowed funds. How efficiently the property is operated, the market, and the amount of competition, of course, also significantly affect investment yields.

Positions in real estate equities without management control are depicted in the lower right quadrant of Figure 1.1. Common examples include limited partnership shares in real estate syndicates and ownership shares in corporations or real estate investment trusts that own real estate equities. These investment vehicles are also discussed in later chapters.

Participants in the various quadrants of Figure 1.1 constantly interact. For example, those who make direct investments in real property (the upper right quadrant) often raise equity funds by selling securities to passive investors (the lower right quadrant) and borrow money by issuing mortgage-secured promissory notes to active investors in debt instruments (the upper left quadrant). Active investors in debt instruments often raise funds by selling both debt and equity securities to passive investors (the two bottom quadrants).

Moreover, only rarely will an investor's activities be confined to a single quadrant. Thus, an equity investor who sells a property will often take back a promissory note in part payment and thereby move solidly into the active debt quadrant. While accumulating liquid reserves for future ventures, active equity and active debt investors often hold real estate–related securities, and thus move into one of the two lower quadrants.

Recent developments have blurred many of the distinctions between equity and debt positions. Credit instruments are typically favored by investors who want predictable, regular cash dividends. Yet the same goal can be pursued by direct ownership of real estate that is rented under a long-term net lease (a lease under which tenants pay operating expenses) to a creditworthy tenant. Conversely, contemporary mortgage lenders often receive debt service payments that vary with an index of general interest rates, such as the ten-year T-bill rate or the London Inter Bank Offered Rate (LIBOR). Some also participate in any increase in the market value of real estate pledged as security for loans. With this latter arrangement, lenders get a fixed rate of return (from below-market interest rates) and additional return from a percentage of appreciation and/or annual income.

EVOLVING INSTITUTIONS AND MARKET TURMOIL

Before the early 1970s, commercial real estate lending practices evolved only modestly over several decades. Debt financing of up to 95 percent of required funds was frequently available. Mortgage-secured loans (other than for construction and development) were almost always payable in equal monthly installments over 25 to 30 years, with interest rates fixed for the entire term. For some classes of properties, loans were on a nonrecourse basis; borrowers were not personally liable for repayment. By the 1990s, with the emergence of conduit financing provided by commercial mortgage-backed securities (CMBS) as a popular form of financing, nonrecourse commercial real estate loans once again became readily available. (Chapter 6 discusses conduit financing and the evolution of real estate lending.)

In such an environment, all lenders knew their place: thrifts (savings and loan associations and savings banks) financed one- to four-family home loans, primarily in their own communities; commercial banks specialized in short-term commercial credit and construction and development loans; life insurance companies concentrated on long-term financing for income properties. The industry was predictable and generally profitable, if relatively unexciting.

During the last half of the 1970s, the pace of change in real estate financing practices and institutions accelerated to a level that was described in a Brookings Institute study as a revolution.[1] That study, published in 1985, ascribed the revolution to factors such as escalating interest rates and lowered average yields on equity capital, intensified competition among lending institutions, partial deregulation of financial markets, and loss of favored income tax treatment for owners of rental real estate. Since the study was published, the cumulative effect of these phenomena and others has intensified and created fiscal stress and dislocation among lending institutions unprecedented since the economic turmoil of the 1930s. This was particularly evident during the years from 1980 through 1994. That this revolution continues unabated can be seen by typing "revolution in real estate finance" into any of the popular Internet search engines.

Stimulative Tax Legislation

In a belated response to the brief economic recession of early 1980, Congress passed the **Economic Recovery Tax Act of 1981 (ERTA)**, which substantially increased the already significant income tax incentives to invest in real estate. Among other things, ERTA permitted investors to claim annual income tax deductions to recover their entire investment in buildings and other improvements to real estate over as little as 15 years, with the bulk of the deductions accruing during the early years. Prior to ERTA this was called **depreciation.** The term was technically changed by ERTA to **cost recovery**, though one still hears real estate practitioners using the old term. The law also reduced marginal income tax rates and introduced attractive new tax credits for rehabilitating older buildings.

A Syndication Explosion

Although real estate limited partnerships began to appear as early as the 1950s, they blossomed in earnest in the 1970s and then accelerated dramatically with passage of ERTA, which often made the tax-avoidance opportunities in real estate more important than its income-earning potential. Publicly registered real estate limited partnerships experienced a compound annual growth rate of about 34 percent for ten years, reaching a zenith of about $8.5 billion in 1986.

Deregulation

During the early 1980s, many government-imposed restraints on the activities that various financial institutions could undertake were removed. Legal ceilings on interest rates paid to savers and depositors by depository institutions were lifted (see the paragraph on usury laws, later), and a much wider variety of mortgage lending arrangements were permitted. Thrifts were permitted to expand the range of financial instruments in which they dealt and the range of investments that they undertook.

In 1980, inflation (the annual rate of increase in the general level of prices) reached 12.5 percent, and the prime lending rate (the rate of interest charged by banks to customers who have the best credit ratings) climbed to an astonishing 21.5 percent. Savers responded by accelerating the pace at which they shifted funds out of banks and thrifts and into bonds and money market mutual funds, a practice that had been growing gradually since the 1960s. This created a liquidity crisis for the lending institutions, and it was in this environment that Congress began tinkering with the long-standing regulatory structure.

In March 1980, Congress passed and President Jimmy Carter signed into law the **Depository Institutions Deregulation and Monetary Control Act.** The act phased out, over a six-year period, limitations on the maximum rates of interest and dividends that depository institutions could pay on deposits and accounts. This could be thought of as a phasing out of usury laws—in reverse. (Though usury laws vary by jurisdiction, in general, they are prohibitions against the charging of exorbitant rates of interest for the loan of money. Usury laws have existed in one form or another in many cultures for thousands of years. In the Old Testament, for example, see Exod. 22:25, Lev. 25:36–37, and Deut. 23:19–20.) It also eliminated geographic limitations on the areas within which institutions could make mortgage loans, and it authorized banks, thrift institutions, and credit unions to offer Negotiable Order of Withdrawal (NOW) accounts, which were the equivalent of interest-bearing checking accounts.

But perhaps most significantly, the act raised the **Federal Deposit Insurance Corporation (FDIC)** coverage for all types of deposits by 150 percent; from $40,000 per account, where it had been fixed in 1974, to $100,000, where it still is today. This gave rise to what are known as **brokered deposits**. Frequently referred to as "hot money," these are funds collected by brokerage firms and deposited in the highest-yielding federally insured certificates of deposit (CDs) that can be found.

With these changes, depository institutions were able to compete more effectively with money market mutual funds. Corporations, pension funds, foreign investors, and wealthy individuals could now deposit an unlimited amount of funds, in $100,000 units, in accounts earning market rates of interest and fully insured by an agency of the federal government.

As money began pouring in to thrift institutions, their liquidity problem was, at least temporarily, abated. But now they found themselves in a profitability squeeze. They had to pay an ever-increasing interest rate to compete for funds, even though their mortgage portfolios, for the most part, locked them into long-term, low-rate loans.

The congressional answer to the institutions' continuing, simmering difficulty was the **Garn-St. Germain Depository Institutions Act of 1982**, which removed all remaining regulatory constraints on maximum rates of interest commercial banks and thrifts could pay for deposits. That act also doubled the portion of their assets that federally chartered depository institutions could put into commercial real estate loans, from 20 percent to 40 percent. According to the FDIC, there were 346 new bank charters that year, a 59.5 percent increase over the previous year.[2] A *Fortune* magazine article said of this complex piece of legislation, which was signed into law in October 1982, "If the objective of government policy had been to destroy the thrift industry, it is doubtful so clever, so toxic, so multifaceted an attack could have been devised."[3]

Partial deregulation removed many barriers that had prevented financial institutions from venturing outside their traditional areas of financial specialization, but it did not sever their special relationship with the federal government. They continued to benefit from federal deposit insurance that enabled them to raise substantial sums of money from depositors at rates that were essentially unrelated to the quality of their portfolios, because the insurance feature sheltered depositors from possible adverse consequences of the institutions' investment practices. Exploiting this special relationship, many financial institutions accumulated large short-term deposits by utilizing the services of brokers and loaned the proceeds on the strength of long-term mortgage-secured notes. This potentially profitable yet highly risky strategy made consummate economic good sense to the parties involved because (1) depositors were insulated from possible adverse consequences by deposit insurance and (2) many institution managers had relatively small personal investments at risk. Thus, the potential gains to both depositors and managers were tremendous, while most of the risk was shifted to the federal agencies that acted as deposit insurers.

Given this almost unlimited flexibility to decide how their federally insured deposits could be invested, thrift institutions engaged in everything from construction lending for office buildings, hotels, shopping centers, and ski lodges to taking equity positions in speculative commercial real estate ventures. The serious overbuilding that occurred in many real estate markets during this period had disastrous ramifications.

Some thrifts even became involved in financing leveraged buyouts (purchases of businesses financed predominantly by debt and with abnormally low amounts of equity) and trading in junk bonds (high-yielding, unsecured debt securities issued by corporations that had low credit ratings or no credit ratings at all).

Reversing the Tax Incentives

There were 11 significant legislative revisions to the Internal Revenue Code between 1971 and 1991, but none of the others rivaled the **Tax Reform Act of 1986 (TRA '86)** in magnitude or significance. This massive legislation (Public Law 101-73, August 9, 1986) influenced almost every aspect of commercial and financial life, and none more so than the real estate industry.

Of the many significant TRA '86 provisions affecting real estate, perhaps the most traumatic to investors was the revised tax treatment of net losses incurred in real estate investments. With only minor exceptions, rental activities and interests in limited partnerships were now deemed "passive" in nature, and net losses from their operation could no longer be offset against otherwise taxable income from other sources. Under the new rules, such losses could be offset only against net income from other passive sources.

The 1986 revision to the tax code also modified the rules for claiming tax deductions to recover one's capital investment in real estate and other relatively long-lived assets. Prior rules permitted very large deductions during the early years of owner-ship, offset by lesser deductions later. Today, most investors must claim deductions for depreciation or cost recovery allowances in equal annual increments, and over a much longer period than provided by previous law.

The 1986 tax revision also eliminated preferential tax treatment for gains on disposal of assets held for lengthy periods (long-term capital gains), and it reduced the incentives for sellers to hold promissory notes from purchasers as a vehicle for financing real estate transactions.

These tax law changes made real estate investment relatively less attractive than in the past, compared with tax-deferred or tax-deductible investment alternatives such as IRAs, 401(k) accounts, tax-deferred annuities, and tax-deferred municipal bonds. (Tax-deferred annuities are an investment account traditionally offered by insurance companies and banks; gains are not taxed until the investor withdraws the funds. Municipal bonds are debt obligations issued by cities, counties, states, and other government entities to raise money for municipal projects such as schools and sewer systems. Most, but not all, municipal bonds offer income that is exempt from both federal and state taxes.)

Solvency Crises

In 1986, the collapse in petroleum prices ravaged the economies of the energy-dependent states of Texas, Louisiana, Colorado, and Oklahoma and exacerbated the already serious problem of real estate overbuilding and mortgage loan default. Serious problems encountered by depository institutions slowed real estate lending activity to a tiny trickle. By early 1991, it was estimated that the federal govern-ment's costs related to deposit insurance obligations at savings associations would amount to $500 billion; more than $2,000 for every person in the United States (the estimate included interest on the total debt incurred to pay for this purpose). Legisla-tive fervor for deregulation was supplanted by growing interest in regulations more stringent than those that had been swept away during the previous two decades.

Government's Response

The savings and loan industry's worst year was 1989, with losses totaling more than $19 billion, according to the FDIC.[4] Congress and the president responded to the growing financial crisis with the landmark **Financial Institutions Reform, Recovery, and Enforcement Act of 1989 (FIRREA)**, signed into law August 9, 1989. FIRREA was a large, tremendously complex, and far-reaching law that, in addition to adding its own new provisions, modified more than 40 existing laws. It abolished the Federal Savings and Loan Insurance Corporation (FSLIC, which had insured deposits in savings and loan associations since the 1930s) and the Federal Home Loan Bank Board (FHLBB, the savings and loan regulatory body), and cre-ated several new government agencies. Principal among the new entities created by FIRREA were the Office of Thrift Supervision (OTS), the Federal Housing and Finance Board (FHFB), and the Resolution Trust Corporation (RTC).

FIGURE 1.2 | Depository Institutions Regulatory Structure

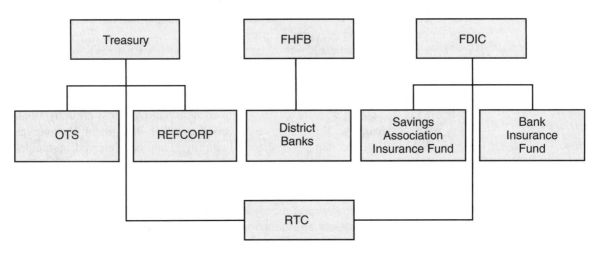

Federal Housing Finance Board (FHFB)
- Responsible for credit allocation by district banks to member banks, in the form of advances

Federal Deposit Insurance Corporation (FDIC)
- Guarantor of deposit insurance funds for banks and savings associations
- Management agent for the Resolution Trust Corporation (RTC)
- Operates FSLIC Resolution Fund, to liquidate assets held by old Federal Savings and Loan Insurance Corporation

Office of Thrift Supervision (OTS)
- Examines and supervises all savings associations

Resolution Funding Corporation (REFCORP)
- Raises funds in capital markets to finance activities of Resolution Trust Corporation

Resolution Trust Corporation (RTC)
- Disposes of assets held by federally insured savings associations that were placed in conservatorship or receivership beginning January 1, 1989

The OTS was established as a new branch of the Treasury Department and given the job of supervising and regulating state and federal thrift institutions. The FHFB was given supervisory responsibility over the Federal Home Loan Bank System, once held by the FHLBB. Figure 1.2 illustrates the new regulatory framework.

The RTC was established to manage and resolve all matters involving thrifts whose accounts were insured by the federal government and for which a conservator or receiver was appointed during the period beginning on January 1, 1989, and ending (initially) on August 8, 1992. This was later extended through September 30, 1993, and then to June 30, 1995.[5] The RTC was instructed to sell or otherwise dispose of the defunct thrifts or their assets, maximizing the return from their sale

FIGURE 1.3 | RTC Conservatorships at the End of the Year 1989–1995

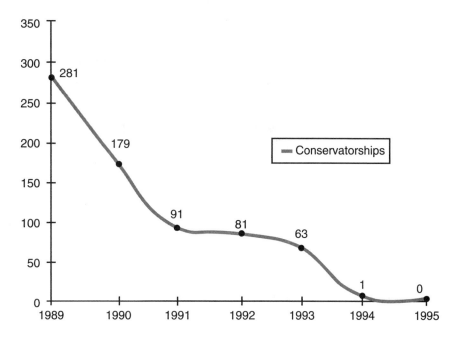

Source: FDIC Annual Reports 1980–1995

or other disposition but subject to the constraint of minimizing the impact of the transactions on local real estate and financial markets.

Almost immediately, the RTC became the single largest owner of real estate in the United States. On August 9, 1989, the RTC assumed control of 262 insolvent thrift associations with total assets of $115.3 billion.[6] During the months that remained in 1989, 56 additional thrifts with total assets of $26.4 billion were placed into the RTC's conservatorship program, for a total of 318 thrifts. The RTC resolved 37 institutions with total assets at the time of resolution of $10.8 billion during that period. A total of 281 thrifts remained in conservatorship at the end of that year. Those 281 thrifts had a total asset book value of $104.9 billion as of December 31, 1989.[7]

The RTC's mandate was to dispose of assets at "market value," a provision that caused no little confusion as well as consternation. Market value as defined by the real estate appraisal industry and the price at which a property is most likely to sell in distressed real estate markets are entirely different concepts.[8]

FIRREA also imposed more stringent limits on institutional lending practices. At the time, many observers argued that FIRREA-mandated rules had a chilling impact on real estate lending and created an unjustified "credit crunch" that exacerbated the already difficult transition through which real estate markets were struggling. Among the new rules that critics cited were statutes prohibiting direct equity investment in real estate by savings associations and a requirement that savings associations must maintain at least 70 percent of their portfolio assets in such things as loans on domestic residential housing.

Thrifts' liabilities were also regulated under FIRREA. The thrifts were now required to maintain a much higher ratio of stable consumer deposits (known in the industry as **core deposits**) to assets than before FIRREA—not less than 3 percent. With a few exceptions, they were now subject to the same limitations on loans to a single borrower as those that pertained to national banks. Any thrift that didn't meet FIRREA-mandated minimum capital requirements was not allowed to accept funds obtained, either directly or indirectly, through brokered deposits. On December 17, 1993, President Clinton signed the **Resolution Trust Corporation Completion Act** into law. The RTC ceased operations on December 31, 1995, and all remaining RTC-related work was transferred to the FSLIC Resolution Fund (FRF), which was managed by the FDIC effective January 1, 1996. From its inception through December 31, 1995, the RTC had disposed of assets with a book value of $445 billion![9] (See Figure 1.3.)

THE NEW FINANCING ENVIRONMENT

The Brookings Institute study cited earlier confirms that the principal consequence of the revolution in real estate finance is the integration of real estate capital markets into the nation's economic mainstream. An ancillary consequence includes a more sophisticated approach to capital markets by real estate practitioners. They have inherited a vastly expanded range of capital structure alternatives but have also been thrown into direct competition for capital resources with all other sectors of the economy.

This environment also caused a blending of real estate debt and equity capital instruments. Previously, the major suppliers of real estate capital provided it in the form of long-term mortgage debt. Now, depending on where the economy is in the economic cycle at a given time, lenders frequently insist on a share of the economic benefits of ownership, by crafting arrangements under which they receive a portion of the cash flow from operations or from the appreciation. In recent years debt increased as a portion of the total capital going into real estate development projects, and, though nonrecourse financing became popular once again, lenders today are underwriting more critically and are typically requiring larger down payments from borrowers.

Altered Lending Practices

A by-product of this shifting environment is confusion about specific activities that can or should be performed by various financial institutions whose roles once were simple and clear. Partial deregulation has spawned integration of financial functions and thereby fostered intensified competition that has upset long-established practices. At the same time, organizational and technological innovation has rendered inefficient many of the old ways of doing business.

Because financial markets in the new environment are more volatile and uncertain, lenders seek ways to protect themselves from market vagaries. Many are less willing to hold mortgage notes in their investment portfolios and have explored and expanded ways to sell these assets in secondary markets. This topic is explored further in Chapter 6.

Changes in Equity Investment Practices

Perhaps the most significant changes affecting equity investments are the trend to securitization of equities and the reduction in income tax incentives that had previously fostered a real estate bias in U.S. capital markets. The rapid securitization of the real estate equities markets has attracted much real estate investment capital that previously would have been channeled into corporate debt or equity securities—in short, it has drawn markets into closer competition.

This competition for limited resources has been played out on a vastly uneven field. In the years preceding TRA '86, the Internal Revenue Code rigged the game in favor of real estate and certain other assets (called **tax shelters**) by offering special tax credits and generous deductions. Most tax advantages for assets other than real estate were erased by major tax code revisions in 1986 and subsequent years. The code changes also greatly attenuated real estate's favored tax status, but left key elements in place. As explained in Chapter 16, some investment tax credits remain, and buildings and other real estate improvements can still be written off over a period that is usually (but not always) shorter than their useful economic lives.

Is It Déjà Vu?

For real estate professionals who had been in the industry for decades, the recent subprime mortgage crisis seemed strangely familiar. The increased foreclosure rates were a consequence of loose underwriting standards and creative financing, two of the key causes of past mortgage crises. Subprime mortgages are riskier than normal loans because the debtors have poor credit. Debtors who would not have been approved for mortgages under past, stricter underwriting standards were given loans that resulted in record numbers of foreclosures. Furthermore, some lenders committed or overlooked fraud, including falsified incomes, which led to inevitable default. The situation was worsened by giving debtors adjustable-rate mortgages (ARMs) with low teaser rates or interest-only (IO) loans that would require large payment increases in the near future. (These loans are described in detail in Chapter 8.) The adjustment of more than $1 trillion of ARMs in the 2007–2008 period resulted in new payments beyond the means of many debtors.

The problems in the lending market are reminiscent of prior crises caused by low underwriting standards, but this time the scope of the debacle is much different. First, so many mortgages today are sold into the secondary mortgage market (discussed in Chapter 6), where they are pooled and converted into securities and purchased by a wide variety of investors, including pension funds and insurance companies. The scope of the dilemma is global because the securities have also been purchased by international investors. Furthermore, the liberal lending standards were not confined to the United States, as British lenders also opened availability of credit in a booming real estate market. Greater use of ARMs and loans of up to 125 percent of a property's value led to problems when the real estate market cooled. Fortunately, another difference from prior crises is the strength of the U.S. and world economies.

SUMMARY

Real estate finance and investment decisions are intertwined to such an extent that neither can be usefully studied in isolation. Investments might be in either debt or equity positions, and most investors are simultaneously debtors and creditors, but not necessarily on the same properties. Revolutionary changes in capital markets during the past two decades have forced real estate practitioners to adopt a more sophisticated approach. They are in more direct competition with other capital markets than previously. In this new environment, capital alternatives have been vastly expanded.

The chain of events over the past 20-plus years that led to the upheaval include the Depository Institutions Deregulation and Monetary Control Act of 1980; the Economic Recovery Tax Act of 1981; the Garn-St. Germain Depository Institutions Act of 1982; widespread overbuilding during the decade of the 1980s; the Tax Reform Act of 1986; the Financial Institutions Reform, Recovery, and Enforcement Act of 1989; and ultimately to the Gramm-Leach-Bliley Act, also known as the Financial Modernization Act of 1999. All are threads in the same revolutionary tapestry.

As we will see in subsequent chapters, the revolution continues through the present day. Any doubt that this is the case can be dispelled by simply typing "revolution in real estate finance" into any of the popular Internet search engines.

KEY TERMS

active activity

brokered deposits

buying

core deposits

cost recovery

Depository Institutions
   Deregulation and
   Monetary Control Act

depreciation

Economic Recovery Tax
   Act of 1981 (ERTA)

Federal Deposit
   Insurance Corporation
   (FDIC)

finance

Financial Institutions
   Reform, Recovery, and
   Enforcement Act of
   1989 (FIRREA)

Garn-St. Germain
   Depository Institutions
   Act of 1982

investment

passive activity

Resolution Trust
   Corporation
   Completion Act

Tax Reform Act of 1986
   (TRA '86)

tax shelter

NOTES

1. Anthony Downs, *The Revolution in Real Estate Finance* (Washington, D.C.: The Brookings Institute, 1985), Chapter 1.

2. Managing the Crisis: The FDIC and RTC Experience Chronological Overview, Federal Deposit Insurance Corporation, Washington, D.C., August 1998.

3. *Fortune*, June 5, 1989, 188.

4. Managing the Crisis: The FDIC and RTC Experience Chronological Overview, Federal Deposit Insurance Corporation, Washington, D.C., August 1998.

5. Ibid.

6. Ibid.

7. Ibid.

8. For a straightforward explanation of various meanings of "price" and "value" see Gaylon E. Greer, *The New Dow Jones-Irwin Guide to Real Estate Investing* (Homewood, IL: Dow Jones-Irwin, 1989), Chapter 3. For a formal definition of market value, see *The Dictionary of Real Estate Appraisal,* Fourth Edition (Chicago: American Institute of Real Estate Appraisers, 2002).

9. Managing the Crisis: The FDIC and RTC Experience Chronological Overview, Federal Deposit Insurance Corporation, Washington, D.C., August 1998.

RECOMMENDED READING

Davies, Paul. "Mortgage Fraud Is Prime." *Wall Street Journal*, August 18, 2007.

Downs, Anthony. *The Revolution in Real Estate Finance*. Washington, D.C.: The Brookings Institute, 1985.

Forsyth, Randall W. "Why the Blow up May Get Worse." *Barron's*, August 13, 2007.

Pizzo, Stephen, Mary Fricker, and Paul Muolo. *Inside Job: The Looting of America's Savings and Loans*. New York: Harper Perennial, 1991.

Rabinowitz, Alan. *The Real Estate Gamble, Lessons from Fifty Years of Boom and Bust*. New York: AMACOM, 1980.

Seidman, L. William. *Full Faith and Credit: The Great S&L Debacle and Other Washington Sagas*. New York: Times Books, a division of Random House, Inc., 1993.

Wannamaker, Edward J. "The Depository Institutions Deregulation and Monetary Control Act of 1980 and Its Effect on Financial Markets and Institutions." Dissertation, University of Montana, 1989.

Yu, Beom J. "The Impact of the Depository Institutions Deregulation and Monetary Control Act (DIDMCA) of 1980 on the Return and Risk Characteristics of Publicly-Traded Depository Institutions." Dissertation, University of Tennessee, 1991.

▌ INTERNET REFERENCES

For numerous links and articles on real estate investment:
www.real-estate-online.com

For a review of the Economic Recovery Tax Act of 1981:
www.fpanet.org/journal/articles/1981_Issues/jfpsu81-art1.cfm

To view the FDIC homepage, containing links to other federal agencies:
www.fdic.gov

For a wealth of articles and information on important banking and finance legislation:
http://library.lp.findlaw.com/administrativelaw_2_8_1.html

For articles and links on real estate finance:
www.mortgagemag.com
www.individual.com (enter mortgage topic)

▌ REVIEW QUESTIONS

1. What are four types of lenders that, at one time or another, have been active real estate lenders?

2. Prior to the early 1970s, savings and loan associations made, primarily, what type of loans?

3. In March 1980, Congress passed and President Jimmy Carter signed into law the *Depository Institutions Deregulation and Monetary Control Act*. In addition to phasing out limitations on the maximum rates of interest and dividends that depository institutions could pay on deposits and accounts, what was it intended to do?

4. List two of the unintended effects the *Garn-St. Germain Depository Institutions Act* had on the thrift industry.

5. Name and describe two changes in income tax laws brought about by the Economic Recovery Tax Act of 1981 that increased the incentives to invest in real estate.

6. Describe two ways in which TRA '86 affected the real estate industry.

7. What was the name of the law passed in August 1989 that created the Resolution Trust Corporation (RTC)? What was the job of the RTC?

8. Distinguish between investment in debt and in equity instruments.

9. How can an investor hold real estate–related assets and still have a relatively liquid portfolio?

10. How does the Internal Revenue Code influence the allocation of capital in the economy?

DISCUSSION QUESTIONS

1. Before the early 1970s, the way commercial real estate projects were financed had, for decades, remained relatively unchanged. But by the mid-1980s, it was difficult to find two projects with the same financial structure. What might have caused these changes?

2. What led to the overbuilding in many major real estate markets during the 1980s, and how did that overbuilding contribute to financial difficulties of the real estate industry in the early 1990s?

3. Before partial deregulation, depository institutions such as banks and savings and loan associations were limited as to how much interest they could pay on deposits. They are now free to compete for deposits in general capital markets. Suggest some arguments for and against this innovation.

4. The government has in the past created and then later taken away a wide array of "tax shelter" opportunities in an apparent effort to achieve various economic and social goals of society by channeling more funds into specific types of investments. Do you favor using the Internal Revenue Code in this manner? Explain your position.

5. Why do you think the tax code gives more advantageous treatment to investors in residential than in nonresidential real estate?

PROBLEMS

1. When a family buys a single-family home, in which quadrant of Figure 1.1 are they participating? If they obtain a mortgage from a financial institution, in which quadrant is the lender participating?

2. If the lender sells a mortgage to Fannie Mae (the Federal National Mortgage Association), in which quadrant of Figure 1.1 is it participating? When Fannie Mae pools that mortgage with others in a security, which quadrant is in action?

3. If a family sells their house and takes back a mortgage (provides financing to the purchaser in place of a conventional lender), in which quadrants of Figure 1.1 are they participating?

Credit Instruments

After studying this chapter, you should be able to explain the functions of notes and mortgages and describe key provisions of various types of mortgage instruments. You should also understand several innovations adopted to suit special types of real property pledges.

Precedent and state statutes have established strict procedural steps and extensive documentation requirements for real estate loans. These documents and procedures are necessary to safeguard security interests and to assert claims against pledged property in the event an underlying debt obligation is not honored.

The most frequently encountered documents are **mortgages** and **promissory notes;** occasionally, these are combined in a single document. The exact nature of credit instruments depends on the character of pledged property and on borrowers' and lenders' objectives. Several alternatives have evolved to meet specialized lending requirements. Deeds of trust are examples of documents that have gained widespread acceptance.

PROMISSORY NOTES

Mortgages and promissory notes serve distinctly different but interrelated functions, and creating a legally enforceable promise to pay and a lien interest in real estate depend on proper application of both instruments. Whereas the note is an acknowledgment of debt and a promise to pay, the mortgage is a pledge of specific assets as security for the promise.[1]

Promissory notes used in real estate financing are generally referred to as *mortgage notes*. They differ from other forms of promissory notes only in their reference to the real estate that serves as security for repayment.

Because it is a private agreement between contracting parties, a promissory note may contain any (legal) provision on which the parties agree. As a practical matter, however, most promissory notes contain basically the same provisions. In point of fact, they are frequently prepared on preprinted forms supplied to a large segment of the industry by the same printing firms.

Figure 2.1 shows a fairly typical real estate promissory note, containing all the provisions that must be present:

1. The amount of the debt
2. The promise to pay
3. The interest rate charged
4. Payment terms (amount and timing of payments)
5. Reference to the real estate pledged in the mortgage or deed of trust

Other clauses that are frequently included, although they are not essential to create a legally binding obligation and security interest, include the following:

6. Acceleration clause, which permits the lender to immediately make the entire balance due if the borrower defaults on any loan terms
7. Default provisions, which usually include a waiver of certain legal rights that might exist in the absence of specific wording to the contrary

FIGURE 2.1 | Promissory Note

PROMISSORY NOTE
(Fixed Rate, Installment Payments)

_____, _____   _____   _____
[Date]   [City]   [State]

_____
[Property Address]

① **1. BORROWER'S PROMISE TO PAY**
②
     In return for a loan that I have received, I promise to pay U.S. $_____ (this amount called "principal"), plus interest, to the order of the Lender. The Lender is _____ _____. I will make all payments under this Note in the form of cash, check, certified funds or money order at the option and direction of Lender. I understand that the Lender may transfer t Note. The Lender or anyone who takes this Note by transfer and who is entitled to receive payments under this I is called the "Note Holder."

2. INTEREST

③
     Interest will be charged on unpaid principal until the full amount of principal has been paid. I will pay interest at a yearly rate of _____ %. The interest rate required by this Section 2 is the rate I pay both before and after any default described in Section 6(B) of this Note.

3. PAYMENTS

(A) Time and Place of Payments

④
     I will pay principal and interest by making a payment every month. I will make my monthly payment or _____ day of each month beginning on _____, _____. I will make these payments every m until I have paid all of the principal and interest and any other charges described below that I may owe under thi Note. Each monthly payment will be applied as of its scheduled due date and will be applied to interest before principal. If, on _____, _____ I still owe amounts under this Note, I will pay tt amounts in full on that date, which is called the "maturity date." I will make my monthly payments at

_____

or at a different place if required by the Note Holder.

(B) Amount of Monthly Payments

     My monthly payment will be in the amount of U.S. $_____.

4. BORROWER'S RIGHT TO PREPAY
{initial desired provision}

_____

⑨

I have the right to make payments of principal at any time before they are due. A payr of principal only is known as a "prepayment." When I make a prepayment, I will tell Note Holder in writing that I am doing so. I may not designate a payment as a prepay if I have not made all the monthly payments due under the Note.
I may make a full prepayment or partial prepayments without paying a prepayment charge. The Note Holder will use my prepayments to reduce the amount of principal t owe under this Note. However, the Note Holder may apply my prepayment to the acc and unpaid interest on the prepayment amount, before applying my prepayment to red the principal amount of the Note. If I make a partial prepayment, there will be no chai in the due date or in the amount of my monthly payment unless the Note Holder agree writing to those changes.

FIGURE 2.1 | Promissory Note *(continued)*

_____ I shall not have the right to prepay this Note unless I pay a prepayment penalty for early prepayment in the amount determined by the Note Holder, not to exceed the maximum amount allowed by the laws of the state where the property is located.

5. LOAN CHARGES

If a law, which applies to this loan and which sets maximum loan charges, is finally interpreted so that the interest or other loan charges collected or to be collected in connection with this loan exceed the permitted limits, then: (i) any such loan charge shall be reduced by the amount necessary to reduce the charge to the permitted limit; and (ii) any sums already collected from me which exceeded permitted limits will be refunded to me. The Note Holder may choose to make this refund by reducing the principal I owe under this Note or by making a direct payment to me. If a refund reduces principal, the reduction will be treated as a partial prepayment.

6. BORROWER'S FAILURE TO PAY AS REQUIRED

(A) Late Charge for Overdue Payments and Receipt of Payments

If the Note Holder has not received the full amount of any monthly payment by the end of _____{enter days before late charges are due under your State's laws} calendar days after the date it is due, I will pay a late charge to the Note Holder. The amount of the charge will be [_____% of my overdue payment of principal and interest or _____ dollars for each late payment]. I will pay this late charge promptly but only once on each late payment. In no event will the late charge exceed the maximum amount allowed by the applicable state law.

Payments to the note holder shall not be considered made until received by the Note Holder at the address specified. Mailing is insufficient to constitute delivery to the Note Holder.

The number of days required for payment of a late charge shall not be considered as a grace period for the payment date required under this Note and the Borrower shall be default if the payment is not paid on the due date.

(B) Default

If I do not pay the full amount of each monthly payment on the date it is due, I will be in default.

(C) Notice of Default

If I am in default, the Note Holder may send me a written notice telling me that if I do not pay the overdue amount by a certain date, the Note Holder may require me to pay immediately the full amount of principal which has not been paid and all the interest that I owe on that amount. That date must be at least 30 days after the date on which the notice is mailed to me or delivered by other means.

(D) No Waiver By Note Holder

Even if, at a time when I am in default, the Note Holder does not require me to pay immediately in full as described above, the Note Holder will still have the right to do so if I am in default at a later time.

(E) Payment of Note Holder's Costs and Expenses

If the Note Holder has required me to pay immediately in full as described above, the Note Holder will have the right to be paid back by me for all of its costs and expenses in enforcing this Note to the extent not prohibited by applicable law. Those expenses include, for example, reasonable attorneys' fees.

FIGURE 2.1 | Promissory Note *(continued)*

7. GIVING OF NOTICES

Unless applicable law requires a different method, any notice that must be given to me under this Note will be given by delivering it or by mailing it by first class mail to me at the Property Address above or at a different address if I give the Note Holder a notice of my different address. Any notice that must be given to the Note Holder under this Note will be given by delivering it or by mailing it by first class mail to the Note Holder at the address stated in Section 3(A) above or at a different address if I am given a notice of that different address.

8. OBLIGATIONS OF PERSONS UNDER THIS NOTE

If more than one person signs this Note, each person is fully and personally obligated to keep all of the promises made in this Note, including the promise to pay the full amount owed. Any person who is a guarantor, surety or endorser of this Note is also obligated to do these things. Any person who takes over these obligations, including the obligations of a guarantor, surety or endorser of this Note, is also obligated to keep all of the promises made in this Note. The Note Holder may enforce its rights under this Note against each person individually or against all of us together. This means that any one of us may be required to pay all of the amounts owed under this Note.

9. WAIVERS

I and any other person who has obligations under this Note waive the rights of presentment and notice of dishonor. "Presentment" means the right to require the Note Holder to demand payment of amounts due. "Notice of dishonor" means the right to require the Note Holder to give notice to other persons that amounts due have not been paid.

10. SECURED NOTE

In addition to the protections given to the Note Holder under this Note, a Mortgage, Deed of Trust or Security Deed (the "Security Instrument"), dated the same date as this Note, protects the Note Holder from possible losses which might result if I do not keep the promises which I make in this Note. That Security Instrument describes how and under what conditions I may be required to make immediate payment in full of all amounts I owe under this Note.

WITNESS THE HAND(S) AND SEAL(S) OF THE UNDERSIGNED

(Seal)

_____
Borrower

(Seal)

_____
Borrower

(Seal)

_____
Borrower

(Seal)

_____
Borrower

8. A waiver of the legal requirement that the borrower must be given notice when each successive payment becomes due

9. Terms under which prepayment may be made, including prepayment penalties if applicable

It is not at all uncommon for a promissory note's terms to appear also in the accompanying mortgage, though this represents unnecessary duplication. In fact, the note and mortgage combined compose the contract between borrower and lender. Should provisions of the two documents conflict, those of the note prevail.

Some authorities discourage the practice of repeating the note's terms in the mortgage itself. They recommend that the note be incorporated in the mortgage by reference only, with no recitation of its specific provisions. Their rationale is that recording a mortgage makes its content a matter of public record and invites competing lenders to "steal" clientele by offering to refinance loans under more advantageous terms.

■ MORTGAGES

Black's Law Dictionary (5th edition) defines a mortgage thus:

> ...a pledge of security of particular property for the payment of a debt or the performance of some obligation, whatever form the transaction may take, but is not now regarded as a conveyance in effect, though it may be cast in the form of a conveyance.[2]

Property pledged via a mortgage may be either realty or personalty, and the obligation it secures may be to repay a debt or to fulfill some other promise. Most mortgages, however, pledge specific assets as security for debt repayment. And because it is immobile and has relatively large unit value, real estate is a very useful asset to be pledged. Moreover, because its high unit value makes it difficult for most buyers to purchase real estate using only their own funds, third-party financing has become an essential element in most transactions. Generally, a mortgage on the property serves as the security instrument for the transaction.

Mortgages are among the oldest and most commonly employed instruments in real estate finance. As such, they carry a heavy burden of legal evolution. They have become complex documents whose legal import is camouflaged by archaic wording and by diverse statutory provisions. As noted by the author of *A History of American Law,* "The outline history of mortgage law is instructive."[3]

Mortgages, in effect, spell out the rights a lender will have in a borrower's estate in the event the borrower defaults on his or her obligation. In the absence of such default, a mortgage creates no interest in the real estate.

As we have seen, the underlying obligation associated with a mortgage is generally spelled out on a separate document called a *promissory note*. This is the borrower's written promise to pay a specified sum of money to another person, called the *payee* or *obligee,* under terms and conditions agreed on by the parties. The borrower is said to be the *maker*, or *obligor.*

Content of a Mortgage

Because state laws vary, mortgage provisions differ from state to state. Inasmuch as they are contracts, though, they are subject to the same limitations as any other contract. That is, they must involve competent parties, offer and acceptance, consideration, and legality of purpose. Because they are subject to the Statute of Frauds (an English law passed in 1677, which developed through common-law courts and was adapted into early American law), they must be in writing to be enforceable, and they must be signed. "[T]he common law was and is a system in which judges, whether following or distinguishing precedent, play a vital role in creating and expounding principles of law. . . In common law many basic rules of law are found nowhere but in the recorded opinions of the judges."[4]

Specific mortgage provisions are largely determined by statute in the state where the mortgaged property is located, no matter where the loan is originated. The following are common to almost all mortgages used to pledge real estate as security for loans and are reflected in the wording of the (fairly typical) mortgage shown in Figure 2.2.

1. Names of the parties. The party pledging property (the borrower) is the **mortgagor**. The party to whom a pledge is made (the lender) is the **mortgagee.** The mortgagor must sign the mortgage, and most states require that the signature be witnessed.

2. A clause pledging the real estate as security for indebtedness, along with identification of the debt so secured. The wording of the pledge often sounds as if there were an actual ownership conveyance, but another clause (**defeasance clause**) renders the transfer inoperative if the note is honored by the borrower.

3. Property description. Pledged property should be sufficiently described so that there can be no reasonable doubt as to just what property is intended. The most prudent approach is to identify property by its legal description, as recorded on the deed.

4. A release clause wherein the lender promises to release the promisor from the mortgage when the note has been fully paid.

Beyond basic minimum contents, mortgage provisions are governed by intent of the parties. A number of additional clauses are typically inserted to cover specific situations and to give added assurances. Phrases and clauses described in the following paragraphs (and referenced by a circled number in Figure 2.2) are common to mortgages in general use:

5. **Covenant of seizin**, in which mortgagors warrant that they are the lawful owners of property being mortgaged.

6. **Covenant to pay taxes**, which comprises the mortgagor's promise to pay all property taxes and assessments levied against the property during the period of the mortgage.

FIGURE 2.2 | Fannie Mae/Freddie Mac Mortgage Form

After Recording Return To:

_____
_____
_____
_____

_____ **[Space Above This Line For Recording Data]** _____

MORTGAGE

DEFINITIONS

Words used in multiple sections of this document are defined below and other words are defined in Sections 3, 11, 13, 18, 20 and 21. Certain rules regarding the usage of words used in this document are also provided in Section 16.

(A) "Security Instrument" means this document, which is dated _____,
____, together with all Riders to this document.

(1) **(B) "Borrower"** is _____. Borrower is the mortgagor under this Security Instrument.

(C) "Lender" is _____. Lender is a
_____ organized and existing under the laws of
_____. Lender's address is _____
_____. Lender is the mortgagee under this Security Instrument.

(D) "Note" means the promissory note signed by Borrower and dated _____,
_____. The Note states that Borrower owes Lender _____
Dollars (U.S. $_____) plus interest. Borrower has promised to pay this debt in regular Periodic Payments and to pay the debt in full not later than

_____.

(E) "Property" means the property that is described below under the heading "Transfer of Rights in the Property."

(F) "Loan" means the debt evidenced by the Note, plus interest, any prepayment charges and late charges due under the Note, and all sums due under this Security Instrument, plus interest.

(G) "Riders" means all Riders to this Security Instrument that are executed by Borrower. The following Riders are to be executed by Borrower [check box as applicable]:

☐ Adjustable Rate Rider ☐ Condominium Rider ☐ Second Home Rider
☐ Balloon Rider ☐ Planned Unit Development Rider ☐ Other(s)[specify] _____
☐ 1-4 Family Rider ☐ Biweekly Payment Rider

ARKANSAS--Single Family--Fannie Mae/Freddie Mac UNIFORM INSTRUMENT   Form 3004   1/01 _(page 1 of 16 pages)_

FIGURE 2.2 | Fannie Mae/Freddie Mac Mortgage Form *(continued)*

(H) "Applicable Law" means all controlling applicable federal, state and local statutes, regulations, ordinances and administrative rules and orders (that have the effect of law) as well as all applicable final, non-appealable judicial opinions.

(I) "Community Association Dues, Fees, and Assessments" means all dues, fees, assessments and other charges that are imposed on Borrower or the Property by a condominium association, homeowners association or similar organization.

(J) "Electronic Funds Transfer" means any transfer of funds, other than a transaction originated by check, draft, or similar paper instrument, which is initiated through an electronic terminal, telephonic instrument, computer, or magnetic tape so as to order, instruct, or authorize a financial institution to debit or credit an account. Such term includes, but is not limited to, point-of-sale transfers, automated teller machine transactions, transfers initiated by telephone, wire transfers, and automated clearinghouse transfers.

(K) "Escrow Items" means those items that are described in Section 3.

(L) "Miscellaneous Proceeds" means any compensation, settlement, award of damages, or proceeds paid by any third party (other than insurance proceeds paid under the coverages described in Section 5) for: (i) damage to, or destruction of, the Property; (ii) condemnation or other taking of all or any part of the Property; (iii) conveyance in lieu of condemnation; or (iv) misrepresentations of, or omissions as to, the value and/or condition of the Property.

(M) "Mortgage Insurance" means insurance protecting Lender against the nonpayment of, or default on, the Loan.

(N) "Periodic Payment" means the regularly scheduled amount due for (i) principal and interest under the Note, plus (ii) any amounts under Section 3 of this Security Instrument.

(O) "RESPA" means the Real Estate Settlement Procedures Act (12 U.S.C. §2601 et seq.) and its implementing regulation, Regulation X (24 C.F.R. Part 3500), as they might be amended from time to time, or any additional or successor legislation or regulation that governs the same subject matter. As used in this Security Instrument, "RESPA" refers to all requirements and restrictions that are imposed in regard to a "federally related mortgage loan" even if the Loan does not qualify as a "federally related mortgage loan" under RESPA.

(P) "Successor in Interest of Borrower" means any party that has taken title to the Property, whether or not that party has assumed Borrower's obligations under the Note and/or this Security Instrument.

TRANSFER OF RIGHTS IN THE PROPERTY

(2) This Security Instrument secures to Lender: (i) the repayment of the Loan, and all renewals, extensions and modifications of the Note; and (ii) the performance of Borrower's covenants and agreements under this Security Instrument and the Note. For this purpose, Borrower irrevocably

ARKANSAS--Single Family--Fannie Mae/Freddie Mac UNIFORM INSTRUMENT   Form 3004   1/01 *(page 2 of 16 pages)*

FIGURE 2.2 | Fannie Mae/Freddie Mac Mortgage Form *(continued)*

mortgages, grants and conveys to Lender the following described property located in the
_____ of _____:

(3)   [Type of Recording Jurisdiction]   [Name of Recording Jurisdiction]

which currently has the address of _____

                                                                            [Street]
_____, Arkansas _____("Property Address"):
             [City]   [Zip Code]

TOGETHER WITH all the improvements now or hereafter erected on the property, and all easements, appurtenances, and fixtures now or hereafter a part of the property. All replacements and additions shall also be covered by this Security Instrument. All of the foregoing is referred to in this Security Instrument as the "Property."

(5)   BORROWER COVENANTS that Borrower is lawfully seised of the estate hereby conveyed and has the right to mortgage, grant and convey the Property and that the Property is unencumbered, except for encumbrances of record. Borrower warrants and will defend generally the title to the Property against all claims and demands, subject to any encumbrances of record.

THIS SECURITY INSTRUMENT combines uniform covenants for national use and non-uniform covenants with limited variations by jurisdiction to constitute a uniform security instrument covering real property.

UNIFORM COVENANTS. Borrower and Lender covenant and agree as follows:
1. Payment of Principal, Interest, Escrow Items, Prepayment Charges, and Late Charges. Borrower shall pay when due the principal of, and interest on, the debt evidenced by the Note and any prepayment charges and late charges due under the Note. Borrower shall also pay funds for Escrow Items pursuant to Section 3. Payments due under the Note and this Security Instrument shall be made in U.S. currency. However, if any check or other instrument received by Lender as payment under the Note or this Security Instrument is returned to Lender unpaid, Lender may require that any or all subsequent payments due under the Note and this Security Instrument be made in one or more of the following forms, as selected by Lender: (a) cash; (b) money order; (c) certified check, bank check, treasurer's check or cashier's check, provided any such check is drawn

FIGURE 2.2 | Fannie Mae/Freddie Mac Mortgage Form *(continued)*

upon an institution whose deposits are insured by a federal agency, instrumentality, or entity; or (d) Electronic Funds Transfer.

Payments are deemed received by Lender when received at the location designated in the Note or at such other location as may be designated by Lender in accordance with the notice provisions in Section 15. Lender may return any payment or partial payment if the payment or partial payments are insufficient to bring the Loan current. Lender may accept any payment or partial payment insufficient to bring the Loan current, without waiver of any rights hereunder or prejudice to its rights to refuse such payment or partial payments in the future, but Lender is not obligated to apply such payments at the time such payments are accepted. If each Periodic Payment is applied as of its scheduled due date, then Lender need not pay interest on unapplied funds. Lender may hold such unapplied funds until Borrower makes payment to bring the Loan current. If Borrower does not do so within a reasonable period of time, Lender shall either apply such funds or return them to Borrower. If not applied earlier, such funds will be applied to the outstanding principal balance under the Note immediately prior to foreclosure. No offset or claim which Borrower might have now or in the future against Lender shall relieve Borrower from making payments due under the Note and this Security Instrument or performing the covenants and agreements secured by this Security Instrument.

2. Application of Payments or Proceeds. Except as otherwise described in this Section 2, all payments accepted and applied by Lender shall be applied in the following order of priority: (a) interest due under the Note; (b) principal due under the Note; (c) amounts due under Section 3. Such payments shall be applied to each Periodic Payment in the order in which it became due. Any remaining amounts shall be applied first to late charges, second to any other amounts due under this Security Instrument, and then to reduce the principal balance of the Note.

If Lender receives a payment from Borrower for a delinquent Periodic Payment which includes a sufficient amount to pay any late charge due, the payment may be applied to the delinquent payment and the late charge. If more than one Periodic Payment is outstanding, Lender may apply any payment received from Borrower to the repayment of the Periodic Payments if, and to the extent that, each payment can be paid in full. To the extent that any excess exists after the payment is applied to the full payment of one or more Periodic Payments, such excess may be applied to any late charges due. Voluntary prepayments shall be applied first to any prepayment charges and then as described in the Note.

Any application of payments, insurance proceeds, or Miscellaneous Proceeds to principal due under the Note shall not extend or postpone the due date, or change the amount, of the Periodic Payments.

3. Funds for Escrow Items. Borrower shall pay to Lender on the day Periodic Payments are due under the Note, until the Note is paid in full, a sum (the "Funds") to provide for payment of amounts due for: (a) taxes and assessments and other items which can attain priority over this Security Instrument as a lien or encumbrance on the Property; (b) leasehold payments or ground rents on the Property, if any; (c) premiums for any and all insurance required by Lender under Section 5; and (d) Mortgage Insurance premiums, if any, or any sums payable by Borrower to Lender in lieu of the payment of Mortgage Insurance premiums in accordance with the provisions of Section 10. These items are called "Escrow Items." At origination or at any time during the term of the Loan, Lender may require that Community Association Dues, Fees, and Assessments, if any,

ARKANSAS--Single Family--**Fannie Mae/Freddie Mac UNIFORM INSTRUMENT**   **Form 3004**   **1/01**   *(page 4 of 16 pages)*

FIGURE 2.2 | Fannie Mae/Freddie Mac Mortgage Form *(continued)*

be escrowed by Borrower, and such dues, fees and assessments shall be an Escrow Item. Borrower shall promptly furnish to Lender all notices of amounts to be paid under this Section. Borrower shall pay Lender the Funds for Escrow Items unless Lender waives Borrower's obligation to pay the Funds for any or all Escrow Items. Lender may waive Borrower's obligation to pay to Lender Funds for any or all Escrow Items at any time. Any such waiver may only be in writing. In the event of such waiver, Borrower shall pay directly, when and where payable, the amounts due for any Escrow Items for which payment of Funds has been waived by Lender and, if Lender requires, shall furnish to Lender receipts evidencing such payment within such time period as Lender may require. Borrower's obligation to make such payments and to provide receipts shall for all purposes be deemed to be a covenant and agreement contained in this Security Instrument, as the phrase "covenant and agreement" is used in Section 9. If Borrower is obligated to pay Escrow Items directly, pursuant to a waiver, and Borrower fails to pay the amount due for an Escrow Item, Lender may exercise its rights under Section 9 and pay such amount and Borrower shall then be obligated under Section 9 to repay to Lender any such amount. Lender may revoke the waiver as to any or all Escrow Items at any time by a notice given in accordance with Section 15 and, upon such revocation, Borrower shall pay to Lender all Funds, and in such amounts, that are then required under this Section 3.

Lender may, at any time, collect and hold Funds in an amount (a) sufficient to permit Lender to apply the Funds at the time specified under RESPA, and (b) not to exceed the maximum amount a lender can require under RESPA. Lender shall estimate the amount of Funds due on the basis of current data and reasonable estimates of expenditures of future Escrow Items or otherwise in accordance with Applicable Law.

The Funds shall be held in an institution whose deposits are insured by a federal agency, instrumentality, or entity (including Lender, if Lender is an institution whose deposits are so insured) or in any Federal Home Loan Bank. Lender shall apply the Funds to pay the Escrow Items no later than the time specified under RESPA. Lender shall not charge Borrower for holding and applying the Funds, annually analyzing the escrow account, or verifying the Escrow Items, unless Lender pays Borrower interest on the Funds and Applicable Law permits Lender to make such a charge. Unless an agreement is made in writing or Applicable Law requires interest to be paid on the Funds, Lender shall not be required to pay Borrower any interest or earnings on the Funds. Borrower and Lender can agree in writing, however, that interest shall be paid on the Funds. Lender shall give to Borrower, without charge, an annual accounting of the Funds as required by RESPA.

If there is a surplus of Funds held in escrow, as defined under RESPA, Lender shall account to Borrower for the excess funds in accordance with RESPA. If there is a shortage of Funds held in escrow, as defined under RESPA, Lender shall notify Borrower as required by RESPA, and Borrower shall pay to Lender the amount necessary to make up the shortage in accordance with RESPA, but in no more than 12 monthly payments. If there is a deficiency of Funds held in escrow, as defined under RESPA, Lender shall notify Borrower as required by RESPA, and Borrower shall pay to Lender the amount necessary to make up the deficiency in accordance with RESPA, but in no more than 12 monthly payments.

Upon payment in full of all sums secured by this Security Instrument, Lender shall promptly refund to Borrower any Funds held by Lender.

FIGURE 2.2 | Fannie Mae/Freddie Mac Mortgage Form *(continued)*

(6)   **4. Charges; Liens.** Borrower shall pay all taxes, assessments, charges, fines, and impositions attributable to the Property which can attain priority over this Security Instrument, leasehold payments or ground rents on the Property, if any, and Community Association Dues, Fees, and Assessments, if any. To the extent that these items are Escrow Items, Borrower shall pay them in the manner provided in Section 3.

Borrower shall promptly discharge any lien which has priority over this Security Instrument unless Borrower: (a) agrees in writing to the payment of the obligation secured by the lien in a manner acceptable to Lender, but only so long as Borrower is performing such agreement; (b) contests the lien in good faith by, or defends against enforcement of the lien in, legal proceedings which in Lender's opinion operate to prevent the enforcement of the lien while those proceedings are pending, but only until such proceedings are concluded; or (c) secures from the holder of the lien an agreement satisfactory to Lender subordinating the lien to this Security Instrument. If Lender determines that any part of the Property is subject to a lien which can attain priority over this Security Instrument, Lender may give Borrower a notice identifying the lien. Within 10 days of the date on which that notice is given, Borrower shall satisfy the lien or take one or more of the actions set forth above in this Section 4.

Lender may require Borrower to pay a one-time charge for a real estate tax verification and/or reporting service used by Lender in connection with this Loan.

(7)   **5. Property Insurance.** Borrower shall keep the improvements now existing or hereafter erected on the Property insured against loss by fire, hazards included within the term "extended coverage," and any other hazards including, but not limited to, earthquakes and floods, for which Lender requires insurance. This insurance shall be maintained in the amounts (including deductible levels) and for the periods that Lender requires. What Lender requires pursuant to the preceding sentences can change during the term of the Loan. The insurance carrier providing the insurance shall be chosen by Borrower subject to Lender's right to disapprove Borrower's choice, which right shall not be exercised unreasonably. Lender may require Borrower to pay, in connection with this Loan, either: (a) a one-time charge for flood zone determination, certification and tracking services; or (b) a one-time charge for flood zone determination and certification services and subsequent charges each time remappings or similar changes occur which reasonably might affect such determination or certification. Borrower shall also be responsible for the payment of any fees imposed by the Federal Emergency Management Agency in connection with the review of any flood zone determination resulting from an objection by Borrower.

If Borrower fails to maintain any of the coverages described above, Lender may obtain insurance coverage, at Lender's option and Borrower's expense. Lender is under no obligation to purchase any particular type or amount of coverage. Therefore, such coverage shall cover Lender, but might or might not protect Borrower, Borrower's equity in the Property, or the contents of the Property, against any risk, hazard or liability and might provide greater or lesser coverage than was previously in effect. Borrower acknowledges that the cost of the insurance coverage so obtained might significantly exceed the cost of insurance that Borrower could have obtained. Any amounts disbursed by Lender under this Section 5 shall become additional debt of Borrower secured by this Security Instrument. These amounts shall bear interest at the Note rate from the date of disbursement and shall be payable, with such interest, upon notice from Lender to Borrower requesting payment.

FIGURE 2.2 | Fannie Mae/Freddie Mac Mortgage Form *(continued)*

All insurance policies required by Lender and renewals of such policies shall be subject to Lender's right to disapprove such policies, shall include a standard mortgage clause, and shall name Lender as mortgagee and/or as an additional loss payee. Lender shall have the right to hold the policies and renewal certificates. If Lender requires, Borrower shall promptly give to Lender all receipts of paid premiums and renewal notices. If Borrower obtains any form of insurance coverage, not otherwise required by Lender, for damage to, or destruction of, the Property, such policy shall include a standard mortgage clause and shall name Lender as mortgagee and/or as an additional loss payee.

In the event of loss, Borrower shall give prompt notice to the insurance carrier and Lender. Lender may make proof of loss if not made promptly by Borrower. Unless Lender and Borrower otherwise agree in writing, any insurance proceeds, whether or not the underlying insurance was required by Lender, shall be applied to restoration or repair of the Property, if the restoration or repair is economically feasible and Lender's security is not lessened. During such repair and restoration period, Lender shall have the right to hold such insurance proceeds until Lender has had an opportunity to inspect such Property to ensure the work has been completed to Lender's satisfaction, provided that such inspection shall be undertaken promptly. Lender may disburse proceeds for the repairs and restoration in a single payment or in a series of progress payments as the work is completed. Unless an agreement is made in writing or Applicable Law requires interest to be paid on such insurance proceeds, Lender shall not be required to pay Borrower any interest or earnings on such proceeds. Fees for public adjusters, or other third parties, retained by Borrower shall not be paid out of the insurance proceeds and shall be the sole obligation of Borrower. If the restoration or repair is not economically feasible or Lender's security would be lessened, the insurance proceeds shall be applied to the sums secured by this Security Instrument, whether or not then due, with the excess, if any, paid to Borrower. Such insurance proceeds shall be applied in the order provided for in Section 2.

If Borrower abandons the Property, Lender may file, negotiate and settle any available insurance claim and related matters. If Borrower does not respond within 30 days to a notice from Lender that the insurance carrier has offered to settle a claim, then Lender may negotiate and settle the claim. The 30-day period will begin when the notice is given. In either event, or if Lender acquires the Property under Section 22 or otherwise, Borrower hereby assigns to Lender (a) Borrower's rights to any insurance proceeds in an amount not to exceed the amounts unpaid under the Note or this Security Instrument, and (b) any other of Borrower's rights (other than the right to any refund of unearned premiums paid by Borrower) under all insurance policies covering the Property, insofar as such rights are applicable to the coverage of the Property. Lender may use the insurance proceeds either to repair or restore the Property or to pay amounts unpaid under the Note or this Security Instrument, whether or not then due.

6. Occupancy. Borrower shall occupy, establish, and use the Property as Borrower's principal residence within 60 days after the execution of this Security Instrument and shall continue to occupy the Property as Borrower's principal residence for at least one year after the date of occupancy, unless Lender otherwise agrees in writing, which consent shall not be unreasonably withheld, or unless extenuating circumstances exist which are beyond Borrower's control.

⑧   **7. Preservation, Maintenance and Protection of the Property; Inspections.** Borrower shall not destroy, damage or impair the Property, allow the Property to deteriorate or commit waste

FIGURE 2.2 | Fannie Mae/Freddie Mac Mortgage Form *(continued)*

on the Property. Whether or not Borrower is residing in the Property, Borrower shall maintain the Property in order to prevent the Property from deteriorating or decreasing in value due to its condition. Unless it is determined pursuant to Section 5 that repair or restoration is not economically feasible, Borrower shall promptly repair the Property if damaged to avoid further deterioration or damage. If insurance or condemnation proceeds are paid in connection with damage to, or the taking of, the Property, Borrower shall be responsible for repairing or restoring the Property only if Lender has released proceeds for such purposes. Lender may disburse proceeds for the repairs and restoration in a single payment or in a series of progress payments as the work is completed. If the insurance or condemnation proceeds are not sufficient to repair or restore the Property, Borrower is not relieved of Borrower's obligation for the completion of such repair or restoration.

Lender or its agent may make reasonable entries upon and inspections of the Property. If it has reasonable cause, Lender may inspect the interior of the improvements on the Property. Lender shall give Borrower notice at the time of or prior to such an interior inspection specifying such reasonable cause.

8. Borrower's Loan Application. Borrower shall be in default if, during the Loan application process, Borrower or any persons or entities acting at the direction of Borrower or with Borrower's knowledge or consent gave materially false, misleading, or inaccurate information or statements to Lender (or failed to provide Lender with material information) in connection with the Loan. Material representations include, but are not limited to, representations concerning Borrower's occupancy of the Property as Borrower's principal residence.

9. Protection of Lender's Interest in the Property and Rights Under this Security Instrument. If (a) Borrower fails to perform the covenants and agreements contained in this Security Instrument, (b) there is a legal proceeding that might significantly affect Lender's interest in the Property and/or rights under this Security Instrument (such as a proceeding in bankruptcy, probate, for condemnation or forfeiture, for enforcement of a lien which may attain priority over this Security Instrument or to enforce laws or regulations), or (c) Borrower has abandoned the Property, then Lender may do and pay for whatever is reasonable or appropriate to protect Lender's interest in the Property and rights under this Security Instrument, including protecting and/or assessing the value of the Property, and securing and/or repairing the Property. Lender's actions can include, but are not limited to: (a) paying any sums secured by a lien which has priority over this Security Instrument; (b) appearing in court; and (c) paying reasonable attorneys' fees to protect its interest in the Property and/or rights under this Security Instrument, including its secured position in a bankruptcy proceeding. Securing the Property includes, but is not limited to, entering the Property to make repairs, change locks, replace or board up doors and windows, drain water from pipes, eliminate building or other code violations or dangerous conditions, and have utilities turned on or off. Although Lender may take action under this Section 9, Lender does not have to do so and is not under any duty or obligation to do so. It is agreed that Lender incurs no liability for not taking any or all actions authorized under this Section 9.

Any amounts disbursed by Lender under this Section 9 shall become additional debt of Borrower secured by this Security Instrument. These amounts shall bear interest at the Note rate from the date of disbursement and shall be payable, with such interest, upon notice from Lender to Borrower requesting payment.

FIGURE 2.2 | Fannie Mae/Freddie Mac Mortgage Form *(continued)*

If this Security Instrument is on a leasehold, Borrower shall comply with all the provisions of the lease. If Borrower acquires fee title to the Property, the leasehold and the fee title shall not merge unless Lender agrees to the merger in writing.

10. Mortgage Insurance. If Lender required Mortgage Insurance as a condition of making the Loan, Borrower shall pay the premiums required to maintain the Mortgage Insurance in effect. If, for any reason, the Mortgage Insurance coverage required by Lender ceases to be available from the mortgage insurer that previously provided such insurance and Borrower was required to make separately designated payments toward the premiums for Mortgage Insurance, Borrower shall pay the premiums required to obtain coverage substantially equivalent to the Mortgage Insurance previously in effect, at a cost substantially equivalent to the cost to Borrower of the Mortgage Insurance previously in effect, from an alternate mortgage insurer selected by Lender. If substantially equivalent Mortgage Insurance coverage is not available, Borrower shall continue to pay to Lender the amount of the separately designated payments that were due when the insurance coverage ceased to be in effect. Lender will accept, use and retain these payments as a non-refundable loss reserve in lieu of Mortgage Insurance. Such loss reserve shall be non-refundable, notwithstanding the fact that the Loan is ultimately paid in full, and Lender shall not be required to pay Borrower any interest or earnings on such loss reserve. Lender can no longer require loss reserve payments if Mortgage Insurance coverage (in the amount and for the period that Lender requires) provided by an insurer selected by Lender again becomes available, is obtained, and Lender requires separately designated payments toward the premiums for Mortgage Insurance. If Lender required Mortgage Insurance as a condition of making the Loan and Borrower was required to make separately designated payments toward the premiums for Mortgage Insurance, Borrower shall pay the premiums required to maintain Mortgage Insurance in effect, or to provide a non-refundable loss reserve, until Lender's requirement for Mortgage Insurance ends in accordance with any written agreement between Borrower and Lender providing for such termination or until termination is required by Applicable Law. Nothing in this Section 10 affects Borrower's obligation to pay interest at the rate provided in the Note.

Mortgage Insurance reimburses Lender (or any entity that purchases the Note) for certain losses it may incur if Borrower does not repay the Loan as agreed. Borrower is not a party to the Mortgage Insurance.

Mortgage insurers evaluate their total risk on all such insurance in force from time to time, and may enter into agreements with other parties that share or modify their risk, or reduce losses. These agreements are on terms and conditions that are satisfactory to the mortgage insurer and the other party (or parties) to these agreements. These agreements may require the mortgage insurer to make payments using any source of funds that the mortgage insurer may have available (which may include funds obtained from Mortgage Insurance premiums).

As a result of these agreements, Lender, any purchaser of the Note, another insurer, any reinsurer, any other entity, or any affiliate of any of the foregoing, may receive (directly or indirectly) amounts that derive from (or might be characterized as) a portion of Borrower's payments for Mortgage Insurance, in exchange for sharing or modifying the mortgage insurer's risk, or reducing losses. If such agreement provides that an affiliate of Lender takes a share of the insurer's risk in exchange for a share of the premiums paid to the insurer, the arrangement is often termed "captive reinsurance." Further:

FIGURE 2.2 | Fannie Mae/Freddie Mac Mortgage Form *(continued)*

(a) Any such agreements will not affect the amounts that Borrower has agreed to pay for Mortgage Insurance, or any other terms of the Loan. Such agreements will not increase the amount Borrower will owe for Mortgage Insurance, and they will not entitle Borrower to any refund.

(b) Any such agreements will not affect the rights Borrower has – if any – with respect to the Mortgage Insurance under the Homeowners Protection Act of 1998 or any other law. These rights may include the right to receive certain disclosures, to request and obtain cancellation of the Mortgage Insurance, to have the Mortgage Insurance terminated automatically, and/or to receive a refund of any Mortgage Insurance premiums that were unearned at the time of such cancellation or termination.

11. Assignment of Miscellaneous Proceeds; Forfeiture. All Miscellaneous Proceeds are hereby assigned to and shall be paid to Lender.

If the Property is damaged, such Miscellaneous Proceeds shall be applied to restoration or repair of the Property, if the restoration or repair is economically feasible and Lender's security is not lessened. During such repair and restoration period, Lender shall have the right to hold such Miscellaneous Proceeds until Lender has had an opportunity to inspect such Property to ensure the work has been completed to Lender's satisfaction, provided that such inspection shall be undertaken promptly. Lender may pay for the repairs and restoration in a single disbursement or in a series of progress payments as the work is completed. Unless an agreement is made in writing or Applicable Law requires interest to be paid on such Miscellaneous Proceeds, Lender shall not be required to pay Borrower any interest or earnings on such Miscellaneous Proceeds. If the restoration or repair is not economically feasible or Lender's security would be lessened, the Miscellaneous Proceeds shall be applied to the sums secured by this Security Instrument, whether or not then due, with the excess, if any, paid to Borrower. Such Miscellaneous Proceeds shall be applied in the order provided for in Section 2.

In the event of a total taking, destruction, or loss in value of the Property, the Miscellaneous Proceeds shall be applied to the sums secured by this Security Instrument, whether or not then due, with the excess, if any, paid to Borrower.

In the event of a partial taking, destruction, or loss in value of the Property in which the fair market value of the Property immediately before the partial taking, destruction, or loss in value is equal to or greater than the amount of the sums secured by this Security Instrument immediately before the partial taking, destruction, or loss in value, unless Borrower and Lender otherwise agree in writing, the sums secured by this Security Instrument shall be reduced by the amount of the Miscellaneous Proceeds multiplied by the following fraction: (a) the total amount of the sums secured immediately before the partial taking, destruction, or loss in value divided by (b) the fair market value of the Property immediately before the partial taking, destruction, or loss in value. Any balance shall be paid to Borrower.

In the event of a partial taking, destruction, or loss in value of the Property in which the fair market value of the Property immediately before the partial taking, destruction, or loss in value is less than the amount of the sums secured immediately before the partial taking, destruction, or loss in value, unless Borrower and Lender otherwise agree in writing, the Miscellaneous Proceeds shall be applied to the sums secured by this Security Instrument whether or not the sums are then due.

If the Property is abandoned by Borrower, or if, after notice by Lender to Borrower that the Opposing Party (as defined in the next sentence) offers to make an award to settle a claim for

---

FIGURE 2.2 | Fannie Mae/Freddie Mac Mortgage Form *(continued)*

damages, Borrower fails to respond to Lender within 30 days after the date the notice is given, Lender is authorized to collect and apply the Miscellaneous Proceeds either to restoration or repair of the Property or to the sums secured by this Security Instrument, whether or not then due. "Opposing Party" means the third party that owes Borrower Miscellaneous Proceeds or the party against whom Borrower has a right of action in regard to Miscellaneous Proceeds.

Borrower shall be in default if any action or proceeding, whether civil or criminal, is begun that, in Lender's judgment, could result in forfeiture of the Property or other material impairment of Lender's interest in the Property or rights under this Security Instrument. Borrower can cure such a default and, if acceleration has occurred, reinstate as provided in Section 19, by causing the action or proceeding to be dismissed with a ruling that, in Lender's judgment, precludes forfeiture of the Property or other material impairment of Lender's interest in the Property or rights under this Security Instrument. The proceeds of any award or claim for damages that are attributable to the impairment of Lender's interest in the Property are hereby assigned and shall be paid to Lender.

All Miscellaneous Proceeds that are not applied to restoration or repair of the Property shall be applied in the order provided for in Section 2.

12. Borrower Not Released; Forbearance By Lender Not a Waiver. Extension of the time for payment or modification of amortization of the sums secured by this Security Instrument granted by Lender to Borrower or any Successor in Interest of Borrower shall not operate to release the liability of Borrower or any Successors in Interest of Borrower. Lender shall not be required to commence proceedings against any Successor in Interest of Borrower or to refuse to extend time for payment or otherwise modify amortization of the sums secured by this Security Instrument by reason of any demand made by the original Borrower or any Successors in Interest of Borrower. Any forbearance by Lender in exercising any right or remedy including, without limitation, Lender's acceptance of payments from third persons, entities or Successors In Interest of Borrower or in amounts less than the amount then due, shall not be a waiver of or preclude the exercise of any right or remedy.

13. Joint and Several Liability; Co-signers; Successors and Assigns Bound. Borrower covenants and agrees that Borrower's obligations and liability shall be joint and several. However, any Borrower who co-signs this Security Instrument but does not execute the Note (a "co-signer"): (a) is co-signing this Security Instrument only to mortgage, grant and convey the co-signer's interest in the Property under the terms of this Security Instrument; (b) is not personally obligated to pay the sums secured by this Security Instrument; and (c) agrees that Lender and any other Borrower can agree to extend, modify, forbear or make any accommodations with regard to the terms of this Security Instrument or the Note without the co-signer's consent.

Subject to the provisions of Section 18, any Successor in Interest of Borrower who assumes Borrower's obligations under this Security Instrument in writing, and is approved by Lender, shall obtain all of Borrower's rights and benefits under this Security Instrument. Borrower shall not be released from Borrower's obligations and liability under this Security Instrument unless Lender agrees to such release in writing. The covenants and agreements of this Security Instrument shall bind (except as provided in Section 20) and benefit the successors and assigns of Lender.

14. Loan Charges. Lender may charge Borrower fees for services performed in connection with Borrower's default, for the purpose of protecting Lender's interest in the Property and rights under this Security Instrument, including, but not limited to, attorneys' fees, property inspection and valuation fees. In regard to any other fees, the absence of express authority in this Security

FIGURE 2.2 | Fannie Mae/Freddie Mac Mortgage Form *(continued)*

Instrument to charge a specific fee to Borrower shall not be construed as a prohibition on the charging of such fee. Lender may not charge fees that are expressly prohibited by this Security Instrument or by Applicable Law.

If the Loan is subject to a law which sets maximum loan charges, and that law is finally interpreted so that the interest or other loan charges collected or to be collected in connection with the Loan exceed the permitted limits, then: (a) any such loan charge shall be reduced by the amount necessary to reduce the charge to the permitted limit; and (b) any sums already collected from Borrower which exceeded permitted limits will be refunded to Borrower. Lender may choose to make this refund by reducing the principal owed under the Note or by making a direct payment to Borrower. If a refund reduces principal, the reduction will be treated as a partial prepayment without any prepayment charge (whether or not a prepayment charge is provided for under the Note). Borrower's acceptance of any such refund made by direct payment to Borrower will constitute a waiver of any right of action Borrower might have arising out of such overcharge.

15. Notices. All notices given by Borrower or Lender in connection with this Security Instrument must be in writing. Any notice to Borrower in connection with this Security Instrument shall be deemed to have been given to Borrower when mailed by first class mail or when actually delivered to Borrower's notice address if sent by other means. Notice to any one Borrower shall constitute notice to all Borrowers unless Applicable Law expressly requires otherwise. The notice address shall be the Property Address unless Borrower has designated a substitute notice address by notice to Lender. Borrower shall promptly notify Lender of Borrower's change of address. If Lender specifies a procedure for reporting Borrower's change of address, then Borrower shall only report a change of address through that specified procedure. There may be only one designated notice address under this Security Instrument at any one time. Any notice to Lender shall be given by delivering it or by mailing it by first class mail to Lender's address stated herein unless Lender has designated another address by notice to Borrower. Any notice in connection with this Security Instrument shall not be deemed to have been given to Lender until actually received by Lender. If any notice required by this Security Instrument is also required under Applicable Law, the Applicable Law requirement will satisfy the corresponding requirement under this Security Instrument.

16. Governing Law; Severability; Rules of Construction. This Security Instrument shall be governed by federal law and the law of the jurisdiction in which the Property is located. All rights and obligations contained in this Security Instrument are subject to any requirements and limitations of Applicable Law. Applicable Law might explicitly or implicitly allow the parties to agree by contract or it might be silent, but such silence shall not be construed as a prohibition against agreement by contract. In the event that any provision or clause of this Security Instrument or the Note conflicts with Applicable Law, such conflict shall not affect other provisions of this Security Instrument or the Note which can be given effect without the conflicting provision.

As used in this Security Instrument: (a) words of the masculine gender shall mean and include corresponding neuter words or words of the feminine gender; (b) words in the singular shall mean and include the plural and vice versa; and (c) the word "may" gives sole discretion without any obligation to take any action.

17. Borrower's Copy. Borrower shall be given one copy of the Note and of this Security Instrument.

FIGURE 2.2 | Fannie Mae/Freddie Mac Mortgage Form *(continued)*

18. Transfer of the Property or a Beneficial Interest in Borrower. As used in this Section 18, "Interest in the Property" means any legal or beneficial interest in the Property, including, but not limited to, those beneficial interests transferred in a bond for deed, contract for deed, installment sales contract or escrow agreement, the intent of which is the transfer of title by Borrower at a future date to a purchaser.

If all or any part of the Property or any Interest in the Property is sold or transferred (or if Borrower is not a natural person and a beneficial interest in Borrower is sold or transferred) without Lender's prior written consent, Lender may require immediate payment in full of all sums secured by this Security Instrument. However, this option shall not be exercised by Lender if such exercise is prohibited by Applicable Law.

If Lender exercises this option, Lender shall give Borrower notice of acceleration. The notice shall provide a period of not less than 30 days from the date the notice is given in accordance with Section 15 within which Borrower must pay all sums secured by this Security Instrument. If Borrower fails to pay these sums prior to the expiration of this period, Lender may invoke any remedies permitted by this Security Instrument without further notice or demand on Borrower.

19. Borrower's Right to Reinstate After Acceleration. If Borrower meets certain conditions, Borrower shall have the right to have enforcement of this Security Instrument discontinued at any time prior to the earliest of: (a) five days before sale of the Property pursuant to any power of sale contained in this Security Instrument; (b) such other period as Applicable Law might specify for the termination of Borrower's right to reinstate; or (c) entry of a judgment enforcing this Security Instrument. Those conditions are that Borrower: (a) pays Lender all sums which then would be due under this Security Instrument and the Note as if no acceleration had occurred; (b) cures any default of any other covenants or agreements; (c) pays all expenses incurred in enforcing this Security Instrument, including, but not limited to, reasonable attorneys' fees, property inspection and valuation fees, and other fees incurred for the purpose of protecting Lender's interest in the Property and rights under this Security Instrument; and (d) takes such action as Lender may reasonably require to assure that Lender's interest in the Property and rights under this Security Instrument, and Borrower's obligation to pay the sums secured by this Security Instrument, shall continue unchanged. Lender may require that Borrower pay such reinstatement sums and expenses in one or more of the following forms, as selected by Lender: (a) cash; (b) money order; (c) certified check, bank check, treasurer's check or cashier's check, provided any such check is drawn upon an institution whose deposits are insured by a federal agency, instrumentality or entity; or (d) Electronic Funds Transfer. Upon reinstatement by Borrower, this Security Instrument and obligations secured hereby shall remain fully effective as if no acceleration had occurred. However, this right to reinstate shall not apply in the case of acceleration under Section 18.

20. Sale of Note; Change of Loan Servicer; Notice of Grievance. The Note or a partial interest in the Note (together with this Security Instrument) can be sold one or more times without prior notice to Borrower. A sale might result in a change in the entity (known as the "Loan Servicer") that collects Periodic Payments due under the Note and this Security Instrument and performs other mortgage loan servicing obligations under the Note, this Security Instrument, and Applicable Law. There also might be one or more changes of the Loan Servicer unrelated to a sale of the Note. If there is a change of the Loan Servicer, Borrower will be given written notice of the change which will state the name and address of the new Loan Servicer, the address to which payments should be made and any other information RESPA requires in connection with a notice

ARKANSAS--Single Family--Fannie Mae/Freddie Mac UNIFORM INSTRUMENT   Form 3004   1/01 *(page 13 of 16 pages)*

FIGURE 2.2 | Fannie Mae/Freddie Mac Mortgage Form *(continued)*

of transfer of servicing. If the Note is sold and thereafter the Loan is serviced by a Loan Servicer other than the purchaser of the Note, the mortgage loan servicing obligations to Borrower will remain with the Loan Servicer or be transferred to a successor Loan Servicer and are not assumed by the Note purchaser unless otherwise provided by the Note purchaser.

Neither Borrower nor Lender may commence, join, or be joined to any judicial action (as either an individual litigant or the member of a class) that arises from the other party's actions pursuant to this Security Instrument or that alleges that the other party has breached any provision of, or any duty owed by reason of, this Security Instrument, until such Borrower or Lender has notified the other party (with such notice given in compliance with the requirements of Section 15) of such alleged breach and afforded the other party hereto a reasonable period after the giving of such notice to take corrective action. If Applicable Law provides a time period which must elapse before certain action can be taken, that time period will be deemed to be reasonable for purposes of this paragraph. The notice of acceleration and opportunity to cure given to Borrower pursuant to Section 22 and the notice of acceleration given to Borrower pursuant to Section 18 shall be deemed to satisfy the notice and opportunity to take corrective action provisions of this Section 20.

21. Hazardous Substances. As used in this Section 21: (a) "Hazardous Substances" are those substances defined as toxic or hazardous substances, pollutants, or wastes by Environmental Law and the following substances: gasoline, kerosene, other flammable or toxic petroleum products, toxic pesticides and herbicides, volatile solvents, materials containing asbestos or formaldehyde, and radioactive materials; (b) "Environmental Law" means federal laws and laws of the jurisdiction where the Property is located that relate to health, safety or environmental protection; (c) "Environmental Cleanup" includes any response action, remedial action, or removal action, as defined in Environmental Law; and (d) an "Environmental Condition" means a condition that can cause, contribute to, or otherwise trigger an Environmental Cleanup. Borrower shall not cause or permit the presence, use, disposal, storage, or release of any Hazardous Substances, or threaten to release any Hazardous Substances, on or in the Property.

Borrower shall not do, nor allow anyone else to do, anything affecting the Property (a) that is in violation of any Environmental Law, (b) which creates an Environmental Condition, or (c) which, due to the presence, use, or release of a Hazardous Substance, creates a condition that adversely affects the value of the Property. The preceding two sentences shall not apply to the presence, use, or storage on the Property of small quantities of Hazardous Substances that are generally recognized to be appropriate to normal residential uses and to maintenance of the Property (including, but not limited to, hazardous substances in consumer products).

Borrower shall promptly give Lender written notice of (a) any investigation, claim, demand, lawsuit or other action by any governmental or regulatory agency or private party involving the Property and any Hazardous Substance or Environmental Law of which Borrower has actual knowledge, (b) any Environmental Condition, including but not limited to, any spilling, leaking, discharge, release or threat of release of any Hazardous Substance, and (c) any condition caused by the presence, use or release of a Hazardous Substance which adversely affects the value of the Property. If Borrower learns, or is notified by any governmental or regulatory authority, or any private party, that any removal or other remediation of any Hazardous Substance affecting the Property is necessary, Borrower shall promptly take all necessary remedial actions in accordance with Environmental Law. Nothing herein shall create any obligation on Lender for an Environmental Cleanup.

FIGURE 2.2 | Fannie Mae/Freddie Mac Mortgage Form *(continued)*

NON-UNIFORM COVENANTS. Borrower and Lender further covenant and agree as follows:

(9) **22. Acceleration; Remedies.** Lender shall give notice to Borrower prior to acceleration following Borrower's breach of any covenant or agreement in this Security Instrument (but not prior to acceleration under Section 18 unless Applicable Law provides otherwise). The notice shall specify: (a) the default; (b) the action required to cure the default; (c) a date, not less than 30 days from the date the notice is given to Borrower, by which the default must be cured; and (d) that failure to cure the default on or before the date specified in the notice may result in acceleration of the sums secured by this Security Instrument and sale of the Property. The notice shall further inform Borrower of the right to reinstate after acceleration and the right to bring a court action to assert the non-existence of a default or any other defense of Borrower to acceleration and sale. If the default is not cured on or before the date specified in the notice, Lender at its option may require immediate payment in full of all sums secured by this Security Instrument without further demand and may invoke any other remedies permitted by Applicable Law. Lender shall be entitled to collect all expenses incurred in pursuing the remedies provided in this Section 22, including, but not limited to, reasonable attorneys' fees and costs of title evidence.

It is understood and agreed to by Borrower that this Security Instrument is subject to the foreclosure procedures of the Arkansas Statutory Foreclosure Law, Act 53 of 1987, as amended from time to time (the "Act"), for Borrower's breach of any covenant or agreement in this Security Instrument. In furtherance and not in limitation of the provisions of Section 12, any forbearance by Lender in exercising any right or remedy under the Act shall not be a waiver of or preclude acceleration and the exercise of any right or remedy under the Act, or at the option of Lender, use of judicial foreclosure proceedings.

(4) **23. Release.** Upon payment in full of all sums secured by this Security Instrument, Lender shall release this Security Instrument. Borrower shall pay any recordation costs. Lender may charge Borrower a fee for releasing this Security Instrument, but only if the fee is paid to a third party for services rendered and the charging of the fee is permitted under Applicable Law.

24. Waivers. Borrower waives all rights of homestead exemption in, and statutory redemption of, the Property and all right of appraisement of the Property and relinquishes all rights of curtesy and dower in the Property.

FIGURE 2.2 | Fannie Mae/Freddie Mac Mortgage Form *(continued)*

BY SIGNING BELOW, Borrower accepts and agrees to the terms and covenants contained in this Security Instrument and in any Rider executed by Borrower and recorded with it.

Witnesses:

_____   _____(Seal)
                                                                    - Borrower

                                     Social Security Number _____

_____   _____(Seal)
                                                                    - Borrower

                                     Social Security Number _____

_____ [Space Below This Line For Acknowledgment] _____

FIGURE 2.2 | Fannie Mae/Freddie Mac Mortgage Form *(continued)*

STATE OF ARKANSAS

COUNTY OF _____

On this the ____ day of _____, _____, before me, _____, the undersigned officer, personally appeared _____, known to me (or satisfactorily proven) to be the person whose name is/are subscribed to the within instrument and acknowledged that he/she/they executed the same for the purposes therein contained.

In witness whereof I hereunto set my hand and official seal.

_____
Notary Public

Printed Name: _____

My Commission Expires:

_____

STATE OF ARKANSAS

COUNTY OF _____

On this the ____ day of _____, _____, before me, _____, the undersigned officer, personally appeared _____, known to me (or satisfactorily proven) to be the person whose name is/are subscribed to the within instrument and acknowledged that he/she/they executed the same for the purposes therein contained.

In witness whereof I hereunto set my hand and official seal.

_____
Notary Public

Printed Name: _____

My Commission Expires:

_____

7. **Covenant of insurance**, in which the mortgagor promises to maintain adequate insurance coverage against fire and other specified hazards.

8. **Covenant against removal**, which is the mortgagor's promise not to remove or destroy any improvement located on mortgaged property without prior permission of the mortgagee.

9. **Acceleration clause**, which permits the mortgagee to declare the remaining balance of the underlying debt due and payable if a mortgagor defaults on any of the agreed-on terms. Although the acceleration clause is routinely inserted in the related promissory note, it is almost universally duplicated in the mortgage.

Additional clauses are inserted in mortgages to meet unusual circumstances or to satisfy special problems. Most frequently encountered are prepayment and assumption clauses.

- Generally, in the absence of specific contractual or statutory provisions to the contrary, mortgagors have no authority to prepay debt secured by a mortgage.[5] **Prepayment clauses** frequently include provision for a penalty for early payment (prepayment penalties on home loans have been virtually outlawed in most states).

- In recent years many lenders have begun inserting an **assumption clause** (often referred to as a **due on sale**, **due on resale**, or **due on alienation clause**), whereby mortgagors agree not to sell mortgaged property subject to the mortgage or to have a buyer assume an existing mortgage without prior approval of the mortgagee. This gives lenders an opportunity to adjust their return to the current market when interest rates have risen by charging an assumption fee or by simply increasing the contract rate as a precondition to approving an assumption. Prohibitions against assumption are not permitted on FHA-insured or VA-guaranteed mortgages, described in Chapter 7.

Right of Assignment

Mortgages are a form of intangible personal property. As such, they can be sold or otherwise conveyed by simple assignment of the lender's interest. Assignment does not require approval of the borrower and does not affect the nature or enforceability of terms of the note and mortgage. Ability to assign mortgage interests is an important element in many lenders' willingness to lend on the security of real property.

Delivery and Acknowledgment

To become a legitimate claim against property, a mortgage must be delivered. **Delivery** is generally considered to have been accomplished when the mortgagor relinquishes physical control over the document with the intent that it should become operative. Lenders usually want to record mortgages to establish their lien interest and to protect themselves from conflicting claims of subsequent creditors or purchasers, and only acknowledged instruments can be recorded. Therefore, acknowledgment—a formal declaration before an authorized official that the document was signed freely and without coercion—is routinely accomplished.

Types of Mortgages

Mortgages are contracts between borrowers and lenders and may be adapted to suit any legal purpose. In practice, several innovations have evolved to suit special types of real property pledges. Popular adaptations include purchase-money mortgages, blanket mortgages, and special mortgages to secure construction loans.

Purchase-Money Mortgages

Any mortgage given by a buyer to a seller to secure a note in part payment of the purchase price is called a **purchase-money mortgage** (also known as a **take-back mortgage**). The seller accepts a purchase-money mortgage in lieu of cash. Structured properly, this type of creative financing can enhance the attractiveness of a real estate transaction for both buyer and seller. A seller eager to dispose of a property may, for example, offer it to a prospective buyer for little or no cash, with a below-market interest rate. An equally eager buyer may be willing to pay a higher rate of interest than the seller otherwise might have been able to obtain. The major distinction between a purchase-money mortgage and a mortgage securing a third-party loan lies in the order of priority of the underlying lien. If a purchase-money mortgage is executed and recorded simultaneously with the deed, it takes precedence over all the mortgagor's subsequent debts.

To protect the priority of a purchase-money mortgage, it must be recorded at the same time as the deed conveying the associated property.

Blanket Mortgages

A borrower may at times pledge two or more parcels of property as security for a single loan. The mortgage thereby created is known as a **blanket mortgage** (also known as a **cross-collateralization agreement**) and may contain special clauses to meet specific borrower needs. Developers and subdividers sometimes give blanket mortgages on large parcels that they intend to subdivide and sell as individual building lots. As each lot is sold, it must be released from the mortgage so that the buyer can pledge the property as security for a loan to finance the transaction. This requires a provision for partial release in the blanket mortgage. A partial release clause typically provides for segments of a mortgaged property to be released after specified lump-sum payments on the mortgage note.

Open-Ended Mortgage

A mortgage can be written so that it will secure future as well as current loans. Even when the exact amount of the subsequent advances cannot be precisely forecast, appropriate wording in a mortgage can provide security for the future obligation without the need to rewrite the mortgage at that time.

Mortgages that provide for future advances are often called **open-ended**, or, more simply, **open mortgages**. The mortgage usually states a ceiling amount for aggregate advances. One of the purposes of an open-ended mortgage is to meet the cost of subsequent construction or property renovation. As construction proceeds, the borrower then has the right to call on the lender for the additional funds under an agreed payout plan. The open-ended mortgage is also utilized in home equity loans in which borrowers use a check or credit card to borrow more funds as they are needed.

The objective of an open-ended mortgage is to protect the lender's position against intervening liens. A properly drawn open mortgage enables the lender to make subsequent payouts and have the lien interest securing these additional funds be senior to other lien interests that may have been created during the interval between payouts. State laws differ, of course, so the rule is not universal.

Construction Loan Mortgages

Perhaps the most common example of open-end mortgages, **construction loan mortgages**, pose special problems. Lenders must ascertain that construction is actually proceeding according to plan and that money from the construction loan is in fact being employed to satisfy claims that might be secured by liens on the mortgaged property.

Construction loans typically provide for disbursement in stages as construction progresses. To protect themselves from intervening liens, construction lenders either disburse proceeds directly to suppliers (**materialmen**) and subcontractors or require affidavits that all such obligations have been satisfied prior to disbursing further funds. (Construction loans are analyzed in more detail in Chapter 12.)

DEEDS OF TRUST

Whereas a regular mortgage is a straightforward contract between two parties (borrower and lender), a **deed of trust** (or **trust deed**) involves a third party designated to act as a trustee in the transaction. The borrower conveys the property to a trustee, who holds title for the lender's benefit. In several states this procedure has largely supplanted regular mortgage arrangements.[6] In others, both mortgages and trust deeds are used.[7] Trust deed contents differ among states where they are employed, but the one in Figure 2.3 is representative.

A trustee takes title via a deed accompanied by a trust agreement (sometimes incorporated into the deed itself), which sets forth terms of the security arrangement and instructs the trustee in the event of default.

Trust agreements incorporate a wide range of trust and mortgage law. They usually provide for a public sale by the trustee in the event of default, to permit easier and quicker closure. (Foreclosure is the legal procedure by which a mortgagee or trustee may take action to "realize on the security for his loan when the covenants of the mortgage have been breached by the borrower. In effect, by filing or giving notice of the foreclosure action, the lender gives the borrower the option of paying in full and redeeming the pledged property or of forfeiting his right to the property so that it can be sold to satisfy the mortgage debt."[8] The topic of default and foreclosure is covered in greater detail in Chapter 11.) In some states, however, foreclosure on a deed of trust requires essentially the same proceeding as with a mortgage. Sales proceeds are distributed in accordance with the trust agreement, the terms of which are usually prescribed by statute. Funds generally are employed first to cover the trustee's expenses, then to satisfy the balance of indebtedness plus accrued interest, with any remaining money going to the defaulting debtor.

State statutes and lender objectives together determine specific provisions in deeds of trust. Like mortgages, however, deeds of trust invariably contain certain basic clauses, which are referenced in Figure 2.3 by the following circled numbers:

1. Names of the parties
2. Description of the property
3. A clause placing ownership in trust as security for a stipulated debt
4. A clause providing for a release when the debt has been fully paid

Also as with a mortgage, the deed of trust will often contain a number of additional phrases or clauses designed to achieve specific objectives. Those clauses, which are essentially the same as described earlier in regards to mortgages, are referenced in Figure 2.3 by the numbers indicated below:

5. Covenant of seizin
6. Covenant to pay taxes
7. Covenant of insurance
8. Covenant against removal
9. Acceleration clause

Deeds of trust appear to have been devised as an attempt to circumvent foreclosure proceedings. In most states today, they are little different functionally from the mortgages for which they serve as alternatives. The deed of trust shown in Figure 2.3 contains a fairly typical power of possession and sale (referenced in the figure as item 9). It authorizes the trustee to take possession and operate the premises as rental property in the event of default, and to sell the premises if the default is not cured as provided for elsewhere in the document.

Deeds of trust do have advantages that transcend attempts to make foreclosure easier and quicker. Selling a note secured by a deed of trust, for example, involves less legal expense and bother than one secured by a conventional mortgage. Moreover, a note secured by a deed of trust can be held without ownership becoming a matter of public record, because the owner of record is the trustee rather than the lender. This is impossible with a mortgage note, because the assignment of a mortgage needs to be recorded to protect the assignee.

FIGURE 2.3 | Deed of Trust

After Recording Return To:

_____

_____

_____

_____

_____ **[Space Above This Line For Recording Data]** _____

DEED OF TRUST

DEFINITIONS

Words used in multiple sections of this document are defined below and other words are defined in Sections 3, 11, 13, 18, 20 and 21. Certain rules regarding the usage of words used in this document are also provided in Section 16.

(A) **"Security Instrument"** means this document, which is dated _____,
_____, together with all Riders to this document.

(1) **(B)** **"Borrower"** is _____. Borrower is the trustor under this Security Instrument.

(C) **"Lender"** is _____. Lender is a _____ organized and existing under the laws of _____.
Lender's address is _____ _____.
Lender is the beneficiary under this Security Instrument.

(D) **"Trustee"** is ____, a resident of _____, Tennessee.

(E) **"Note"** means the promissory note signed by Borrower and dated _____,
_____. The Note states that Borrower owes Lender _____
Dollars (U.S. $_____) plus interest. Borrower has promised to pay this debt in regular Periodic Payments and to pay the debt in full not later than _____.
The maximum principal indebtedness for Tennessee recording tax purposes is $_____.

(F) **"Property"** means the property that is described below under the heading "Transfer of Rights in the Property."

(G) **"Loan"** means the debt evidenced by the Note, plus interest, any prepayment charges and late charges due under the Note, and all sums due under this Security Instrument, plus interest.

TENNESSEE--Single Family--Fannie Mae/Freddie Mac UNIFORM INSTRUMENT   Form 3043 1/01 _(page 1 of 16 pages)_

FIGURE 2.3   Deed of Trust *(continued)*

(H) **"Riders"** means all Riders to this Security Instrument that are executed by Borrower. The following Riders are to be executed by Borrower [check box as applicable]:

☐ Adjustable Rate Rider   ☐ Condominium Rider   ☐ Second Home Rider
☐ Balloon Rider   ☐ Planned Unit Development Rider   ☐ Other(s) [specify] _____
☐ 1-4 Family Rider   ☐ Biweekly Payment Rider

(I) **"Applicable Law"** means all controlling applicable federal, state and local statutes, regulations, ordinances and administrative rules and orders (that have the effect of law) as well as all applicable final, non-appealable judicial opinions.

(J) **"Community Association Dues, Fees, and Assessments"** means all dues, fees, assessments and other charges that are imposed on Borrower or the Property by a condominium association, homeowners association or similar organization.

(K) **"Electronic Funds Transfer"** means any transfer of funds, other than a transaction originated by check, draft, or similar paper instrument, which is initiated through an electronic terminal, telephonic instrument, computer, or magnetic tape so as to order, instruct, or authorize a financial institution to debit or credit an account. Such term includes, but is not limited to, point-of-sale transfers, automated teller machine transactions, transfers initiated by telephone, wire transfers, and automated clearinghouse transfers.

(L) **"Escrow Items"** means those items that are described in Section 3.

(M) **"Miscellaneous Proceeds"** means any compensation, settlement, award of damages, or proceeds paid by any third party (other than insurance proceeds paid under the coverages described in Section 5) for: (i) damage to, or destruction of, the Property; (ii) condemnation or other taking of all or any part of the Property; (iii) conveyance in lieu of condemnation; or (iv) misrepresentations of, or omissions as to, the value and/or condition of the Property.

(N) **"Mortgage Insurance"** means insurance protecting Lender against the nonpayment of, or default on, the Loan.

(O) **"Periodic Payment"** means the regularly scheduled amount due for (i) principal and interest under the Note, plus (ii) any amounts under Section 3 of this Security Instrument.

(P) **"RESPA"** means the Real Estate Settlement Procedures Act (12 U.S.C. §2601 et seq.) and its implementing regulation, Regulation X (24 C.F.R. Part 3500), as they might be amended from time to time, or any additional or successor legislation or regulation that governs the same subject matter. As used in this Security Instrument, "RESPA" refers to all requirements and restrictions that are imposed in regard to a "federally related mortgage loan" even if the Loan does not qualify as a "federally related mortgage loan" under RESPA.

(Q) **"Successor in Interest of Borrower"** means any party that has taken title to the Property, whether or not that party has assumed Borrower's obligations under the Note and/or this Security Instrument.

TRANSFER OF RIGHTS IN THE PROPERTY

③ This Security Instrument secures to Lender: (i) the repayment of the Loan, and all renewals, extensions and modifications of the Note; and (ii) the performance of Borrower's covenants and agreements under this Security Instrument and the Note. For this purpose, Borrower irrevocably

FIGURE 2.3 | Deed of Trust *(continued)*

grants and conveys to Trustee, in trust, with power of sale, the following described property located in the _____ of _____:

[Type of Recording Jurisdiction]   [Name of Recording Jurisdiction]

②

Derivation Clause

The instrument constituting the source of the Borrower's interest in the foregoing described property was a [Warranty Deed] [Quitclaim Deed] [Other] recorded [at Book _____, Page _____] [under Instrument No. _____] in the Register's Office of _____ County, Tennessee.

which currently has the address of _____

                                                              [Street]

_____, Tennessee _____ ("Property Address"):

            [City]   [Zip Code]

TO HAVE AND TO HOLD, the aforedescribed property, together with all the hereditaments and appurtenances thereunto belonging to, or in anywise appertaining, unto the Trustee, its successors in trust and assigns, in fee simple forever.

TOGETHER WITH all the improvements now or hereafter erected on the property, and all easements, appurtenances, and fixtures now or hereafter a part of the property. All replacements and additions shall also be covered by this Security Instrument. All of the foregoing is referred to in this Security Instrument as the "Property."

⑤ BORROWER COVENANTS that Borrower is lawfully seised of the estate hereby conveyed and has the right to grant and convey the Property and that the Property is unencumbered, except for encumbrances of record. Borrower warrants and will defend generally the title to the Property against all claims and demands, subject to any encumbrances of record.

THIS SECURITY INSTRUMENT combines uniform covenants for national use and non-uniform covenants with limited variations by jurisdiction to constitute a uniform security instrument covering real property.

UNIFORM COVENANTS. Borrower and Lender covenant and agree as follows:

TENNESSEE--Single Family--Fannie Mae/Freddie Mac UNIFORM INSTRUMENT   Form 3043 1/01 *(page 3 of 16 pages)*

FIGURE 2.3 | Deed of Trust *(continued)*

1.   Payment of Principal, Interest, Escrow Items, Prepayment Charges, and Late Charges. Borrower shall pay when due the principal of, and interest on, the debt evidenced by the Note and any prepayment charges and late charges due under the Note. Borrower shall also pay funds for Escrow Items pursuant to Section 3. Payments due under the Note and this Security Instrument shall be made in U.S. currency. However, if any check or other instrument received by Lender as payment under the Note or this Security Instrument is returned to Lender unpaid, Lender may require that any or all subsequent payments due under the Note and this Security Instrument be made in one or more of the following forms, as selected by Lender: (a) cash; (b) money order; (c) certified check, bank check, treasurer's check or cashier's check, provided any such check is drawn upon an institution whose deposits are insured by a federal agency, instrumentality, or entity; or (d) Electronic Funds Transfer.

Payments are deemed received by Lender when received at the location designated in the Note or at such other location as may be designated by Lender in accordance with the notice provisions in Section 15. Lender may return any payment or partial payment if the payment or partial payments are insufficient to bring the Loan current. Lender may accept any payment or partial payment insufficient to bring the Loan current, without waiver of any rights hereunder or prejudice to its rights to refuse such payment or partial payments in the future, but Lender is not obligated to apply such payments at the time such payments are accepted. If each Periodic Payment is applied as of its scheduled due date, then Lender need not pay interest on unapplied funds. Lender may hold such unapplied funds until Borrower makes payment to bring the Loan current. If Borrower does not do so within a reasonable period of time, Lender shall either apply such funds or return them to Borrower. If not applied earlier, such funds will be applied to the outstanding principal balance under the Note immediately prior to foreclosure. No offset or claim which Borrower might have now or in the future against Lender shall relieve Borrower from making payments due under the Note and this Security Instrument or performing the covenants and agreements secured by this Security Instrument.

2.   Application of Payments or Proceeds. Except as otherwise described in this Section 2, all payments accepted and applied by Lender shall be applied in the following order of priority: (a) interest due under the Note; (b) principal due under the Note; (c) amounts due under Section 3. Such payments shall be applied to each Periodic Payment in the order in which it became due. Any remaining amounts shall be applied first to late charges, second to any other amounts due under this Security Instrument, and then to reduce the principal balance of the Note.

If Lender receives a payment from Borrower for a delinquent Periodic Payment which includes a sufficient amount to pay any late charge due, the payment may be applied to the delinquent payment and the late charge. If more than one Periodic Payment is outstanding, Lender may apply any payment received from Borrower to the repayment of the Periodic Payments if, and to the extent that, each payment can be paid in full. To the extent that any excess exists after the payment is applied to the full payment of one or more Periodic Payments, such excess may be applied to any late charges due. Voluntary prepayments shall be applied first to any prepayment charges and then as described in the Note.

Any application of payments, insurance proceeds, or Miscellaneous Proceeds to principal due under the Note shall not extend or postpone the due date, or change the amount, of the Periodic Payments.

3.   Funds for Escrow Items. Borrower shall pay to Lender on the day Periodic Payments are due under the Note, until the Note is paid in full, a sum (the "Funds") to provide for payment of

FIGURE 2.3 | Deed of Trust *(continued)*

⑥ amounts due for: (a) taxes and assessments and other items which can attain priority over this
⑦ Security Instrument as a lien or encumbrance on the Property; (b) leasehold payments or ground rents on the Property, if any; (c) premiums for any and all insurance required by Lender under Section 5; and (d) Mortgage Insurance premiums, if any, or any sums payable by Borrower to Lender in lieu of the payment of Mortgage Insurance premiums in accordance with the provisions of Section 10. These items are called "Escrow Items." At origination or at any time during the term of the Loan, Lender may require that Community Association Dues, Fees, and Assessments, if any, be escrowed by Borrower, and such dues, fees and assessments shall be an Escrow Item. Borrower shall promptly furnish to Lender all notices of amounts to be paid under this Section. Borrower shall pay Lender the Funds for Escrow Items unless Lender waives Borrower's obligation to pay the Funds for any or all Escrow Items. Lender may waive Borrower's obligation to pay to Lender Funds for any or all Escrow Items at any time. Any such waiver may only be in writing. In the event of such waiver, Borrower shall pay directly, when and where payable, the amounts due for any Escrow Items for which payment of Funds has been waived by Lender and, if Lender requires, shall furnish to Lender receipts evidencing such payment within such time period as Lender may require. Borrower's obligation to make such payments and to provide receipts shall for all purposes be deemed to be a covenant and agreement contained in this Security Instrument, as the phrase "covenant and agreement" is used in Section 9. If Borrower is obligated to pay Escrow Items directly, pursuant to a waiver, and Borrower fails to pay the amount due for an Escrow Item, Lender may exercise its rights under Section 9 and pay such amount and Borrower shall then be obligated under Section 9 to repay to Lender any such amount. Lender may revoke the waiver as to any or all Escrow Items at any time by a notice given in accordance with Section 15 and, upon such revocation, Borrower shall pay to Lender all Funds, and in such amounts, that are then required under this Section 3.

Lender may, at any time, collect and hold Funds in an amount (a) sufficient to permit Lender to apply the Funds at the time specified under RESPA, and (b) not to exceed the maximum amount a lender can require under RESPA. Lender shall estimate the amount of Funds due on the basis of current data and reasonable estimates of expenditures of future Escrow Items or otherwise in accordance with Applicable Law.

The Funds shall be held in an institution whose deposits are insured by a federal agency, instrumentality, or entity (including Lender, if Lender is an institution whose deposits are so insured) or in any Federal Home Loan Bank. Lender shall apply the Funds to pay the Escrow Items no later than the time specified under RESPA. Lender shall not charge Borrower for holding and applying the Funds, annually analyzing the escrow account, or verifying the Escrow Items, unless Lender pays Borrower interest on the Funds and Applicable Law permits Lender to make such a charge. Unless an agreement is made in writing or Applicable Law requires interest to be paid on the Funds, Lender shall not be required to pay Borrower any interest or earnings on the Funds. Borrower and Lender can agree in writing, however, that interest shall be paid on the Funds. Lender shall give to Borrower, without charge, an annual accounting of the Funds as required by RESPA.

If there is a surplus of Funds held in escrow, as defined under RESPA, Lender shall account to Borrower for the excess funds in accordance with RESPA. If there is a shortage of Funds held in escrow, as defined under RESPA, Lender shall notify Borrower as required by RESPA, and Borrower shall pay to Lender the amount necessary to make up the shortage in accordance with

TENNESSEE--Single Family--Fannie Mae/Freddie Mac UNIFORM INSTRUMENT   Form 3043 1/01 *(page 5 of 16 pages)*

FIGURE 2.3 │ Deed of Trust *(continued)*

RESPA, but in no more than 12 monthly payments. If there is a deficiency of Funds held in escrow, as defined under RESPA, Lender shall notify Borrower as required by RESPA, and Borrower shall pay to Lender the amount necessary to make up the deficiency in accordance with RESPA, but in no more than 12 monthly payments.

Upon payment in full of all sums secured by this Security Instrument, Lender shall promptly refund to Borrower any Funds held by Lender.

⑥   **4. Charges; Liens.** Borrower shall pay all taxes, assessments, charges, fines, and impositions attributable to the Property which can attain priority over this Security Instrument, leasehold payments or ground rents on the Property, if any, and Community Association Dues, Fees, and Assessments, if any. To the extent that these items are Escrow Items, Borrower shall pay them in the manner provided in Section 3.

Borrower shall promptly discharge any lien which has priority over this Security Instrument unless Borrower: (a) agrees in writing to the payment of the obligation secured by the lien in a manner acceptable to Lender, but only so long as Borrower is performing such agreement; (b) contests the lien in good faith by, or defends against enforcement of the lien in, legal proceedings which in Lender's opinion operate to prevent the enforcement of the lien while those proceedings are pending, but only until such proceedings are concluded; or (c) secures from the holder of the lien an agreement satisfactory to Lender subordinating the lien to this Security Instrument. If Lender determines that any part of the Property is subject to a lien which can attain priority over this Security Instrument, Lender may give Borrower a notice identifying the lien. Within 10 days of the date on which that notice is given, Borrower shall satisfy the lien or take one or more of the actions set forth above in this Section 4.

Lender may require Borrower to pay a one-time charge for a real estate tax verification and/or reporting service used by Lender in connection with this Loan.

⑦   **5. Property Insurance.** Borrower shall keep the improvements now existing or hereafter erected on the Property insured against loss by fire, hazards included within the term "extended coverage," and any other hazards including, but not limited to, earthquakes and floods, for which Lender requires insurance. This insurance shall be maintained in the amounts (including deductible levels) and for the periods that Lender requires. What Lender requires pursuant to the preceding sentences can change during the term of the Loan. The insurance carrier providing the insurance shall be chosen by Borrower subject to Lender's right to disapprove Borrower's choice, which right shall not be exercised unreasonably. Lender may require Borrower to pay, in connection with this Loan, either: (a) a one-time charge for flood zone determination, certification and tracking services; or (b) a one-time charge for flood zone determination and certification services and subsequent charges each time remappings or similar changes occur which reasonably might affect such determination or certification. Borrower shall also be responsible for the payment of any fees imposed by the Federal Emergency Management Agency in connection with the review of any flood zone determination resulting from an objection by Borrower.

If Borrower fails to maintain any of the coverages described above, Lender may obtain insurance coverage, at Lender's option and Borrower's expense. Lender is under no obligation to purchase any particular type or amount of coverage. Therefore, such coverage shall cover Lender, but might or might not protect Borrower, Borrower's equity in the Property, or the contents of the Property, against any risk, hazard or liability and might provide greater or lesser coverage than was previously in effect. Borrower acknowledges that the cost of the insurance coverage so obtained might significantly exceed the cost of insurance that Borrower could have obtained. Any amounts disbursed by Lender under this Section 5 shall become additional debt of Borrower secured by this Security Instrument. These amounts shall bear interest at the Note rate from the date of disbursement and shall be payable, with such interest, upon notice from Lender to Borrower requesting payment.

All insurance policies required by Lender and renewals of such policies shall be subject to Lender's right to disapprove such policies, shall include a standard mortgage clause, and shall name Lender as mortgagee and/or as an additional loss payee. Lender shall have the right to hold the policies and renewal certificates. If Lender requires, Borrower shall promptly give to Lender all receipts of paid premiums and renewal notices. If Borrower obtains any form of insurance coverage, not otherwise required by Lender, for damage to, or destruction of, the Property, such policy shall include a standard mortgage clause and shall name Lender as mortgagee and/or as an additional loss payee.

In the event of loss, Borrower shall give prompt notice to the insurance carrier and Lender. Lender may make proof of loss if not made promptly by Borrower. Unless Lender and Borrower otherwise agree in writing, any insurance proceeds, whether or not the underlying insurance was required by Lender, shall be applied to restoration or repair of the Property, if the restoration or repair is economically feasible and Lender's security is not lessened. During such repair and restoration period, Lender shall have the right to hold such insurance proceeds until Lender has had an opportunity to inspect such Property to ensure the work has been completed to Lender's satisfaction, provided that such inspection shall be undertaken promptly. Lender may disburse proceeds for the repairs and restoration in a single payment or in a series of progress payments as the work is completed. Unless an agreement is made in writing or Applicable Law requires interest to be paid on such insurance proceeds, Lender shall not be required to pay Borrower any interest or earnings on such proceeds. Fees for public adjusters, or other third parties, retained by Borrower shall not be paid out of the insurance proceeds and shall be the sole obligation of Borrower. If the restoration or repair is not economically feasible or Lender's security would be lessened, the insurance proceeds shall be applied to the sums secured by this Security Instrument, whether or not then due, with the excess, if any, paid to Borrower. Such insurance proceeds shall be applied in the order provided for in Section 2.

If Borrower abandons the Property, Lender may file, negotiate and settle any available insurance claim and related matters. If Borrower does not respond within 30 days to a notice from Lender that the insurance carrier has offered to settle a claim, then Lender may negotiate and settle the claim. The 30-day period will begin when the notice is given. In either event, or if Lender acquires the Property under Section 22 or otherwise, Borrower hereby assigns to Lender (a) Borrower's rights to any insurance proceeds in an amount not to exceed the amounts unpaid under the Note or this Security Instrument, and (b) any other of Borrower's rights (other than the right to any refund of unearned premiums paid by Borrower) under all insurance policies covering the Property, insofar as such rights are applicable to the coverage of the Property. Lender may use the insurance proceeds either to repair or restore the Property or to pay amounts unpaid under the Note or this Security Instrument, whether or not then due.

FIGURE 2.3 | Deed of Trust *(continued)*

6. Occupancy. Borrower shall occupy, establish, and use the Property as Borrower's principal residence within 60 days after the execution of this Security Instrument and shall continue to occupy the Property as Borrower's principal residence for at least one year after the date of occupancy, unless Lender otherwise agrees in writing, which consent shall not be unreasonably withheld, or unless extenuating circumstances exist which are beyond Borrower's control.

7. Preservation, Maintenance and Protection of the Property; Inspections. Borrower shall not destroy, damage or impair the Property, allow the Property to deteriorate or commit waste on the Property. Whether or not Borrower is residing in the Property, Borrower shall maintain the Property in order to prevent the Property from deteriorating or decreasing in value due to its condition. Unless it is determined pursuant to Section 5 that repair or restoration is not economically feasible, Borrower shall promptly repair the Property if damaged to avoid further deterioration or damage. If insurance or condemnation proceeds are paid in connection with damage to, or the taking of, the Property, Borrower shall be responsible for repairing or restoring the Property only if Lender has released proceeds for such purposes. Lender may disburse proceeds for the repairs and restoration in a single payment or in a series of progress payments as the work is completed. If the insurance or condemnation proceeds are not sufficient to repair or restore the Property, Borrower is not relieved of Borrower's obligation for the completion of such repair or restoration.

Lender or its agent may make reasonable entries upon and inspections of the Property. If it has reasonable cause, Lender may inspect the interior of the improvements on the Property. Lender shall give Borrower notice at the time of or prior to such an interior inspection specifying such reasonable cause.

8. Borrower's Loan Application. Borrower shall be in default if, during the Loan application process, Borrower or any persons or entities acting at the direction of Borrower or with Borrower's knowledge or consent gave materially false, misleading, or inaccurate information or statements to Lender (or failed to provide Lender with material information) in connection with the Loan. Material representations include, but are not limited to, representations concerning Borrower's occupancy of the Property as Borrower's principal residence.

9. Protection of Lender's Interest in the Property and Rights Under this Security Instrument. If (a) Borrower fails to perform the covenants and agreements contained in this Security Instrument, (b) there is a legal proceeding that might significantly affect Lender's interest in the Property and/or rights under this Security Instrument (such as a proceeding in bankruptcy, probate, for condemnation or forfeiture, for enforcement of a lien which may attain priority over this Security Instrument or to enforce laws or regulations), or (c) Borrower has abandoned the Property, then Lender may do and pay for whatever is reasonable or appropriate to protect Lender's interest in the Property and rights under this Security Instrument, including protecting and/or assessing the value of the Property, and securing and/or repairing the Property. Lender's actions can include, but are not limited to: (a) paying any sums secured by a lien which has priority over this Security Instrument; (b) appearing in court; and (c) paying reasonable attorneys' fees to protect its interest in the Property and/or rights under this Security Instrument, including its secured position in a bankruptcy proceeding. Securing the Property includes, but is not limited to, entering the Property to make repairs, change locks, replace or board up doors and windows, drain water from pipes, eliminate building or other code violations or dangerous conditions, and have utilities turned on or off. Although Lender may take action under this Section 9, Lender does not have to do so and is not

FIGURE 2.3 | Deed of Trust *(continued)*

under any duty or obligation to do so. It is agreed that Lender incurs no liability for not taking any or all actions authorized under this Section 9.

Any amounts disbursed by Lender under this Section 9 shall become additional debt of Borrower secured by this Security Instrument. These amounts shall bear interest at the Note rate from the date of disbursement and shall be payable, with such interest, upon notice from Lender to Borrower requesting payment.

If this Security Instrument is on a leasehold, Borrower shall comply with all the provisions of the lease. If Borrower acquires fee title to the Property, the leasehold and the fee title shall not merge unless Lender agrees to the merger in writing.

10. Mortgage Insurance. If Lender required Mortgage Insurance as a condition of making the Loan, Borrower shall pay the premiums required to maintain the Mortgage Insurance in effect. If, for any reason, the Mortgage Insurance coverage required by Lender ceases to be available from the mortgage insurer that previously provided such insurance and Borrower was required to make separately designated payments toward the premiums for Mortgage Insurance, Borrower shall pay the premiums required to obtain coverage substantially equivalent to the Mortgage Insurance previously in effect, at a cost substantially equivalent to the cost to Borrower of the Mortgage Insurance previously in effect, from an alternate mortgage insurer selected by Lender. If substantially equivalent Mortgage Insurance coverage is not available, Borrower shall continue to pay to Lender the amount of the separately designated payments that were due when the insurance coverage ceased to be in effect. Lender will accept, use and retain these payments as a non-refundable loss reserve in lieu of Mortgage Insurance. Such loss reserve shall be non-refundable, notwithstanding the fact that the Loan is ultimately paid in full, and Lender shall not be required to pay Borrower any interest or earnings on such loss reserve. Lender can no longer require loss reserve payments if Mortgage Insurance coverage (in the amount and for the period that Lender requires) provided by an insurer selected by Lender again becomes available, is obtained, and Lender requires separately designated payments toward the premiums for Mortgage Insurance. If Lender required Mortgage Insurance as a condition of making the Loan and Borrower was required to make separately designated payments toward the premiums for Mortgage Insurance, Borrower shall pay the premiums required to maintain Mortgage Insurance in effect, or to provide a non-refundable loss reserve, until Lender's requirement for Mortgage Insurance ends in accordance with any written agreement between Borrower and Lender providing for such termination or until termination is required by Applicable Law. Nothing in this Section 10 affects Borrower's obligation to pay interest at the rate provided in the Note.

Mortgage Insurance reimburses Lender (or any entity that purchases the Note) for certain losses it may incur if Borrower does not repay the Loan as agreed. Borrower is not a party to the Mortgage Insurance.

Mortgage insurers evaluate their total risk on all such insurance in force from time to time, and may enter into agreements with other parties that share or modify their risk, or reduce losses. These agreements are on terms and conditions that are satisfactory to the mortgage insurer and the other party (or parties) to these agreements. These agreements may require the mortgage insurer to make payments using any source of funds that the mortgage insurer may have available (which may include funds obtained from Mortgage Insurance premiums).

As a result of these agreements, Lender, any purchaser of the Note, another insurer, any reinsurer, any other entity, or any affiliate of any of the foregoing, may receive (directly or indirectly)

TENNESSEE--Single Family--**Fannie Mae/Freddie Mac UNIFORM INSTRUMENT**   Form 3043 1/01 *(page 9 of 16 pages)*

FIGURE 2.3 | Deed of Trust *(continued)*

amounts that derive from (or might be characterized as) a portion of Borrower's payments for Mortgage Insurance, in exchange for sharing or modifying the mortgage insurer's risk, or reducing losses. If such agreement provides that an affiliate of Lender takes a share of the insurer's risk in exchange for a share of the premiums paid to the insurer, the arrangement is often termed "captive reinsurance." Further:

(a) **Any such agreements will not affect the amounts that Borrower has agreed to pay for Mortgage Insurance, or any other terms of the Loan. Such agreements will not increase the amount Borrower will owe for Mortgage Insurance, and they will not entitle Borrower to any refund.**

(b) **Any such agreements will not affect the rights Borrower has – if any – with respect to the Mortgage Insurance under the Homeowners Protection Act of 1998 or any other law. These rights may include the right to receive certain disclosures, to request and obtain cancellation of the Mortgage Insurance, to have the Mortgage Insurance terminated automatically, and/or to receive a refund of any Mortgage Insurance premiums that were unearned at the time of such cancellation or termination.**

11. Assignment of Miscellaneous Proceeds; Forfeiture. All Miscellaneous Proceeds are hereby assigned to and shall be paid to Lender.

If the Property is damaged, such Miscellaneous Proceeds shall be applied to restoration or repair of the Property, if the restoration or repair is economically feasible and Lender's security is not lessened. During such repair and restoration period, Lender shall have the right to hold such Miscellaneous Proceeds until Lender has had an opportunity to inspect such Property to ensure the work has been completed to Lender's satisfaction, provided that such inspection shall be undertaken promptly. Lender may pay for the repairs and restoration in a single disbursement or in a series of progress payments as the work is completed. Unless an agreement is made in writing or Applicable Law requires interest to be paid on such Miscellaneous Proceeds, Lender shall not be required to pay Borrower any interest or earnings on such Miscellaneous Proceeds. If the restoration or repair is not economically feasible or Lender's security would be lessened, the Miscellaneous Proceeds shall be applied to the sums secured by this Security Instrument, whether or not then due, with the excess, if any, paid to Borrower. Such Miscellaneous Proceeds shall be applied in the order provided for in Section 2.

In the event of a total taking, destruction, or loss in value of the Property, the Miscellaneous Proceeds shall be applied to the sums secured by this Security Instrument, whether or not then due, with the excess, if any, paid to Borrower.

In the event of a partial taking, destruction, or loss in value of the Property in which the fair market value of the Property immediately before the partial taking, destruction, or loss in value is equal to or greater than the amount of the sums secured by this Security Instrument immediately before the partial taking, destruction, or loss in value, unless Borrower and Lender otherwise agree in writing, the sums secured by this Security Instrument shall be reduced by the amount of the Miscellaneous Proceeds multiplied by the following fraction: (a) the total amount of the sums secured immediately before the partial taking, destruction, or loss in value divided by (b) the fair market value of the Property immediately before the partial taking, destruction, or loss in value. Any balance shall be paid to Borrower.

In the event of a partial taking, destruction, or loss in value of the Property in which the fair market value of the Property immediately before the partial taking, destruction, or loss in value is

FIGURE 2.3 | Deed of Trust *(continued)*

less than the amount of the sums secured immediately before the partial taking, destruction, or loss in value, unless Borrower and Lender otherwise agree in writing, the Miscellaneous Proceeds shall be applied to the sums secured by this Security Instrument whether or not the sums are then due.

If the Property is abandoned by Borrower, or if, after notice by Lender to Borrower that the Opposing Party (as defined in the next sentence) offers to make an award to settle a claim for damages, Borrower fails to respond to Lender within 30 days after the date the notice is given, Lender is authorized to collect and apply the Miscellaneous Proceeds either to restoration or repair of the Property or to the sums secured by this Security Instrument, whether or not then due. "Opposing Party" means the third party that owes Borrower Miscellaneous Proceeds or the party against whom Borrower has a right of action in regard to Miscellaneous Proceeds.

Borrower shall be in default if any action or proceeding, whether civil or criminal, is begun that, in Lender's judgment, could result in forfeiture of the Property or other material impairment of Lender's interest in the Property or rights under this Security Instrument. Borrower can cure such a default and, if acceleration has occurred, reinstate as provided in Section 19, by causing the action or proceeding to be dismissed with a ruling that, in Lender's judgment, precludes forfeiture of the Property or other material impairment of Lender's interest in the Property or rights under this Security Instrument. The proceeds of any award or claim for damages that are attributable to the impairment of Lender's interest in the Property are hereby assigned and shall be paid to Lender.

All Miscellaneous Proceeds that are not applied to restoration or repair of the Property shall be applied in the order provided for in Section 2.

12. Borrower Not Released; Forbearance By Lender Not a Waiver. Extension of the time for payment or modification of amortization of the sums secured by this Security Instrument granted by Lender to Borrower or any Successor in Interest of Borrower shall not operate to release the liability of Borrower or any Successors in Interest of Borrower. Lender shall not be required to commence proceedings against any Successor in Interest of Borrower or to refuse to extend time for payment or otherwise modify amortization of the sums secured by this Security Instrument by reason of any demand made by the original Borrower or any Successors in Interest of Borrower. Any forbearance by Lender in exercising any right or remedy including, without limitation, Lender's acceptance of payments from third persons, entities or Successors in Interest of Borrower or in amounts less than the amount then due, shall not be a waiver of or preclude the exercise of any right or remedy.

13. Joint and Several Liability; Co-signers; Successors and Assigns Bound. Borrower covenants and agrees that Borrower's obligations and liability shall be joint and several. However, any Borrower who co-signs this Security Instrument but does not execute the Note (a "co-signer"): (a) is co-signing this Security Instrument only to mortgage, grant and convey the co-signer's interest in the Property under the terms of this Security Instrument; (b) is not personally obligated to pay the sums secured by this Security Instrument; and (c) agrees that Lender and any other Borrower can agree to extend, modify, forbear or make any accommodations with regard to the terms of this Security Instrument or the Note without the co-signer's consent.

Subject to the provisions of Section 18, any Successor in Interest of Borrower who assumes Borrower's obligations under this Security Instrument in writing, and is approved by Lender, shall obtain all of Borrower's rights and benefits under this Security Instrument. Borrower shall not be released from Borrower's obligations and liability under this Security Instrument unless Lender

FIGURE 2.3 | Deed of Trust *(continued)*

agrees to such release in writing. The covenants and agreements of this Security Instrument shall bind (except as provided in Section 20) and benefit the successors and assigns of Lender.

14. Loan Charges. Lender may charge Borrower fees for services performed in connection with Borrower's default, for the purpose of protecting Lender's interest in the Property and rights under this Security Instrument, including, but not limited to, attorneys' fees, property inspection and valuation fees. In regard to any other fees, the absence of express authority in this Security Instrument to charge a specific fee to Borrower shall not be construed as a prohibition on the charging of such fee. Lender may not charge fees that are expressly prohibited by this Security Instrument or by Applicable Law.

If the Loan is subject to a law which sets maximum loan charges, and that law is finally interpreted so that the interest or other loan charges collected or to be collected in connection with the Loan exceed the permitted limits, then: (a) any such loan charge shall be reduced by the amount necessary to reduce the charge to the permitted limit; and (b) any sums already collected from Borrower which exceeded permitted limits will be refunded to Borrower. Lender may choose to make this refund by reducing the principal owed under the Note or by making a direct payment to Borrower. If a refund reduces principal, the reduction will be treated as a partial prepayment without any prepayment charge (whether or not a prepayment charge is provided for under the Note). Borrower's acceptance of any such refund made by direct payment to Borrower will constitute a waiver of any right of action Borrower might have arising out of such overcharge.

15. Notices. All notices given by Borrower or Lender in connection with this Security Instrument must be in writing. Any notice to Borrower in connection with this Security Instrument shall be deemed to have been given to Borrower when mailed by first class mail or when actually delivered to Borrower's notice address if sent by other means. Notice to any one Borrower shall constitute notice to all Borrowers unless Applicable Law expressly requires otherwise. The notice address shall be the Property Address unless Borrower has designated a substitute notice address by notice to Lender. Borrower shall promptly notify Lender of Borrower's change of address. If Lender specifies a procedure for reporting Borrower's change of address, then Borrower shall only report a change of address through that specified procedure. There may be only one designated notice address under this Security Instrument at any one time. Any notice to Lender shall be given by delivering it or by mailing it by first class mail to Lender's address stated herein unless Lender has designated another address by notice to Borrower. Any notice in connection with this Security Instrument shall not be deemed to have been given to Lender until actually received by Lender. If any notice required by this Security Instrument is also required under Applicable Law, the Applicable Law requirement will satisfy the corresponding requirement under this Security Instrument.

16. Governing Law; Severability; Rules of Construction. This Security Instrument shall be governed by federal law and the law of the jurisdiction in which the Property is located. All rights and obligations contained in this Security Instrument are subject to any requirements and limitations of Applicable Law. Applicable Law might explicitly or implicitly allow the parties to agree by contract or it might be silent, but such silence shall not be construed as a prohibition against agreement by contract. In the event that any provision or clause of this Security Instrument or the Note conflicts with Applicable Law, such conflict shall not affect other provisions of this Security Instrument or the Note which can be given effect without the conflicting provision.

FIGURE 2.3 | Deed of Trust *(continued)*

As used in this Security Instrument: (a) words of the masculine gender shall mean and include corresponding neuter words or words of the feminine gender; (b) words in the singular shall mean and include the plural and vice versa; and (c) the word "may" gives sole discretion without any obligation to take any action.

17. Borrower's Copy. Borrower shall be given one copy of the Note and of this Security Instrument.

18. Transfer of the Property or a Beneficial Interest in Borrower. As used in this Section 18, "Interest in the Property" means any legal or beneficial interest in the Property, including, but not limited to, those beneficial interests transferred in a bond for deed, contract for deed, installment sales contract or escrow agreement, the intent of which is the transfer of title by Borrower at a future date to a purchaser.

If all or any part of the Property or any Interest in the Property is sold or transferred (or if Borrower is not a natural person and a beneficial interest in Borrower is sold or transferred) without Lender's prior written consent, Lender may require immediate payment in full of all sums secured by this Security Instrument. However, this option shall not be exercised by Lender if such exercise is prohibited by Applicable Law.

If Lender exercises this option, Lender shall give Borrower notice of acceleration. The notice shall provide a period of not less than 30 days from the date the notice is given in accordance with Section 15 within which Borrower must pay all sums secured by this Security Instrument. If Borrower fails to pay these sums prior to the expiration of this period, Lender may invoke any remedies permitted by this Security Instrument without further notice or demand on Borrower.

19. Borrower's Right to Reinstate After Acceleration. If Borrower meets certain conditions, Borrower shall have the right to have enforcement of this Security Instrument discontinued at any time prior to the earliest of: (a) five days before sale of the Property pursuant to any power of sale contained in this Security Instrument, (b) such other period as Applicable Law might specify for the termination of Borrower's right to reinstate; or (c) entry of a judgment enforcing this Security Instrument. Those conditions are that Borrower: (a) pays Lender all sums which then would be due under this Security Instrument and the Note as if no acceleration had occurred; (b) cures any default of any other covenants or agreements; (c) pays all expenses incurred in enforcing this Security Instrument, including, but not limited to, reasonable attorneys' fees, property inspection and valuation fees, and other fees incurred for the purpose of protecting Lender's interest in the Property and rights under this Security Instrument; and (d) takes such action as Lender may reasonably require to assure that Lender's interest in the Property and rights under this Security Instrument, and Borrower's obligation to pay the sums secured by this Security Instrument, shall continue unchanged. Lender may require that Borrower pay such reinstatement sums and expenses in one or more of the following forms, as selected by Lender: (a) cash; (b) money order; (c) certified check, bank check, treasurer's check or cashier's check, provided any such check is drawn upon an institution whose deposits are insured by a federal agency, instrumentality or entity; or (d) Electronic Funds Transfer. Upon reinstatement by Borrower, this Security Instrument and obligations secured hereby shall remain fully effective as if no acceleration had occurred. However, this right to reinstate shall not apply in the case of acceleration under Section 18.

20. Sale of Note; Change of Loan Servicer; Notice of Grievance. The Note or a partial interest in the Note (together with this Security Instrument) can be sold one or more times without prior notice to Borrower. A sale might result in a change in the entity (known as the "Loan

FIGURE 2.3 | Deed of Trust *(continued)*

Servicer") that collects Periodic Payments due under the Note and this Security Instrument and performs other mortgage loan servicing obligations under the Note, this Security Instrument, and Applicable Law. There also might be one or more changes of the Loan Servicer unrelated to a sale of the Note. If there is a change of the Loan Servicer, Borrower will be given written notice of the change which will state the name and address of the new Loan Servicer, the address to which payments should be made and any other information RESPA requires in connection with a notice of transfer of servicing. If the Note is sold and thereafter the Loan is serviced by a Loan Servicer other than the purchaser of the Note, the mortgage loan servicing obligations to Borrower will remain with the Loan Servicer or be transferred to a successor Loan Servicer and are not assumed by the Note purchaser unless otherwise provided by the Note purchaser.

Neither Borrower nor Lender may commence, join, or be joined to any judicial action (as either an individual litigant or the member of a class) that arises from the other party's actions pursuant to this Security Instrument or that alleges that the other party has breached any provision of, or any duty owed by reason of, this Security Instrument, until such Borrower or Lender has notified the other party (with such notice given in compliance with the requirements of Section 15) of such alleged breach and afforded the other party hereto a reasonable period after the giving of such notice to take corrective action. If Applicable Law provides a time period which must elapse before certain action can be taken, that time period will be deemed to be reasonable for purposes of this paragraph. The notice of acceleration and opportunity to cure given to Borrower pursuant to Section 22 and the notice of acceleration given to Borrower pursuant to Section 18 shall be deemed to satisfy the notice and opportunity to take corrective action provisions of this Section 20.

21. Hazardous Substances. As used in this Section 21: (a) "Hazardous Substances" are those substances defined as toxic or hazardous substances, pollutants, or wastes by Environmental Law and the following substances: gasoline, kerosene, other flammable or toxic petroleum products, toxic pesticides and herbicides, volatile solvents, materials containing asbestos or formaldehyde, and radioactive materials; (b) "Environmental Law" means federal laws and laws of the jurisdiction where the Property is located that relate to health, safety or environmental protection; (c) "Environmental Cleanup" includes any response action, remedial action, or removal action, as defined in Environmental Law; and (d) an "Environmental Condition" means a condition that can cause, contribute to, or otherwise trigger an Environmental Cleanup.

Borrower shall not cause or permit the presence, use, disposal, storage, or release of any Hazardous Substances, or threaten to release any Hazardous Substances, on or in the Property. Borrower shall not do, nor allow anyone else to do, anything affecting the Property (a) that is in violation of any Environmental Law, (b) which creates an Environmental Condition, or (c) which, due to the presence, use, or release of a Hazardous Substance, creates a condition that adversely affects the value of the Property. The preceding two sentences shall not apply to the presence, use, or storage on the Property of small quantities of Hazardous Substances that are generally recognized to be appropriate to normal residential uses and to maintenance of the Property (including, but not limited to, hazardous substances in consumer products).

Borrower shall promptly give Lender written notice of (a) any investigation, claim, demand, lawsuit or other action by any governmental or regulatory agency or private party involving the Property and any Hazardous Substance or Environmental Law of which Borrower has actual knowledge, (b) any Environmental Condition, including but not limited to, any spilling, leaking, discharge, release or threat of release of any Hazardous Substance, and (c) any condition caused by

FIGURE 2.3 | Deed of Trust *(continued)*

the presence, use or release of a Hazardous Substance which adversely affects the value of the Property. If Borrower learns, or is notified by any governmental or regulatory authority, or any private party, that any removal or other remediation of any Hazardous Substance affecting the Property is necessary, Borrower shall promptly take all necessary remedial actions in accordance with Environmental Law. Nothing herein shall create any obligation on Lender for an Environmental Cleanup.

NON-UNIFORM COVENANTS. Borrower and Lender further covenant and agree as follows:

⑨ **22. Acceleration; Remedies. Lender shall give notice to Borrower prior to acceleration following Borrower's breach of any covenant or agreement in this Security Instrument (but not prior to acceleration under Section 18 unless Applicable Law provides otherwise). The notice shall specify: (a) the default; (b) the action required to cure the default; (c) a date, not less than 30 days from the date the notice is given to Borrower, by which the default must be cured; and (d) that failure to cure the default on or before the date specified in the notice may result in acceleration of the sums secured by this Security Instrument and sale of the Property. The notice shall further inform Borrower of the right to reinstate after acceleration and the right to bring a court action to assert the non-existence of a default or any other defense of Borrower to acceleration and sale. If the default is not cured on or before the date specified in the notice, Lender at its option may require immediate payment in full of all sums secured by this Security Instrument without further demand and may invoke the power of sale and any other remedies permitted by Applicable Law. Lender shall be entitled to collect all expenses incurred in pursuing the remedies provided in this Section 22, including, but not limited to, reasonable attorneys' fees and costs of title evidence.**

If Lender invokes the power of sale, Trustee shall give notice of sale by public advertisement in the county in which the Property is located for the time and in the manner provided by Applicable Law, and Lender or Trustee shall mail a copy of the notice of sale to Borrower in the manner provided in Section 15. Trustee, without demand on Borrower, shall sell the Property at public auction to the highest bidder at the time and under the terms designated in the notice of sale. Lender or its designee may purchase the Property at any sale.

Trustee shall deliver to the purchaser Trustee's deed conveying the Property without any covenant or warranty, expressed or implied. The recitals in the Trustee's deed shall be prima facie evidence of the truth of the statements made therein. Trustee shall apply the proceeds of the sale in the following order: (a) to all expenses of the sale, including, but not limited to, reasonable Trustee's and attorneys' fees; (b) to all sums secured by this Security Instrument; and (c) any excess to the person or persons legally entitled to it. If the Property is sold pursuant to this Section 22, Borrower, or any person holding possession of the Property through Borrower, shall immediately surrender possession of the Property to the purchaser at the sale. If possession is not surrendered, Borrower or such person shall be a tenant at will of the purchaser and hereby agrees to pay the purchaser the reasonable rental value of the Property after sale.

④ **23. Release.** Upon payment of all sums secured by this Security Instrument, Lender shall release this Security Instrument. Lender may charge Borrower a fee for releasing this Security

FIGURE 2.3 | Deed of Trust *(continued)*

Instrument, but only if the fee is paid to a third party for services rendered and the charging of the fee is permitted under Applicable Law.

24. Substitute Trustee. Lender, at its option, may from time to time remove Trustee and appoint a successor trustee to any Trustee appointed hereunder by an instrument recorded in the county in which this Security Instrument is recorded. Without conveyance of the Property, the successor trustee shall succeed to all the title, power and duties conferred upon Trustee herein and by Applicable Law.

25. Waivers. Borrower waives all right of homestead, equity of redemption, statutory right of redemption and relinquishes all other rights and exemptions of every kind, including, but not limited to, a statutory right to an elective share in the Property.

BY SIGNING BELOW, Borrower accepts and agrees to the terms and covenants contained in this Security Instrument and in any Rider executed by Borrower and recorded with it.

IN WITNESS WHEREOF, Borrower has executed this Security Instrument.

Witnesses:

_____   _____ (Seal)
                                                                            - Borrower

                                             Social Security Number _____

_____   _____ (Seal)
                                                                            - Borrower

                                             Social Security Number _____

_____ **[Space Below This Line For Acknowledgment]** _____

FIGURE 2.3 | Deed of Trust *(continued)*

STATE OF TENNESSEE

COUNTY OF _____

On this _____ day of _____, 20 _____, before me personally appeared
_____, to me known to be the person (or persons)
described in and who executed the foregoing instrument, and acknowledged that such person (or
persons) executed the same as such person (or person's) free act and deed.

_____

Notary Public

Printed Name: _____

Commission Expires:

_____

STATE OF TENNESSEE

COUNTY OF _____

On this _____ day of _____, 20 _____, before me personally appeared
_____, to me known to be the person (or persons)
described in and who executed the foregoing instrument, and acknowledged that such person (or
persons) executed the same as such person (or person's) free act and deed.

_____

Notary Public

Printed Name: _____

Commission Expires:

_____

SAMPLE

SUMMARY

A promissory note represents a promise to pay a debt and specifies the terms and conditions. The promise may be secured or unsecured. If real estate is to be pledged as security for the promise, this is usually accomplished by a mortgage. Mortgages appear to be actual transfers of ownership, but they contain a defeasance clause that renders the transfer inoperative if the promissory note is honored by the borrower.

Common variations of mortgage instruments include purchase-money mortgages, blanket mortgages, open-ended mortgages, and construction loan mortgages. Purchase-money mortgages secure notes given to a seller in part payment for property, while blanket mortgages pledge two or more parcels of property as security for a single loan. Open-ended mortgages are written so that additional funds can be advanced under the security of the same mortgage. Construction loan mortgages involve special problems for lenders, because funds are advanced on the security of improvements that are not yet in existence.

In many jurisdictions, deeds of trust are used instead of mortgages. The trust deed transfers property ownership to a trustee who is obligated to act in accordance with a trust agreement that spells out what the trustee must do in event of default on the loan.

KEY TERMS

acceleration clause	covenant against removal	mortgagee
assumption clause (due on sale, due on resale, due on alienation clause)	covenant of insurance	mortgagor
	covenant of seizin	open-ended mortgage (open mortgage)
	covenant to pay taxes	prepayment clause
	deed of trust (trust deed)	promissory notes
blanket mortgage (cross-collateralization agreement)	defeasance clause	purchase-money mortgage (take-back mortgage)
	delivery	
construction loan mortgage	materialmen	
	mortgage	

NOTES

1. In some states—notably Delaware and Pennsylvania—bonds are employed instead of mortgages. This specialized kind of bond differs little from a mortgage.

2. Reprinted from *Black's Law Dictionary*, Henry Campbell Black and Michael J. Connolly, 5th edition, 1979, with permission of West Group.

3. L.M. Friedman, *A History of American Law,* 2nd ed. New York: Touchstone Publishers, 1986; Robert H. Skilton, "Developments in Mortgage Law and Practice," *Temple Law Quarterly* 17 (1943): 315.

4. Friedman, 17–18.

5. Many states have enacted statutory provisions for prepayment without penalty under specified circumstances. These laws generally cover only mortgages on personal residences. FHA-insured and VA-guaranteed mortgage notes must permit prepayment without penalty under specially prescribed circumstances.

6. California, Colorado, Connecticut, Mississippi, Missouri, Oregon, Tennessee, Texas, Virginia, West Virginia.

7. Alaska, Delaware, Idaho, Kansas, Kentucky, Nevada, South Carolina.

8. Alvin L. Arnold, *Real Estate Investor's Deskbook,* 3rd ed., §11:32.

▌RECOMMENDED READING

Downs, Anthony. *The Revolution in Real Estate Finance*. Washington, D.C.: The Brookings Institute, 1985.

Greenberg, Alan. "Back to Basics: Negotiating Financing in the 1990s." *Real Estate Finance Journal* 7, no. 3 (Winter 1992): 33–37.

Stein, Joshua. "Cures for the (Sometimes) Needless Complexity of Real Estate Documents." *Real Estate Review* 25, no. 3 (Fall 1995): 63–67.

For a summary of many of the forms of promissory notes and mortgages preferred by local usage see the following:

Martindale-Hubbell Law Digest: United States Law Digests, 2005. Part I, Digests of the Laws of the States, The District of Columbia, Puerto Rico and The Virgin Islands. Martindale-Hubbell, a Division of Reed-Elsevier Inc.

Friedman, L.M. *A History of American Law*, 2nd ed. New York: Touchstone Publishers, 1986.

▌INTERNET REFERENCES

For information on Mortgage Law:
www.law.cornell.edu/topics/mortgages.html

▌REVIEW QUESTIONS

1. How do mortgage notes differ from other promissory notes?

2. List five provisions that must be included in mortgage notes.

3. What functions do mortgages serve?

4. List five items that are included in almost all mortgages.

5. What is a covenant of seizin?

6. What is the purpose of an assumption clause?

7. Because acknowledgment is not necessary for a valid mortgage, why would a lender bother to have a borrower's signature acknowledged?

8. How do purchase-money mortgages differ from other mortgages?

9. What is an open-ended mortgage?

10. What is the primary difference between a regular mortgage and a deed of trust?

11. Describe the role of the trustee in a trust deed arrangement.

12. What is the Statute of Frauds?

DISCUSSION QUESTIONS

1. Why is there so much variety in loan documentation among the various states? Would a uniform national system be useful?

2. It has been argued that the wording on loan documents favors lenders over borrowers, while courts' interpretations favor borrowers over lenders. Discuss.

3. If mortgaged property is in one state and the mortgage lender is in another, which state's laws should govern the mortgage loan transaction?

4. Do rational property owners voluntarily insure their property and pay their property taxes? Why, then, do lenders routinely insist on a covenant of insurance and a covenant to pay taxes as part of the mortgage?

5. How might the mortgage loan market be different if the sale of a note by a lender required the borrower's approval?

CHAPTER 3

Credit Procedures

LEARNING OBJECTIVES

After studying this chapter, you should know how lenders evaluate loan applications and the basic standards for underwriting. You should understand each step in the application and approval process and both public and private credit enhancements.

Even though all mortgage lenders deal in the same product—money—and render essentially the same service—temporary access to capital—their customs and practices often differ significantly. Even so, they do have essential similarities in their approaches to mortgage lending, and these standard procedures are important guideposts for real estate practitioners who want quick and easy access to mortgage loan funds at reasonable rates.

THE LOAN APPLICATION PROCESS

Lenders want to know as much as possible about issues affecting the safety of their loans. Consequently, prospective borrowers must file documents telling about themselves and about the real estate that will be pledged as collateral for the loan. This permits the lender to evaluate both the borrower and the security.

Information about the Applicant

Knowledge of the borrower's ability and willingness to honor repayment obligations is more important than knowing about the real estate that is being financed. The real estate's value becomes of paramount importance only if the lender is forced to foreclose on a defaulted loan. Thus, foreclosure is the lender's last line of defense; the borrower's ability and willingness are the first line.

Borrowers' reputations and experience are key considerations. To assess these characteristics, lenders require that applicants file extensive information about themselves. Information about creditworthiness and stability of employment will be checked with reliable sources.

Information about the Real Estate

Lenders want to know the real estate's market value and, for commercial projects, its income-earning ability. Projecting the **net operating income (NOI)** is important because the property's income will be a valuable source (sometimes, the sole source) of revenue with which to meet the borrower's debt service obligation. The market value is determined using the market data, cost, and income approaches to appraisal discussed in Chapter 14. The project's market value becomes a key issue if the lender is forced to seek the sale of the project in a foreclosure action, a topic that is explored at length in Chapter 11.

THE LOAN UNDERWRITING PROCESS

Underwriting is the practice of analyzing information relating to risk (an uncertain event) and making decisions designed to manage risk appropriately. Underwriting practices stem from carefully considered attempts to manage risk, from a need to comply with federal and state government regulations, and from a complex, little-understood mix of institutional culture and industry tradition. The decision to underwrite may be based on the three Cs of underwriting: **character**, **capacity**, and **collateral**.

Mortgage lenders shoulder a particularly delicate underwriting task because they must not only weigh the likelihood that borrowers will honor their promises to pay but also be concerned with the marketability of mortgage notes. If a loan is not attractive to investors, it cannot be sold in the secondary market without a substantial discount.

Uniform underwriting guidelines for all mortgage-secured loans would be inappropriate. Even for loans on the same type of property, underwriting criteria differ owing to the influence of mortgage insurers or guarantors (e.g., the FHA and VA) and private mortgage insurance firms. Even so, many of the differences affect loan processing procedures more than they do actual evaluation of the application. This is convenient, because it enables us to present a composite set of general guidelines and merely note when a particular agency imposes significantly different standards. Furthermore, underwriting factors vary between residential and commercial mortgages.

Character (Determination to Repay)

Ability to honor a debt obligation is meaningless without the determination to do so. Accordingly, lenders first investigate credit records to estimate applicants' willingness to fulfill repayment obligations. Past credit problems may cause a lender to disapprove an application even when current income is more than adequate. Credit scores are given on the debtor's credit report. The higher the score, the higher the likelihood of approval and that the loan will be at a low interest rate. Low credit scores will result in rejection of the loan or higher interest rates for a subprime loan. The Fair Credit Reporting Act sets standards for collecting information about credit applicants and limits how the information may be used. For commercial mortgages, lenders analyze the track record of experience in the type of property involved.

Capacity (Ability to Repay)

No matter how well-intentioned the borrower, credit obligations will not be met if there is insufficient income for that purpose. Key indicators of capacity to honor the repayment obligation are stable employment, liquid asset reserves, and adequate earning power. For commercial mortgages, the income of the property is analyzed, as discussed in Chapters 13 and 14.

To determine the adequacy of an applicant's capacity, prospective lenders insist on verification of employment. They ask applicants' employers to report on the amount and source of current income and the length and stability of employment, as well as the probability of continued employment. Other income, such as that from self-employment, alimony, and child support, can also be considered.

The Equal Credit Opportunity Act (ECOA) of 1976, discussed in Chapter 7, imposes on lenders the obligation of applying the same underwriting criteria to all applicants. The law requires that income from all sources (including public assistance) be considered when determining the adequacy of income. It prohibits discrimination based on race, color, national origin, gender, marital status, the possibility of pregnancy, age (provided the applicant is of legal age to contract), or that a portion of income stems from public assistance. If credit is denied, the act requires that the applicant be informed of the specific reasons.

Once an applicant's income has been established, its adequacy is assessed in terms of the relationship between financial responsibilities and the income out of which they must be met. For income-generating projects, this relationship is reflected in the debt coverage ratio (NOI from the property, divided by the debt service obligation), which shows the amount of annual NOI expected for each dollar required to service the mortgage loan. The lender's underwriting guidelines will specify minimum debt coverage ratios for various classes of income property loans.

For owner-occupied residences and for very small residential rental projects, lender guidelines establish minimum permissible ratios between income and housing expenses and between income and all recurring expenditures (essentially, housing expenses plus payments on long-term debt). The precise ratios themselves, as well as the exact mechanics of their determination, will differ, depending on whether the loan is to be insured or guaranteed by a private company or a government agency or whether it will be uninsured. Housing expenses include principal, interest, property taxes, and insurance on the property. Other debt obligations are included in the total debt service.

Accumulated assets are a crucial aspect of an applicant's capacity to repay. Experience suggests that higher down payments result in substantially less risk that the borrower will default. A cushion of reserve assets will carry a debtor through temporary unemployment or other economic adversity without the necessity to suspend payments on the mortgage note. Some lenders consider these assets as another C of underwriting: Capital. In addition to the reserve assets and the down payment, the required monies for closing costs are analyzed by the lender as to amount and source.

Collateral

Once a loan has been made, the lender is, to a substantial extent, at the borrower's mercy. No criminal penalties apply to a defaulting borrower unless fraud can be proved. Creditors' ability to attach current income or accumulated assets is severely circumscribed. If efforts to collect delinquent payments are fruitless, the lender's final recourse is to foreclose on property pledged as security for the debt. Thus, determining the adequacy of security is a key element in the underwriting process.

Toward this end, lenders set a maximum loan-to-value (LTV) ratio, which limits the loan to a specified percentage of the property's market value. Allowable LTV ratios differ for various types of property and types of loans. They also differ among classes of lenders. High LTV ratio loans (above 80 percent) generally require some type of credit enhancement such as a government guarantee or mortgage insurance, discussed later in the chapter.

The adequacy of security is determined by an appraisal. The appraisal report is used to estimate the current value of pledged property and the likely trend in its value over the lending period. The valuation of both residential and commercial properties is discussed further in Chapter 14.

Capital and Conditions

Sometimes, underwriting includes a fourth and a fifth C: **capital** and **conditions**. Capital includes the money needed to pay the down payment if the loan does not have 100 percent LTV and the closing costs required for the loan. These monies must be in place before the loan is closed and usually cannot come from another loan.

Conditions that may be considered include personal conditions, such as non-income money sources (alimony, child support) or lower living expenses. For mortgages on commercial real estate, the impact of general and regional economic conditions and the financial strength of the borrower's (and sometimes the lease-holder's) enterprise are also major considerations.

Economic conditions, especially in the geographic area where the income property is located, can affect a property's ability to generate cash flows and, hence, the borrower's ability to repay a loan. The borrower's asset and liability structure, including the degree of financial leverage already employed and the relationship between short-term and long-term assets and liabilities, may be valuable indicators of ability to honor the debt service obligation.

THE MORTGAGE LENDING DECISION: RISK AND RETURN TRADE-OFFS

Chapter 10 is devoted to costs and benefits accruing to borrowers. Buy what about the lender? The residential mortgage lending decision is a balancing act between risk and expected return.

Subprime and "Low-Doc" Lending

For many years, conventional financial institutions made residential mortgage loan decisions on a pass-or-fail basis. If an applicant did not meet the lender's criteria, the loan was denied. However, many lenders today weigh the amount of risk associated with each loan and charge a higher interest rate on loans that are deemed more risky but still acceptable.

Loans that entail higher than normal risk are called **subprime**. The higher return generated by subprime loans might be achieved by charging a higher contract interest rate, by charging fees designed to increase the effective interest rate, or by a combination of a higher nominal rate and fees. The practice of subprime lending has enhanced lenders' expected returns, and it has expanded the size of the mortgage market by increasing the number of loan applications that are deemed acceptable. But it has also elevated the aggregate risk in loan portfolios.

Most of the risk assumed by lenders in the subprime loans relates to financial risk and is estimated by analyzing credit reports. For a brief period in the 1980s, and again recently, lenders attempted to streamline the approval and closing process by minimizing loan documentation ("doc"). Underwriters of the "no-doc" or "low-doc" loans sometimes overlooked costly risks and found themselves holding problem loans. Some lenders still offer "low-doc" loans but usually only to borrowers who are deemed excellent credit risks.

Mortgage Loans as Portfolio Assets

One of the key financial problems encountered by depository-type mortgage lenders in the past has been a mismatch between long-term assets (primarily mortgage loans) and short-term liabilities (primarily depositor accounts). When market interest rates jumped, lenders found themselves paying higher interest rates on short-term liabilities than they earned on their long-term assets.

A major strategy employed to avoid a replay of this problem has been recourse to the secondary mortgage market. Depository-type lenders can sell their loans to other institutions that are less reliant on short-term liabilities for financing. Prime candidates for these transactions are life insurance companies and pension funds. The securitization of mortgages, discussed in Chapter 6, also offered a solution to the depository-type lender's need for a better match between the term structure of assets and liabilities. Commercial mortgage-backed securities enable investor of all sizes to participate in the mortgage market.

▌ THE LOAN COMMITMENT

Commitments—agreements to make financing available to qualified borrowers under specified terms and conditions—are commonly used for all kinds of real estate financing; construction loans, standby loans, gap loans, sale-leaseback arrangements, and so forth, as well as for long-term mortgage loans. **Loan commitments** are legally binding agreements that oblige the lender to disburse stipulated or determinable sums, although the commitments themselves are often expressed in very general terms. One consequence of this is frequent lawsuits charging breach of promise to lend.

Real estate attorneys emphasize the importance of loan commitments by calling them "blueprints for the deal." Yet, because it is a preliminary document that merely summarizes what *might* occur, the commitment cannot possibly contain all the terms and conditions of the contemplated transaction. The summary nature of commitment documents often leaves the parties uncertain about their rights and obligations. Consequently, it is vital that the commitment contain all the significant terms of the loan. It follows that the more involved the loan, the more lengthy and detailed will be the commitment letter.

Offers to purchase are usually contingent on obtaining a loan commitment under terms and conditions acceptable to the buyer. If the commitment cannot be obtained by the time specified in the offering document, the offer is usually rendered null and void and all monetary deposits are returned. Commitments for loans to finance property construction or rehabilitation (discussed in Chapter 12) are often contingent on the borrower's obtaining a binding commitment for a long-term loan from a source acceptable to the construction lender.

Commitment fees are routinely charged. All or a portion of the fee is sometimes in the form of a promissory note or a bank letter of credit. If the prospective borrower willfully fails to complete the transaction, the commitment fee is forfeited.

▌ CREDIT ENHANCEMENTS

Investors seeking more money than lenders are willing to commit sometimes try to enhance their borrowing power by reducing the lender's risk exposure. Toward this end, they seek third-party assurances that the lender will be protected against losses from default. Because credit enhancement reduces lenders' exposure to default risk, they will often advance a greater sum on the security of a mortgage note with the enhancement. Lenders that insist on an 80 percent LTV ratio, for example, might be willing to lend 95 percent of a property's value if repayment of the additional funds is guaranteed by a creditworthy third party.

An additional benefit of credit enhancement may be a lower interest rate. Offsetting this benefit, however, are the fees associated with the enhancement itself. An additional disadvantage is the extra time that must be scheduled into the financing process. Credit enhancements, particularly those provided by the federal government, require considerable administrative detail that can be vexing and time-consuming.

Government-Sponsored Credit Enhancements

Mortgage insurance or payment guarantees from the federal government enable investors and prospective homeowners to borrow more than would otherwise be available. Payment insurance from the Department of Housing and Urban Development (HUD) makes possible high LTV ratio loans for homes, residential rental units intended for low- to moderate-income tenants, and medical and congregate care facilities. Both HUD and the Department of Veterans Affairs (VA) administer special programs designed to extend homeownership to population segments that might not otherwise be able to get mortgage financing.

Mortgage Insurance

The best known and most widely used program of government mortgage insurance is authorized by Section 203(b) of the **National Housing Act** (as amended), for new or existing one- to four-family homes. This is the program most commonly referred to as *FHA*, although as a part of HUD, the Federal Housing Administration oversees many programs.[1] Loans under Section 203(b) cannot exceed 97 percent of the first $25,000 of acquisition cost and 95 percent of acquisition cost in excess of $25,000, up to a maximum that is determined by HUD.

The maximum allowable loan amount varies by geographic area. The highest maximum is in Alaska. Until 1991, all of the buyer's closing costs could also be financed, but now only 57 percent of the closing costs can be financed. The seller is allowed to pay up to 6 percent of the sales price for closing costs and prepays. FHA's supporters maintain that in addition to making affordable financing available to homebuyers, this program has improved the quality of housing by requiring that units meet minimum property standards (MPS) before receiving approval for loans. Example 3.1 illustrates the relationship between acquisition and closing costs and the allowable loan.

EXAMPLE 3.1

Both the price and the appraised value of a home are $90,000, and the purchasers are paying their own closing costs, which the FHA estimates to be $2,700. The amount on which the allowable loan is computed is $91,539, determined as follows:

Value and purchase price	$90,000
Add: 0.57 × $2,700	1,539
Total	$91,539

The maximum allowable loan is $87,462, determined as follows:

0.97 × $25,000	$24,250
Add: 0.95 × ($91,539 – $25,000)	63,212
Maximum allowable loan	$87,462

Section 221(d)(4) of the National Housing Act permits HUD to insure mortgage loans for construction or major rehabilitation of housing units intended for moderate-income tenants. The loans can extend for as long as 40 years and can cover up to 90 percent of project cost. The remaining 10 percent of cost can include builders' and sponsors' deferred profit, provided there is at least token overlap of ownership between developer and builder.

HUD also has a program [Section 223(f)] for financing the "moderate" rehabilitation of multifamily rental property. This generally implies rehabilitation costs of less than 15 percent of total project value.

Other HUD programs include mortgage insurance for up to 90 percent of the cost of various classes of congregate care facilities for the elderly (Section 232) and for construction and outfitting of hospitals (Section 242). Insured congregate care mortgage loans can extend for as long as 40 years; those for hospitals are limited to 25 years.

Precise terms and conditions of HUD mortgage insurance programs shift with government policy, which is notoriously unstable. There are also significant differences in the rules among the various programs. All of the programs outlined above, however, share the following features:

- All facilities must meet minimum construction standards embodied in local codes approved by HUD.

- HUD charges a commitment fee, expressed as a percentage of the proposed mortgage loan. The fee must be paid (usually in stages) during the period in which the application is being processed.

- Borrowers pay an annual mortgage insurance premium of one-half of 1 percent of the outstanding balance of the insured loan. The premium is added to the monthly mortgage payment.

- The mortgages are **nonrecourse**, which means the borrower has no personal liability for the debt. The federal government looks only to the value of the mortgaged property for compensation in the event of default.

- Mortgage insurance does not completely eliminate lender risk. The lender bears the risk associated with 30 days of unpaid interest, and must pay HUD 1 percent of the outstanding balance as an assignment fee when a defaulted loan is assigned to HUD. On certain loan insurance programs, HUD payment is made in cash. On others, payment is in the form of 20-year FHA debentures, which may carry a below-market interest rate.

Payment Guarantees

As World War II drew to a victorious close, a grateful nation prepared to ease its warriors' reintegration into civilian life. High-LTV-ratio, low-interest home loans figured prominently into the package of benefits designed to accomplish this objective. Under varying terms and conditions, since 1944 mortgage loans for qualifying veterans and their families have been available with payment guaranteed by an agency of the federal government.

Initially, the **Veteran's Loan Guarantee Program** was administered by the Comptroller General. Within a year of its inception, however, the program was extensively revamped and moved to the newly created Veterans Administration, now the Department of Veterans Affairs. Early versions of enabling legislation required that veterans exercise their entitlement within specific time limits after becoming eligible. All termination dates were removed by the **Veteran's Housing Act** of 1970.

Unlike HUD, the VA does not actually insure a portion of the mortgage loan. Instead, it provides an absolute guarantee of payment. The agency becomes immediately liable for the entire guaranteed amount when a veteran defaults. The guarantee covers only a fraction of each loan, however. A maximum of 60 percent of the loan may be guaranteed initially, with the total amount of the guarantee adhering to the loan as the remaining loan balance is reduced. There is a maximum dollar limit on the amount of each guarantee, but the limit has been increased several times and will undoubtedly be increased again. Above the prescribed maximum purchase price, therefore, a VA guarantee becomes less than 60 percent.

VA-guaranteed home loans enable qualifying veterans to buy homes with little or no down payment. Without the guarantee, a lender might finance only a fraction of the purchase price. With the top 60 percent guaranteed, however, lenders can finance as much as 100 percent of the purchase price without increasing their risk exposure beyond that associated with a conventional (that is, unguaranteed) loan equaling only 40 percent of the mortgaged property's value. Therefore, although the current maximum guarantee is limited, lenders will loan four times the guarantee on a 100 percent LTV ratio mortgage.

Eligible veterans can obtain VA-guaranteed loans for alteration or purchase of real estate intended primarily as a personal residence. Loans on property intended strictly as investments do not qualify, but a personal residence may contain as many as four dwelling units as long as the veteran intends one of the units for personal use. Where two or more veterans take title jointly, a property may contain four units plus one additional unit for each veteran. Thus, two veterans could jointly qualify for a guaranteed loan on a six-unit building if each intended to occupy one of the units.

The VA and HUD are the primary federal government sources of mortgage loan enhancement, but they are not the sole sources. The Small Business Administration and the **Rural Housing Service (RHS)**, formerly the Farmer's Home Administration, for example, each have significant programs. RHS offers loans to rural areas for farms, houses, and community facilities. RHS loans have the advantages of no down payments or mortgage insurance and are not limited to first-time homebuyers. Like other government programs, there are maximums for the loan amount and other requirements, such as personally occupying the property. Miscellaneous other programs are scattered through the government's alphabet agencies. Specific provisions are specialized and details are too transitory to be usefully incorporated here.

Private Credit Enhancements

Generalizations about private arrangements to enhance mortgage credit are rendered difficult by the sheer variety available. The most common examples include private mortgage insurance and letters of credit.

Private Mortgage Insurance

Private mortgage insurance (PMI) has a long history in the United States, and it was an important element in the mortgage market as early as the 1920s. Early "insurers" were actually mortgage originators that sold the mortgage notes with a guarantee against default. They made no special provisions to ensure funds would be available to deliver on their guarantees, however. Most of the mortgage "insurers" of that era failed during the Depression of the 1930s, bringing financial ruin to investors who relied on their guarantees. This precipitated a crisis of confidence so extensive that PMI virtually disappeared. It did not reemerge for almost three decades.

The role of the Federal Housing Administration in filling the void left by the collapse of private mortgage insurers was described earlier. Government-backed mortgage insurance helped overcome the crisis of confidence that had virtually destroyed the mortgage market in the early 1930s. The government pioneered standards that would ultimately serve as a model to launch a renewed PMI industry on a sounder financial footing.

PMI was reintroduced in 1957 with creation of the Mortgage Guarantee Insurance Corporation (MGIC, promptly dubbed Magic). Its pioneering role enabled MGIC to establish a commanding lead over copycat firms that followed. Although it stumbled badly at one point and lost much of its market share, MGIC remains a major force in a vastly expanded market.

Today's PMI industry bears little resemblance to its pre-Depression predecessor. Private mortgage insurers are now evaluated by rating agencies such as Moody's and Standard and Poor's. Whereas early insurers were virtually unregulated, their successors' activities are controlled both by the laws of states in which they are domiciled and by those of states in which they do business. Underwriting standards and loss reserves required by these regulatory authorities have resulted in an industry that appears capable of withstanding any foreseeable financial collapse.

Private mortgage insurers cover only a portion of the mortgage loan. The amount insured depends on the type of mortgage and the LTV ratio. For example, with a 90 percent LTV ratio a private mortgage insurer might insure 20 percent of the loan against default. This would reduce the lender's risk exposure to only 72 percent of the mortgaged property's value.

Insurance premiums are usually quoted on an annual basis, but are paid monthly as a part of the mortgage loan payment. A typical premium on a $90,000 mortgage with a 95 percent LTV ratio is approximately $75 per month. The premium payments can continue even after the loan balance is reduced to a level that would not have required mortgage insurance in the first place, unless the borrower makes arrangements to have it canceled. At least one state (California) requires that borrowers be notified when the mortgage insurance can be canceled. A borrower can seek to eliminate the PMI when the ratio of loan balance to market value drops below 80 percent.

Several private companies write mortgage insurance on commercial as well as residential property. Private insurance works very much like that provided by HUD. The cost includes both an application fee and mortgage insurance premiums.

Letters of Credit

Commercial banks often issue **letters of credit** for a small portion of the mortgage loan. With a letter of credit securing a loan amount equal to, say, 10 percent of a property's value, the lender can loan 80 percent of the value yet be exposed to default risk on only 70 percent. The degree of enhancement accomplished by a letter of credit depends on the credit rating of the bank that issues the letter. The issuing bank will look to the general credit rating of the applicant and to any other collateral that the borrower may post.

Letters of credit are often used for other purposes as well. They are a common means, for example, of assuring a municipality that public improvements will be installed by a subdivision developer. Posting an irrevocable letter of credit, which can be drawn on to pay the cost of the improvements if the developer defaults, is often an acceptable substitute for a cash escrow deposit or a surety bond. In other cases, the letter of credit is posted with the bonding company as an inducement to issue the surety bond.

Lenders typically charge a monthly fee equal to a fractional percentage of the face amount of the letter of credit outstanding. Because they may result in disbursements by the lender, the face amounts of letters of credit are treated as a part of the financing extended to a borrower, with appropriate provisions for collateral security.

SUMMARY

Before advancing funds, lenders investigate applicants' loan repayment records, to determine their willingness to honor their obligations; their earning power, to determine their ability to repay; and the property that will be pledged as collateral to estimate its value and marketability. The process of assessing the risk associated with a loan is called *underwriting*. Lenders agree to make a mortgage loan by providing a commitment letter, which states in general terms the conditions under which the loan will be made and the provisions that will be incorporated into the actual lending documents.

Credit enhancements are arrangements that induce lenders to provide larger loans than would otherwise be available. The federal government provides enhancements in the form of mortgage insurance or loan repayment guarantees. Private sources of credit enhancement most commonly consist of mortgage insurance or letters of credit.

KEY TERMS

capacity	loan commitments	private mortgage insurance (PMI)
capital	mortgage insurance	
character	National Housing Act	Rural Housing Service (RHS)
collateral	net operating income (NOI)	subprime
conditions		underwriting
Equal Credit Opportunity Act (ECOA)	nonrecourse	Veteran's Housing Act
letters of credit	payment guarantees	Veteran's Loan Guarantee Program
	private credit enhancements	

NOTE

1. When the Department of Housing and Urban Development (HUD) was created in 1965, one of the previously independent agencies that was merged with the new department was the Federal Housing Administration (FHA). Although the FHA is no longer an independent agency, many HUD programs are still referred to as *FHA programs*, and HUD's Assistant Secretary for Housing also has the title of FHA Commissioner. Thus, for credit enhancement and housing subsidy programs, HUD and FHA should be considered synonymous and interchangeable terms.

RECOMMENDED READING

Programs of HUD. Washington, D.C.: U.S. Department of Housing and Urban Development, 2006.

For VA loan information: Title 38, U.S. Code of Federal Regulations, Section 1801.

INTERNET REFERENCES

For an example of a loan application checklist:
www.sba.gov/services/financialassistance/sbaloantopics/index.html

For additional information on the FHA Home Loan underwriting process:
www.fha-home-loans.com/underwriting_process_fha_loans.htm

Veteran's Loan Guarantee Program:
www.homeloans.va.gov

Find additional information about private mortgage insurance at:
www.hsh.com/pamphlets/mgicpmi.html

For information on Rural Housing Service:
http://rurdev.usda.gov/rhs

For information on qualifying and affordability:
www.hsh.com/calc-amort.html

REVIEW QUESTIONS

1. What does the term *loan underwriting* mean?
2. Describe the relative significance of a mortgaged property's net operating income and market value to the mortgage lender.
3. What key obligation does the Equal Credit Opportunity Act of 1976 impose on lenders?
4. What federal law sets standards for collecting information about loan applicants and limits how the information may be used?
5. What is collateral?
6. What is the document that sets out the general terms and conditions of a loan and specifies the preconditions under which a lender promises to make a loan?
7. What key government agencies provide mortgage loan credit enhancements?
8. What are key private sources of mortgage loan credit enhancements?
9. What are letters of credit, and what institutions issue them?

▌ DISCUSSION QUESTIONS

1. Character, capacity, and collateral have been described as "the three Cs of credit." What do these terms mean, and what is their relative significance to the loan underwriting process?

2. As a prospective lender, would a valid and binding letter of credit from a commercial bank induce you to advance funds to the bearer? What additional assurances might you seek?

3. Are there significant differences in the credit enhancement arrangements afforded by the Department of Veterans Affairs and HUD? If uniform arrangements were going to be instituted, which of these models would you, as a citizen and taxpayer, prefer?

4. Lenders that incorporate character judgments into their underwriting process depend primarily on the applicant's record of repaying previous loans. This poses an obvious problem for applicants with no prior credit history. Discuss the issue in terms of fairness, social policy, and possible alternatives.

5. Private mortgage insurers are regulated by the governments of states in which they are domiciled and states in which they do business. Discuss the merit of uniform national standards imposed by the federal government to (a) supplant state regulations or (b) to ensure minimum standards where state standards are overly lax.

Interest Rate Determinants

LEARNING OBJECTIVES

After studying this chapter, you should understand how governments and economic influences interact to determine interest rates. You should also be able to explain the term structure of interest rates and the role of expectations.

Although we speak of "the mortgage market" as if it were a monolithic aggregate, there are in fact a number of submarkets within which **interest rates** and fund availability vary. Submarket stratification exists because mortgage markets are less efficient, in an economic sense, than are many related credit markets. Housing markets, for example, are local by their very nature. But the financing of housing need not be a function of local sources only, when some lenders, perhaps located in other cities with plentiful supplies of cash, are searching for opportunities.

Recent years have seen great strides toward reducing allocative inefficiencies and merging mortgage markets more firmly into the general credit system. An unavoidable by-product of this convergence has been increasing complexity of credit instruments and institutional arrangements associated with real estate finance.

Government fiscal and monetary policies (influenced, among other things, by the powerful U.S. bond market) are today major determinants of the cost and availability of mortgage funds. Government wields its influence by controlling the supply of loanable funds and by exercising regulatory authority over major lenders. On the demand side, the U.S. Treasury affects interest rates by the frequency and extent of its borrowing.

Recognizing the degree to which government influences interest rates and fund availability, borrowers and lenders alike attempt to divine intent from government actions and pronouncements, and then act to protect themselves from adverse consequences. Expectations thus become a powerful additional factor amplifying shifts in interest rates and willingness of lenders to make mortgage funds available.

Today, cost and availability of loanable funds in the real estate sector are closely tied to general capital market conditions. This is a mixed blessing. On the one hand, real estate no longer bears the brunt of government monetary policy designed to dampen economic activity at the top of the cycle. On the other hand, mortgage lending is now subject to exactly the same sweeping and sometimes unpredictable changes that have traditionally haunted markets for corporate securities.

In the new mortgage market a corporate treasurer would feel at home. Analysis and forecasting of cost and availability of funds for mortgage lending must now proceed along the same lines of inquiry as do those in other areas. Investigation of contemporary mortgage markets must begin with a review of basic supply and demand phenomena, which determine prices in any market system. This leads to understanding how government influence over supply factors distorts market reactions and makes cost and availability of loanable funds a government policy variable.

THE ROLE OF FINANCIAL INTERMEDIARIES

Unique supply determinants are a distinguishing characteristic of financial markets. Unlike most other products, the aggregate quantity of funds supplied is not determined solely by price. Relative prices (i.e., interest rates) do influence the channeling of available funds among the sectors of financial markets. Total supply, however, is more heavily influenced by such factors as the aggregate level of economic activity, Federal Reserve policy, and the propensity of the populace to save a portion of their pay.

Loanable funds are generated by economic units (households, business firms, or government bodies) that consume less than they earn. This difference between earnings and consumption makes up aggregate savings within the economy. Savings are employed by other economic units that either temporarily consume more than they produce or that anticipate that they can earn a higher rate of return on investments than the interest rate they must pay for borrowed funds. Financial markets are the mechanism through which funds generated by savers are transmitted to user-borrowers. Although such funds may be loaned directly by savers to ultimate user-borrowers, most are transmitted through financial intermediaries.

Intermediaries are simply institutions such as commercial banks, savings associations, savings banks, and credit unions, which act as middlemen between ultimate savers and user-borrowers. Intermediaries issue their own liabilities—in effect, borrow from ultimate savers—and make loans to user-borrowers. They provide a valuable service by absorbing the risk associated with lending and by generating market information required for intelligent lending operations. Their compensation is the "spread" between the interest rates they pay to ultimate savers and those they charge user-borrowers.[1]

Real estate specialists are accustomed to thinking of mortgage markets as isolated phenomena. Traditional concepts notwithstanding, mortgage lenders must compete for savings in more generalized financial markets. Moreover, mortgage loans are just one of a number of alternative investments available to financial intermediaries. Mortgage markets are thereby connected to general financial markets. The more efficiently financial markets function, the closer will be the relationship between interest rates and fund availability in various sectors of the economy.

PRIMARY AND SECONDARY FINANCIAL MARKETS

In recent years, another powerful relationship between mortgage markets and other financial markets has been forged. A number of institutional arrangements now permit mortgage lenders to compete for funds through the secondary mortgage market.

Primary mortgage markets are those in which mortgages originate. This is where financial intermediaries make mortgage-secured loans directly to borrowers who are buying or improving real estate. The primary mortgage market includes:

- Depository institutions such as commercial banks and thrifts
- Nondepository institutions such as mortgage banks, mortgage brokers, pension funds, thrifts, and life insurance companies (though pension funds and life insurance companies have become less active as direct real estate lenders and have trended toward investments in mortgage-backed securities)

Secondary financial markets, in contrast, comprise arrangements for buying and selling existing financial instruments in organized trading markets such as the various stock exchanges. The **secondary mortgage market,** accordingly, is the market in which existing mortgages or securities based on mortgages are traded. Principal secondary market conduits are the following:

- Fannie Mae—the Federal National Mortgage Association
- Ginnie Mae—the Government National Mortgage Association
- Freddie Mac—the Federal Home Loan Mortgage Corporation
- Private investors

An efficiently functioning secondary market provides greater liquidity for primary mortgage lenders, and permits them to compete more effectively for funds.

Secondary mortgage market instruments and institutions are discussed more completely in Chapter 6. Because of the close connection (wrought by the secondary market) between mortgage interest rates and the general interest rate spectrum, economic phenomena that affect one sector of financial markets affect all sectors. Interest-rate differentials now primarily reflect differences in market expectations concerning risk and liquidity, rather than mere market inefficiencies.

SUPPLY, DEMAND, AND MARKET-CLEARING INTEREST RATES

Analysis of supply and demand for loanable funds and their role in determining market rates of interest represent a straightforward application of basic economic concepts. In any competitive market, whether for agricultural products, manufactured goods, or personal services, price and quantity exchanged are determined by the interaction of supply and demand. Financial markets are no exception. Interest represents the price of borrowing or the reward for lending, and the level of *interest rates* (price of funds) depends on the relative positions of suppliers (lenders) and demanders (borrowers) in the marketplace.

Figure 4.1 is a standard supply and demand diagram such as might be included in any basic economics textbook. It illustrates price determination with supply and demand schedules. The fact that the commodity involved is loanable funds and that the price is expressed as a rate of interest is only coincidental. If at a particular interest rate (say, 8 percent) borrowers are anxious to borrow more funds than lenders are willing to provide, then the interest rate will rise as borrowers bid against each other for available funds. On the other hand, if the interest rate is, say, 12 percent, the rate will fall as anxious lenders drop their asking price (rate) in an effort to put idle funds to work. In the market depicted by Figure 4.1, only at 10 percent will borrowers be able to find all the funds desired (at that price) and lenders be able to put all their available funds to work.

Changes in Demand

Demand for loans varies inversely with market interest rates. As interest rates increase, real estate projects that were feasible at lower rates no longer are economical. As the number of viable projects decreases due to the increased cost of borrowed funds, demand for such funds declines. Conversely, as interest rates drop, previously

FIGURE 4.1 | Supply and Demand of Loanable Funds

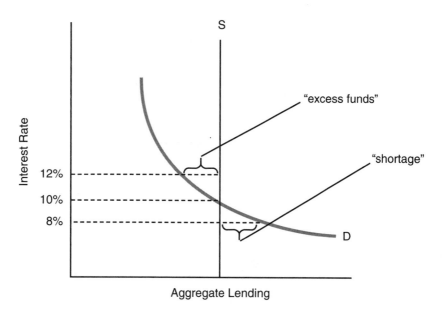

Aggregate Lending

unfeasible projects become economical and the demand for project loans accelerates. This relationship is depicted by line D in Figure 4.1.[2]

Several underlying economic factors interact to determine the location and slope of the demand function in Figure 4.1. Among these are expected demand for the product being produced, cost of productive elements other than capital, changes in technology and innovation, and shifting expectations concerning the future economic and political environment.

Expectations are often the most volatile of the factors affecting demand for loanable funds. Entrepreneurs who are optimistic about the market potential of their product will vigorously expand their operations and thereby increase aggregate demand for loans. Souring expectations, on the other hand, have a chilling impact on willingness to borrow and invest. Increased pessimism is reflected in Figure 4.2 by a shift in the relationship between interest rates and investment funds from that depicted by line D to that shown by line D'.

Market-Induced Supply Changes

Substantial and impressive research supports the generally accepted position that saving is primarily a function of the level of disposable income. By definition, householders either spend their income (personal consumption expenditures) or save

FIGURE 4.2 | Shift in Demand for Loanable Funds

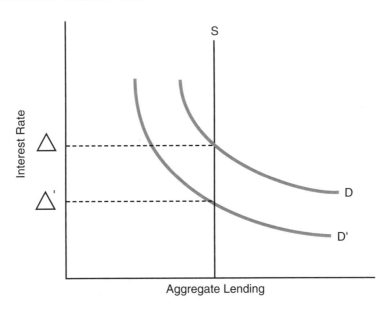

it. From the end of World War II until the 1980s, the percentage of aggregate income saved each year in the United States was surprisingly constant. During the 1980s, however, savings as a percentage of income declined somewhat.

Government-Induced Supply Changes

Authority to borrow or lend massive amounts of funds, coupled with control over required bank reserves, enables the Board of Governors of the Federal Reserve System ("the Fed") to exercise substantial discretionary control over the money supply. It primarily accomplishes this by using three powerful tools of monetary policy:

1. The purchase and/or sale of government bonds via its open market operations
2. Changing the percentages of certain types of deposits banks must keep on hand (reserve requirements)
3. Varying the discount rate (the interest rate the Fed charges banks for short-term loans)

Should expanding economic activity or growing investor optimism increase aggregate demand for loanable funds, the Federal Reserve can accommodate the change by expanding total supply, thereby preventing any increase in interest rates. Conversely, it can force interest rates up by being less accommodating, or even contracting the supply of loanable funds. Though unable to "fine-tune" the consequences, the Federal Reserve has consistently been able to determine the direction of change in market rates of interest by intervening in financial markets.

Because the quantity of money required to finance general business operations and to satisfy day-to-day demands of householders (generally called **transactions balances**) remains relatively stable at a given level of economic activity, the impact of government-induced money supply changes falls almost entirely on loanable funds. As a consequence, relatively small changes in total money supply can result in wide swings in market interest rates.

If the economy is "overheated" and burgeoning demand threatens unacceptable increases in the rate of inflation, monetary policy can lower the general level of demand. The Federal Reserve reduces the money supply (or lessens its rate of increase), thus lessening credit availability and forcing up interest rates. The impact is felt throughout the economy, but the burden is unequally shared. Housing construction and general real estate activity are among those sectors of the economy that bear the brunt of restrictive monetary policy.

Although the Federal Reserve arguably has been the most powerful quasi-public institution in America since its creation in 1913, the influence of the U.S. bond market on the Fed's monetary policy decisions has become increasingly significant. Monetary policy is, of course, not directed specifically at the real estate industry. Yet, real estate activity is inordinately affected by Federal Reserve action. Several factors contribute to the unusual susceptibility of real estate and construction to interest rate fluctuations.

Interest as a Cost Component

Because real estate transactions depend on massive infusions of borrowed funds, interest expense is a large component of total cost. Interest rate changes are thus immediately reflected in the cost of real estate production and ownership.

Mortgage Lenders Have Fewer Funds

As interest rates escalate, savers look for opportunities to increase their yields. Major institutional lenders who serve as intermediaries between savers and real estate borrowers are regulated by various government agencies, who in the past have limited interest rates offered to savers. Seeking better yields, people sometimes withdrew their savings from these institutions and participated directly in financial markets. This process is called **disintermediation**. The limitations on interest rates have been greatly reduced in recent years and, therefore, there has been less disintermediation. Furthermore, the operation of the secondary mortgage market provides liquidity for lenders who sell their mortgages.

Lenders Become Reluctant to Make Loans

Even lenders who have funds may prefer to shift away from mortgage loans during such periods. Causes of preference shifts are diverse. Tight money may reduce mortgage lending profitability at the same time as it increases attendant risk. Lenders respond by moving funds into alternative uses. This seems to be a general pattern

FIGURE 4.3 | Long-Term versus Short-Term Rates

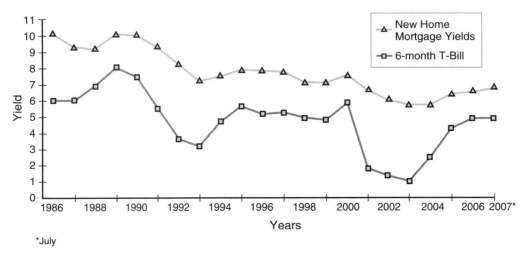

*July

followed by the commercial banking and thrift industries. When credit tightens, mortgages decline as a portion of their total asset portfolios.

EXPECTATIONS AND THE TERM STRUCTURE OF INTEREST RATES

Reference to the market rate of interest is imprecise. There is, in fact, a spectrum of interest rates, which differ due to perceived risk differentials and varying term structures of underlying debt. This entire spectrum tends to move up or down in response to market forces, but movements within the spectrum are not uniform. The variation in interest rates due to differences in perceived risk is illustrated by the yield curves for mortgages and treasury bill instruments. (See Figure 4.3.) As overall rates change, relative rates for short-term and long-term loans may also vary. This represents an alteration in the entire term structure of interest rates.

During periods of high interest rates and scarce funds, mortgage lenders' preferences for nonmortgage alternatives are reinforced by the impact market forces have on the term structure of interest rates. When the term structure shifts to make short-term loans relatively more attractive, lenders may prefer to avoid long-term mortgage loans.

Expectations and Liquidity Preference Theories

If lenders anticipate no future change in interest rates, they will prefer to hold short-term rather than long-term credit instruments unless compensated for longer-term loans by receiving higher rates of interest. Interaction of supply and demand, therefore, results in a positive relationship between interest rates and the length to maturity.

Expectations of future changes in interest rates may alter the preference for short-term over long-term assets. Unless appropriately compensated, lenders generally prefer to hold even shorter-term instruments if they anticipate an increase in the general level of interest rates in the near future and to hold long-term assets if they expect a downward adjustment.

Understanding the relationship between current interest rates and the market value of existing debt instruments makes clear the logic of such preferences. To illustrate, consider a one-year promissory note with a face value (that is, the amount due at maturity) of $100, and a contract interest rate of 8 percent. Suppose the note calls for payment of accrued interest plus the face amount of the note at maturity at the end of one year. During the holding period, therefore, the holder receives no cash payments. At the end of the final month of the holding period, however, she will receive $108. Now imagine that, immediately after receiving the note, the holder wishes to sell it in the secondary market. What price can she expect to receive for this note?

Before market value can be estimated, we must know what interest rate applies to newly created notes of the same type. If a new note similar in maturity and risk carries a contract interest rate of 8 percent, then the existing note will have a market value of approximately $100, that is, its face value. Assuming no difference in perceived risk, a holder of cash balances will be indifferent between buying the existing note for $100, thus earning 8 percent per annum for one year, and lending $100 at 8 percent for one year on a new one-year note.

What happens, then, to the value of the existing note if market interest rates go above 8 percent? If the current interest rate of a new one-year note is 10 percent, a lender can earn 10 percent per annum for one year either by lending on a new 10 percent, one-year note or by purchasing the existing 8 percent note (with one year remaining) for $98.18. Competition between holders of cash balances will, therefore, drive the market price of this and similar notes down to approximately $98.18. This price is determined as follows:

Anticipated proceeds from existing 8 percent one-year note:

Face amount of note	$100.00
Add: interest for one year	8.00
Total due in one year	$108.00

Thus, the amount that must be invested at 10 percent to earn $108.00 in one year is:

$$\$108.00/1.10 = \$98.18$$

Now assume the same facts as before, except that the market rate of interest on a new one-year note declines to 6 percent. A lender can earn 6 percent either by lending money at 6 percent per annum or by purchasing the existing 8 percent note at a premium that yields 6 percent at maturity. The lender will be indifferent between lending on a new note or purchasing the 8 percent $100 note for $101.89. Any lesser price will yield more than the current market rate of 6 percent, so competition between cash holders will bid the market price up to this amount. The price is determined as follows:

Amount to be received when note matures:

Face amount	$100.00
Accrued interest for one year	8.00
Total	$108.00

Therefore, the market value when discounted at 6 percent is

$$\$108.00/1.06 = \$101.89$$

These examples demonstrate the inverse relationship between market rates of interest and the market value of existing debt instruments. The higher the current rate of interest, the lower the market value of existing debt. Conversely, the lower the current rate, the greater the market value of existing instruments. The examples are relatively simple and straightforward, but even the most complex cases can be analyzed in the same way by utilizing present value analysis, as demonstrated in Appendix B. Purchasers of mortgages in the secondary mortgage market use the same analysis, setting prices according to the present value calculated with their desired effective yield instead of the market interest rate.

Given the capital-loss consequence of an increase in current market rates of interest, why will anyone accept the risk of holding debt instruments (frequently called **interest rate risk**—the possibility of a reduction in the value of an investment resulting from the fluctuation in interest rates) when there is even the remotest possibility of such an increase? Rational people will do so only if expected compensation makes the risk worthwhile. The alternatives of holding cash or nonfinancial assets instead of debt instruments are also costly, because they entail sacrificing the interest a debt instrument could be earning.

To recapitulate, the reward for holding debt is the contract rate of interest plus the possibility of capital gains due to an increase in market value should market interest rates decline during the holding period. The risk is that the market rate of interest will increase, causing a capital loss due to a drop in market value of the existing instrument.[3]

Holders of speculative balances, therefore, face a choice. They can hold interest-bearing assets and benefit from interest income, while bearing the risk of capital loss should the market rate of interest increase. Or they can hold non-interest-bearing (i.e., extremely liquid) instruments and avoid risk of capital loss, at the cost of interest income thereby foregone. Facing an uncertain future, most people compromise.

Changes in the market value of interest-bearing assets, coincident with change in the current market rate of interest on new assets of the same type, depend primarily on the length of time until the old assets mature. Other factors remaining equal, the greatest impact on market price will be experienced by those existing assets that have the longest remaining time to maturity.

To illustrate, consider two 8 percent $100-face-value notes. Assume the first note to have a one-year term, with both interest and principal due on maturity. Assume the second 8 percent note to have a five-year term, with accrued interest paid annually. Now, immediately after creation of the two notes, assume the market rate of interest changes from 8 percent to 10 percent, and observe what happens to relative market values.

The one-year note declines in value from $100 to $98.1818, a decline of approximately 1.8 percent. The five-year note, however, declines almost 7.6 percent, from $100 to $92.4184. Here are the computations:

Market value of note having . . .

Length to Maturity of	1 Year	5 Years
Discounted at 8%	$100.00	$100.00
Discounting at 10%[4]	98.1818	92.4184
Decline in market value	$1.8181	$7.5816

CALCULATOR APPLICATION

n = 1	n = 5
I = 10	i = 10
	PMT = 8
FV = 108.00	FV = 100.00
Solve for PV:	*Solve for PV:*
PV = $98.1818	PV = $92.4184

Generalizing from the above, the longer the remaining term to maturity, the greater will be the capital gain or loss attendant to a change in the market rate of interest. Strategy implications for holders of speculative cash balances are clear and unequivocal. The stronger the conviction that interest rates will move up in the near future, the shorter should be the term structure of assets in one's portfolio. This reduces potential capital loss should anticipated changes actually occur.

At the extreme, an investor might choose to reject interest-bearing assets entirely. The possibility of capital loss is thereby reduced to zero, and the investor is positioned to exploit changes in interest rates by buying at reduced rates when prices drop. This is a potentially costly strategy, however, since it sacrifices all interest income during the waiting period. It is a rational course of action only when the investor is thoroughly convinced that a significant move to higher rates is imminent.[5] If all holders of speculative balances are convinced that rates can go no lower and must imminently move up, no one will be willing to hold interest-bearing assets.

At the other extreme, if everyone is convinced that interest rates can go no higher and that they, indeed, must decline imminently, all will seek to hold interest-bearing assets instead of cash. Moreover, unless relative interest rates shift to compensate for differences in potential capital gains, everyone will desire debt instruments of the longest possible length to maturity. Because it is obviously impossible for everyone to hold only long-term debt instruments, relative interest rates in fact shift, so that higher interest rates on short-term instruments offset their lesser potential for capital gains.

Consensus, however, is rare in our society. We can't even agree on the significance of current happenings, much less on what is likely to occur in the future. Thus, at any time some people will prefer longer-term debt instruments in anticipation of interest rate declines, while others will prefer to hold speculative cash balances in anticipation of interest rate increases. Others will hedge their position by holding some long-term and some short-term instruments. The higher current interest rates are, the greater will be the general conviction that rates will soon move down, and thus the greater will be the aggregate preference for long-term interest-bearing assets such as bonds and mortgages. Conversely, the lower the current rates (relative to their historical levels), the more nearly will there be a consensus that rates will soon move up and, therefore, the greater will be the aggregate preference for liquid financial positions.

SUMMARY

Federal Reserve fiscal and monetary policies are today major determinants of the cost and availability of mortgage funds. The Fed wields its influence by controlling the supply of loanable funds through the purchase and/or sale of government bonds via its open market operations and by exercising its authority over major lenders through changes in the discount rate and regulating the amount of money banks must hold in reserve.

Savings are generated by economic units that consume less than their total income. These savings are channeled to users either as loans or as equity investments. Much of the economy's aggregate savings are channeled through financial intermediaries. In many cases, however, savers place their resources directly with ultimate users.

Mortgage loans are made in the primary mortgage market, largely by financial intermediaries. Existing mortgages are traded in the secondary mortgage market. An efficiently functioning secondary mortgage market makes lenders more willing to commit funds in the primary market, and thereby lowers the interest rates that mortgage borrowers must pay.

Market-clearing prices are determined by the interaction of supply and demand. In the mortgage loan market, prices (the cost of borrowed money) are called **interest rates**. The market clearing prices are altered when supply or demand functions shift, and shifts can be induced by market forces or government policy. Shifts also result from altered expectations of market participants.

▌ KEY TERMS

disintermediation

government-induced
   supply changes

interest rates

interest rate risk

market-induced supply
   changes

primary mortgage market

secondary mortgage
  market

transactions balance

▌ NOTES

1. Serious real estate students should pursue these related subjects by taking courses or reading in the area of economics and finance.

2. Economists sometimes call the demand schedule for loanable funds a *schedule of marginal efficiency of investment*. Profit-motivated businessmen will continue to expand the level of their business activities as long as the return on invested capital (after accounting for the "normal" level of profit as compensation for risk taking) is greater than the cost of investable funds.

3. There is, of course, also the risk that the borrower will default. This risk, however, is not directly related to movements in market rates of interest and will have been incorporated into the contract rate. It might seem that one could avoid a capital loss due to decline in market value simply by holding an instrument until maturity. Yet this is not so. The loss occurs, nevertheless, but is reflected in a lesser return on investment than could have been earned by lending only after the upward movement in interest rates. Thus, holding an instrument instead of selling only translates the (potential) capital loss into an opportunity cost having the same negative value as a capital loss would have had if the instrument had been sold. In terms of current value, the two eventualities are identical.

4. Calculations:

   Value of one-year note, discounted at 10%:

   Maturity value = $1.08 \times \$100$ = \$108.00

   Maturity value, discounted at
   10% (\$108 / 1.10)   = \$98.1818

   Value of five-year note, discounted at 10%:

   Cash flow during holding period

   ($\$100 \times 0.08$) = \$8.00 per annum

   Value of \$8 per annum for five years, discounted at 10%:

   $$= \$8 \sum_{t=1}^{5} 1 / (1.10)^{t} = \$30.3263$$

   Add: value of \$100 at maturity, discounted at 10% for 5 years

   ($\$100 / (1.10)^{5}$ = \$62.0921

   Total \$92.4184

5. Under these circumstances, a sensible strategy will be not only to liquidate all debt instruments from the portfolio, but also to become a net borrower. Then, after interest rates move up, borrowed funds can be loaned at the new higher rates.

RECOMMENDED READING

Galbraith, John Kenneth. *Money: Whence It Came, Where It Went.* Boston: Houghton Mifflin Co., 2001.

Polakoff, Murray E., Thomas A. Durkin, et al. *Financial Institutions and Markets,* 2nd ed. Boston: Houghton Mifflin Co., 1981.

INTERNET REFERENCES

To view the Economic Report of the President:
http://w3.access.gpo.gov/usbudget/fy2007.pdf

For information on interest rates:
www.bai.org
www.bloomberg.com
www.interest.com
www.newyorkfed.org

To view the Federal Reserve's homepage, go to:
www.federalreserve.gov

For more information regarding the risk and term structure of interest rates:
www.digitaleconomist.com

For a survey of 15 and 30-year fixed rate mortgages:
www.realinfo.net/15year.pdf
www.realinfo.net/30year.pdf

REVIEW QUESTIONS

1. What are financial intermediaries, and why are they important to mortgage borrowers and lenders?
2. What is meant by the term *primary mortgage markets?*
3. Explain how secondary mortgage markets differ from primary mortgage markets.
4. What is the "cost" of borrowed money, and how is it determined in a market system?
5. How do entrepreneurial expectations affect the shape and location of demand curves for borrowed funds?
6. How does government monetary policy affect the cost of borrowing?

7. How does liquidity preference affect the relative cost of long-term and short-term borrowing?

8. If you were confident that interest rates in general were going to drop, would you prefer to own long-term or short-term promissory notes? Would you prefer to be a long-term or short-term borrower?

9. In the secondary market, are current values of long-term or short-term mortgage-secured promissory notes likely to be more volatile?

DISCUSSION QUESTIONS

1. Should the federal government pursue a policy that encourages low interest rates, thus making home ownership less costly? Why or why not?

2. How might actions of the U.S. Treasury and the Federal Reserve system affect individual preferences for long-term and short-term credit instruments?

CHAPTER 5

Capital Costs and the Incentive to Borrow—Leverage

After studying this chapter, you should understand the benefits and the risks of financial leverage and know how to compute the cost of both debt and equity funds. You should also be able to compute the widely employed ratios associated with the use of financial leverage.

THE COST OF CAPITAL

Real estate investment funds might come from an investor's own resources (equity) or they might be borrowed (debt). In most cases, some of the needed money will come from each of these sources. And, of course, the funds have a cost in both instances. The most desirable mix, from the equity investor's point of view, will depend in part on the relative cost of debt and equity funds.

THE COST OF EQUITY

For individuals and for closely held corporations, the cost of equity funds is usually measured by the opportunity cost principle. Resources may be invested in the contemplated project or they may be otherwise employed. The **opportunity cost** of investing in the project is the yield that could have been earned with an alternative use that involves about the same degree of risk. The opportunity cost provides the minimum interest rate that an investor should accept on invested funds or the maximum rate she should pay on any additional borrowed funds. There are two ways to quickly approximate the opportunity cost of equity funds.

Mortgage Cost Plus Risk Premium

Although it is an ad hoc subjective procedure, the cost of equity funds can be estimated by adding a risk premium to the interest rate an investor is paying on outstanding mortgage indebtedness. One could use equity funds to retire outstanding loans and thus earn the mortgage rate of interest without increasing investment risk. Amplifying risk exposure by putting money into a new risky project instead of paying off outstanding debt will be justified only if the new venture's earnings prospects are sufficiently higher.

How much greater the new venture's earning potential must be to justify the additional risk depends on one's attitude toward risk and is affected by, among other things, the aggregate risk to which one is already exposed. This approach does not produce an accurate measure of the cost of equity funds, but it does get one "into the right ballpark."

Discounted Cash Flow

Investigating the relationship between price and anticipated cash flows from recently sold property similar to the contemplated acquisition will give an indication of yields available in the market. This involves forecasting the cash flows from the property and finding the discount rate that makes the present value of the cash flows equal the acquisition cost of the property. This technique is addressed in textbooks on real estate investment analysis. (See, for example, Kolbe and Greer, *Investment Analysis for Real Estate Decisions,* 6th edition.)

TABLE 5.1 | Monthly Payment to Amortize a $1 Debt

Number of Years	Annual Interest Rate						
	6.0%	**7.0%**	**8.0%**	**9.0%**	**10.0%**	**12.0%**	**14.0%**
1	.086066	.086527	.086988	.087451	.087916	.088849	.089787
2	.044321	.044773	.045227	.045685	.046145	.047073	.048013
3	.030422	.030877	.031336	.031800	.032267	.033214	.034178
4	.023485	.043946	.024413	.024885	.025363	.026334	.027326
5	.019333	.019801	.020276	.020758	.021247	.022244	.023268
6	.016573	.017049	.017533	.018026	.018526	.019550	.020606
7	.014609	.015093	.015586	.016089	.016601	.017653	.018740
8	.013141	.013634	.014137	.014650	.015174	.016253	.017372
9	.012006	.012506	.013019	.013543	.014079	.015184	.016334
10	.011102	.011611	.012133	.012668	.013215	.014347	.015527
11	.010367	.010884	.011415	.011961	.012520	.013678	.014887
12	.009759	.010284	.010825	.011380	.011951	.013134	.014371
13	.009247	.009781	.010331	.010897	.011478	.012687	.013951
14	.008812	.009354	.009913	.010489	.011082	.012314	.013605
15	.008439	.008988	.009557	.010143	.010746	.012002	.013317
16	.008114	.008672	.009249	.009845	.010459	.011737	.013077
17	.007831	.008397	.008983	.009588	.010212	.011512	.012875
18	.007582	.008155	.008750	.009364	.009998	.011320	.012704
19	.007361	.007942	.008545	.009169	.009813	.011154	.012559
20	.007164	.007753	.008364	.008997	.009650	.011011	.012435
25	.006443	.007068	.007718	.008392	.009087	.010532	.012038
30	.005996	.006653	.007338	.008046	.008776	.010286	.011849

THE COST OF BORROWED CAPITAL

The cost of borrowing is usually expressed as an effective interest rate. This is the rate charged by the lender plus an additional amount to amortize any up-front borrowing costs over the period of the loan. To get a handle on the issue, we look first at the concepts of debt service and loan amortization. Then we consider the impact of front-end costs and the relationship between the nominal and effective interest rates.

The **nominal interest rate** is the stated rate on the loan, while the **effective interest rate** is the rate actually paid for the use of borrowed funds. The effective interest rate is a function of the amount borrowed and the amount and timing of required repayment.

Debt Service and Loan Amortization

Most real estate loans require periodic payments, usually equal monthly amounts, designed to pay the accumulated interest and to retire a portion of the principal. As the remaining balance of the loan is gradually reduced, interest on the unpaid balance declines. Such a loan is said to be *fully amortizing*. As time passes, an ever-greater portion of the monthly payment is applied to reduce the principal. The final payment in the amortization period reduces the principal balance to zero.

The size of the required payments (**debt service**) depends on the loan amount, the interest rate, and repayment provisions. The monthly debt service for a loan of a predetermined size with a specified interest rate can be computed by reference to a table of amortization factors. Prior to financial calculators, such tables were utilized to make all calculations; an abbreviated excerpt is shown as Table 5.1. To use the table, find the interest rate by reading across the top of the columns, then read down the appropriate column to the row corresponding with the number of years over which the loan is to be amortized.

Consider, for example, a $100,000, 25-year, fully amortizing loan with interest at 8 percent per annum, requiring monthly debt service payments. The number found at the intersection of the 25-year row and the 8 percent column in Table 5.1 is the monthly payment required to fully amortize a $1 loan: 0.007718. The monthly payment on the $100,000 loan is simply 100,000 times this amount: $771.80, or with a financial calculator the answer is $771.82.

CALCULATOR APPLICATION

n = 300 (12 months × 25 years)
i = .666667 (8 ÷ 12)
PV = 100,000

Solve for PMT:
PMT = $771.82

A portion of each monthly payment is in satisfaction of the interest that has accrued since the last payment. The balance is applied to reduce the principal amount of the loan. As the principal is gradually reduced, the portion of each payment needed to satisfy accrued interest declines and the amount applied to retire the principal increases. The final payment at the end of 25 years will include only a tiny interest increment, and the rest of the payment will reduce the principal balance

FIGURE 5.1 | Mortgage Amortization Schedule of Balance for a $100,000, 25-Year, Fully Amortizing Loan at 8 Percent

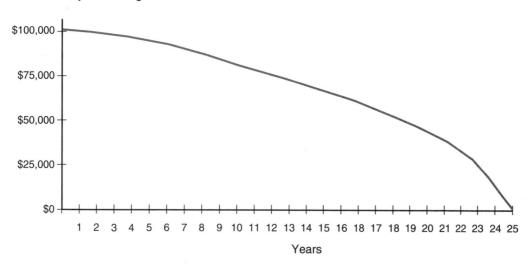

to zero. Figure 5.1 illustrates the slow payoff of principal in the earlier years of the loan. By way of illustration, consider the amortization of this loan over its first three months and its last three months. Because the annual interest rate is 8 percent, the monthly rate, expressed as a fraction, will be 0.00666667. The calculations are shown in Table 5.2.

A section of Appendix B, called "Payments to Amortize a Loan," explains the derivation of the factors in Table 5.1. In actual practice, inexpensive financial calculators have largely supplanted the tables. The calculators are fast, light, and accurate, and generally cost less than a book of tables. Calculator solutions will generally differ slightly from solutions using tables, because the tables introduce rounding error. Examples of numerous calculator computations are presented in Appendix C.

Fully amortizing loans, such as the one illustrated in Table 5.2, are the most common real estate lending arrangement. But partially amortizing loans and term loans are sometimes employed. A **term loan** (also known as a **bullet loan** or **straight loan**) requires payments consisting wholly of accrued interest (no principal) during the term of the loan, with the entire principal amount due and payable when the loan matures.

A **partially amortizing** (also known as **partly amortized**) **loan** includes some repayment of principal during the loan period, with a remaining balance, frequently called a **balloon payment**, due at the end. A partially amortizing loan is set up just like a fully amortizing loan, but the remaining balance becomes due partway through the amortization period. This is one of the ways lenders shorten the terms of loans and thereby shift interest rate risk to borrowers.

TABLE 5.2 | Amortizing a $100,000, 25-Year, Fully Amortizing Loan with Interest at 8 Percent

	Month 1	Month 2	Month 3
Beginning Principal Balance	$100,000.00	$99,894.85	$99,789.00
× Monthly Rate	0.00666667	0.00666667	0.00666667
Interest Amount	$666.67	$665.97	$665.26
Monthly Payment	$771.82	$771.82	$771.82
Less: Interest	$666.67	$665.97	$665.26
Principal Paid	$105.15	$105.85	$106.56
Ending Principal Balance			
	$99,894.85	$99,789.00	$ 99,682.44
	Month 298	**Month 299**	**Month 300**
Beginning Principal Balance	$2,284.93	$1,528.34	$766.71
× Monthly Rate	0.00666667	0.00666667	0.00666667
Interest Amount	$15.23	$10.19	$5.11
Monthly Payment	$771.82	$771.82	$771.82
Less: Interest	$15.23	$10.19	$5.11
Principal Paid	$756.59	$761.63	$766.71
Ending Principal Balance	$1,528.34	$766.71	$0.00

For example, John Smith borrows $200,000 at 10 percent per annum interest. The lender wants to loan the money for only 10 years, but will calculate the payment based on a 30-year amortization term. Mr. Smith's monthly payment will be $1,755.14 (using the factors in Table 5.1, the payment is $1,755.20; a six-cent rounding error using the table).

CALCULATOR APPLICATION
n = 360 (12 months × 30 years)
i = .833333 (10 ÷ 12)
PV = 200,000

Solve for PMT:
PMT = $1,755.14

Smith will have a balloon payment at the end of year 10 equal to the remaining balance, based on the 30-year amortization term: $181,876 (rounded to the nearest whole dollar). The balance is calculated with a financial calculator by determining the present value of the remaining payments discounted at the nominal rate on the loan. For the above loan, the remaining 240 payments are discounted at 10 percent. See Appendix C for more examples of the use of a financial calculator in calculating a balloon payment.

CALCULATOR APPLICATION

n = 240 (12 months × 20 years)
i = .833333 (10 ÷ 12)
PMT = 1,755.14

Solve for PMT:
PV = $181,875.71

Mortgage Discount Points

Effective interest rates are those borrowers actually pay for the use of borrowed funds. They often differ strikingly from rates quoted by lenders. Common instances of differences between nominal or stated interest rates (rates quoted by a lender) and effective interest rates (those actually paid by a borrower) on loans occur when the lender charges a loan origination fee or discount points and disburses only the remaining balance (a discount point equals 1 percent of the face value of the loan).

By reducing the loan amount without changing the debt service, lenders are able to increase their return or yield above the contract rate. Loans are often arranged by intermediaries between borrowers and lenders, and the intermediaries charge loan origination fees. This does not increase the yield to the lender, but it does increase the effective cost of borrowing. In both instances, because the borrower makes payments on funds not received (net of the fee or discount), the effective interest rate exceeds the stated or nominal rate. This topic is explored in more detail in Chapter 10, and additional examples are provided in Appendix B.

The Annual Constant

Debt service requirements are often expressed as a **mortgage constant** or a **debt constant** (**debt service constant**). The most common way of expressing the constant is as a percent of the face amount of a loan. The annual constant (C) associated with a 25 year, 12 percent, $100,000 loan ($L$), with monthly payments (P) of $1,053.20, is 0.126384, or 12.64 percent. Here is the calculation:

$$C = P/L$$
$$= (\$1,053.20 \times 12)/\$100,000$$
$$= \$12,638.40/\$100,000$$
$$= 0.126384, \text{ or } 12.64 \text{ percent}$$

The loan constant is sometimes expressed as the debt service obligation per $100 of indebtedness. This is nothing more than the percentage calculation expressed in dollar terms. The 12.64 percent in the preceding calculation therefore becomes $12.64.

Debt service may be expressed as an **annual constant** or a **monthly constant**, depending on the use to be made of the information. Because an annual constant (assuming monthly payment) is simply 12 times the monthly constant, the distinction is trivial. A monthly constant can be read directly from a loan amortization table such as the excerpt shown as Table 5.1. The annual constant is 12 times the monthly factor from the amortization table.

WHY REAL ESTATE INVESTORS BORROW: THE LURE OF FINANCIAL LEVERAGE

Real estate investors usually borrow a major portion of project funds. In many cases, this is the only way they can finance a large real estate project. Even where it is not absolutely necessary, however, investors frequently use borrowed money to enhance the rate of return on equity resources.

Using borrowed funds to amplify the outcome of equity investment creates **financial leverage**. The greater the ratio of borrowed funds to equity, the greater the financial leverage employed. When the cost of borrowing is less than the rate of return on assets, borrowing increases the return to the equity investor, and this is said to be **favorable leverage**. Leverage is unfavorable when borrowing costs more than the rate of return on assets.

The difference between the rate of return on assets and the cost of borrowing is often called the **spread**. Even a small favorable spread magnifies return on equity on a highly leveraged investment. A small negative spread (unfavorable leverage) on such a project, however, results in a magnified negative rate of return to the equity position.

EXAMPLE 5.1

A property that has a market value of $5.5 million is expected to generate annual net operating income (gross rental revenue minus operating expenses) of $660,000. The investor can borrow $3.85 million with interest at 8 percent per annum and equal monthly payments to retire the loan over 20 years. The monthly payment will be $32,203 (rounded to the nearest whole dollar; using factors from Table 5.1 yields a payment of $32,202, a difference attributable to rounding error in the table). Annual debt service is simply 12 times this amount, or approximately $386,436.

TABLE 5.3 | Expected Outcomes from Example 5.1

	No Loan	$3,850,000 Loan	$4,400,000 Loan
Actual Net Operating Income	$660,000	$660,000	$660,000
Less: Debt Service (Annual)	0	386,436	458,208
Actual Before-Tax Cash Flow	$660,000	$273,564	$201,792
Purchase Price	$5,500,000	$5,500,000	$5,500,000
Less: Loan	0	3,850,000	4,400,000
Equity	$5,500,000	$1,650,000	$1,100,000
Annual Debt Service/Loan	n.a.	10.04%	10.41%
Cash Flow/Equity	12.00%	16.58%	18.34%

Example 5.1 illustrates the potential impact of financial leverage. If the investors in this example elect not to borrow, they will have to put up $5.5 million of equity funds. The entire $660,000 of expected net operating income will accrue to them, and the expected rate of return on the investment, expressed as a current yield (cash flow/equity), will be 12 percent. The first column of Table 5.3 summarizes this information.

If the investors avail themselves of the available $3.85 million loan, $386,436 of the expected annual net operating income must be paid to the mortgage lender. This leaves only $273,564 of expected annual cash flow for the equity investors. This alters the expected rate of return on equity funds, as shown in the second column of Table 5.3.

Now see what happens when even greater financial leverage is employed. Assume that a loan equal to 80 percent of the property's market value will require interest at 8.5 percent per annum (higher interest rate to compensate for the greater risk of a higher loan-to-value ratio) and will also be paid off in equal monthly installments over 20 years. The monthly payment required by this $4.4 million loan will be approximately $38,184 (rounded to the nearest whole dollar), and the annual debt service will be 12 times this amount, or approximately $458,208. Thus the cash flow to the equity position will be reduced to $201,792. But the equity investors will need to put up only $1.1 million of their own money. Because the cost of borrowing is still significantly below the return on assets, the larger loan further enhances the return on equity funds expressed as a percentage of the initial equity investment. The result is summarized in the third column of Table 5.3.

Look at the ratios computed at the bottom of Table 5.3. Note that expected annual net operating income is 12 percent of the property's market value (cash flow/equity, with no borrowed money), and that annual debt service is less than 12 percent (specifically, either 10.04 percent or 10.41 percent). Using borrowed funds decreases

TABLE 5.4 | Outcomes from Example 5.1 with Less Than Expected Net Operating Income

	No Loan	$3,850,000 Loan	$4,400,000 Loan
Actual Net Operating Income	$440,000	$440,000	$440,000
Less: Debt Service (Annual)	0	386,436	458,208
Actual Before-Tax Cash Flow	$440,000	$53,564	$(18,208)
Purchase Price	$5,500,000	$5,500,000	$5,500,000
Less: Loan	0	3,850,000	4,400,000
Equity	$5,500,000	$1,650,000	$1,100,000
Annual Debt Service/Loan	n.a.	10.04%	10.41%
Cash Flow/Equity	8.00%	3.25%	–1.66%

the amount of equity funds required by a proportionately greater amount than it decreases cash flow to the equity position. As a consequence, the current yield to equity (cash flow/equity) is increased.

But the salutary effects of financial leverage are easy to overemphasize. Remember that the operating results in Example 5.1 are mere expectations. What if the actual outcome proves to be less than expected? If net operating income, as a percent rate of return on assets, drops below the annual debt service constant, financial leverage will reduce the current return on equity.

To illustrate, consider again the data in Example 5.1. The expected net operating income of $660,000 notwithstanding, assume the actual net operating income is just $440,000. The consequences of having used financial leverage based on an overoptimistic cash-flow forecast are illustrated in Table 5.4.

Note the ratios at the bottom of this table. As in Table 5.3, the debt service on the two alternative loans is, respectively, 10.04 percent or 10.41 percent of the loan amount. But the actual net operating income is only 8 percent of the property's market value. Because this is less than the debt service as a percent of the loan, borrowing reduces the cash flow to the equity investors, expressed as a percent of the equity investment.

OTHER BENEFITS OF FINANCIAL LEVERAGE

Rational investors, it is frequently assumed, will not knowingly accept unfavorable financial leverage. Yet during periods of very high interest rates and rapid inflation, financial leverage *as traditionally measured* is almost certain to be unfavorable. Many astute investors nevertheless do enter into highly leveraged deals during such periods.

This seeming paradox stems from the conventional practice of computing annual rates of return as a current yield on a before-tax basis (cash flow before income taxes/ equity) and ignoring anticipated growth in market value during the holding period. Yet during periods of rapid inflation, appreciation may constitute a significant portion of expected benefit from such an investment. Moreover, income tax effects are so pervasive that any investment calculation that ignores them is virtually useless.

Leverage Amplifies the Tax Shelter

Income tax laws create a major incentive to use borrowed money. With certain limitations, interest payments are deductible from taxable income on a dollar-for-dollar basis. Also, investors are allowed a deduction from taxable income for an estimate of the wearing away of buildings and other improvements to real estate, whether or not any actual reduction in market value occurs. This allowance, called a *depreciation* or *cost recovery allowance*, is based on the total purchase price of buildings and other improvements, without reference to whether borrowed funds are employed. Depreciation is explored in more detail in Chapter 16.

Let's look at an example. An investor with $100,000 of cash could purchase a $100,000 depreciable real estate asset without using leverage. Or by borrowing 75 percent of the purchase price, the investor could purchase a $400,000 property (using $100,000 of equity funds and borrowing $300,000). Employing financial leverage will have increased the investor's annual depreciation or cost recovery allowance by 300 percent with no additional requirement of equity investment.

Leverage Amplifies the Consequences of Disposal

Pressure from population growth and urban sprawl has made land in most parts of the United States experience a more or less continuous increase in value during the post–World War II period. This has been particularly true during periods of rapid monetary inflation. Financial leverage can multiply the potential gain from such appreciation. Consider the land investment opportunity outlined in Example 5.2.

EXAMPLE 5.2

A parcel of land well situated to benefit from rapid urban growth can be acquired for $60,000. A prospective investor expects that the land will double in value during the next five years (an annual rate of return of 14.9 percent), at which time he plans to sell. During the interim, the land can be leased to a turnip farmer for an annual rental that just covers the property tax liability, so there will be zero annual cash flow before debt service and income taxes.

The land can be purchased for $60,000 cash, or the present owner will accept a $15,000 down payment accompanied by a note and purchase-money mortgage for $45,000. Both the principal and the accumulated interest on the note will be due and payable at the end of the fifth year, with interest accumulating at a compound annual rate of 10 percent.

The expected rates of return on the equity funds invested in Example 5.2 will differ significantly, depending on the source of funds. Because the interest rate on the purchase-money mortgage (10 percent) is less than the expected rate of increase in the market value of the property (14.87 percent), leverage is expected to be favorable. The expected annual rates of return on equity, calculated on a pretax basis both with and without the seller-financing alternative, are presented in Table 5.5.

The $72,473 balance due on the purchase-money note shown in Table 5.5 represents the value, after five years, of a $45,000 deposit (the face amount of the note) that grows at a compound rate of 10 percent per annum (the accumulating interest income). The annual rates of return on the equity investments (14.87 percent and 25.94 percent) represent compound annual growth rates that will make the initial cash outlays under each alternative financing arrangement approximately equal to the net proceeds from sale after five years. Appendix B explains how such computations are made.

CALCULATOR APPLICATION

n = 5	n = 5
PV = 15,000 (enter as negative amount)	PV = 60,000 (enter as negative amount)
FV = 47,527	FV = 120,000
Solve for i:	*Solve for i:*
i = 25.94%	i = 14.87%

MEASURING FINANCIAL LEVERAGE

Financial leverage can be measured as (1) the relationship between debt and equity funds or (2) the relationship between borrowed funds and the total market value of assets acquired. Corporate financial analysts frequently express this relationship as a **debt-to-equity ratio**, the ratio between borrowed funds and equity funds. For reasons having to do as much with its origin as with its usefulness, the ratio between borrowed funds and the market value of the asset being financed (a **loan-to-value ratio**) is more commonly employed in real estate circles.

The loan-to-value (LTV) ratio provides mortgage lenders with a tool for estimating the margin of safety associated with mortgage-secured loans, and it is for this purpose that the measure was initially devised. Should a borrower default on an obligation to repay a mortgage loan, the lender expects to recoup the loss from the proceeds of a sale of the mortgaged property. In most states, sale is by public auction, with the property going to the highest bidder. (Chapter 11 explains the procedure in greater detail.) Should the lender be the winning bidder (many times the lender is the only bidder), it could suffer financial loss when it sells the property.

TABLE 5.5 | The Impact of Financial Leverage

	With Leverage	Without Leverage
Proceeds from Sale after 5 Years	$120,000	$120,000
Less: Balance Due on Note	72,472	0
Net Proceeds before Tax	$47,527	$120,000
Initial Cash Outlay	$15,000	$60,000
Approximate Annual Pretax Rate of Return	25.94%	14.87%

Expressing loans as a percentage of the value of the mortgaged property provides some indication of the risk of such a loss. The LTV ratio associated with the property in Example 5.1 ($3,850,000/$5,500,000, or 70 percent) expresses that, in the event of immediate default, the property could net in a sale as much as 30 percent below its current value before the lender would suffer a significant loss.

Loan-to-value ratios serve an entirely different function for the investment analyst. They provide a measure of the dollar amount of real estate that can be controlled with a given amount of equity funds. If, for example, the available LTV ratio is 0.70, the investor can control $3.33 [$1/(1 − 0.70)] of real estate for every $1 of equity funds invested. This is the case in the $3.85 million loan in Example 5.1, where $1.65 million of equity funds confers control of a $5.5 million asset. For the $4.4 million loan alternative shown in Table 5.3, the investor controls the $5.5 million in real estate with only $1.1 million of equity, an LTV ratio of 0.80. The LTV ratio, therefore, serves as a measure of available financial leverage.

The debt-to-equity ratio expresses the degree of leverage available in a slightly different fashion. In Example 5.1 the debt-to-equity ratio for the first loan is $3.85 million to $1.65 million, or 2.33 to 1. This indicates that the investor can borrow $2.33 for every $1 of equity funds employed (note that adding the $1 of equity money to the debt/equity ratio takes you back to the loan/value ratio). For the second loan in Table 5.3 the investor can borrow $4 for every $1 of equity, a debt-to-equity ratio of four to one ($4.4 million/$1.1 million).

It should be emphasized here that the higher LTV ratio for the $4.4 million loan in Example 5.1 is riskier for the lender. Consequently, the lender charged a higher interest rate than for the lower LTV mortgage.

▮ FINANCIAL LEVERAGE FROM THE LENDER'S PERSPECTIVE

Greater leverage increases the risk that cash flow from an investment will be insufficient to meet the debt service obligation. The greater the amount of financial leverage employed (therefore, the greater the required debt service), the greater is the likelihood that equity investors will have to invest additional funds or default on a loan. Risk that cash flow from investments will be insufficient to service mortgage debt is called *financial risk*. It is a direct consequence of employing financial leverage.

Debt Coverage Ratio

The degree to which actual net operating income (gross rental income minus operating expenses) can fall below expectations and still be sufficient to meet the debt service obligation is expressed as a **debt coverage ratio**, also known as a *debt service ratio*. This is simply the ratio between net operating income and the debt service obligation. In equation form, this is

Debt Coverage Ratio = Net Operating Income/Debt Service

The debt coverage ratio for the $3.85 million loan in Example 5.1 is 1.71, calculated by dividing the expected $660,000 net operating income by the $386,436 annual debt service requirement. (See Table 5.3.) This expresses an expectation that annual cash flow before debt service will be approximately 1.7 times the amount required to service the debt. It indicates a substantial cushion for underestimated operating expenses or overestimated gross rental revenues before actual net operating income falls below that required to service the mortgage indebtedness. The additional risk associated with the $4.4 million loan in Table 5.3 is illustrated by its lower debt coverage ratio: $660,000/$458,208 = 1.44.

Debt Coverage Ratios and Available Financing

On all except very small investment properties, lenders can expect that investors will honor their debt service obligations only if the property that is security for the loan generates sufficient cash flow for this purpose. Moreover, because a mortgaged property's value depends on its ability to generate income, the property value will drop if the expected income does not materialize. This makes the debt coverage ratio an important measure of a lender's risk exposure; it indicates how far the net operating income can fall before it becomes inadequate to meet the borrower's debt service obligation.

Recognizing the relationship between net operating income and the likelihood that borrowers will honor their debt service obligations, lenders often specify minimum acceptable debt coverage ratios. These minimum standards will vary by industry and market. In such cases it is possible to estimate the available mortgage financing by starting with permissible ratios. Dividing the estimated annual net operating income by the minimum acceptable debt coverage ratio yields the maximum amount of annual debt service the property will support. Dividing this amount by the annual loan constant for the most likely loan terms results in an estimate of the loan that the property will support. Example 5.3 illustrates this.

EXAMPLE 5.3

A lender specifies a minimum debt coverage ratio of 1.20 for a certain property profile. The market interest rate for a loan of this type is 8 percent per annum, with a 20-year amortization period and monthly payments. The property is expected to yield first-year net operating income of $500,000.

To satisfy the lender requirement in Example 5.3, the expected $500,000 net operating income from the property must be at least 1.2 times as great as the annual debt service obligation. The debt service obligation, therefore, cannot exceed $500,000/1.2, or $416,667. The amortization table in Appendix D at the end of the text (and the excerpt in Table 5.1) reveals that an 8 percent, 20-year, fully amortizing loan requires monthly payments of $0.0083644 per dollar borrowed. The annual debt service per dollar borrowed is simply 12 times this amount, or $0.10037281. Because the maximum debt service the net operating income will support is $416,667, the property will support a maximum loan of $416,667/0.10037281, or $4,151,190.

SUMMARY

Financial leverage, the use of borrowed money, enables an investor to acquire a much more expensive property than would otherwise be possible. It also permits acquiring more separate properties, and thus may reduce aggregate risk through diversification.

Risk that cash flow from an investment will be insufficient to meet associated mortgage-debt payments is called *financial risk*. Adding to financial leverage increases financial risk. The borrowing decision involves weighing offsetting elements of enhanced earnings potential and increased financial risk.

Financial leverage can be measured as the ratio between equity funds and borrowed funds: the debt-to-equity ratio. A more common measure in real estate is the loan-to-value ratio, which expresses the portion of a property's value that is financed with borrowed money. Lenders often specify a maximum permissible loan-to-value ratio. They also frequently insist on a specific amount of expected net operating income for each dollar of annual debt service on the mortgage loan, a measure called a *debt coverage ratio*.

Like debt, equity funds are employed by rational investors only if the difference between fund cost and yield justifies the attendant risk. Cost estimating is more difficult for equity than for borrowed funds, however. Two commonly employed techniques are (1) to add a risk premium to the yield available by repaying outstanding indebtedness and (2) to estimate the yield on equity associated with other investments viewed as equally risky. Appendix B: Mathematics of Compounding and Discounting and Appendix C: Compounding and Discounting with Financial Calculators are useful adjuncts to this chapter.

KEY TERMS

annual constant	debt-to-equity ratio	nominal interest rate
balloon payment	effective interest rate	opportunity cost
bullet loan	favorable leverage	partially amortizing loan
debt constant (debt	financial leverage	(partly amortized)
service constant)	loan-to-value ratio	spread
debt coverage ratio	monthly constant	straight loan
debt service	mortgage constant	term loan

RECOMMENDED READING

Axelrod, Allan, Curtis J. Berger, and Quintin Johnstone. *Land Transfer and Finance.* Boston: Little, Brown and Company, 1993, 877–986.

Bagby, Joseph R. *Real Estate Financing Desk Book*, 3rd ed. Englewood Cliffs, N.J.: Institute for Business Planning, 1981.

Beaton, William R. *Real Estate Finance,* 2nd ed. Englewood Cliffs, N.J.: Prentice-Hall, 1981, 233–236.

Britton, James A., Jr., and Lewis O. Kerwood, eds. *Financing Income-Producing Real Estate: A Theory and Casebook.* New York: McGraw-Hill, 1977.

Kolbe, Phillip T., and Gaylon E. Greer. *Investment Analysis for Real Estate Decisions,* 6th ed. Chicago: Dearborn Real Estate Education, 2006.

Wiedemer, John P. *Real Estate Finance,* 9th ed. Reston, Va.: Reston Publishing Company, Inc., 2007.

INTERNET REFERENCES

To try some calculations involving discount points and interest rates:
www.bai.org
www.getsmart.com
www.interest.com

For further information on financial leverage in real estate:
www.ifecorp.com

For additional loan-to-value information:
www.mortgageresearchcenter.com/mortgages/ltv.php

▊ REVIEW QUESTIONS

1. How do income tax laws create an incentive to borrow money?
2. When financial leverage is used, what is the potential impact on before-tax cash flow and the current yield to the equity position?
3. How do fully amortizing loans differ from partially amortizing loans?
4. Explain the meaning of the loan-to-value ratio from a mortgage lender's perspective and from the viewpoint of an investor.
5. Describe financial risk in real estate investment and explain a useful method of measuring financial risk.
6. How can the debt coverage ratio be used to determine the amount of available financing for a project?
7. Financial leverage can amplify the gain realized on the disposal of a prop- Why might an astute investor knowingly enter into a financing arrangement that appears nominally unfavorable?

▊ DISCUSSION QUESTIONS

1. The interest rate charged on fixed-rate, 15-year mortgage loans is lower than that charged on fixed-rate, 30-year loans.
   a. Why is this so?
   b. As a borrower, what are some factors you should consider in deciding whether to accept a 15-year or a 30-year fixed-rate loan, when the 15-year rate is somewhat lower than the 30-year rate?
2. William Zeckendorf, a legendary real estate developer and promoter, is said to have commented during a real estate negotiation, "You can name the price if I can name the terms." What was the logic (if any) of Zeckendorf's position?
3. Two loans are negotiated for the same amount of money at the same annual interest rate. They require equal periodic payments to fully amortize the loans over 20 years. One loan calls for level monthly payments, the other for level annual payments.
   a. Will the annual payment loan require a payment of exactly 12 times the monthly payment on the other loan? Explain.
   b. Over the full 20-year repayment period, will the cumulative total interest paid on the two loans be the same? Explain.

▮ PROBLEMS

1. Mr. and Mrs. Average Consumer have been approved for an 80 percent loan-to-value fully amortizing mortgage for their $100,000 house. If the interest rate on this 30-year mortgage is 9 percent, what will their monthly payment be? If the Consumers pay all 360 payments on time, what is the effective cost of borrowing or the yield to the lender?

2. If the Consumers in Problem 1 had a partially amortizing mortgage with the same terms, what would be the balloon payment due in ten years?

3. Dent-the-Tenant Apartments has a market value of $800,000 and an annual net operating income of $100,000. If Igor Investor purchased the apartments with cash, what would be Igor's rate of return (before-tax cash flow/ equity)?

4. If Igor obtained a fully amortizing loan for 70 percent loan-to-value at 10 percent for 15 years, what would be his rate of return and annual debt service/loan?

5. If Igor financed 80 percent loan-to-value at 11 percent for 15 years, what would be the rate of return and annual debt service/loan?

6. If Igor's interest rate on the 80 percent LTV loan in Problem 5 is 13 percent, what would the two ratios be?

7. What is the debt coverage ratio for the loan in Problem 6?

CHAPTER 6

Sources and Uses of Real Estate Credit

After studying this chapter, you should understand the basic structure and history of real estate capital markets, key mortgage loan variations, and the common sources of mortgage loan funds, including commercial mortgage-backed securities.

An extensive and complex financial network caters to real estate industry needs. Many mortgage lenders are depository institutions that accumulate individual depositor's savings and originate mortgage loans. Chief among these are thrifts (savings associations and savings banks) and commercial banks. Federal credit unions are less significant in terms of the dollar volume of mortgage loans, but their importance, particularly to smaller home loans, cannot be ignored. This chapter describes the principal activities of each of these institutions.

Nondepository institutions such as life insurance companies, real estate investment trusts, mortgage companies, pension and trust funds, and, of course, conduit financing provided by commercial mortgage-backed securities also lend vast sums on the security of real estate mortgages.

It has been said that extraordinary times call for extraordinary measures. This was certainly the case for mortgage lenders during the decades of the 1970s and 1980s. That period brought financial upheavals unprecedented since World War II. To cope with widely fluctuating interest rates coupled with scary inflationary spurts and economically disrupting corrective action by government policymakers, lenders pioneered several mortgage innovations that are still with us today. Some of these are variations on older themes; others represent entirely new initiatives. The more significant innovations are discussed in Chapter 8: Alternative Financing Methods and Products.

WHERE THE MONEY COMES FROM

Ultimately, loans represent the application of savings accumulated by individuals, businesses, and institutions. Because most savers do not themselves make loans, the system requires a network of financial intermediaries, or middlemen, who aggregate funds from many savers and handle myriad details associated with lending operations.

The Structure of Real Estate Financial Markets

Money moves through a complex network of financial institutions, from those who save to those who invest in real estate assets. These institutions form only a portion of the country's total financial market structure, but they are a key segment because mortgage indebtedness is a major element in the nation's total debt structure.

Figure 6.1 illustrates the central figures in real estate financial markets: savers, savings depository institutions, mortgage originators, secondary market expediters, and final capital users. Some institutions perform multiple roles, but most concentrate primarily on one aspect of the real estate finance game.

Savers, quite simply, are individuals and institutions that spend less than they earn. Businesses and government agencies sometimes fit this definition, but only temporarily. Moreover, most business or government agency savings are offset by

FIGURE 6.1   Institutional Structure of the Mortgage Market

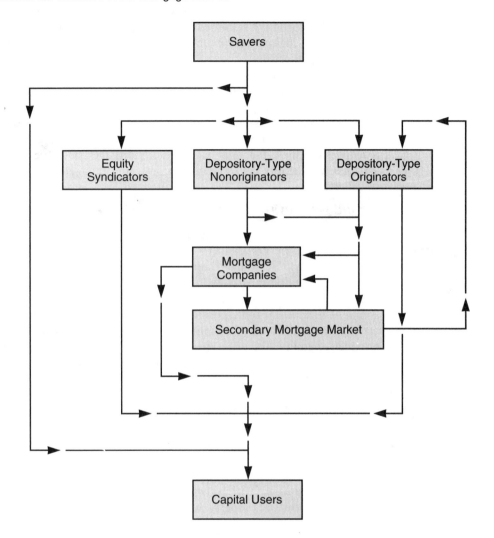

similar units elsewhere in the economy that borrow at least as much. After considering all economic sectors, therefore, individual households are the country's only consistent net savers.

Total savings per period depend primarily on aggregate income. Households as a group save a fairly consistent portion of their income each year, but the percentage saved does vary over time. While personal saving as a percentage of disposable personal income declined significantly through the late 1990s, the trend began to reverse in 2000. Figure 6.2 shows personal savings in the United States as a percentage of national income for recent years.

Although some savers make direct investments, most place their money with financial intermediaries such as banks and savings associations, which then invest the funds in productive activities, including real estate. Other intermediaries include life insurance companies, mutual savings banks, pension funds, credit unions, and real estate syndicators.

Real estate is but one of the many outlets financial intermediaries employ to gainfully invest funds. The intermediaries invest in real estate equities, buy real estate secured by promissory notes on the secondary market (where existing mortgage instruments are purchased and sold), make real estate loans themselves, and buy real estate–backed securities. Figure 6.1 divides the intermediaries into those that originate loans and those that only buy notes or mortgage-backed securities in the secondary market; in reality the same institutions often engage in both activities.

An Industry in Transition

Three types of financial intermediaries—commercial banks, thrift institutions, and life insurance companies—traditionally dominated the real estate mortgage lending industry. But today their relative positions and their roles in the industry have been radically transformed by legislation and by the march of economic events. From time to time a fourth group, pension funds, has entered the mortgage lending arena. At the present time, pension funds are disinclined to move into the commercial real estate market as a significant provider of debt, but they remain an important provider of equity. Today, a type of lending known as **conduit financing**, provided by commercial mortgage–backed securities, has emerged as one of the most popular and dominant forms of financing for commercial real estate.

For more than 20 years after World War II, mortgage lending was a predictable, unexciting, but generally profitable business where each type of intermediary filled a special niche. Each understood the others' roles and how its own function melded into the entire scheme of things. The thrift's job was to make high loan-to-value ratio loans on residential real estate within 100 miles of the lender's home office, with an occasional loan on nonresidential projects. Banks made construction and development loans (primarily within their local market area) and long-term loans on commercial and industrial property, with only an occasional long-term mortgage loan on multifamily residential property. Life insurance firms made large loans nationwide (but principally through local loan correspondents) on large commercial and multifamily residential projects.

The old order was gradually disintegrating, even as the players were becoming comfortable with the status quo. The system's foundation was grounded on low-cost funds provided by savers who had few alternatives but to place their funds with depository-type financial intermediaries at interest rates kept artificially low by law or custom. People began revolting against the established order during the 1960s. They started bypassing banks and thrifts, electing instead to invest directly in financial markets or to place their savings with money market mutual funds.

FIGURE 6.2 | Relationship between Aggregate Savings and National Income

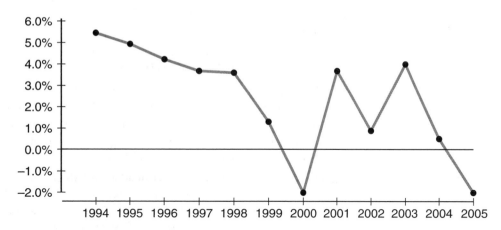

Interest rates paid by banks and savings and loan associations (S&Ls) were fixed by law during this early period at a very low level, thus assuring the intermediaries of a generous spread between their cost of funds and the rates they could earn in the market. Federal law also permitted savings associations to pay a slightly higher rate than commercial banks, a comfortable arrangement that assured them a stable source of funds with a built-in profit margin. A charter to start a federal S&L was a license to make money with low risk and little need to innovate or improvise.

In 1966 and 1969, then again in 1973–1974, interest rates increased sharply on instruments where the rate was not fixed by law. In 1965, for example, the average annual yields on treasury bonds and on S&L deposits were almost identical, at around 3 percent, with the savings deposit rate actually slightly higher. By 1966, government bonds were yielding slightly more (21 basis points: one **basis point** = 1/100 of 1 percent) than the rate paid by S&Ls; by 1969, the difference had grown to the point where the government bond yield was more than one-fourth higher (85 basis points).

Consumers responded by moving their savings into unregulated markets. In 1966, the rate of growth in deposits at savings institutions other than commercial banks dropped by almost half. They dropped again—by about one-third—with the 1969 rate divergence. The drop in the 1974–1975 period was less radical, yet remained a troublesome concern. Securities industry professionals seized the opportunity to introduce money market mutual funds that offered small-scale savers the same market-determined rates that had previously been available only to the relatively wealthy. By early 1978, deposits with money market mutual funds had grown to $11 billion (they would grow to more than $200 billion during the ensuing four years), and thrift institutions were feeling the competitive pinch.

CHRONOLOGY OF CONVERGENCE

By the mid-1980s, a series of laws and regulatory initiatives had virtually obliterated the distinctions between commercial banks and savings and loan associations. Key events in this convergence of characteristics were:

1970   **Housing Act of 1970** permits S&Ls to make preauthorized funds transfers from savings accounts for household-related bills.

1974   Money market mutual funds begin offering shareholders withdrawals by check, an innovation that makes the funds more competitive with banks and S&Ls.

1978   The Federal Reserve Board authorizes commercial banks to automatically transfer funds from interest-bearing savings accounts to checking accounts whenever funds are needed to cover a check.

1980   The **Depository Institutions Deregulation and Monetary Control Act** becomes law. It authorizes negotiated orders of withdrawal (NOW accounts) for S&Ls nationwide, extending the types of assets that S&Ls are authorized to own, imposing the Federal Reserve System's reserve requirements on all depository institutions that offer checking accounts or certificates of deposit with maturities of less than four years, increasing deposit insurance to a level of $100,000 per account in each insured institution, and setting up the Depository Institutions Deregulatory Committee to gradually eliminate interest rate differentials among institutions.

1982   The **Garn-St. Germain Depository Institutions Act** is enacted. It permits interstate mergers of depository institutions and removes interest rate ceilings on short-term accounts that have a minimum balance of at least $2,500.

1989   The **Financial Institutions Reform, Recovery, and Enforcement Act (FIRREA)** is enacted. It abolishes the Federal Savings and Loan Insurance Corporation and the Federal Home Loan Bank Board and creates the Office of Thrift Supervision, the Federal Housing and Finance Board, and the Resolution Trust Corporation. It provides a common insurance agency for deposits in commercial banks and thrifts.

1991   The **Federal Deposit Insurance Corporation Improvement Act (FDICIA)** is enacted. It enacts additional reforms to the system of bank supervision and to federal deposit insurance. The FDICIA is the final legislative response to the thrift crisis of the 1980s.

1994   The **Riegle-Neal Act** removes most of the remaining limitations on the consolidation of the interstate banking system.

1999   The **Gramm-Leach-Bliley Act** becomes law. Also known as the **Financial Modernization Act of 1999**, it arguably represents the single most important set of regulatory reforms of the financial services industry since the Glass-Steagall Act of 1933. The Gramm-Leach-Bliley Act repeals and/or amends many of the key provisions of the Glass-Steagall Act and of the Bank Holding Company Act of 1956. Specifically, it repeals provisions of the 1933 Glass-Steagall Act that separated commercial and investment banking, and it repeals

provisions of the Bank Holding Company Act of 1956 that restricted affilia
tions of banking and insurance. Now for the first time banks and other financial
firms are allowed to establish so-called financial holding companies which can
include securities underwriting, commercial and merchant banking, and insurance underwriting.

To stem this economic hemorrhaging, federal regulators created new financial
instruments designed to let the thrifts pay rates closer to the market. This slowed the
rate of deposit losses, but it saddled thrifts with a much higher cost of funds. The
rates they paid on deposits rose steadily—from an average of 6.44 percent in 1977
to 11.53 in late 1981—and squeezed profit margins that were already burdened by
the high number of lower-interest, long-term mortgages the thrifts were carrying in
their portfolios. Federal officials broadened the range of activities in which S&Ls
could engage, virtually obliterating the distinction between commercial banks and
thrifts. The old order was destroyed, and traditional repositories for individual savings had to adapt or die. This ultimately led to the solvency crisis discussed in detail
in Chapter 1.

MAJOR MORTGAGE LENDERS

Collectively, commercial banks, thrifts, life insurance companies, and mortgage
companies accounted for more than 85 percent of all new mortgages in 2000, but
nowthe majority of real estate loans are held by institutions and agencies with mortgage pools. (See Figure 6.3.) Each lender exhibits distinct preferences as to type
of borrower, loan size, and type of real estate pledged as security. Differences are
attributable to variations in sources of funds and accompanying need for portfolio
liquidity, as well as to varying characteristics of the regulatory framework under
which lenders operate.

Commercial Banks

Commercial banks are one of the largest sources of new real estate mortgage
loans. According to the Board of Governors of the Federal Reserve System, mortgage holdings by commercial banks reached $1.776 trillion in 2005. This type of
lending activity is now the mainstay of the commercial banking industry, with real
estate representing about 62 percent of commercial bank lending. (See Figure 6.4.)
Because their loans are heavily concentrated in construction financing, commercial
banks are by far the largest source of such loans.

There may be no such thing as a "typical" commercial bank in the United States.
Commercial banks may be either state or federally chartered. Commercial banks
vary in size from less than $1 million to well over $5 billion in assets. State banking
regulations differ dramatically across the nation, and local practices vary accordingly. According to the Federal Deposit Insurance Corporation (FDIC), the number
of commercial banks in the United States has fallen. This decline is attributable

FIGURE 6.3 | Distributive Market Shares among Real Estate Mortgage Holders, 2005

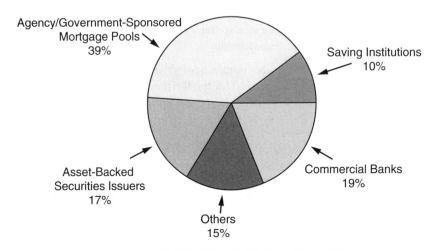

Source: *Statistical Abstract of The United States*, 2006

primarily to the large number of commercial bank mergers and buyouts, while the number of new banks entering the market continues to decline.

Traditionally, commercial bankers have been reluctant to commit themselves deeply to the long-term mortgage market. Their principal sphere of activity has been short-term credit. Where they have entered the mortgage lending field, they have generally concentrated on construction financing, which is the short-term end of the mortgage lending spectrum. They are vital to the construction industry because they provide more than 75 percent of all construction loan funds. Figure 6.3 illustrates the relative significance of commercial banks to the lending industry and the industry's importance to banks.

Commercial bankers' role in the mortgage lending industry goes far beyond their direct participation in loan origination, however. Nondepository mortgage lenders (whom we will consider shortly) frequently look to commercial banks as a source of loanable funds. Pledging their inventory of existing mortgage loans as security for additional short-term funds enables these lenders to carry a mortgage-loan portfolio several times as large as would be possible were they to depend solely on their personal equity capital.

The practice of borrowing money on the strength of an existing mortgage portfolio with which to further expand the size of the portfolio in anticipation of eventually assigning the pledged mortgages to other investors is called **mortgage warehousing.** Consequently, bank loans to facilitate the practice are called **mortgage warehousing loans**.

Private mortgage companies that look to commercial banks for mortgage warehousing loans are often called **mortgage bankers.** Commercial banks have themselves

FIGURE 6.4 | Percentage Distribution of New Commercial Bank Loans

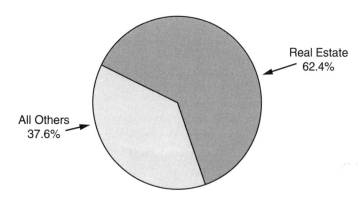

Source: *Statistical Abstract of The United States*, 2005

become increasingly active in mortgage banking. This has proven a lucrative source of additional bank revenue, and it does not significantly diminish the commercial bank's treasured liquidity.

Savings Associations and Savings Banks

For many years, thrifts—savings associations and savings banks—limited their lending operations almost exclusively to financing the purchase of new or existing homes or the refinancing of outstanding home loans. They sometimes made loans to finance land, for mobile-home purchases, or for education. Yet their *raison d'être* was long-term, fully amortizing home mortgage loans.

The Garn-St. Germain Depository Institutions Act of 1982 (described more fully in Chapter 1) erased virtually all distinctions between savings banks and savings associations and, in fact, authorized institutions to easily convert their charters from savings banks to savings associations and vice versa. Subsequently, the number of savings banks grew rapidly, more than doubling (to 984) by 1987. Like savings associations, savings banks may hold either state or federal charters, but presently only about a third of the states charter them.

Although their degree of dominance nose-dived during the past three decades (from an all-time high of 55.8 percent in 1976, their market share declined to about 21 percent by 1991), thrifts continue to be a source of residential mortgage loans, but more typically they offer second mortgages, home improvement loans, and installment loans. At the peak of their market dominance, however, they embarked on a radically different financial path. The Garn-St. Germain Act placed thrifts in direct competition with commercial banks. The act eliminated a federally mandated differ-

TABLE 6.1 | Mortgage Loans Outstanding in 2005, by Investor Type (one-family to four-family properties)

Type of Investor	Morgage Loans Outstanding ($ Billions)
Agency/Government-Sponsored Mortgage Pools	3,547
Commercial Banks	1.776
Asset-Backed Securities Issuers	1.592
Savings Institutions	955
Government-Sponsored Enterprises	354
Credit Unions	246
Finance Companies	233
REITs	147
All Other Investors	299
Total Outstanding	9.149

Source: Statistical Abstract of the United States, 2006

ential in cost of funds that had favored thrifts over banks, and permitted the thrifts to compete with banks in a wide arena from which they had previously been excluded.

Thrifts responded by shifting a substantial portion of their assets into areas other than mortgage loans. In 1981, mortgage loans accounted for more than 78 percent of total savings association assets. After enactment of the Garn-St. Germain Act they declined steadily until, by 1987, they constituted less than 56 percent of the total. Meanwhile, as noted earlier, their share of the residential mortgage market declined precipitously.

These numbers understate the continuing importance of savings associations as a generator of mortgage money, however, because the associations have moved aggressively into mortgage banking. Mortgage bankers originate loans that they then sell to investors. The increasing role of savings associations in this arena is reflected in loans sold compared with the percentage of loans originated. This percentage crept up gradually from around 5 percent in 1970 to about 20 percent in 1981. Sales exploded in 1982, exceeding 88 percent of new loans originated. They settled back after the initial excitement of deregulation, but the average annual sales as a percentage of average new loan originations from 1984 through 1987 remained slightly above 50 percent.

Although their overall share of the real estate lending market is dwarfed by that of commercial banks—only $955 billion in 2005 versus commercial banks' $1.776 trillion—savings associations continue as a key source of long-term residential mortgage loans.

Federal Credit Unions

Credit unions provide loans and a means of regular savings to their members, who must have a common bond such as membership in an affinity group or a common source of employment. The federal government agency that supervises, charters, and insures federal credit unions is the National Credit Union Administration (NCUA). The NCUA also insures state-chartered credit unions that apply and qualify for insurance. The unions are consumer cooperatives; officers are members who (mostly) serve without compensation. A manager is usually hired to run the credit union's business affairs.

Although they are presently relatively small players in mortgage lending ($246 billion in 2005), federal credit unions as a source of funds, particularly smaller mortgages, should not be ignored. According to the National Association of Federal Credit Unions, over the past several years credit unions consistently approved more than 90 percent of all mortgage loan applications. From 2001 to 2005 the dollar amount of mortgages held by credit unions has jumped 75 percent.

Federal legislation dating from 1977 allows credit unions to expand into areas from which they have traditionally been excluded. These new operations—savings certificates, interest-bearing checking accounts, credit cards, and so forth—should make credit unions more competitive with savings associations. This bodes well for their future as a source of mortgage funds.

Mortgage Companies

In the past, real estate mortgage lending, by its very nature, was a localized activity. Loan solicitation, application processing, and property inspection all required a loan representative on-site. Mortgage lenders were often geographically remote from borrowers and found it uneconomical to establish a network of branch offices to perform on-site loan functions. The coming of age of the Internet is changing much of this.

As local surrogates for absentee lenders, local mortgage companies frequently handle the myriad details attendant on mortgage lending. Sometimes they function as mortgage bankers, making loans by disbursing their own (or borrowed) funds, then selling the mortgages to a final lender. Alternatively, they sometimes act as **mortgage brokers**, functioning as an intermediary between borrowers and lenders. Many (still) serve as correspondents for lenders such as pension funds or life insurance companies. They generally service loans on behalf of the final lender: collecting payments, handling record-keeping chores, and so forth. In some of these roles they process loan applications, check credit references, arrange for property appraisals, and act as the lenders' agents in closing loan transactions and disbursing funds. The real estate supplement sections of most large city Sunday newspapers are full of advertisements for these companies.

Mortgage companies' importance is disproportionate to the capital they commit to mortgage lending. Though they themselves are not major holders of mortgage portfolios, they are a significant link in the chain that connects lenders with borrowers. It is likely that the Web's encroachment into the traditional mortgage business will continue making the process more efficient.

Today, for example, online companies such as LendingTree (*www.lendingtree .com*) connect the prospective borrower to a network of lenders who compete for their business. All the user has to do is complete an online questionnaire to request a loan. The company sends the applicant's loan request to a number of lenders in its network. The lenders respond with a decision about the loan request, and after evaluating the offer(s), the prospective borrower chooses the loan and lender he or she feels is best. (Key "shopping for a mortgage lender" into any of the popular Internet search engines such as Google™ to see how this works.)

Real Estate Investment Trusts

Since 1960 the Internal Revenue Code has provided income tax advantages to corporations that qualify as **real estate investment trusts** (commonly called **REITs**; rhymes with sweets). REITs operate much like closed-end mutual funds. They are required by the Internal Revenue Code to be organized in such a manner that they will be treated as corporations for tax purposes (though they may actually be organized under state laws as business trusts or associations). Shares must be readily transferable, and operating policy must be set by a board of directors or trustees. REITs owe their popularity with investors to Sections 856 through 860 of the Code. They must distribute 90 percent of annual income as dividends to shareholders. For the REIT, all of this income is exempt from taxation, but the dividends are taxed as ordinary income to shareholders. This permits investors to gain the principal advantages of corporate ownership without the offsetting disadvantage of earnings being taxed twice—once as income to the corporation itself and again as dividend income to investors.

REITs raise funds by issuing their own shares, bonds, and commercial paper and by borrowing from other financial institutions. They invest in real estate debt and equity. Many REITs specialize in short-term lending to finance construction and development projects; others focus on long-term mortgage loans. Most prefer to take an ownership position in income-producing properties such as warehouses, apartments, offices, self-storage facilities, and clinics. Still others include both mortgages and equities in their portfolios. Certain REITs have found a market niche by concentrating on some specialized aspect of mortgage lending, such as wraparound mortgages or sale-leasebacks. (Alternative financing is discussed in Chapter 8.)

Early REITs confined themselves almost exclusively to equity investment. Reflecting their asset preference, they are called *equity REITs*. With the run-up in interest rates and tight money during the late 1960s and early 1970s, REIT investment patterns and growth trends changed dramatically. From 1969 through 1972, REIT shares constituted more than 11 percent of all new corporate shares sold in the United States. REIT borrowing grew from $90 million in 1968 to more than $10 billion by 1973. The favored REIT investment during this period was short-term construction and development lending. (REITs that invest primarily in mortgages, whether short-term or long-term, are called *mortgage REITs*; those that hold a balanced portfolio of equities and mortgages are called *hybrid REITs*.)

Beginning in 1973, the REIT industry's glow turned to gloom. High borrowing costs, combined with excessive construction and consequent high vacancy rates, created financial turmoil that caused REIT shares to lose half their aggregate value in one year. Within two years, industry assets declined from their 1974 high of about $20 billion to around $5 billion. By 1976, the industry had largely restructured and began once more expanding its lending activity. It wasn't until 1984, however, that total REIT assets began to grow appreciably. The industry's upward progress has been more or less constant since. Recent REIT fortunes from 1995 through 2006 are reflected in the graph in Figure 6.5.

According to the National Association of Real Estate Investment Trusts (NAREIT), there are about 300 REITs operating in the United States today. Their assets total over $300 billion. About two-thirds of these trade on the national stock exchanges.

Life Insurance Companies

Life and other insurance companies originate far fewer real estate mortgage loans than do commercial banks or savings associations. (See Figure 6.3.) They are more inclined, however, to retain the loans in their portfolios and, in fact, buy substantial

---

FIGURE 6.5 | Public Offerings of Securities by REITs

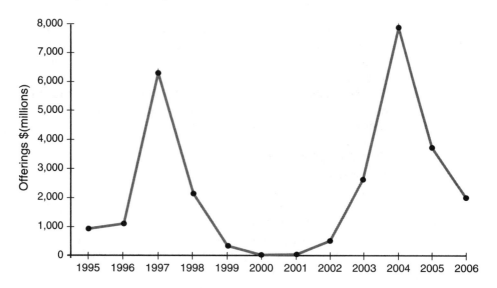

Printed with permission from the National Association of Real Estate Investment Trusts®.

amounts of loans from other originators. With more than 20 percent of their assets committed to real estate mortgage loans, they cannot be ignored. Moreover, many take equity positions in major real estate development projects.

Insurance companies are headquartered all across the country, but the industry has traditionally been concentrated in northeast states. Relatively lenient regulatory environments have made Texas, Louisiana, and Arizona increasingly popular head-quarters states in recent years; these three states house approximately half of all life insurance firms in the nation. But companies domiciled in northeastern states still control a disproportionate share of life insurance industry assets.

Life insurers show a distinct preference for permanent loans on large "class A" high quality commercial and industrial properties located in top-tier markets, particularly large shopping centers anchored by credit tenants and "trophy" office buildings. Because of the geographic diversity of their lending operations, most are not well positioned to make single-family loans; less than 7 percent of their mortgage loan portfolios represented one- to four-family dwellings.

Mortgage operations are usually controlled from a company's head office, but loan origination and servicing practices differ widely among firms. Many employ mortgage correspondents (independent agents) for this function. Others make frequent use of independent loan brokers.

Because regulations governing their loan activities are less restrictive than those imposed on banks and savings associations, life insurance companies are often more responsive to relatively flexible financing proposals, such as less onerous early repayment terms. They themselves sometimes take the initiative in suggesting new arrangements.

Pension Funds

Historically, pension funds have had a significant interest in real estate lending. Today, they are only bit players in the mortgage lending market (in contrast to the equity market, where they enthusiastically embrace high quality real estate investments), but this understates pension fund commitments to real estate, because it does not include the funds' portfolio of mortgage-backed securities (instead, they are lumped with bonds in flow of funds accounts) or their commitment to the total U.S. equity real estate (excluding debt) market.

REGULATIONS' BY-PRODUCT: INFORMATION

Pension funds have entered the real estate equities market via commingled real estate funds (CREFs). Managed by independent management firms, CREFs are like an open-ended equity REIT with an exclusive set of investors. CREF assets are appraised quarterly so that the value of each pension fund's shares can be estimated. This quarterly appraisal, coupled with reliable purchase, sale, and net operating income information, has created an extremely valuable but heretofore unavailable source of time-series data on the performance of major real estate investments. Several researchers have used CREF data to estimate risk and return series for real estate investments.

The Secondary Mortgage Market

One problem that, in the past (prior to the 1930s) caused the mortgage lending industry to be particularly sensitive to cyclical economic downturns, has already been mentioned—a term structure that required that mortgage notes be renegotiated every three to five years. During the loan term, only accrued interest was paid, and this typically only every six months. The principal amount, of course, became due when mortgage notes matured. Seldom did a mortgagor have sufficient funds to retire a maturing mortgage note, however. Reliance on ability to renew the face amount of a note was almost universal.

The peculiar nature of mortgage loans made them susceptible to liquidity problems, even without more generalized economic difficulties. Secured as they were by local realty, they had limited market appeal. Because lending practices and mortgage formats varied widely from place to place, investors in mortgage notes seldom were willing to commit resources outside the geographic area in which their representatives were active. No nationwide secondary mortgage market (a market in which existing mortgage notes are bought and sold) existed, and under such conditions none could be expected.

Lacking a secondary market, lenders were loath to place a substantial portion of their assets in mortgages. Those who did so (principally S&Ls) generally were forced to carry the notes in their own portfolios until maturity. In a financial crisis, these assets could not readily be converted into cash.

Investors in corporate securities generally did not consider mortgage notes an acceptable alternative. Rates of return, therefore, varied greatly between corporate bonds and mortgage notes, and even between mortgage notes in different localities. There could be a surplus of funds available for corporate bonds, while the real estate

TABLE 6.2 | Mortgage Loan Characteristics and Intended Loan Proceeds

Loan Characteristic	Loan Type		
	Interim	Standby	Permanent
Interest Rate	Higher	Intermediate	Lower
Administrative Burden	High	Low	Low
Amortizing?	No	Sometimes	Yes
Maturity	Short-term	Intermediate	Long-term
Purpose	Construction, development, rehabilitation	Substitute for long-term loan	Repay interim or standby; finance a purchase

industry starved for lack of money. Likewise, a real estate boom in one part of the nation might be accompanied by a virtual depression in another.

Some interarea flow of mortgage funds did occur through correspondent relationships between midwestern (predominantly) mortgage companies and eastern (predominantly) life insurance companies. But these loans were usually secured by farm mortgages at loan-to-value ratios that almost never exceeded 50 percent.

To remedy some of these problems, the federal government created a number of agencies intended to increase liquidity and allocative efficiency in mortgage markets. Chief among these were the Federal Housing Administration (FHA), the Federal National Mortgage Association (FNMA, now Fannie Mae), the Government National Mortgage Association (GNMA, now Ginnie Mae), and the Federal Home Loan Mortgage Corporation (FHLMC, now Freddie Mac). (These agencies are described in more detail in Chapter 7.)

WHERE THE MONEY GOES

Unique requirements and special circumstances have spawned mortgage lenders that specialize in catering to specific types of borrowers. Lending conveniently divides into development and construction financing, standby financing, and long-term financing. Table 6.2 summarizes key differences.

Interim Loans

Roughly one third of all real estate mortgage loans are originated to finance new construction. This is the sector of the industry in which value is created. Developers interpret market data, make development decisions, and thereby determine the future shape and size of our cities and towns. Construction lending is perhaps the most risky of all real estate loans. Lenders provide funds for both labor and materials in advance of construction. They frequently must disburse substantial amounts on the security of nonexistent or incomplete structures.

Most construction loans do eventually prove profitable, but there is no advance assurance of this. Unforeseeable events such as labor strife, inclement weather, or material shortages may delay a project indefinitely. Consequent cost overruns can easily drive a developer into bankruptcy. Lenders may then find themselves in possession of unfinished and perhaps ill-conceived projects.

As indicated in Table 6.2, construction loans, also called **interim loans**, are the most complicated type of mortgage financing to administer. Lenders must protect themselves against unsatisfied claims of laborers and suppliers to whom a developer might become indebted. In many legal jurisdictions, claims of these individuals can represent liens to which a lender's mortgage is subordinate. To safeguard against such problems, lenders closely monitor construction activity. Loans are usually disbursed in stages as construction progresses. Lenders frequently pass money directly to subcontractors and suppliers, or they may require affidavits that subcontractors' and suppliers' claims have been satisfied before disbursing the final installment of construction loan proceeds.

Reflecting their higher risk and greater administrative burden, construction loans command a higher interest rate than do those secured by existing buildings. Because of its quick turnover, this type of loan appeals to lenders that need substantial liquidity, including institutions that collect short-term savings from depositors. Moreover, lenders profit from significant fees and discounts levied on borrowers. Effective yields are, therefore, enhanced by quick loan turnover. Lenders prefer maturities that require at least one loan renewal during the construction period, because this gives them greater control over the borrowers' activities. Construction and development loans are examined further in Chapter 12.

Permanent Financing

Loans on completed structures, called **permanent**, **takeout**, or **end loans**, differ in key respects from construction loans. Whereas construction loans are repaid in a lump sum when the project is completed, permanent loans usually call for monthly payments to amortize the loan over its term. In contrast to the short-term nature of construction lending, permanent loans may have maturities of 30 years or longer. Loans on one- to four-family residences are typically amortized over 15 to 30 years. Maturities on other permanent loans usually range from 10 to 20 years, but those with the shorter maturities often permit payments based on a much longer amortization period, with a lump-sum "balloon" payment of the balance due at the end of the term. These loans are the partially amortizing loans described in Chapter 5.

Because of the vastly different administrative requirements and the radical variations in asset liquidity associated with interim and permanent financing, lenders usually have a distinct preference for one type of loan over the other. Indeed, those that are active in permanent lending frequently provide interim financing only as a precondition to making the end loan.

In contrast to interim loans, permanent loans are attractive to those lenders with more predictable fund flows that require opportunities to leave funds "at risk" for considerable periods of time.

Standby Financing

Most developers expect to retire maturing construction loan obligations with proceeds from a permanent, or end, loan. To assure themselves of repayment, interim lenders may require a binding endloan commitment as a precondition to the actual disbursement of construction loan funds. For a number of reasons, though, a developer may be unable or unwilling to arrange a permanent loan so early in the development process. Instead, the developer might seek standby financing to carry the project after completion until a permanent loan is obtained.

There are several reasons why a developer may use standby financing to allow a delay in obtaining a permanent loan commitment:

- Prevailing interest rates may be abnormally high, and the developer may prefer to delay long-term financing until rates fall back.

■ Value created in the design and construction phases or anticipated positive changes in economic conditions during construction might enable the developer to negotiate a larger loan at a later time. (One example of this might be the planned opening of a newly constructed highway off-ramp in the immediate area of a development.)

■ A permanent mortgage commitment may be contingent on the existence of long-term leases on the building. Yet the developer may be unable to lease the required portion of the building in advance of construction, or it may prefer to delay leasing in contemplation of higher rents when space becomes less available at a later stage in the business cycle.

Whatever their motivation, developers that wish or are forced to delay binding agreements for permanent financing have a problem. Interim lenders recognize that a completed project will have to be sold or refinanced before they can expect to recover funds advanced for construction. To reduce their risk, most will want the borrower to acquire a firm commitment from a permanent lender that will "take out" the interim construction loan. Lenders that are willing to advance interim funds without a take-out commitment will demand a higher interest rate or greater fees (frequently both) to compensate for increased risk exposure.

Standby loan commitments are a common solution. They constitute binding obligations on lenders, but are in the nature of options for developers. Such loans ensure that funds will be available if takeout loans cannot be obtained under more favorable terms before the interim loan matures.

Standby commitments are lucrative for lenders because no one—neither developer nor lender—expects that a loan will actually be made. Standby commitments call for higher interest rates and shorter amortization periods than are characteristic for permanent loans, and therefore are exercised only as a last resort. Yet, for the mere assurance that funds will be available if needed, developers pay a nonrefundable fee based on the dollar amount of the commitment.

Conduit Lending and CMBS

Conduit loans, also known as **commercial mortgage-backed securities (CMBS)**, are a special type of securitized debt that arguably has become one of the most important forms of long-term, fixed-rate mortgage financing for commercial and industrial real estate in use today. Securitization is simply the process of converting assets (receivables, mortgages, or other financial assets) into securities (marketable financial instruments) backed by those assets. It is the financial magic that transmutes illiquid, risky individual loans into more liquid, less risky securities.

It is difficult to understand the basics of CMBS without some feel for the history of the mortgage-backed securities market. For a brief history lesson we turn to remarks made by Chairman Alan Greenspan before a conference on Mortgage Markets and Economic Activity sponsored by America's Community Bankers, Washington, D.C., November 2, 1999:

The mortgage-backed securities market grew dramatically, beginning in 1970 with the issuance of the first Ginnie Mae [Government National Mortgage Association] pass-through security [pass-through means the security passes through to the purchaser the principal and interest scheduled for payment each month from the mortgagors on the remaining balance of the loans that comprise the security] and followed by Freddie Mac's [Federal Home Loan Mortgage Corporation] sale of mortgage-backed securities backed by conventional loans in 1971, reflecting the wide acceptance of these securities by the investor community. This was also an era when the principal mortgage lenders, savings and loans, were sometimes constrained from satisfying mortgage demands by binding Regulation Q [a regulation that imposed interest rate ceilings on most deposit accounts at financial institutions—effectively phased out by the Depository Institutions Deregulation and Monetary Control Act of 1980] ceilings that eroded their deposit base when interest rates rose. In those difficult times, the development of the mortgage-backed securities market helped to provide a safety valve and, as a result, the standard residential mortgage today need no longer be funded or originated by specialized financial institutions.

By the mid-1980s, the channels for mortgage originations and holdings had become quite diverse, with the traditional depositories competing against mortgage brokers and mortgage bankers, who sold their loans not only to Fannie Mae [Federal National Mortgage Association] and Freddie Mac but to others as well. This greater institutional diversity in the sources of mortgage finance played a key role in maintaining the uninterrupted flow of mortgage credit during the then-biggest financial debacle since the Great Depression—the S&L crisis of the late 1980s. The resiliency of the mortgage credit market during that period highlights the value of having a diverse set of financial institutions and financial markets that serve a key sector of the economy, such as housing.

Although CMBS have been around in one form or another since the 1970s, they really took off during the recessionary period of the early 1990s when the Resolution Trust Corporation (RTC) started using debt securitization as a tool to help dispose of its portfolio of nonperforming properties held by S&Ls. In June 1991, the RTC initiated its residential securitization program. Securities backed by single-family and (usually) one-family to four-family mortgages were issued. The first of these was AA rated and was backed by $440 million of mortgages from one RTC conservatorship. (The credit rating of a security depends on the company's ability to pay back its debt. AAA- and AA-rated bonds are considered high quality with little chance of default.) From the program's inception through the end of 1994, almost $45 billion in performing and nonperforming loans were securitized (source: FDIC). Since that time, the role of CMBS in commercial real estate finance has exploded. Today, in the United States, conduit financing has become one of the most important components of long-term, fixed-rate mortgage financing for commercial real estate. According to data provided by Commercial Mortgage Alert, CMBS volume in the United States was $74.4 billion in 2001.

Although frequently referred to as *conduit loans*, residential mortgage-backed securities (RMBS) and CMBS are not loans in and of themselves. The entity securitizing its mortgage loans guaranteed (if CMBS) by commercial or industrial properties (typically office buildings, warehouses, shopping centers, and self-storage properties) is not borrowing money; rather, it is selling its stream of cash flows. CMBS are actually financial instruments in which many individual real estate mortgages are grouped together (pooled) and used as collateral for bond offerings. The way CMBS are constructed allows the bonds to provide yields that are as good as or better than corporate bonds (or similar fixed income investments) with comparable levels of risk. Because bond investors are attracted by the relative safety and yield of CMBS, Wall Street investment banks are eager to sell them to institutional investors.

Why Is This So Important?

The terms under which financial institutions make mortgage loans to real estate borrowers typically require periodic payments (usually monthly) over an extended period of time—10 to 30 years for commercial loans and 15 to 30 years for residential loans. During this time, the lender's invested capital (the funds the lender has "invested" in the mortgage loan to the borrower) is only gradually being replenished through the loan amortization process. Securitization provides an almost perfect solution. Because CMBS are so alluring to investors, lenders see them as an ideal way to replenish their loaned funds at a profit by accommodating the needs of a source of financing (Wall Street) that seems to have an almost unlimited capacity to supply funding for quality real estate loans. According to data provided by Commercial Mortgage Alert, CMBS U.S. volume was $205.6 billion in 2006, up from $169.2 billion in 2005, and the global market for CMBS is large and growing. A listing of annual CMBS (U.S. only) issuance since 1985 is shown as Table 6.3.

Long-term lenders of all types have increasingly adapted their underwriting guidelines and loan requirements to the CMBS market. With so many "traditional" commercial mortgage lenders (life insurance companies, commercial banks and pension funds, and even "nontraditional" real estate lenders such as General Electric's GE Capital Real Estate and GMAC Commercial Mortgage) rushing to securitize and sell their loans, the interests, needs, and requirements of CMBS investors are of paramount importance. It's as if every homebuilder in the United States gradually discovered that homebuyers were interested only in homes with whirlpool baths. Would many homebuilders be motivated to install anything else?

So that their loans can be easily understood by CMBS investors, conduit lenders endeavor to use a fairly standard format for terms, conditions, and documentation for all loans. This serves to enhance the marketability of the bond offering, which, after all, is the whole idea. Though CMBS loan documents have many things in common with traditional commercial/industrial real estate loans, those destined to become CMBS are more complex and can easily run 60 pages or more.

The following are some of the more important "standard" CMBS lender requirements.

TABLE 6.3 | U.S. CMBS by Year, All in U.S. $ in Millions

Year	Total	No. of Deals
1985	204.0	1
1986	90.0	1
1987	1,707.3	9
1988	1,299.7	15
1989	3,584.0	23
1990	2,885.5	21
1991	5,330.6	31
1992	13,866.5	51
1993	16,733.9	114
1994	17,404.1	115
1995	17,848.8	94
1996	28,764.0	106
1997	40,441.7	92
1998	77,726.1	92
1999	58,481.8	101
2000	48,870.5	88
2001	74,375.7	115
2002	66,383.0	98
2003	77,800.0	98
2004	93,100.0	85
2005	169,200.0	99
2006	205,600.0	102
2007*	136,991.2	46

*First half year

Source: Commercial Mortgage Alert (*www.CMAlert.com*)

Single-Purpose Entity

Conduit financing provided by CMBS requires that the borrower be a single purpose entity (SPE), that is, an ownership structure that has only one asset, the property to be mortgaged. In theory, in the event of foreclosure this form of ownership ensures that the process will be relatively quick and clean for the lender. Investment bankers refer to this as bankruptcy remoteness. This structure also insulates the lender from potential problems that could occur with the borrower's other assets. Among other things, the SPE must

- be a legal entity separate and distinct from any other entity and hold itself out to the public as such;
- not own any asset or property other than the property to be mortgaged (this, of course, does not include things that are incidental to operation of the property to be mortgaged);
- not engage in any business other than the ownership, management, and operation of the property to be mortgaged;
- not incur any debt other than the mortgage and operational debt incurred in the ordinary course of business with trade creditors;
- not make any loans to any third parties;
- maintain separate books and records, financial statements, and bank accounts; and
- file its own separate tax returns.

Carve-Outs

Conduit loans are typically nonrecourse. This means the lender's only recourse in the event of default is the property; the borrower is not personally liable. While this is great for the borrower, it's not so great for the lender or the investor. For that reason, conduit loans contain language that makes the borrower personally liable for specific acts such as fraud or commission of a criminal act. These are called **carve-outs** and typically include:

- Criminal acts
- Failure to comply with certain provisions of the loan agreement
- Fraud or misrepresentation
- Failure to maintain required insurance
- Failure to comply with environmental regulations
- Misapplication of rents or other payments
- Brokerage fees

Prepayment Protection

Conduit loans prohibit prepayment for a number of years. Indeed, prepayment protection is one of the, if not the, major attractions of CMBS for the bond investors. Typical loans are closed or locked out from prepayment in full or in part until 60 to 90 days prior to the date on which the entire loan is required to be paid in full (the maturity date). After, typically, two to five years, however, the borrower may obtain release of the property from the lien of the mortgage, most usually under a defeasance provision.

Today, if a conduit loan can be paid off before maturity at all (and for practical purposes, they frequently cannot be), it must be defeased. **Defeasance** is a process that enables a borrower to prepay a collateralized loan by substituting it with a package of U.S. Treasury or equivalent securities selected by the lender into an entity the lender establishes and designates for that purpose. The Treasuries must be in an amount that will as closely as possible reproduce all of the cash flows (principal and interest) from the prepaid loan. Once this is done, bondholders' rights and interests are terminated, and their lien on the mortgaged property is extinguished. From the bond investor's perspective, defeasance doesn't just replicate the cash flows. The use of U.S. Treasuries actually improves the credit quality because now the credit risk is presumed to be virtually zero. For this reason, investors prefer defeasance to either yield maintenance fees or prepayment penalty points. But defeasance is complicated and expensive; in fact, it is intended to be a disincentive. In today's environment, only owners with a very compelling need to release property from a loan encumbrance would opt for defeasance.

The speed with which this type of financing has evolved is extraordinary. In the not-so-distant past, once the lockout period had expired it was possible to pay off a conduit loan with a large prepayment penalty fee, referred to as a *yield maintenance fee*. The yield maintenance fee (in classic finance textbook form) is typically determined by calculating the net present value of the future cash flows to the lender from the mortgage loan (i.e., all of the benefits of the investment to the lender) discounted at a rate equal to the yield of a U.S. Treasury bond with the same average life as the loan. This method still exists, but because it is less desirable to CMBS investors than defeasance, its popularity is diminishing. Prepayment penalty **points** have also been used. Each point is a percentage of the face value of the bond, and payment effectively raises the yield received by the investor. To CMBS investors, this is the least attractive method of prepayment.

Escrowed or Impounded Funds

Most permanent loans for income-producing real estate require that the borrower set aside (escrow) an adequate amount of money for payment of property taxes, for insurance, and frequently for a reserve for replacements. Conduit lending has raised this practice to an art form. Though they can be structured in different ways, loans that are to become part of a CMBS commonly require that the borrower escrow a monthly deposit of 1/12th of the following:

- Taxes the lender estimates will be payable during the next 12 months in order to accumulate with the lender sufficient funds to pay the real estate taxes

- Insurance premium that the lender estimates will be payable to renew the insurance policies it requires

- Amount the lender estimates will be necessary each year for repairs and replacements

The best aspect of these requirements (from the lender's perspective) is that the funds so deposited frequently may be held by the lender without interest and may be commingled with the lender's general funds.

Underwriting Standards

Conduit lenders try to use standard underwriting practices for the same reason they endeavor to use fairly standard documentation for their loans. It makes the CMBS easier to understand and evaluate and enhances the marketability of the bond offering. The more thorough the underwriting, the easier the loan will be to securitize.

It's important to understand that CMBS involve multitiered underwriting, and the term frequently means different things, depending on the context in which it is being used. The institution making a mortgage loan destined to become a CMBS; the bank, investment bank, or other firm that creates the securities backed by the pool of mortgages; the rating agencies; and the investors all "underwrite" with their own particular needs and requirements in mind. An underwriter, technically, is the purchaser of newly issued bonds or mortgage notes for ultimate resale to investors. But the term **underwriting** is frequently also used to refer to the practice (common to all of the groups listed above) of reviewing and evaluating the quality of and risk factors associated with loans. When used in this way it would be more accurate to use the term **due diligence.** It is, nevertheless, common to hear banks and other institutions involved in both commercial and residential real estate lending make reference to *underwriting standards*. It is in this context that a few criteria common to all of the above may be found.

As with traditional commercial/industrial loans with no borrower recourse, CMBS valuations are, to a large extent, based on two critical quantitative measures: debt coverage ratio (DCR) and loan-to-value (LTV) ratio. As the DCR and the LTV ratio were discussed in Chapter 5, they are only briefly reviewed below.

The DCR is simply the ratio of the net operating income (NOI) to the total mortgage payment. Using a DCR of 1:1.2, a lender is saying that it is looking for $1.20 in net income for each $1.00 mortgage payment. This is a measurement of the capacity of the cash flow from the underlying property to adequately service principal and interest on the debt. Each property in the CMBS pool is evaluated as a separate business. The higher the DCR, the more conservative the loan. A DCR of less than 1.0 means that the property is not providing enough cash flow to service the debt.

The loan-to-value (LTV) ratio is the ratio of the loan amount divided by the value of the property that is collateral for the loan. (Remember, CMBS are nonrecourse loans.) As a measurement of leverage, LTV ratios are important as tools for estimating the margin of safety associated with mortgage-secured loans. The higher the LTV ratio, the greater the likelihood of default and the less money that the lender will be able to recoup from the proceeds of sale of the mortgaged property in the event of default.

A Word or Two about the Bond's Structure

Because it is important for CMBS investors to be at ease with the composition of the underlying properties in the pool, CMBS deals are structured so as not to expose investors to a large concentration of any one property type. The pools are, accordingly, diversified by loan size, geographic location, property type, and industry concentration.

Credit Tranching

The word **tranche** is a French word, meaning *slice*. Tranching is one of the keys to creating CMBS bonds. It allows the creation of multiple securities that appeal to investors with varying risk/return tolerances. This is done by creating different classes of securities, each having a different risk factor, payment priority, and timing. Each tranche represents a separate security with its own maturity date and credit rating assigned by nationally recognized rating agencies, such as Moody's Investors Service, Inc.; Standard & Poor's Rating Group; Duff & Phelps Credit Rating Co.; and Fitch IBCA, Inc. As with other bonds, these ratings are the agencies' judgments of the investment quality of each security. AAA-rated tranches, for example, are analogous to high quality corporate bonds.

Ratings are a straightforward, easy-to-understand classification of the risk. As with corporate bonds, as the rating goes down (from AAA, AA, A, BBB, BB, to B), the price of the security decreases relative to its nominal or face value (par value), and the investor is compensated with commensurately higher yields. The higher-rated tranches, referred to as *senior classes tranches*, receive first priority or the first cash flows. Should a delinquency or default occur, the lower-rated tranches, called *subordinated* or *junior tranches*, have their cash flows diverted to make payments to the senior classes tranches. If the loss is of such magnitude that this level is insufficient, then the next higher rated tranche's principal is reduced, and so on. This is typically referred to as a *waterfall of credit classes*. This prioritizing of losses to a lower credit class is what allows issuers to create securities with varying levels of quality.

▌ SUMMARY

Mortgage funds are channeled, through a complex network of institutions, from savers to borrowers. For many years the industry was fairly simple and relatively stable in terms of organization and operations. A rapidly changing financial and political environment has roiled the mortgage lending waters with increasing ferocity since the mid-1960s, however, and contemporary mortgage lending is a far more sophisticated industry than its predecessor of only two decades ago.

Mortgage loans can be conveniently classified according to their purpose. Development and construction loans are relatively high interest, short-term loans to finance the development/construction phases. Takeout, or end, loans provide funds to liquidate construction and development loans and represent the bulk of resources committed to real estate. These loans are usually partially amortizing over 20 to 30 years (with 5- or 10-year stops), and generally carry an interest rate somewhat below that of construction and development loans. Standby loan commitments are used to ensure the availability of funds to retire construction loans, should an end loan be unavailable or be unacceptably costly.

Funds generated by savers (primarily households) are channeled into the mortgage market through financial intermediaries, principally commercial banks, savings associations, savings banks, and life insurance companies. Other important intermediaries include credit unions, mortgage companies, pension funds, and real estate investment trusts.

CMBS, a special type of securitized debt, have become one of the most common forms of long-term, fixed-rate mortgage financing for commercial and industrial real estate in use today. CMBS may well be a real example of the old cliché that "the whole is greater than the sum of its parts." Their popularity brings to mind another cliché: the "win/win scenario." Owners of mortgage loans get to increase the liquidity associated with mortgage lending by securitizing and selling their real estate loans. Investors get to purchase investments with yields that are as good as or better than corporate bonds with public debt rating, diversification, and subordination protection. And, for quality projects, the borrower gets access to nonrecourse loans at attractive fixed rates (presumably), even during downturns in the economy. CMBS really are a win/win for all participants; they are here to stay.

As one studies the financing of commercial real estate, its dynamic nature becomes increasingly clear. The debt and equity markets are nothing if not opportunistic. They are constantly changing and evolving to accommodate the needs of borrowers, lenders, and equity investors. It is a good bet that they will continue to do so.

▌ KEY TERMS

basis point

carve-outs

commercial mortgage-backed securities (CMBS)

conduit financing

defeasance

Depository Institution Deregulation and Monetary Control Act

due diligence

Federal Deposit Insurance Corporation Improvement Act (FDICIA)

Financial Institutions Reform, Recovery, and Enforcement Act (FIRREA)

Garn-St. Germain Depository Institutions Act

Gramm-Leach-Bliley Act (Financial Modernization Act of 1999)

Housing Act of 1970

interim loans

mortgage bankers

mortgage brokers

mortgage warehousing

mortgage warehousing loans

permanent, take-out, end loans

points

real estate investment trust (REIT)

Riegle-Neal Act

tranche

underwriting

RECOMMENDED READING

Block, Ralph. *The Essential REIT, A Guide to Profitable Investing in Real Estate Investment Trusts*. San Francisco, Calif.: Brunston Press, 1997.

Downs, Anthony. *The Revolution in Real Estate Finance*. Washington, D.C.: The Brookings Institution, 1985.

Fabozzi, Frank J.. *Handbook of Mortgage Backed Securities*, 6th ed. New York: McGraw-Hill Professional, 2005.

Rabinowitz, Alan. *The Real Estate Gamble, Lessons from 50 Years of Boom and Bust*. New York: AMACOM, 1980.

The 2003 Financial Services Goldbook: A Comprehensive Guide to Real Estate Capital from Wall Street to Main Street. Published by Commercial Property News, Phillip Wren Publisher, New York.

INTERNET REFERENCES

Federal Housing and Finance Board homepage:
www.fhfb.gov/FDIC law, regulations, and related acts
www.fdic.gov/regulations/laws/rules

For more on the Gramm-Leach-Bliley Act:
www.ftc.gov/privacy/glbact

For information on Real Estate Investment Trusts:
www.investinreits.com
www.nareit.com/home.cfm
www.reitcafe.com/REITcafe.html
www.reitnet.com

National Association of Federal Credit Unions:
www.nafcu.org

Office of Thrift Supervision:
www.ots.treas.gov

REVIEW QUESTIONS

1. What is a financial intermediary?
2. Who are the "big four" in mortgage lending?
3. Describe the principal source of the change in the relative cost of funds for commercial banks and thrift associations.

4. What is a savings bank? How does it differ from a commercial bank?

5. How does the usual repayment pattern of construction and development loans differ from that of takeout, or end, loans?

6. Why are interest rates on construction and development loans usually higher than those on takeout, or end, loans?

7. List three reasons that a developer might use standby financing to allow delay in obtaining a permanent loan commitment.

8. Because standby loan commitments are seldom exercised, and thus no interest ever accrues, how can these commitments be profitable to lenders?

9. What is the secondary mortgage market, and why does it exist? What are the three primary agencies operating in this market?

10. What are CMBS, and why were they initially developed?

11. How much has U.S. CMBS volume grown between 1991 and 2001, in dollars and in percentage growth?

12. List two traditional and two nontraditional real estate lenders.

13. What is/are the following:

    a. Single-purpose entities, and why are they used in CMBS loans?

    b. Carve-outs? List three.

    c. Three methods of prepayment protection listed?

    d. Defeasance and how does it work?

    e. Impounded funds?

14. Why do CMBS lenders endeavor to use common loan documentation and underwriting?

15. What is credit tranching, and why is it important?

DISCUSSION QUESTIONS

1. If you were a construction and development lender, what evidence would you demand as assurance that a loan would be repaid on completion of construction?

2. Because construction and development loans generally carry higher interest rates than do takeout, or end, loans, why don't all mortgage lenders concentrate on this segment of the market? Moreover, why doesn't the movement of funds out of the end-loan market and into the construction loan market (i.e., shifts in supply schedules) cause interest rates in these two segments of the mortgage market to be equal?

3. Should the government use interest rate regulations (rate ceilings, for example) to channel more funds into segments of the market that are considered more needy? Why or why not?

4. Why doesn't the government treat all financial intermediaries the same? Would a single set of regulations that apply to all be more equitable?

5. Why is a CMBS like a corporate bond?

6. How are CMBS valuations influenced by the rating agencies?

Government's Role in Mortgage Markets

After studying this chapter, you should understand how social and economic upheavals during the 1930s spawned government intervention in real estate finance markets, and you should be able to describe key government agencies and federal laws that affect the industry.

Some proponents of free enterprise exhibit a curious dualism in their attitudes: They clamor for freedom from government constraints, seeking at the same time certain assurances of government support and protection from adversity. The real estate finance industry has discovered that government intervention works both ways. While providing some cushion against disastrous disruptions of the mortgage market, government has established itself as a ubiquitous presence in every aspect of the industry. Regulations specify many things that lenders *cannot* do and perhaps an equal number that they absolutely *must* do.

This chapter reviews economic disruptions that led to major government intervention in financial markets early in the century. It then explains major elements of government's current regulatory efforts.

ORIGINS OF THE FEDERAL GOVERNMENT'S INVOLVEMENT IN THE MORTGAGE MARKET

Today's mortgage market differs drastically from that which existed before the economic depression of the 1930s. Both primary and secondary mortgage markets were then local in nature, and were not well-interconnected with general financial markets. Events flowing from the Depression years set in motion a chain of developments that radically altered the institutional environment of real estate finance.

Real estate mortgage notes in the pre-Depression era typically matured in five years. During that term, borrowers paid only accrued interest, with the entire principal amount due on maturity. Maturing notes were typically "rolled over" (that is, refinanced) with a renegotiated interest rate reflecting market changes during the interim. Mortgage notes were generally held to maturity by lending institutions because there was little or no demand for them in secondary financial markets.

When the Money Stopped

Massive mortgage loan defaults and panic withdrawal of funds from banks and other depository institutions during the early 1930s created more stress than the system could handle. Lenders became cautious, anticipating that more depositors would take flight. Trying frantically to increase their liquidity, the better to cope with such an eventuality, many lenders began to call loans. Thus, mortgage borrowers found they could no longer refinance maturing mortgage notes as they had done so easily in the past.

Individual banks' efforts to improve liquidity proved inadequate. Inevitably, some ran short of cash. Word of their inability to honor obligations to depositors spread rapidly, panic ensued, and a "run" on the banking system was in full swing.

In such a climate, bank failures were inevitable. Nor were such failures unprecedented. What shocked people was the extent of the phenomenon and the rapidity with which the contagion spread. With news that a bank was in trouble, people came in ever-increasing droves to withdraw deposits. Soon, even the soundest banks were hard-pressed to meet depositors' demands for cash. In 1929, there were

659 bank failures; in 1930, there were 1,352; in 1931, 2,294. By the close of 1933, approximately 50 percent of the nation's banks had suspended operations.

Those banks that survived the panic did so only after suffering near fatal financial hemorrhage. In their frantic search for liquidity, they withdrew their interbank deposits and called interbank loans. Even the soundest banks were forced to curtail lending activity and call maturing loans. They effectively converted themselves to safety deposit institutions.

Stabilizing the System

Political events in 1933 were both propitious and ominous. Adolf Hitler came to power in Germany that year, and Franklin Delano Roosevelt was elected President of the United States. The campaigns of both men were aided by public outrage at their governments' inability to cope with economic dislocation that bordered on chaos.

In both countries new regimes wrought drastic changes in the old order. Political power became more centralized in each. Beyond this, of course, similarities cease. The U.S. Constitution provides for a balance of power, which diluted Roosevelt's ability to dictate to the nation, even as the Congress foiled his efforts to pack the Supreme Court.

Legislators cooperated, however, in completely revamping the country's financial system. There resulted a stronger, more viable set of financial institutions capable of weathering cyclical swings in the economy. Periodic rashes of bank failures, with which the nation had been plagued throughout its history, ceased. Today, a bank failure may mean suffering and loss for stockholder-investors, but seldom for depositors.

To stem the tide of bank failures and to more nearly ensure that banks would be operated prudently in the future, regulatory authority was concentrated in the **Federal Reserve System**. Prior to 1933, power was widely dispersed among the 12 district reserve banks. A series of new laws enacted between 1933 and 1935 significantly revised the system. The Board of Governors was given extensive and wide-ranging authority to directly regulate activities of all member banks.

Perhaps equally important was legislation in 1933 that created the **Federal Deposit Insurance Corporation (FDIC)**. Deposit insurance thereby became available to all banks, which either chose or were required to join the system. Not since the creation of the FDIC have lines of frightened depositors forming outside a member bank generated widespread financial panic. Indeed, seldom have such lines formed at all. Nor is there reason for them to do so. The FDIC stands ready immediately and without equivocation to provide whatever funds are needed to cover insured deposits. The initial coverage was $2,500 per account; today, the coverage is $100,000 per account.

Federal Reserve Board authority and FDIC insurance, however, originally applied only to commercial banks (although today it applies to thrift institutions as well). These commercial banks were (and continue to be) a substantial source of mortgage credit, but the giant in mortgage lending has been the nation's network of savings associations. Organized along lines similar to the Federal Reserve System, the Federal Home Loan Bank System was created in 1933 to provide regulatory guidance and financial assistance to the savings and loan industry.

As a temporary measure to reduce hardship stemming from widespread home mortgage foreclosures, the Congress in 1933 also created the **Home Owners' Loan Corporation**, which exchanged government-backed bonds for home mortgages in default. These defaulted mortgage notes were then refinanced with provisions for installment payments to fully amortize balances over a 15-year term. Started at a time when more that 40 percent of the nation's home mortgage debt was in default, Home Owners' Loan Corporation operated for a three-year period. During this time it refinanced more than 1 million nonfarm home mortgages and enabled thousands of homeowners to avoid the financial disaster frequently attendant to foreclosure. Its emphasis on long-term, fully amortizing mortgages virtually revolutionized the mortgage lending industry.

Federal Housing Administration

In 1934, the Congress authorized formation of the **Federal Housing Administration (FHA)**, to create an environment conducive to growth of a truly national secondary mortgage market. The FHA sought to overcome what were perceived as major impediments to an active secondary market by standardizing mortgage terms and formats and by insuring holders of mortgage notes against losses due to default.

The FHA initiated a transition in mortgage instruments. The problems created by the short-term nature of home mortgage loans were resolved by introducing a 30-year, fixed-rate, fully amortizing mortgage insured by the FHA. By dictating minimum property standards for FHA-insured loans, the agency also improved the quality of housing in the nation.

With FHA insurance providing necessary elements of dependability, transferability, and minimal risk, mortgage funds began flowing more freely across geographic boundaries. Using FHA standards, life insurance companies expanded the scope of their nationwide lending activities through correspondent mortgage companies.

Insurance companies thus embraced the FHA-insured mortgage concept. Yet FHA programs were received with less enthusiasm by other major home mortgage lenders. Savings and loan associations and commercial banks continued to lend primarily on a local basis, using mostly conventional mortgages.

Today, the FHA is the key mortgage insurer; it is not a mortgage lender. It insures mortgage lenders against loss due to default. About 70 percent of all FHA mortgage insurance is written on one- to four-family dwellings. The balance encompasses certain nonresidential structures, multifamily rental housing projects, cooperative housing projects, and housing for the elderly. FHA-insured home loans must be assumable, and they cannot carry prepayment penalties. With the FHA insurance, lenders will lend at a higher loan-to-value (LTV) ratio, up to 97 percent.

The FHA can be considered a partial success; it did extend home ownership, as did the Veterans Administration (VA, now the Department of Veterans Affairs) later with its guarantee on VA loans for qualified veterans and their families. (VA loans require only a $1 down payment, virtually a 100 percent LTV ratio.) FHA also brought a degree of stability to mortgage markets and enabled funds to move more freely between regions. Yet, despite FHA-created conditions, no truly national secondary mortgage market emerged during the decade of the 1930s.

SECONDARY MORTGAGE MARKET AGENCIES

Federal National Mortgage Association

To promote a government-sponsored secondary market for FHA-insured mortgages, the Congress created in 1938 the **Federal National Mortgage Association (FNMA)**, known today as **Fannie Mae**. Where there existed no private market for existing mortgages, FNMA was empowered to purchase FHA-insured mortgages from primary lenders, thus providing the lenders with additional loanable funds.

Money for FNMA secondary market activities was raised by selling government-backed FNMA securities and by selling certificates backed by a pool of FHA-insured mortgages held by FNMA. For the first time, investors in corporate and government bond markets began to look at mortgage-related instruments as an alternative to their traditional investment outlets.

Historians are fond of saying of the Holy Roman Empire that it was neither holy nor Roman. Similarly, one can say today that Fannie Mae is neither federal nor an association. It became a predominantly privately owned corporation in 1968, although it is still under some regulatory control of the Department of Housing and Urban Development (HUD), which also now oversees the FHA. More than 50 million shares of Fannie Mae stock are privately held and are actively traded on the New York Stock Exchange.

Under private auspices, Fannie Mae continues to make an active secondary market for approved mortgages. It extensively taps private capital markets to finance its activities, selling both short-term and long-term obligations. We look more closely at these activities in a later section.

Government National Mortgage Association

The 1968 law that transferred Fannie Mae from federal to private ownership also created a new organization to carry on certain activities of the old FNMA. This new entity, the **Government National Mortgage Association (GNMA)** came, perhaps inevitably, to be called **Ginnie Mae**. It took over loan servicing and portfolio liquidation duties from Fannie Mae, and assumed subsidy aspects of the old FNMA activities.

Ginnie Mae guarantees timely payment of both principal and interest on securities backed by a package of approved home mortgages. This program has met with enthusiastic investor response, and it has served as a model for a number of similar programs involving conventional mortgages. These are secured by private mortgage insurers and are offered through investment banking houses by a variety of primary mortgage lenders.

Federal Home Loan Mortgage Corporation

Savings associations whose deposits are insured by the Federal Deposit Insurance Corporation have access to secondary mortgage markets via activities of the **Federal Home Loan Mortgage Corporation (FHLMC)**. This organization (today called **Freddie Mac**) purchases mortgage loans from approved lending institutions. It finances its purchases primarily by selling mortgage participation certificates that permit holders to participate in the proceeds of a group of mortgages backing the certificates.

▋ FEDERAL LAWS REGULATING MORTGAGE LENDING ─────────

As in most areas of contemporary life, federal laws and regulations have in recent years intruded massively into what had been primarily a private affair between borrowers and lenders. Whatever the merit and motivation, this trend is likely to accelerate.

Truth in Lending

Officially known as **Title I of the Consumer Protection Act**, the federal **Truth-in-Lending Act** was enacted in 1969 with the avowed purpose to assure a meaningful disclosure of credit terms so that the consumer will be able to compare more readily the various credit terms available to him and avoid the uninformed use of credit.[1]

The act requires disclosure of specified information in connection with all consumer credit transactions. The act is implemented by **Regulation Z**, issued by the Board of Governors of the Federal Reserve System.

Regulation Z and the Truth-in-Lending Act apply to any real estate transaction in which a seller extends credit to a buyer, if the seller, "in the ordinary course of business regularly extends or arranges for the extension of credit." Therefore, it does not apply to the private seller of a home who takes back a purchase-money mortgage in part payment. It does apply to an investor who regularly sells property and who "extends or arranges for the extension of" financing for the transactions.

Those required to comply with Regulation Z must provide each borrower with a statement that shows the annual percentage rate (APR) and includes the amount and nature of all finance charges. The regulation gives credit purchasers the right to rescind certain transactions.

Amount of Finance Charge

Regulation Z defines the finance charge as being the sum of all charges payable directly or indirectly by a borrower that are imposed directly by the lender as a precondition to granting a loan. It specifically includes the following as a part of the finance charge:

- Interest charges, discount points, or any amount payable under a discount provision or other system of additional charges
- Service fees, transaction fees, activity fees, or carrying charges
- Loan fees, finder's fees, or similar charges
- Charges or premiums for insurance (other than insurance against loss or damage to property), where there is the actual or implied requirement for insurance as a precondition for the loan
- Charges or premiums for insurance against loss or damages to property if obtained through the creditor, unless the lender clearly states in writing that the debtor may choose his or her own insurer
- Premiums or charges for insurance or guarantees against the debtor's default (private mortgage insurance)

Many costs that are normal and incidental to obtaining credit are not included in the finance charge. These include fees for title examination, title abstract, title insurance, escrow payments, notary fees, appraisal fees, credit report costs, and fees for preparation of deeds and other documents associated with the transaction.

Annual Percentage Rate

Lenders are required to express the cost of borrowing as an APR based on actual loan proceeds. The Truth-in-Lending Act and Regulation Z require that the APR be disclosed to within one-quarter of 1 percent and specifies precisely how the rate is to be computed. Chapter 9 illustrates how to calculate APR or yield.

Right to Rescind

Individuals have the right to rescind any credit transaction that will result in a lien on their personal residence, unless the transaction involves acquisition of a personal residence. This means the individual may terminate the agreement, and all parties will return to the legal position or relationship existing prior to the transaction.

Where the right to rescind is required, a borrower has three business days to exercise the right. The rescission period starts with the later of (1) the date of the loan transaction or (2) the date of receipt of notice of the right to rescind.

Within ten days of notice that a borrower is exercising the (valid) right to rescind, the lender must return any consideration tendered in the transaction. Of course, the borrower must also return any cash or item of value received in the transaction.

Equal Credit Opportunity

Intended to ensure that "no credit applicant shall be denied the credit he or she needs or wants on the basis of characteristics that have nothing to do with his or her credit worthiness,"[2] the **Equal Credit Opportunity Act (ECOA)** was enacted in 1974. The act requires that the Board of Governors of the Federal Reserve System promulgate implementing regulations. The Federal Reserve responded with Regulation B, which delegates responsibility for enforcement to various other government agencies.

Creditors, the act specifies, must notify applicants of decisions within 30 days of receipt of application. On request, applicants must be informed of reasons for any adverse decision. Lenders cannot consider factors that are based on race, color, national origin, religion, age, gender, or marital status.

Home Mortgage Disclosure Act

Every depository lending institution with a home office or a branch office in a metropolitan statistical area (MSA) must, under the **Home Mortgage Disclosure Act (HMDA)**, compile a report that reveals the extent to which mortgage loans are being made within the MSA, compared with loans being made outside the MSA. The report, which the lender is required to keep available for public inspection, must also indicate the distribution of loans within the MSA, by either census tract or postal ZIP code number. The avowed purpose of the HMDA is to discourage **redlining**, which is defined as loan practices that discriminate against mortgagors of real estate solely because a property is located in a specific geographic area. Redlining, the framers of the act reasoned, contributes to the deterioration of neighborhoods and is often based on racial factors. HMDA, the **Community Reinvestment Act**, and many other federal laws have done much to ensure equity in housing financing by preventing discrimination in real estate financing.

Real Estate Settlement Procedures Act (RESPA)

All residential real estate transactions that have federally related first mortgages are covered by the **Real Estate Settlement Procedures Act (RESPA)**. This 1974 act was passed to ensure that both buyers and sellers receive information on settlement costs. RESPA is administered by HUD and requires that all loan applicants must receive an informational booklet, entitled *Settlement Costs and You*, which gives general information on settlement costs. Additionally, a good-faith estimate of the specific settlement costs for a transaction must be given to the borrower within three days of loan application. Actual closing costs must be on a *Uniform Settlement Statement* (HUD-1 Form) and can be inspected one day before closing. RESPA also prohibits kickbacks such as unearned referral fees.

National Flood Insurance Act

The National Flood Insurance Act of 1968 and other flood control insurance laws have made real estate mortgages possible for the many households living in flood-prone areas. Without this federal assistance, a large amount of real estate financing would have been denied or greatly restricted. The act encourages lending and credit institutions to assist in furthering the objectives of flood insurance programs.

MAINSTREAMING THE MORTGAGE MARKET

Mortgage loans are originated in the primary mortgage market; existing loans are bought and sold in the secondary mortgage market. Just as organized stock exchanges enhance the ability of listed corporations to sell new stock, so an active secondary mortgage market amplifies the ability and willingness of primary lenders to originate new mortgage loans.

Primary mortgage lenders use secondary markets in several ways. When demand for new mortgage loans exceeds available funds, lenders raise additional cash by selling previously originated loans from their portfolios. When cash balances temporarily exceed the need for mortgage funds in their market area, lenders put excess liquidity to work by buying existing mortgages on the secondary market. Because the secondary market includes provision for purchase and sale of mortgages for future delivery, primary lenders can shift to willing speculators the risk that interest rates will change in a manner that adversely affects the value of existing mortgage portfolios.

Savings associations, commercial banks, and mutual savings banks are among the largest mortgage lenders. These institutions all depend on deposits for loanable funds. Their success in attracting depositors has traditionally determined their ability to originate loans. During periods of unusually high demand for loans, or when depositors' balances are uncharacteristically low, these lenders would be unable to meet borrowers' needs if it were not for secondary mortgage markets.

Mortgage bankers, unlike depository institutions, typically do not hold a substantial portion of their loans in their own investment portfolios. Selling their old mortgage loans and relending the proceeds enables mortgage bankers to originate loans far exceeding their own capital resources. By selling mortgages nationwide, they effectively shift loanable cash from regions of temporary excess liquidity to those where funds are in short supply. An active secondary market is essential to mortgage banking success.

Fannie Mae

Among those organizations active in the secondary market, Fannie Mae (previously the Federal National Mortgage Association, or FNMA) looms as a giant. More home mortgage loan funds are generated by Fannie Mae activities than by any other secondary market operation. Fannie Mae pioneered the practice of purchasing mortgage loans from primary lenders with funds raised by selling its own debt instruments in general financial markets.

Like all corporations, Fannie Mae is operated by a corps of officers appointed by the board of directors. Atypically, though, one third of Fannie Mae's directors are appointed by the federal government. The remainder are elected by shareholders in the usual manner. Enabling legislation requires that one federally appointed director be chosen from the homebuilding industry, one from the mortgage lending industry, and one from the general real estate industry.

Headquartered in Washington, D.C., Fannie Mae maintains regional offices across the country. Its purpose, as specified in enabling legislation, is to facilitate housing finance by enhancing the supply of mortgage funds. The association has set for itself several specific goals. These include the following:[3]

- Sufficient profitability to attract needed funds in the capital markets
- To the extent consistent with its profitability goal, and subject to limitations imposed by prudent business and financial practices, to promote a stable supply of mortgage funds at the minimum possible cost to homebuyers
- To provide industry leadership by developing new housing finance programs and techniques, while maintaining high standards of corporate citizenship

Fannie Mae has largely accomplished its goals. It has successfully tapped new sources of long-term funds for mortgage finance. Its secondary mortgage market operations have provided additional liquidity during periods of tight money and have absorbed excess liquidity when necessary. It has played a major role in developing a truly national secondary market for residential mortgage notes.

By issuing its own securities in general financial markets, Fannie Mae taps sources of money that would not otherwise be directed into residential mortgages. Its activities permit mortgage borrowers to indirectly compete with issuers of corporate bonds and notes.

Fannie Mae's operations are national in scope. When its commitments are sold at auction, bidders from areas of high mortgage demand are able to bid more competitively than those from areas of lesser demand relative to the local supply of loanable funds. Thus, funds provided from Fannie Mae operations are directed to the geographic areas of higher relative demand. This leads to much greater convergence of regional interest rates than was previously the case.

Because Fannie Mae is willing to make forward purchase commitments for mortgage-secured loans, primary lenders are able to hedge their positions against adverse movements in market interest rates. This reduction in interest-rate risk makes lenders more willing to advance funds during periods of economic uncertainty and volatile interest rates.

By purchasing mortgage loans from lenders that are active in the primary mortgage market, Fannie Mae injects liquidity into the system. It can regulate the degree of liquidity by varying the level of its purchases. The scope of its secondary market operations has made Fannie Mae the nation's single largest supplier of residential mortgage credit. Since its inception, Fannie Mae has purchased almost half of all home mortgage loans insured by the FHA. Several innovations have, over the years, drastically altered Fannie Mae's operations. Today, it commits to buy mortgage notes for future delivery (**standby forward commitments**), as well as continuing to buy notes for immediate delivery.

Standby Forward Commitments

To reduce the uncertainty faced by primary lenders, Fannie Mae sells standby forward commitments to purchase mortgages at a yield that is specified in advance. The commitments are binding on Fannie Mae, but are optional for the primary lender. Thus, a lender may exercise its option to deliver mortgages at the auction-determined price; it may instead sell the mortgages to another secondary market purchaser at the prevailing spot price, or it may decide to continue holding the mortgage in its own portfolio. The lender must pay one-half of 1 percent of the loan portfolio amount as a commitment fee. Additionally, the lender must pay a delivery fee of another one-half of 1 percent if the lender executes the option.

Pricing System

Fannie Mae purchases project loans for immediate delivery at specified yield rates. Standby commitments, however, are priced by competitive bidding or on a noncompetitive basis computed with reference to average bid prices. Prior to each auction, Fannie Mae announces the dollar quantity of commitments it will sell at competitive bids. It sells this amount by accepting those bids that provide the highest yield. Additional commitments are sold on a noncompetitive basis to certain lenders at a price determined by the average yield commitments sold at the auction.

Bulk Purchase from Ginnie Mae

Fannie Mae makes some bulk purchases of mortgage loans from Ginnie Mae (previously the Government National Mortgage Association, or GNMA, discussed in the next section), at a price yielding Fannie Mae a "market" rate if interest rates rise. Ginnie Mae must absorb any discount resulting from having bought mortgage loans issued at a discount below the market rate of interest. About 16 percent of Fannie Mae's portfolio consists of mortgages acquired from Ginnie Mae in this manner. This joining of Fannie Mae and Ginnie Mae is known as the tandem plan. Through the tandem plan Fannie Mae can purchase high-risk, low-yield loans at full market rates, while Ginnie Mae guarantees payment and absorbs the difference between the low yield and current market prices.

Ginnie Mae

Created by Congress in 1968 as part of the Department of Housing and Urban Development, the Government National Mortgage Association (GNMA), now Ginnie Mae, was initially charged with three primary functions. Two of these, **special assistance** and **management and liquidation**, were inherited from Fannie Mae when that institution became a privately owned corporation. The third function, **guaranteeing payment on mortgage-backed securities**, may well prove to be Ginnie Mae's greatest contribution to meeting the nation's need for a rapidly expanding housing stock.

The special assistance function consists primarily of providing funding for projects in support of the federal government's housing policy. This may entail purchasing mortgages issued at below-market interest rates or mortgages that have not become acceptable in the private mortgage market. Ginnie Mae also purchases large pools of mortgage loans on low or moderately priced housing, to increase liquidity in this segment of the market during periods of tight money.

Various government agencies acquire mortgages and other real estate–related assets as a part of designated subsidy programs. Ginnie Mae manages these portfolios and liquidates the government's interest by selling participation certificates. The agency also guarantees payment on bonds backed by pools of mortgages held by Fannie Mae or Freddie Mac and participation certificates issued by approved private companies.

Ginnie Mae's **certificate payment guarantee program** has almost become a classic case of "the tail wagging the dog." Although mortgage pools backing these certificates are held by the issuing agencies, Ginnie Mae's guarantee is such a crucial element that the certificates themselves have become known as *Ginnie Mae pass-throughs*. The certificates are backed by pools of FHA, Farmers Home Administration, or VA mortgages, and represent pro-rata shares therein.

Several variations of **pass-through certificates** have been tested in the marketplace. Of these, the most popular, and thus most common, passes a pro-rata share of mortgage principal and interest payments through to certificate holders on a monthly basis. This version is generally identified as a **modified pass-through.**

All Ginnie Mae certificates are registered securities. They can be transferred or assigned. They are freely negotiable and may be bought and sold like any other registered security.

Approved mortgage bankers wishing to sell Ginnie Mae pass-through certificates must first assemble an appropriate pool of mortgage loans. Ginnie Mae then issues a guarantee of payment, which makes the pass-through certificates marketable. The originator continues to service the loans, passing interest and principal payments through to certificate holders. When all mortgages in a pool have been repaid, the certificates will thereby have been retired.

Pass-through certificates and mortgage-backed bonds are virtually free of default risk. Certificate issuers and servicers must be approved by Ginnie Mae, which sets minimum capitalization requirements. Moreover, Ginnie Mae is authorized to reassign the servicing function. Ginnie Mae's payment guarantee extends to both principal and interest on the pooled mortgage loans. The guarantee is backed by the "full faith and credit" of the United States, and Ginnie Mae has the power to borrow from the U.S. Treasury if necessary to ensure timely payment.

Freddie Mac

To create a secondary market for conventional home mortgage loans similar to that maintained by Fannie Mae for government-insured mortgages through Title III of the Emergency Home Finance Act, the Congress in 1970 authorized formation of the Federal Home Loan Mortgage Corporation (FHLMC), now known as Freddie Mac. Freddie Mac issues its own securities to raise money for purchase from savings associations of conventional single- and multifamily residential mortgage loans.

Freddie Mac (also sometimes called *The Mortgage Corporation*) is organized as a corporation, and until recently its $100 million worth of stock (all nonvoting) was held by the 12 Federal Home Loan Banks. It was governed by a board whose members were drawn from the boards of the Federal Home Loan Bank System. It was authorized to leverage its equity capital by borrowing from the Federal Home Loan Banks or by selling its own securities in financial markets. As detailed in Chapter 1, recent legislation has transformed much of the federal bureaucracy. Today Freddie Mac is under the Department of the Treasury and the Office of Thrift Supervision.

To raise money in financial markets, Freddie Mac sells mortgage participation certificates and guaranteed mortgage certificates. Both of these securities are pass-through certificates, but they differ in the pattern and timing of the pass-through of interest and principal on the underlying mortgages. Participation certificates pass both interest and principal payments through on a monthly basis, in the same manner as Ginnie Mae modified pass-throughs. Guaranteed mortgage certificates, in contrast, pay interest semiannually and pass principal payments through only on an annual basis. Both certificates compete directly with corporate bonds, channeling into the mortgage market funds that would otherwise be reserved for the corporate sector.

Freddie Mac is authorized to purchase residential mortgages from originators whose deposits are insured by an agency of the federal government. Acquired mortgages may be government-insured/guaranteed (FHA and VA), but are predominantly conventional. Purchases may be either for immediate or for future delivery.

Immediate Delivery Commitments

Mortgages for immediate delivery are bought at auction, with commitments going to lenders whose bids offer Freddie Mac the highest yields. Mortgage loans must be delivered within 60 days of these commitments.

Forward Commitments

Freddie Mac also sells commitments to purchase mortgage loans for delivery six months and eight months in the future. These commitments also go to bidders offering Freddie Mac the highest yield. Auctions are held monthly.

Conventional Mortgage-Backed Securities

Mortgage-backed securities (MBS) are not a Ginnie Mae monopoly. Increasingly, mortgage bankers and large institutional lenders are selling securities backed by a pool of conventional mortgages. The securities may be bonds, which usually remain a direct obligation of the issuer, or participation certificates, wherein the issuer's interest in the mortgage pool is assigned to a trustee for the benefit of certificate holders.

Most conventional mortgage pools consist of first mortgage loans on owner-occupied single-family residences, including condominiums. Mortgage loans may carry either fixed or variable interest rates. Amortization periods are 30 years or less. Mortgaged properties are located within the United States, and all mortgages are insured by a private mortgage insurance company.

Securities backed by conventional mortgages are usually issued through an investment banker that is experienced in sale and distribution of securities to the investing public. The sale may be a public issue or a private placement. Public issues are usually larger, typically above $50 million. The Securities and Exchange Commission (SEC) monitors all interstate securities sales and requires that each issuer file an extensive prospectus. Private placements are smaller in dollar volume and may be exempt from SEC rules governing public issues. An issuer may be able to sell a private placement without the assistance of an investment banker.

Public issues are usually rated by one of the securities rating services such as Moody's or Standard and Poor's. This permits comparison with alternative investment opportunities and broadens the market by making securities eligible for inclusion in institutional investors' portfolios. Rating services consider the experience and capability of servicer and trustee and the financial soundness of the mortgage insurer. They also weigh the size and nature of the equity reserve fund, the nature of the mortgage pool itself, and the amount of "all-risk" hazard insurance provided.

▌ SUMMARY

Federal government efforts to alleviate economic disruption during the Depression years of the 1930s evolved into an extensive array of programs that regulate mortgage finance and enhance credit availability to select groups of applicants.

The Federal Reserve System was empowered to control the nation's supply of money and credit and to influence the direction and rate of change in interest rates. The Federal Deposit Insurance Corporation insures depositors against losses. Fannie Mae, Freddie Mac, and Ginnie Mae are active in the secondary mortgage market.

The Federal Housing Administration, now part of the Department of Housing and Urban Development, provides mortgage insurance and some degree of subsidized housing finance. The Department of Veterans Affairs guarantees a portion of qualifying mortgage loans to veterans.

Since 1969, the federal government has increasingly acted to regulate the activities of mortgage lenders. Title I of the Consumer Protection Act was passed that year. It requires that lenders disclose specified information about credit terms, including the amount and nature of all finance charges and the effective annual percentage rate of interest, and gives borrowers in certain situations the right to rescind transactions within three days with no penalty. The Equal Credit Opportunity Act forbids denying credit on the basis of characteristics that do not affect creditworthiness. The Home Mortgage Disclosure Act requires that lenders disclose the portion of their loans that are made within the metropolitan statistical area in which they are located.

KEY TERMS

certificate payment guarantee program

Community Reinvestment Act

Equal Credit Opportunity Act (ECOA)

Federal Deposit Insurance Corporation (FDIC)

Federal Home Loan Mortgage Corporation (FHLMC), Freddie Mac

Federal Housing Administration (FHA)

Federal National Mortgage Association (FNMA), Fannie Mae

Federal Reserve System

Government National Mortgage Association (GNMA), Ginnie Mae

guaranteeing payment on mortgage-backed securities

Home Mortgage Disclosure Act (HMDA)

Home Owners' Loan Corporation

management and liquidation

modified pass-through

pass-through certificates

Real Estate Settlement Procedures Act (RESPA)

redlining

Regulation Z

special assistance

standby forward commitments

Title I of the Consumer Protection Act, Truth-in-Lending Act

NOTES

1. 15 U.S.C., Sec 1601.

2. Committee on Banking, Housing and Urban Affairs, Senate Report Number 94-589, 94th Congress, 2nd Session, 406.

3. Federal National Mortgage Association, *A Guide to Fannie Mae* (Washington, D.C.: Federal National Mortgage Association, 1979), ix.

INTERNET REFERENCES

For information on Federal Housing Administration (FHA):
www.hud.gov/offices/hsg/index.cfm

Federal National Mortgage Association (FNMA or Fannie Mae):
www.fanniemae.com/index.jhtml

Government National Mortgage Association (GNMA or Ginnie Mae):
www.ginniemae.gov/index.asp

Federal Home Loan Mortgage Corporation:
www.freddiemac.com

For more information on Regulation Z:
www.mortgage-mart.com

For information on the Equal Credit Opportunity Act:
www.usdoj.gov/crt/housing/housing_ecoa.htm

▌ REVIEW QUESTIONS

1. Describe the role of the FDIC in mortgage financing.
2. What is the principal function of the FHA?
3. Who owns Fannie Mae?
4. How does Fannie Mae raise money for its secondary mortgage market operations?
5. How does Ginnie Mae's activity contribute to the success of the secondary mortgage market?
6. What does the Truth-in-Lending Act require of lenders?
7. Individuals have the right to rescind any credit transaction that results in a lien on their personal residence, unless the transaction involves acquisition of a personal residence. What does this mean?
8. What is redlining?
9. What is meant by equity in housing financing and what federal agencies and laws regulate this objective?

▌ DISCUSSION QUESTIONS

1. Discuss the roles of Fannie Mae and Ginnie Mae. How do they differ, and in what ways are they complementary? Are both really needed?
2. Should government agencies designed to assist a specific segment of the U.S. population (such as homebuyers or mortgage lenders) be self-supporting, or is it appropriate to support them out of general tax revenues? Discuss.

3. Real estate mortgages before 1933 typically matured in five years. From World War II until the 1980s, nearly all mortgage loans (other than for construction) were fully amortizing over 20 to 30 years. During the 1980s there was a shift back to short maturities for mortgage loans on large commercial properties. Does this create conditions that might lead to another major credit debacle, such as that following the stock market crash of 1929? Discuss.

4. If the FHA and the VA experienced such massive defaults and low values for foreclosed properties that their resources were insufficient to honor their obligations, would the Treasury Department provide all the needed funds? Should it? Discuss.

PART TWO

The Borrowing and Lending Decisions

"No money down!" The battle cry of leverage proponents has drawn many people to become debtors in the real estate mortgage market. Tales of making fortunes by using other people's money sound too good to be true. The perceived ease of such deals is beyond the realm of reality, and the complexity of the arrangement requires careful analysis. While the benefits of leverage have been overstated by the popular press, the analysis of costs and benefits is critical to proper decision making. The nitty-gritty of borrowing and lending is explored in Part Two. It presents analysis of alternative financing, mortgage yields and values, the key decisions on loans, and the issue of problem loans.

Alternative Financing Methods and Products

LEARNING OBJECTIVES

After studying this chapter, you should be aware of a wide range of mortgage loan arrangements and the major shortcomings and merits of each. You should also understand the nature of and the motivation for recent lending innovations.

Religion and law are perhaps Western culture's most tradition-bound institutions, and real estate lending has been heavily influenced by both. New lending arrangements have appended themselves to the real estate finance superstructure without fully supplanting the old. Thus, today's lending practices reflect efforts to contend with contemporary legal and financial conundrums as well as to cope with crises from problems of the past.

Real estate loans have traditionally employed fully amortizing, long-term, fixed-rate promissory notes secured by mortgages or deeds of trust that pledge the realty as collateral. Increasingly, however, standard interest and repayment provisions are being modified to give lenders more attractive yields under uncertain economic conditions, to shift risk from lenders to borrowers, or to make loans more obtainable in a high-interest-rate milieu. Alternative security arrangements have been extensively adopted in response to the evolution of mortgage foreclosure rules that increasingly put lenders' interests at risk when borrowers default.

ALTERNATIVE CREDIT ARRANGEMENTS

Persistent price inflation and rising interest rates combined during the decade of the 1970s to ravage mortgage lenders' profitability, even to threaten their long-range survival. Many lenders had loaned money on long-term mortgages at fixed rates, which were then below the rising rates paid to savers. Interest rate–associated risk led to a reduced supply of funds and to the failure of many financial institutions. Lenders responded with a spate of innovative financing arrangements. As always in a market system, consumers (in this case, borrowers) determined which would last and which would quickly fade.

Homeowners have been the primary target in this revolution in available mortgage credit instruments, but commercial borrowers have a number of new alternatives as well. Following are several innovations that have gained sufficient consumer acceptance to become a permanent part of the lending landscape.

Tax-Exempt Bonds

State and local governments are empowered to issue bonds, which are attractive to investors in high income tax brackets because the interest income is exempt from federal and (in some states) state income taxes. Local governments have long used this authority as a means of financing private businesses, on the grounds that it helps attract economic activity to the area and creates employment opportunities or furthers social goals such as creating mass transportation or affordable housing. The bonds are usually payable only out of revenue from the activity being financed (thus, they are called **revenue bonds**); therefore, they are not a true obligation of the issuer. The tax-exempt status of such bonds has permitted them to carry a much lower interest rate than conventional private-source bonds.

Private Activity Bonds

Beginning in 1986, the Internal Revenue Code (in Section 142) restricted the use of tax-exempt bonds issued to finance private commercial activities. Such instruments (called **private activity bonds**, or **PABs**, by the Code) are now permitted only for specified projects:

- Airports, docks and wharves, and mass communication facilities that are to be owned by government units, though they may be leased to private companies under strictly limited conditions

- Water, sewage, and solid or hazardous waste disposal facilities, as well as local or district utilities, that will provide services available to the general public

- Qualified residential projects. Residential rental projects will qualify for tax-exempt PABs only if, during a "qualified project period," which may last for 15 years or longer, a prescribed portion of the tenants are sufficiently impoverished. At least 40 percent of the units must be occupied by tenants whose income does not exceed 60 percent of the area median, or at least 20 percent must be occupied by tenants whose income does not exceed 50 percent of the area median.

Redevelopment Bonds

Tax-exempt redevelopment bonds may be issued to finance land acquisition and preparation (razing existing structures, and so forth), for relocating tenants out of the redevelopment area, and for rehabilitating buildings in areas designated as "blighted" by local government. The debt service on redevelopment bonds must be underwritten to a significant degree by a local government, either by pledging general tax revenue or the incremental property tax revenue that will result from enhanced property values in the redeveloped area.[1]

Variable Rate Loans

Depository-type lenders have used funds from short-term deposits to finance long-term mortgage loans. The difference between interest earned on loans and interest paid to depositors (the *spread*) constitutes their return for bearing administrative costs and risks.

Such institutions are particularly vulnerable to unanticipated interest rate increases. Because deposits are relatively short term, interest rates on them tend to move up fairly quickly with prevailing market rates. Interest rates on conventional mortgage loans, in contrast, are "locked in" for the term of the loan. Lenders thus face the danger that increasing market interest will reduce the spread between rates paid on deposits and rates received on mortgage loans. Lenders have responded by creating adjustable-rate and renegotiable-rate loans, both of which involve interest rates that vary over the term of the loan.

FIGURE 8.1 | Historical Interest Rates (Fixed and Variable)

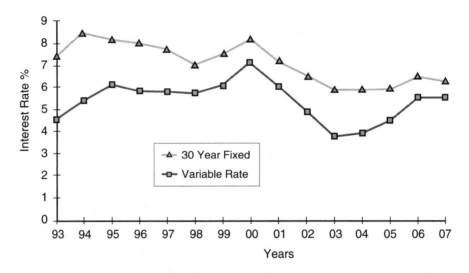

Adjustable-Rate Mortgages

To shift a portion of the risk of unanticipated changes in interest rates from lender to borrower, lenders have aggressively marketed **adjustable-rate mortgages (ARMs)**. For their part, many borrowers find ARMs attractive because the adjustable provision enables them to borrow at lower initial interest rates. Figure 8.1 shows the relationship between effective interest rates on fixed-rate and adjustable-rate conventional home loans during recent years. When interest rates climb, ARMs become increasingly popular because they reduce the extent to which the high rates make housing unaffordable.

In some places, ARMs are called by other names, including **variable rate mortgages (VRMs)**. VRMs actually include all types of mortgages with varying rates or payments to counteract the effect of inflation and interest rate changes. Whatever the local name, borrower and lender agree that interest charged on the loan will vary with some specified market index, such as the average yield on Treasury securities, the average cost of funds to insured lenders, LIBOR (London Interbank Offer Rate), COFI (Cost of Funds Index), the Prime Rate charged by that institution, or average mortgage rates. The borrower pays interest at a rate that changes with the index. For example, the rate may be two and one-half percentage points over the Treasury bill rate. The additional percentage points over the index are the **margin** that is added each adjustment period and stays fixed for the life of the loan. The index might be measured one of two ways: Date certain or moving average. **Date certain** utilizes the index value on a specific day for each adjustment period. Better for smoothing possible spikes in the index is the **moving average method**, which uses an average index value for a specified period, such as six months.

In most instances, there is a prescribed maximum permissible interest rate increase per adjustment period for ARMs (periodic cap), as well as a maximum rate that can be charged over the life of the loan (lifetime cap). There may also be a maximum amount by which the adjustment can increase the monthly payment (payment cap). For example, the French ARM caps the payment so that it can increase by no more than the rate of inflation, and the Mexican ARM is capped to rise no more than the increase in average wages.

Adjustments may be accommodated either by changing the monthly debt service payment or by altering the maturity period (term) of the note. If ARM rates increase, the latter approach may involve negative amortization: monthly payments that are less than the monthly interest. When this happens, the unpaid interest is added to the principal amount of the loan.

ARMs have become a major factor in housing finance. During the recent period of low interest rates, ARMs have become less popular. ARMs recently began at a "teaser" rate that is usually one to two percentage points below the interest rate on fixed-rate mortgages.

Advocates observe that ARMs reduce borrowing costs by allowing debtors to shoulder a portion of the interest rate risk. The greater the portion of the risk a borrower bears, the nearer the mortgage interest rate will be to short-term rates. Critics respond that borrowers are less able than lenders to bear this risk, and cite a lack of evidence that sufficient interest rate differentials exist between fixed-rate and adjustable-rate mortgages. Moreover, there is some concern that a rapid run-up in ARM interest payments could trigger wholesale default.

EXAMPLE 8.1

A homebuyer obtains an 80 percent loan-to-value ratio, 15-year ARM on his $125,000 house. The $100,000 loan begins at a teaser interest rate of 6 percent and has a one-year adjustment period with an annual cap of one percentage point. The ARM is indexed to the one-year Treasury bill rate plus a margin of 2.5 percentage points.

To see how ARM adjustment provisions work, consider Example 8.1. If the Treasury Bill rate in the example is, say, 5.5 percent at the first-year adjustment point, the interest rate on the ARM should adjust to 8 percent. The adjusted rate would be 8 percent (the index of 5.5 percent plus the 2.5 percent margin), except for the cap provision, which limits annual adjustments to one percentage point. Therefore, the new rate would go up only to 7 percent because the periodic cap limits the increase for the year to 1 percent. If the Treasury bill rate is still at 5.5 percent at the second-year adjustment point, the rate on the ARM will go up to 8 percent.

As noted earlier, ARM interest rate adjustments can be accomplished by adjusting the monthly payment or by adjusting the amortization period. The data below show changes in payments for the ARM in Example 8.1 during each of the first three years, assuming that the Treasury bill rate goes to 5.5 percent and remains there for the entire period. The payment on the variable-payment ARM is recalculated for the new interest rate and balance at the time of the adjustment. Changes in the term (maturity) are made if payments are fixed. For the variable-term, fixed-payment

ARM, the term (maturity) is recalculated by changing the interest rate, keeping the payment the same, and solving for the new term or number of payments: n on financial calculators.

		Adjustment Mechanism			
		Variable Payment		Variable Term	
Year	Interest Rate	Payment	Maturity	Payment	Maturity
1	6%	$843.86	15 years	$843.86	15 years
2	7	895.73	14 years	843.86	15.6 years
3	8	946.10	13 years	843.86	16.4 years

The balances at the end of the first year are the same for both types of ARMs ($95,758.69) because they have the same payment and interest rate in that first year. The variable-payment ARM finances the first-year balance at the second-year rate of 7 percent for the remaining 14 years. The new payment is $895.73. After the second year, the new balance for this ARM is $91,580.99, which is then financed at 8 percent for the remaining 13 years, resulting in the third-year payment of $946.10. For the fixed-payment, variable-term ARM, the first-year balance of $95,758.69 is financed at the new 7 percent rate by holding the payment at $843.86 and recalculating the term/maturity. After two years, the balance on this ARM is $92,386.07. This new balance is then financed at 8 percent, resulting in a new term of 16.4 years.

CALCULATOR APPLICATION

PMT = $843.86
n = 168 (12 months × 14 years)
i = .5 (6 ÷ 12)

Solve for PV:
PV = $95,758.69

For fixed payment ARM	*For variable payment ARM*
PMT = 843.86 (enter as negative number)	n = 168 (12 months × 14 years)
PV = 95,758.69	i = .5833 (7 ÷ 12)
i = .5833 (7 ÷ 12)	PV = 95,758.69
Solve for n:	*Solve for PMT:*
n = 187 months	PMT = $895.73

Interest rate differentials exist between ARMs and conventional loans because ARM borrowers bear a large portion of the interest rate risk. Moreover, lenders sometimes set initial ARM rates at low **teaser rates** to attract borrowers. A differential between fixed-rate and adjustable-rate mortgages is particularly attractive to borrowers when fixed rates are high, because it is then that these borrowers have trouble qualifying for loans.

ARMs are also attractive to short-term homeowners, those who are only going to own the home for several years. The low teaser rate and periodic cap allow the short-term homeowner to save money with lower ARM payments and to build up more equity in the home than the owner could do with a fixed-rate mortgage. ARMs are also attractive to debtors when interest rates are headed down, especially if the index is going lower, as was the case in the first years of the 21st century with T-Bill rates approaching historic lows in late 2002.

Renegotiable-Rate Mortgages

Renegotiable-rate mortgages (RRMs) are fixed-rate, level-payment instruments with payments designed to amortize the loan over 20 to 30 years. After a relatively short period, however (typically, three to five years), the principal balance is due and payable. Hence, the RRM acts like the partially amortizing mortgage described in Chapter 5. The key difference in the RRM is that at the end of the initial payment period, the balance is refinanced by the lender over the remaining years at currently prevailing interest rates, with the remaining principal balance falling due once again in three to five years. Unlike the partially amortizing mortgage, the RRM lender must continue to give the debtor the right to pay for the next period. With the partially amortizing loan, the lender can call the balance due at the stop. The interest rate of the RRM is adjusted to the market periodically over the entire amortization term. This type of mortgage is used extensively in Canada.

For residential mortgage loans, government regulations typically place a limit on the magnitude of the RRM interest rate adjustment, and the lender does not have the option of calling the loan but must offer the option of extending for another period at the new rate. This leaves borrowers with the option of extending or seeking alternative financing sources. These protective rules often do not apply for investment property loans or for partially amortizing mortgages.

Convertible Loans

There are two common types of **convertible** mortgage **loans**. The first is a variable-rate loan that gives the borrower an option, for a limited time and on payment of a specified conversion fee, to convert to a fixed-rate loan. This feature appeals to many borrowers. It permits them to enjoy the lower cost associated with variable-rate loans during a period of high or rising interest, to benefit from the lower cost associated with fixed-rate loans during a period of declining interest, and to "lock in" a lower fixed rate if one should occur.

The second type of convertible loan gives holders of mortgage-secured notes an option to convert their mortgage loan positions into equity interests. The usual approach is to permit the unamortized principal balance to be surrendered in exchange for equity at a specified price or at a price to be determined by a property appraisal on

TABLE 8.1 | Annual Payment PLAM

Year	Payment	Interest (4%)	Principal	Balance	Infl. Rate	Balance + Inflation
1	$5,756.23	$2,560.00	$3,196.23	$60,803.77	10%	$66,884.14
2	6,331.85	2,675.37	3,656.48	63,227.66	10	69,550.43
3	6,965.04	2,782.02	4,183.02	65,367.41	10	71,904.15
4	7,661.54	2,876.17	4,785.37	67,118.78	10	73,830.66
5	8,427.70	2,953.23	5,474.47	68,356.19	10	75,191.81
6	9,270.47	3,007.67	6,262.80	68,929.01	5	72,375.46
7	9,733.99	2,895.02	6,838.97	65,536.49	5	68,813.31
8	10,220.69	2,752.53	7,468.16	61,345.15	5	64,412.41
9	10,731.73	2,576.50	8,155.23	56,257.14	5	59,070.04
10	11,268.31	2,362.80	8,905.51	50,164.53	5	52,672.76
11	11,831.73	2,106.91	9,724.82	42,947.94	5	45,095.34
12	12,423.32	1,803.81	10,619.51	34,475.83	5	36,199.62
13	13,044.48	1,447.98	11,596.50	24,603.12	5	25,833.27
14	13,696.70	1,033.33	12,663.37	13,169.90	5	13,828.40
15	14,381.53	553.14	13,828.39	0.01	5	0.01

the conversion date. This arrangement often appeals to lenders because it provides a hedge against inflation. The lender is assured that the loan will receive the contract rate of interest and has the potential for substantially higher yields should the project be spectacularly successful. Meanwhile, maintaining the status of a mortgage lender may give more control than would be available as a minority equity owner.

The debt-to-equity conversion feature often appeals to borrowers because they get a somewhat lower interest rate than would be available with a conventional mortgage loan. The disadvantage is loss of control over the timing of conversion because the option rests with the lender.

Price Level-Adjusted Mortgages

Federal regulators are experimenting with mortgage loans whose contract rate of interest is based on historical real (that is, inflation-adjusted) rates but whose principal balance adjusts to reflect inflation during the loan term. The contract interest rate on these **price level–adjusted mortgages (PLAMs)** is based on the rate of return that would apply if the expected inflation rate were zero and the rate were to remain constant over the life of the loan. The outstanding principal balance and the monthly payments, however, are adjusted annually to account for inflation. As a consequence, monthly payments over the entire term of the mortgage remain constant in purchasing power terms.

EXAMPLE 8.2

A homebuyer obtains an 80 percent loan-to-value (LTV) ratio, 15-year, price level-adjusted mortgage for her $80,000 house. The $64,000 loan is at 4 percent per annum because inflation has been subtracted from the interest rate. Assume that inflation is at 10 percent for the first 5 years and then at 5 percent for the remainder of the mortgage. Calculate the annual payments and balances.

Example 8.2 illustrates how a PLAM operates. It also shows one of the key problems with a PLAM: the remaining balance grows instead of declining during the early years. For ease of explanation, the loan is assumed to require annual, rather than monthly payments. The amortization schedule in Table 8.1 shows how the loan balance and (consequently) the payments for the loan increase with the rate of inflation.

CALCULATOR APPLICATION

PMT = 5,756.23   PV = 66,884.14 ($60,803.77 × 1.10)
n = 14   n = 14
i = 4   i = 4

Solve for PV: *Solve for PMT:*
PV = Balance = $60,803.77   PMT = $6,331.85

Graduated Payment Mortgages

An unfortunate by-product of price inflation is that housing costs frequently escalate faster than wages and profits. Prices, moreover, are only one element of home ownership costs. A major factor determining affordability is the relationship between monthly income and monthly residential mortgage loan payments. Increased home prices combined with escalating interest rates make debt service on traditional fixed-term mortgage notes too great to be managed by many people at an early stage in their working lives.

One response to this problem has been the **graduated payment mortgage (GPM)**. Initial monthly payments on GPMs are often less than the monthly interest accrual, so the remaining balance of the loan actually grows during the early years. The payments are gradually increased so that the initial principal and all the interest is repaid over the total loan period.

Mortgage loans insured by the Federal Housing Administration (FHA) or guaranteed by the Department of Veterans Affairs (VA) together account for between 15 and 20 percent of all mortgage loans on one- to four-family dwellings in the United States, so these agencies are a major force in determining available mortgage loan arrangements (FHA and VA were discussed in detail in Chapter 7). FHA plans include several GPM alternatives for single-family dwellings. Its Plan III program (similar to the GPM program available on VA-guaranteed loans) provides for increasing monthly payments by 7.5 percent each year for five years, after which the monthly payment remains constant for the remaining term.

EXAMPLE 8.3

An FHA Plan III mortgage for $60,000 is to be amortized over 30 years with interest at 10.5 percent per annum. Initial payments of principal and interest will be $418.44, as calculated from the FHA III model. Payments will increase 7.5 percent each year, however, for the first five years.

Example 8.3 illustrates the negative amortization feature of the GPM. At the stipulated rate of 10.5 percent per annum, the first month's interest will be [$60,000 × (0.105/12)], or $525. But, as noted in the example, the monthly payment during the first year is only $418.44; not enough to cover the interest. The unpaid interest accumulates and itself earns interest at the contract rate. As a consequence of this negative amortization, the loan balance will have grown to approximately $63,624 by the end of the fifth year, as shown in Table 8.2.

After five years, the monthly payment in Example 8.3 will level off at $600.72, which is just sufficient to amortize the accumulated loan balance over the remaining 25 years.

Growing Equity Mortgages

Initial payments on **growing equity mortgages (GEMs)** are determined by using a regular fully amortizing, 25- or 30-year level payment schedule. Subsequent payments, however, are increased by a predetermined percentage, with the increased amount of the payment being applied directly to principal reduction. This, of course, means that the interest portion of all subsequent payments declines and the principal portion grows accordingly. The percentage of each payment that applies to reduction of the principal balance of the mortgage increases in a manner reminiscent of a snowball's growth as it plummets down a hill.

Borrowers who are more concerned with equity buildup than with the income tax advantages of deductible interest expense may be attracted to GEMs; others will wonder about the wisdom of paying down the principal quickly and thus reducing the time period over which their loan origination fees are amortized—a practice that increases the effective cost of borrowing (Chapter 9 explains why this is so). A more attractive option might be a standard fully amortizing loan with no prepayment penalty. The borrower then has the option of making additional principal payments if doing so appears beneficial. A reduced interest rate appears to be the only rational

TABLE 8.2 | Loan Balance for GPM in Example 8.3

Months	Monthly Payment	One Month's Interest (10.5%)	Ending Loan Balance
1	$418.44	$525.00	$60,106.56
2	418.44	525.93	60,214.05
3	418.44	526.87	60,322.49
4	418.44	527.82	60,431.87
5	418.44	528.78	60,542.21
6	418.44	529.74	60,653.51
7	418.44	530.72	60,765.79
8	418.44	531.70	60,879.05
9	418.44	532.69	60,993.30
10	418.44	533.69	61,108.55
11	418.44	534.70	61,224.81
12	418.44	535.72	61,342.09
13 through 24	449.82	Increases with growing balance until month 49	62,436.86
25 through 36	483.56		63,227.33
37 through 48	519.83		63,648.15
49 through 60	558.81		63,624.31
61 through 300	600.72		0

incentive for borrowers to accept GEM terms. The key negative aspect of GEMs is the fact that the borrower is locked into paying the increased payment each year. With the standard fully amortizing loan, prepaying an increased payment is optional.

Lenders may be attracted by the rapidly increasing borrower equity as additional security for GEM loans and by the prospect of turning funds over more quickly. If forced to offer significant interest rate concessions to induce borrowers to accept GEMs, however, lenders will find them less enticing.

Reverse Annuity Mortgages

Whereas with a conventional mortgage loan borrowers (mortgagors) make monthly payments to the lender (mortgagee), in a **reverse annuity mortgage (RAM)** the lender sends the borrower a monthly check. At the end of the term, the sum of all the monthly disbursements plus accumulated interest is due and payable. Reverse annuity mortgages may be for a fixed term (usually 10 to 15 years), may run until a designated LTV ratio is achieved, or, for homeowners who have reached a qualifying age, they may continue for life or as long as the homeowners continue to use the mortgaged property as their principal residence. Homeowners can receive a lump sum, monthly payments, and/or a line of credit.

Reverse annuity mortgages are most attractive to lenders during inflationary periods, because inflation-driven price increases help ensure that the mortgaged home's value will stay substantially ahead of the growing balance of the loan. This is a delicate problem for lenders, who must structure such loans carefully to keep the loan balance within permissible LTV guidelines.

From a borrower's perspective, the most attractive version is probably the life-time annuity RAM. For elderly homeowners with a large home equity, this offers an attractive way to enhance retirement income. The payments have no income tax consequences during the borrowers' lifetimes (assuming they continue using the homes as their principal residences, thus avoiding loan maturity) and do not affect qualification for Social Security pension receipts.

RAMs are also known as HECMs (home equity conversion mortgages). The loan-to-value ratio varies with the age of the mortgagor, starting at 50 percent for age 62 and going up to 70 percent for age 82. A ten-year RAM is shown in Example 8.4. Since the payments are the opposite of a normal mortgage, the balances are calculated by solving for FV of the payments paid to the mortgagor. If the example was for a lifetime RAM, instead of a ten-year term, the term would be the number of years the mortgagor is expected to live—taken from actuarial tables as used in the life insurance industry. RAMs are also available with payments that increase with inflation.

EXAMPLE 8.4

A couple owns a home valued at $300,000. Since they are both 62 years old, their lender will give them a 50 percent loan-to-value RAM at 7 percent for ten years.

CALCULATOR APPLICATION
FV = $150,000
n = 120 (12 months × 10 years)
i = .5833 (7 ÷ 12)

Solve for PMT:
PMT = $866.63

For first-year balance:
n = 12 (12 months × 1 year)
i = .5833 (7 ÷ 12)
PMT = $866.63

Solve for FV:
FV = $10,739.79

TABLE 8.3 | Payments and Balances for a Ten-Year RAM at 7 Percent

Year	Monthly Payment to Mortgagor	Ending Loan Balance
0	$866.63	$0
1	866.63	10,739.79
2	866.63	22,255.95
3	866.63	34,604.62
4	866.63	47,845.98
5	866.63	62,044.56
6	866.63	77,269.55
7	866.63	93,595.16
8	866.63	111,100.94
9	866.63	129,872.23
10	866.63	150,000.49

Interest-Only Mortgages

Interest-only (IO) loans have made a comeback in recent years. These mortgages, also known as term, straight, or bullet loans, were actually the dominant type of mortgage 100 years ago. The attractiveness of the loans today is the low payment, since it includes no principal. The lack of principal is also the biggest drawback because the entire principal balance is due at the end of the IO loan. Most debtors have no means of paying this large balloon payment at the end.

The calculation of the monthly payment is simple. The balance is multiplied by the annual interest rate and then divided by 12, as illustrated in Example 8.5.

EXAMPLE 8.5

A debtor was approved for a 15-year, $100,000, IO mortgage at 7 percent. Her monthly payment is: $100,000 \times 0.07 \div 12 = 583.33.

Equity Participation Loans

Financial institutions observed developers and large investors reaping the benefits of sustained inflation while primary lenders bore the brunt of risk associated with new projects. Hence, they began experimenting with ways to share the largess from successful projects while continuing to insulate themselves from the consequences of poor performance.

These experiments spawned a covey of contract clauses that permit lenders to receive a portion of economic benefits that previously accrued solely to developers. These benefits were in addition to the lenders' interest charges.

Common forms of equity participation involve sharing (33 to 50 percent) in gross revenues above some specified base figure and sharing in capital appreciation on ultimate sale of a project (or, if the project isn't sold, when the mortgage is retired or at a designated stop). Some lenders insure increased yields by measuring the appreciation as a percentage of the mortgage amount, rather than of the original property value. Also, lenders do not share in a loss if a property value goes down.

Many developers initially resisted this incursion on what had been their exclusive turf. After a period of reflection and adjustment, however, they appear to have grown more willing to grant some degree of participation to persuade lenders to favor their applications during periods of increasingly tight markets for mortgage funds. Furthermore, the lower rates offered by lenders on participation loans can make project profitability more plausible.

The two most common types of participation mortgages are the **shared appreciation mortgage (SAM)** and the **shared equity participation (SEP)**. In the SAM the lender shares in only the appreciation, but in the SEP the lender receives a percentage of equity each year (cash flows) and at the end of the term. The participation by lenders is not actual ownership, but instead is contingent interest, also known as an **equity kicker**. The equity kicker is paid out of sales proceeds, or if the house is not sold, it is paid from refinancing.

EXAMPLE 8.6

A homebuyer obtains an 80 percent LTV, 30-year SAM for her $120,000 house, with a stated/nominal rate of 5 percent and an appreciation equity kicker of 33 percent. If annual inflation on the house is 10 percent for each of the first three years and 5 percent for the next three years, calculate the payment and equity kicker to the lender.

The $96,000 SAM is at a below-market rate of 5 percent. The loan payment is $515.35. During the six years, the house will appreciate $64,896, going from the purchase price of $120,000 to $184,896. The first three years the value will grow by 10 percent per year, to $159,720. Then, in the next three years, the value will appreciate by 5 percent per year, to $184,896. At the end of the six years the mortgagor will pay the equity kicker of $21,416 to the lender: $64,896 × 0.33 = $21,416.

Wraparound Mortgages

Also called an **all-inclusive mortgage**, the face amount of a **wraparound mortgage** note includes the balance due on an existing note in addition to any amount to be disbursed on the new note. The wraparound lender assumes responsibility for meeting debt service obligations on the old mortgage note that has been "wrapped."

Wraparound loans—sometimes called, more simply, **wraps** or **WAMS**—are frequently used to stretch out payments on an existing loan, thus reducing a borrower's periodic debt service obligation. Or they might be used to raise additional money. Sometimes, of course, a wraparound loan does both.

EXAMPLE 8.7

A property owner still has ten years to pay on a $250,000, 7 percent, 30-year first mortgage note. Monthly payments, including both principal and interest, are $1,663, and the remaining principal balance is approximately $143,228.

To see how a stretched-out payment wrap might work, consider Example 8.7. The borrower might reduce the monthly payments by negotiating a new long-term wraparound mortgage loan for exactly the remaining balance of the existing note: $143,228.

If the wraparound note is payable in monthly payments over 25 years with interest at 9.5 percent, monthly payments will be only $1,251. No funds are actually disbursed as a consequence of the new note. Instead, the wraparound lender makes all further payments on the underlying first mortgage note. The borrower will thereby have reduced the monthly payment obligation by $412 (the old payment of $1,663 minus the new payment of $1,251), at the cost of extending the payment period from the ten years remaining on the old mortgage to the 25-year term of the new.

Remaining payments on the old loan ($1,663 monthly for ten years) will become an obligation of the wraparound lender, who will incur a monthly net cash outflow of $412:

Monthly payment on "wrapped" loan	$1,663.00
Monthly receipt from wraparound note	1,251.00
Monthly net outlay for remaining life of "wrapped" note	$ 412.00

After 10 years, the old note is retired and the lender's monthly payment obligation ceases. Monthly receipts, however, will continue for another 15 years. The lender's cash-flow expectation at the time the wraparound note is negotiated is:

Years	Monthly Cash Flow		
	Inflow	Outflow	Net
1 through 10	$1,251	$1,663	($412)
11 through 25	1,251	-0-	1,251

Assuming (for simplicity) that the lender receives no loan origination fee and charges no discount points, the average annual yield on funds actually extended will be the discount rate that makes the present value of the forecast cash flow exactly zero. This higher yield for the lender explains why lenders offer the wraparound at a lower rate than a standard mortgage and (especially) lower than a risky second mortgage. Briefly, the yield rate is determined by solving for the discount rate that makes the present value of the negative flows exactly equal to that of the positive flows and multiplying by 12 (Appendix B explains how to do the calculation).

Wraparound mortgages are sometimes used to raise additional funds as well. If, in Example 8.5, the borrower wished to raise, say, $75,000, then the amount of the wraparound note would include the $143,228 balance of the old mortgage plus $75,000. Monthly payments on a 9.5 percent, 25-year wraparound mortgage note for this amount would be $1,907, compared with payments of $1,663 on the underlying first mortgage. The monthly cash flows would then be as follows:

Years	Monthly Cash Flow		
	Inflow	Outflow	Net
Zero	-0-	$75,000	($75,000)
1 through 10	$1,907	1,663	244
11 through 25	1,907	-0-	$1,907

The wraparound mortgage may be an attractive alternative for a borrower who is considering a second mortgage loan, because the interest rate on the wraparound is usually lower than that for a second mortgage. If the borrower in the above example had obtained a new second mortgage for the $75,000, the lender would charge a higher interest rate to compensate for the additional risk. If that rate was at, say, 12 percent, the combined payment on the first and the second mortgage notes ($1,663 plus $790, for a total of $2,453) would be substantially higher than the $1,907 payment on the wrap.

ALTERNATIVE SECURITY INSTRUMENTS

Real estate financing instruments reflect centuries of ceaseless legal struggle between debtors and creditors, each vying for advantage either by influencing new legislation or by developing legal maneuvers to circumvent existing laws. Out of the fury have evolved two alternative security instruments, which have become widely accepted and employed today.

Installment Sales Contract

When a seller is willing to finance a portion of the sales price, an **installment sales contract** may be employed instead of a note and mortgage. Also called **land contracts**, **contracts for deed**, or **articles of agreement**, installment sales contracts spell out the terms and conditions under which sellers (**vendors**) are obligated to render deeds of conveyance to buyers (**vendees**) at some future date. During the interim, vendors retain title in their own names and continue as owners of record. The contracts remain **executory** (incomplete) until all preconditions have been met and the deeds are delivered. Sellers often prefer these contracts because income taxes are only due when principal is received, thereby deferring taxes.

Because the seller retains legal title under an installment sales contract, a buyer has only those rights granted by contract terms or by specific provisions of state statutes. Typical contract arrangements give buyers the right to possession during the term of their contracts but require that they pay all property taxes and assessments, acquire and maintain hazard insurance, and maintain property in good repair. Sellers are generally not required to have good title during the term of the contract, but they must *acquire* title if they are to convey as prescribed in the contract.

Often, an installment sales contract provides that default extinguishes all of a vendee's rights in the property. Where such provisions are enforceable, defaulting vendees lose not only their rights to possession and collection of rents but also forfeit any equity accumulated due to debt retirement or increases in property value. Some states have legislated that if the property is an owner-occupied home, vendees lose equity equal to fair market rent only.

Prudent buyers may strengthen their positions in installment sales contract transactions by requiring that the seller provide title insurance and insisting that the transaction be recorded. The prior step ensures that the vendor has good title (or reveals exceptions as listed on the insurance document); the latter gives constructive notice of the buyer's claim against the property.

In many cases, vendees have successfully petitioned the courts to set aside contract provisions that, in the court's view, are punitive in nature. Where a forfeiture clause has wrought no unconscionable penalties on a buyer, however, courts have tended to view the clauses as awarding liquidation damages to the vendor. In this latter case, courts have been inclined to strictly enforce contract provisions.

Sale and Leaseback

Although **sale and leaseback** is not really a lending arrangement, it does serve as an alternative means of financing. Owners desiring to free their capital for other uses sell property to an investor and simultaneously lease the facility from its new owner. The rental rate is usually sufficient to ensure a return of invested capital, provide an acceptable return, and provide income tax advantages.

Land sales and leasebacks are a popular strategy for generating development capital. By selling a shopping center site and leasing it back with a provision that the landowners will subordinate their interest to a mortgage taken out by the lessee, a developer might be able to completely eliminate any requirement for its own equity capital.

Builders and developers also use sale and leaseback arrangements to generate funds to retire construction loans. This might involve selling the entire project to a group of investors and leasing it back on a long-term net lease. Alternatively, the land might be sold and leased back by the developer, who retains ownership of the buildings and other improvements and who then has the right to claim depreciation deductions for income tax purposes. With this arrangement, the developer will often raise additional funds by borrowing on the leasehold interest and the fee ownership of the improvements.

Homebuilding firms sometimes sell their model homes and furnishings to investors and lease them back on a net-lease basis for the anticipated duration of the sales period. The initial lease period typically runs for 12 to 24 months, with a provision that lets the builder lease on a month-to-month basis if more than the anticipated selling time is needed. This enables builders to free their capital for other uses.

Income tax law peculiarities have also contributed to the practice of selling and leasing back model homes. The Internal Revenue Service has ruled (in Revenue Ruling 89-25) that homebuilders cannot claim depreciation deductions on their models, because they are held primarily for resale in the ordinary course of business (inventory). Investors who buy the models and lease them back to builders, however, are permitted such depreciation deductions. Meanwhile, the entire carrying cost of the rented model becomes a tax-deductible operating expense to the builder.

SUMMARY

From the late 1930s until the mid-1970s, most real estate mortgage loans were long-term, fully amortizing instruments. Persistent price inflation and widely fluctuating interest rates in recent years have forced lenders to innovate or perish. As a consequence, numerous alternative credit instruments have flourished.

Mortgage loan innovations that have been used in home mortgage financing, but are either less popular or unavailable for use with investment property financing, include growing equity mortgages, reverse annuity mortgages, graduated payment mortgages, and price level–adjusted mortgages. Growing equity mortgages require that borrowers pay gradually increasing amounts that are applied to reducing the principal amount of the mortgage loan. Reverse annuity mortgages involve loan disbursement to the borrower over an extended period, with principal and accrued interest due and payable when the loan matures.

Graduated payment loans often involve negative amortization during the early years, during which the loan amount continues to grow. Then, during later years, the borrower must make larger monthly payments to fully amortize the balance over the remaining term. Price level–adjusted mortgages have their remaining principal balance and payments adjusted regularly for changes in the general price level. Adjustable-rate loans are a type also applicable to commercial loans. ARMs carry an interest rate that is indexed to some economic indicator and thus is altered periodically over the loan term.

Convertible loans give creditors the option of converting their position into equity and provide an attractive hedge against inflation. Equity participation loans take this a step farther by permitting lenders to share in earnings or appreciation without relinquishing their positions as creditors. Wraparound mortgages are junior financing devices that enable junior lienholders to control payments to the senior lienholders.

State and local governments issued a spate of tax-exempt bonds as a real estate financing device. Income tax law revisions in the 1980s drastically curtailed the uses to which such bond financing can be put.

Installment sales contracts are an alternative financing arrangement wherein the seller agrees to deliver a deed to the property only after the buyer satisfies contractual arrangements—usually payment of the purchase price plus interest. Sale and leaseback arrangements also substitute for conventional mortgage financing. In this arrangement the financier buys the property and leases it back to the user.

KEY TERMS

adjustable-rate mortgage
(ARM)

convertible loans

date certain

equity kicker

equity participation loans

executory

graduated payment
mortgage (GPM)

growing equity mortgage
(GEM)

installment sales contract
(land contract, contract
for deed, articles of
agreement)

interest-only mortgage

margin

moving average method

price level–adjusted
mortgage (PLAM)

private activity bonds
(PABs)

redevelopment bonds

renegotiable rate
mortgage (RRM)

revenue bonds

reverse annuity mortgage
(RAM)

sale and leaseback

shared appreciation
mortgage (SAM)

shared equity
participation (SEP)

tax-exempt bonds

teaser rate

variable rate mortgage
(VRM)

vendee

vendor

wraparound mortgage
(all-inclusive
mortgage, wrap, WAM)

NOTE

1. Internal Revenue Code Section 144(c).

INTERNET REFERENCES

To view the Federal Reserve Boards Consumer Handbook on Adjustable-Rate
Mortgages:
www.federalreserve.gov/pubs/brochures/arms/arms.pdf

For more information on reverse mortgages:
www.aarp.org/money/revmort
www.ftc.gov/bcp/conline/pubs/homes/rms.htm
www.hud.gov/buying/rvrsmort.cfm

REVIEW QUESTIONS

1. What is the attraction of government bond financing for real estate
   developers?
2. For what real estate uses can tax-exempt bond financing be used under current income tax regulations?
3. What do lenders find attractive about convertible loans?
4. What is the potential advantage to borrowers of convertible loans?

5. How does a convertible loan differ from an equity participation loan?

6. What are some representative uses of wraparound mortgage loans?

7. Distinguish between a growing equity mortgage and a graduated payment mortgage.

8. Describe how an elderly homeowner might use a lifetime reverse annuity mortgage as a retirement financing device.

9. What are the characteristics of an ARM?

10. Are adjustable-rate loans more risky for borrowers than long-term, fixed-rate loans? If so, what is the nature of the additional risk?

11. What is the attraction of adjustable-rate loans to borrowers? To lenders?

12. What are the elements of a sale and leaseback transaction?

▌ DISCUSSION QUESTIONS

1. What is to keep an unscrupulous seller under an installment contract from mortgaging the property after the installment contract has been negotiated, so that the buyer discovers a first mortgage lien on the property when the deed is eventually delivered?

2. Why might a business elect to dispose of its buildings in a sale and lease-back arrangement, even though it will continue to need the premises for an indefinite period? Why not keep ownership of the property as an additional investment, thereby avoiding having to pay rent?

3. There were very few successful mortgage loan innovations in this country during the decades of the 1950s and 1960s. Then the following two decades witnessed a spate of innovations. What might have caused this abrupt shift in the rate of innovation?

4. What are the advantages and disadvantages of a price level-adjusted mortgage for a borrower and lender? What risks are involved? Are there any tax advantages for the borrower?

▌ PROBLEMS

1. Howard Homebuyer is contemplating the use of a 30-year ARM to buy his new $125,000 house (a $100,000 loan). If the ARM begins at a teaser rate of 5.5 percent and has a six-month adjustment period with a cap of one-half of 1 percent and a lifetime cap of 4 percent, what will be the highest interest rate possible on the ARM after one year? The highest over the entire term? Calculate the monthly payment if rates hit the lifetime cap.

2. If the ARM in Problem 1 is a fixed payment ARM, what would the monthly payment and term be after one year?

3. If Howard decides on a GPM at 7 percent with a first-year monthly payment of $542.42 instead of the ARM in Problem 1, will he have negative amortization? If so, by how much in the first month? What will be the second month's interest, principal, and ending balance?

4. Howard's wife, Helen, wants to use a PLAM to finance their home instead of the alternatives in Problems 1, 2, and 3. If the PLAM is at 3 percent per annum and if inflation is 6 percent the first year and 4 percent per annum thereafter, what will be the monthly payments and the ending loan balances for the first three years?

5. Howard's brother, H.R., suggests that he should use a 5 percent SAM, which requires a 33 percent equity kicker at the end of five years. If the home appreciates at the rate of inflation in Problem 4, what is Howard's monthly payment and his equity kicker to be paid to the lender in five years?

6. Ben Babyboomer and his wife, Betty, are both 62 years old and want to get a RAM to supplement their retirement income. If their house is valued at $400,000 and the lender will give them a 50 percent LTV RAM at 7.25 percent, what will be the monthly payments to Ben and Betty if they obtain a ten-year RAM? What will the balance be on this RAM in four years? In seven years? If instead of the ten-year RAM, Ben and Betty obtained a lifetime RAM and the actuarial tables predict they will live another 20 years, what would be their monthly payment on a 7.25 percent RAM?

Calculating Mortgage Values and Yields

After studying this chapter, you should understand the relationship between interest rates and mortgage values and the effect of discount points and loan origination fees on mortgage yield. You should also be able to calculate the values and yields for mortgages under various interest rate and prepayment assumptions.

The concept of the time value of money, discussed earlier in the book and explored extensively in Appendix B, is the key to understanding mortgage yields and values in the secondary mortgage market. The value of a mortgage note to a current or prospective investor is affected by changes in market rates of interest because an asset's value can be viewed as the present value of the benefits expected to flow from ownership. Because cash flows from mortgage loans occur in the future, they must be discounted by an appropriate **discount rate** to determine the loan's current value. Mortgages are valued in the same way by discounting the cash flows that will go to an investor holding that mortgage. The appropriate discount rate is the market rate of current mortgages. This rate is used because it is the rate that could be earned if a lender were to issue a new mortgage loan today. In other words, the lender could invest its money in that new mortgage.

The relationship between the actual cash invested today in a mortgage and the expected future cash receipts determines the yield to the investor. This relationship applies whether the owner is a lender originating a new loan or an investor purchasing an existing loan.

THE MARKET VALUE OF A MORTGAGE

Mortgages will be valued at **par** (at face value), **above par** (at a premium), or **below par** (at a discount), depending on whether the **contract interest rate** (the rate the borrower must pay) is the same as, more than, or less than the current market rate on mortgage loans of similar duration and quality. The key determinant of value is the rate used to discount anticipated future cash flows. The cash flows received by the holder of a mortgage note are the payments from the borrower. The appropriate discount rate is the current market rate on similar mortgages; that is, the rate a lender could earn by originating a new loan.

EXAMPLE 9.1

A newly originated 30-year, fully amortizing, $100,000 mortgage note has a contract interest rate of 7 percent. The mortgage note requires monthly payments of $665.30.

CALCULATOR APPLICATION

PV = 100,000

n = 360 (12 months × 30 years)

i = .5833 (7 ÷ 12)

Solve for PMT:

PMT = $665.30

Whenever a mortgage is discounted at its nominal or contract rate (the rate specified on the loan document), the loan is valued at par, an amount equal to the remaining balance of the loan. By way of illustration, consider the loan described in Example 9.1. Current value is calculated by discounting the future cash flows (payments) by the market rate of 7 percent. The future cash flows are monthly payments of $665.30 over the next 360 months. Discounting those payments by 7 percent (divided by 12 because of monthly payments) gives a present value of the payments of $100,000 or the par of the mortgage, its current balance.

Value = PV of 360 payments of $665.30 discounted at 0.58333 (7/12)
= $100,000

Interest Rate Fluctuations Influence Value

The market value of a mortgage moves inversely with current market interest rates. When the market rate on similar mortgages goes up, the market value of existing mortgages will decline; when market rates go down, the value of existing mortgages will go up. If the market rate jumps to 8 percent after the loan is originated, the value of the $100,000, 30-year, 7 percent mortgage note discussed in Example 9.1 will decline below $100,000. If the market rate changes immediately after the loan is originated and *if market participants assume the mortgage will be outstanding for its full 30-year term*, the market value will be the present value of 360 monthly payments when discounted at 8 percent per annum.

Value = PV of 360 payments of $665.30 discounted at 0.666667 (8 ÷ 12)
= $90,669.41

CALCULATOR APPLICATION
n = 360 (12 months × 30 years)
i = .666667 (8 ÷ 12)
PMT = 665.30

Solve for PV:
PV = $90,669.41

The increase in market interest rates has driven the market value of the existing mortgage well below its $100,000 par. Because lenders can originate new $100,000 loans at the higher market rate of 8 percent, they will insist on a price that will generate an 8 percent return if they buy the existing 7 percent mortgage loan from its current holder.

But suppose market interest rates, instead of increasing to 8 percent immediately after the loan in Example 9.1 is originated, immediately decline to 6 percent. Rather than originate a new loan at 6 percent, a lender will be willing to buy the existing 7 percent loan at any price that will yield more than 6 percent per annum. *If market participants make the assumption that the loan will be outstanding for its full*

30-year term, the interaction of supply and demand in the marketplace will drive the market value of loans such as the one in Example 9.1 to a price such that the monthly debt service receipts of $665.30 for 360 months will yield the purchaser of the mortgage just 6 percent; the loan will sell at a premium over par. To determine the market price, discount the monthly payments at the prevailing 6 percent interest rate.

Value = PV of 360 monthly payments of $665.30 discounted at 6% per annum
= $110,966.46

CALCULATOR APPLICATION

n = 360 (12 months × 30 years)
i = .50 (6 ÷ 12)
PMT = 665.30

Solve for PV:
PV = $110,966.46

The impact of changes in market interest rates on the market value of existing loans creates risk that the market value of loan portfolios will change. This is called **interest rate risk**. Lenders seek to manage interest rate risk by selling mortgages in the secondary mortgage market and by marketing other variable rate instruments.

Prepayment Assumptions Influence Value

To isolate the impact of changes in market interest rates, our exploration of mortgage values has incorporated two simplifying assumptions: (1) that the interest rate change occurs immediately after the loan is originated and (2) that buyers and sellers in the secondary mortgage market assume mortgages will remain outstanding for their full term. The simplifying assumption that market participants expect mortgage loans to run full term must be dropped, because lenders do not generally expect that to happen. Borrowers pay loans off early (prepay) for a variety of reasons, but the most common motivation is the sale of the mortgaged property or refinancing when interest rates fall.

Because of this tendency to pay off mortgage loans before maturity, lenders typically base their analysis on the assumption that loans will be paid off after five to seven years. This assumption affects the calculation of market values of existing mortgage loans.

EXAMPLE 9.2

The contract interest rate on 30-year, $100,000 mortgages is 7 percent. Prepayment is expected to occur in five years. The current market interest rate is 8 percent.

CALCULATOR APPLICATION

PV = 100,000

n = 360 (12 months × 30 years)

i = .5833 (7 ÷ 12)

Solve for PMT:

PMT = $665.30

n = 300 (because 25 years remain) (12 × 25)

Solve for PV:

PV = $94, 131.24

Consider Example 9.2, which is the same as Example 9.1, except that it incorporates an assumption that the mortgage will be paid off after five years. The holder of the mortgage note will receive monthly payments until the payoff, and will receive the remaining principal balance at that time. The lender or investor who places a value on the note will discount the monthly payments and the expected lump-sum payoff at the current market rate of interest to determine the mortgage value of the note. The first step in the analysis is to determine the principal balance after five years. The procedure, explained in Appendixes B and C, reveals that the balance will be $94,131.24. If the market rate moves to 8 percent per annum immediately after the mortgage note is originated, the market value of the mortgage note will drop to $95,993.66.

Value = PV of 60 monthly payments of $665.30 discounted at 8% per annum + balance of $94,131.24 discounted for five years at 8%

= $95,993.43

CALCULATOR APPLICATION

PMT = 665.30

n = 60 (12 months x 5 years)

i = .6667 (8 ÷ 12)

FV = $94,131.24

Solve for PV:

PV = $95,993.43

Compare this value with that determined earlier for the same note under the simplifying assumption that buyers and sellers of such mortgage notes expect them to remain outstanding for their full 30-year term. In both illustrations, the contract interest rate of 7 percent in an 8 percent interest rate environment drives the market value below par. But when the below-market rate is not expected to continue for the full term of the mortgage note, the discount is much smaller. The longer the mortgage note with a below-market interest rate is expected to remain outstanding, the closer its market value will be to $90,669.41, its value with no expected prepayment.

Market value with an expected payoff after five years $95,993.43

Market value with no expected early payoff $90,669.41

Now revisit the illustration of the change in market value when market interest rates drop below the rate on an existing note. Recall that the change in rates drives the market value to a premium above par. To determine the market value, use the current higher interest rate to discount the $665.30 monthly debt service for the expected period that the mortgage loan will remain outstanding and the remaining principal balance at that time. If the market rate is 6 percent and the expected period before prepayment is five years, the market value will be $104,199.30.

Value = PV of 60 monthly payments of $665.30 discounted at 8% per annum +
      balance of $94,131.24 discounted for five years at 8%

    = $95,993.43

Value = PV of 60 monthly payments of $665.30 discounted at 6% per annum +
      balance of $94,131.24 discounted for five years at 6%

    = $104,199.30

This figure is less than the illustration of the premium with the simplifying assumption that the loan will remain outstanding full term. The longer the expected time before prepayment, the closer the market value will come to the larger number.

Market value with an expected payoff after five years $104,199.30

Market value with no expected early payoff $110,966.46

CALCULATOR APPLICATION

PMT = 665.30	FV = 94,131.24
n = 360 (12 months × 30 years)	PMT = 665.30
i = .5 (6÷12)	n = 60 (12 months × 5 years)
	i = .5 (6÷12)
Solve for PV:	*Solve for PV:*
PV = $110,966.46	PV = $104,199.30

The remaining simplifying assumption in the illustrations—that interest rate changes occur immediately after the mortgage loan is originated—must also be dropped. A mortgage note may be sold long after it is originated, and in fact may be sold several times before it is finally paid off. All the while, market interest rates will be fluctuating. These changes in interest rates and the steadily declining principal balance as the borrower makes payments on the loan will affect the mortgage note's value in the secondary market. To see the impact of the mortgage note's age at the time it is sold, consider Example 9.3.

EXAMPLE 9.3

Two mortgage loans, each for $100,000, are originated at the same time. Both are fully amortizing over 20 years with monthly payments and earn interest at 7 percent. Monthly payments are $775.30. The loans have been outstanding for three years, so both have 17 years remaining and have current balances of $92,334.92 (determined by financial calculator or by using the procedures in Appendix B or C). From the perspective of an investor, the loans are considered equally risky in all aspects other than the time until they will be prepaid. If Loan A is prepaid as expected, it will run for a total of eight years (the three years it has already existed plus the five until it is prepaid). If Loan B is prepaid as expected, it will run for a total of ten years (the three years it has already existed plus the seven until it is prepaid).

Suppose the notes in Example 9.3 are sold at a price to yield the investor 6.5 percent per annum. Because their contract rates are above the market-determined discount rate, both loans will have above-par market values. But Loan B, which is expected to generate interest at the above-market rate for two years longer than Loan A, will have the greater value premium over par.

The remaining balance at the time of prepayment on Loan A will be $75,390.34. Therefore, a purchaser of the mortgage will expect to receive the monthly payment of $775.30 for 60 months (five years) plus $75,390.34 at the end of the 60th month. Discounting at the market rate of 6.5 percent per annum (6.5%/12 or 0.54167% per month) yields a market value of $94,143.94. The loan is currently worth $1,809.02 above par.

Market value	$94,143.94
Par value (principal balance today)	$92,334.92
Premium over par	$1,809.02

The remaining balance at the time of prepayment on Loan B will be $66,773.76. Therefore, a purchaser of the mortgage will expect to receive $775.30 per month for 84 months (seven years) plus $66,773.76 at the end of the 84th month. Discounting at the market rate of 6.5 percent per annum yields a market value of $94,627.26. The loan is currently worth $2,292.34 above par.

Market value	$94,627.26
Par value (principal balance today)	$92,334.92
Premium over par	$2,292.34

CALCULATOR APPLICATION

Loan A	*Loan B*
PMT = 775.30	PMT = 775.30
n = 144 (12 months × 12 years)	n = 120 (12 months × 10 years)
i = .5833 (7 ÷ 12)	i = .5833 (7 ÷ 12)

Solve for PV:	*Solve for PV:*
Balance = PV = $75,390.34	Balance = PV = $66,773.76

FV = 75,390.34	FV = 66,773.76
PMT = 775.30	PMT = 775.30
n = 60 (12 months × 5 years)	n = 84
i = .54167 (6.5 ÷ 12)	i = .54167 (6.5 ÷ 12)

Solve for PV:	*Solve for PV:*
PV = $94,143.94	PV = $94,627.26

Consider the impact of the shorter expected period until payoff when current market interest rates move above the contract rate on outstanding loans. When this happens, the existing loans will have below-par market values, and the loan with the longest expected period until payoff will sell for less. Suppose market rates on loans such as those in Example 9.3 move above the contract rate and the market-determined discount rate moves to 7.5 percent. Because this is above the contract rate, both loans will have below-par market values. But because the holder of Loan B will be locked into the below-market rate for two years longer, the value of this loan will be less than that of Loan A. Here are the calculations based on the revised assumption about current interest rates.

Market value of Loan A = PV of 60 monthly payments of $775.30 +
                            PV of $75,390.34 discounted for five years,
                            at 7.5% per annum
                         = $90,567.06

Market value of Loan B = PV of 84 monthly payments of $775.30 +
                            PV of $66,773.76 discounted for seven years,
                            at 7.5% per annum
                         = $90,111.72

▌ MORTGAGE YIELDS

The yield on a mortgage is calculated by solving for the rate of return that equates the future cash flows to the initial investment. This rate is also known as the **internal rate of return**, or **IRR**. If a lender lends $100,000, charges no fees or points, and there is no prepayment penalty, the yield is the same as the stated/nominal rate on the loan. But if a lender charges an origination fee, if the loan is prepaid and there is a prepayment penalty, or if an investor buys a loan in the secondary market for more or less than par, the yield will differ from the contract rate.

See Appendix C for a demonstration of the use of a financial calculator in calculating IRR.

EXAMPLE 9.4

For a 30-year, 7 percent mortgage of $100,000 with no fees or points a lender has an initial investment of $100,000 and will receive 360 monthly payments of $665.30, assuming no prepayment.

Example 9.4 illustrates the concept. The rate of return can be calculated by determining the rate of discount that equates the present value of the future cash flows to the investment cost or value. Because the lender "purchased" the loan at par, the rate of return or IRR for this investment is 7 percent—the same as the stated rate on the loan.

$$\text{PV @ IRR (360 payments of \$665.30)} = \text{Initial investment}$$
$$= \$100,000$$
$$\text{IRR} = 7\%$$

If the lender could find an investor that would pay $101,000 for the new mortgage, the yield to the new investor would be lower than that for the original loan at par. An initial investment of $101,000 for the 360 monthly payments would result in a yield below the stated/nominal rate on the loan. The rate of return for the new investor is 6.90 percent.

$$\text{PV @ IRR (360 payments of \$665.30)} = \text{Initial investment}$$
$$= \$101,000$$
$$\text{IRR} = 6.90\%$$

CALCULATOR APPLICATION

This type of problem may also be solved on a financial calculator by solving for i.

PV = 100,000 (enter as negative number)
PMT = 665.30
n = 360 (12 months × 30 years)

Solve for i
i = 7% (.5833 × 12)

If the lender sold the loan to an investor for $97,000, the yield to this new investor would be enhanced. The new investor would receive the same 360 monthly payments, but paid only $97,000 for them. Any time an investor pays less than the par or balance on a loan, the yield will be increased over the nominal rate on the loan. For the example of a discounted $97,000 purchase price, the rate of return will be 7.3 percent, above the stated/nominal rate of 7 percent. In the same way, a lender who charges three points on the loan pays only $97,000 for the right to receive the payments for the term of the loan. Each point is one percent of the original or face loan amount. Because points are paid up front at the beginning of the mortgage, a lender is actually lending less money. In the above example, at the time of closing the lender is lending only $97,000 ($100,000 – $3,000 in points = $97,000). The lender's yield is increased by the points.

$$\text{PV @ IRR (360 payments of \$665.30)} = \text{Initial investment}$$
$$= \$97,000$$
$$\text{IRR} = 7.30\%$$

The yield to a lender is what is calculated when computing the annual percentage rate (**APR**). The **Truth-in-Lending Act** and **Regulation Z** mandate that lenders report the APR to the borrower within one-eighth percentage point of the true APR (one-quarter percentage point for adjustable-rate mortgages). Errors in calculations of lenders' computers can be resolved only if the lenders have taken reasonable steps to verify the accuracy of the computer programs. It is obvious that lenders need to know how to calculate APR.

IRR can be used to calculate the APR. If a lender receives points, it actually reduces the amount loaned. The amount loaned is also reduced by any other finance charges paid to the lender by the borrower. For example, if no points were paid in the 7 percent loan discussed earlier but the lender charged $900 for underwriting, a tax review, and an amortization schedule, the yield to the lender would be above the contract rate of 7 percent. The borrower would be paying $900 and the lender would be investing only $99,100 for the $100,000 loan. The yield is increased to 7.09 percent, above the stated rate on the mortgage.

The Truth-in-Lending Act and Regulation Z require reporting of all charges over the life of the mortgage, including credit life and mortgage insurance premiums, points, and other financing fees. Furthermore, the lender must report the sum total of payments and interest charges. The total payments are easy to calculate because the payments in a fully amortizing mortgage remain the same. The term multiplied by the payment is the sum total. In the above example, 360 times the payment of $665.30 equals $239,508. The total interest can be easily calculated by subtracting the principal amount ($100,000) from the total.

$$\text{Total payments} - \text{Principal} = \text{Interest}$$
$$\$239,508 - \$100,000 = \$139,508$$

Fortunately, Regulation Z requires reporting of the APR only on the basis of full-term loans. The yield or APR varies if the mortgage is prepaid. Most mortgages are not paid for their entire term; most borrowers prepay their loans. A variety of prepayment assumptions have been used in the treatment of mortgage pools. The 12-year assumption is based on an average ownership period of 12 years—no prepayment for 12 years and then all mortgages paid off. The Federal Housing Administration experience is based on historical statistics and actuarial predictions, with a certain percentage of mortgages paid off each year. In the single monthly mortality (SMM) model, experience rates are used to estimate the percentage of outstanding principal that will be prepaid in a month on average. The Public Securities Association (PSA) has designed a dynamic SMM model as an industry standard. The 100 percent PSA estimates annual prepayment rates of 0.2 percent and incremental increases of 0.2 percent until the 6 percent level is reached in the 30th month. The 50 percent PSA starts at 0.1 percent and rises to 3 percent in the 30th month.

EXAMPLE 9.5

For a 7 percent, monthly payment, 30-year mortgage of $100,000, a borrower pays a fee of $900.

Whatever the assumptions, prepayment affects the yield on a mortgage if there are finance fees or points. Consider Example 9.5. To see what happens to the lender's yield if the mortgage is prepaid after only ten years, first calculate the balance that will be due at the time of prepayment. After ten years, there will be 240 payments left. Discounting those at the contract rate of interest reveals that the balance will be $85,812.06. The yield to the lender is the rate of return that sets the present value of the first 120 payments of $665.30 plus the lump sum of $85,812.06 equal to the lender's initial investment.

CALCULATOR APPLICATION

PMT = 665.30

n = 240 (12 months × 20 years)

i = .5833 (7 ÷ 12)

Solve for PV:

PV = $85,812.06

That initial investment is the face amount of the loan minus the fees collected by the lender: $100,000 − $900, or $99,100. Solving for the IRR reveals that the yield will be 7.13 percent per annum.

$$\$99,100 = (PV @ IRR \text{ of } \$665.30 \text{ per month for } 120 \text{ months}) +$$
$$(PV @ IRR \text{ of } \$85,812.06 \text{ due after ten years})$$

$$IRR = 7.13\%$$

CALCULATOR APPLICATION
PMT = 665.30
FV = 85,812.06
PV = 99,100 (enter as negative number)
n = 120 (12 months × 10 years)

Solve for i:
i = .5944 (.5944 × 12 = 7.13)

The yield on the loan in Example 9.5 is increased by prepayment because the period over which the front-end fee is amortized is shortened. The yield would be even higher if the borrower prepaid still earlier, say, in five years. The balance in five years will be $94,131.24, and the yield on the loan would be 7.22 percent.

Prepayment also affects the yield to investors who buy existing mortgage notes in the secondary market. If a loan is bought at a discount from par, early prepayment increases the yield; if it is bought at a premium above par, early prepayment will decrease the yield.

SUMMARY

The market value of a mortgage fluctuates with changes in prevailing market interest rates and the assumptions investors make about probable prepayment patterns. If the market interest rate is the same as the contract rate, the value will be equal to the balance on the loan, or par value. However, if the market rate is different from the stated or nominal rate on the loan, the loan will be affected in relation to the market rate. When the market rate differs from the contract rate on a mortgage, prepayment of the mortgage affects the market value positively if the market is above the stated rate and negatively if it is below the nominal rate.

The yield on a mortgage is the rate of return to the lender or holder of the mortgage note. The yield will be the market yield when an investor pays par for the loan. This relationship is true even if the loan is prepaid. However, the yield on a loan is increased if an investor pays less than the balance, as when a lender receives points and/or fees at origination. The yield is diminished if an investor pays a premium for a mortgage. The yields are also affected by prepayment if the loan was purchased at a premium or a discount. The yield is negatively impacted by prepayment when a premium is paid and positively impacted by prepayment when the loan is purchased at a discount.

KEY TERMS

above par (at a premium)

APR

below par (at a discount)

contract interest rate

discount rate

interest rate risk

internal rate of return
  (IRR)

par (face value)

Regulation Z

Truth-in-Lending Act

INTERNET REFERENCES

For further information on mortgage yields:
  http://money.cnn.com/index.html (search for "mortgage yields")

Survey of real estate trends from the FDIC:
  www.fdic.gov

REVIEW QUESTIONS

1. What is the relationship of market interest rates to value of a mortgage?

2. How does prepayment of a mortgage affect the value of a mortgage if the market rate is the same as the stated rate on the mortgage?

3. How does prepayment affect the value of a mortgage if the market rate is above the nominal rate on the loan?

4. How does prepayment affect the value of a mortgage if the market rate is below the nominal rate on the loan?

5. What is the relationship of purchase price of a mortgage to yield?

6. How does prepayment affect yield when a loan is purchased at par?

7. How does prepayment affect yield when a mortgage is purchased at a premium?

8. How does prepayment affect yield when a mortgage is purchased at a discount?

DISCUSSION QUESTIONS

1. In the past few years, market rates on mortgages have risen from to historical lows. What impact did this rise have on existing mortgages with lower rates?

2. When market interest rates are substantially below the stated/nominal rate on a mortgage, why should an investor not pay the premium value for this loan?

3. If a lender held a mortgage that had a nominal rate below the market rate, how could the lender motivate the borrower to prepay the loan? Why would the lender want prepayment?

4. Why do lenders want borrowers to pay points on a mortgage? What advantage do debtors realize from paying points?

5. What prepayment assumption is most valid for residential mortgages today?

6. What prepayment assumption would be most appropriate for baby boomers?

7. How would a lender estimate the prepayment on a commercial loan?

▌ PROBLEMS

1. What is the value of a 7.5 percent, 30-year mortgage with a monthly payment of $699.21 if the borrower does not prepay and the current market rate is 8 percent?

2. What is the value of a 7.5 percent, 30-year mortgage with a monthly payment of $699.21 if the borrower does not prepay and the current market rate is 7 percent?

3. What is the value of a 7.5 percent, 30-year mortgage with a monthly payment of $699.21 if the borrower does not prepay and the current market rate is 7.5 percent?

4. What is the value of a 7.5 percent, 30-year mortgage with a monthly payment of $699.21 if the borrower prepays in 10 years and the current market rate is 8 percent?

5. What is the value of a 7.5 percent, 30-year mortgage with a monthly payment of $699.21 if the borrower prepays in 10 years and the current market rate is 7 percent?

6. What is the value of a 7.5 percent, 30-year mortgage with a monthly payment of $699.21 if the borrower prepays in 10 years and the current market rate is 7.5 percent?

7. If a 7 percent, $140,000, 30-year monthly payment mortgage was purchased for $133,209.48, what would be the yield for the purchaser? Assume no prepayment.

8. What would be the yield of a 7 percent, $140,000, 30-year monthly payment mortgage if the purchase price for the mortgage was $121,134.56? Assume no prepayment.

9. What would be the IRR of a 7 percent, $140,000, 30-year monthly payment mortgage if the purchase price for the mortgage was $140,000? Assume no prepayment.

10. If a 7 percent, $140,000, 30-year monthly payment mortgage is to be pre-paid in 6 years, what will be the yield to a buyer who paid $140,000?

11. If a 7 percent, $140,000, 30-year monthly payment mortgage is to be pre-paid in 6 years, what will be the yield to the buyer who paid $136,729.58?

12. If a 7 percent, $140,000, 30-year monthly payment mortgage is to be pre-paid in 6 years, what will be the yield to a buyer who paid $143,361.54?

Residential Borrowing and Lending Decisions

After studying this chapter, you should understand the risk and return trade-offs facing lenders and debtors to determine whether it is more advantageous to buy or to rent, and be able to estimate what percentage of a purchase price should be financed. Additionally, you should be able to compute how much a purchaser can borrow, when it is advantageous to pay points, and when to refinance an existing mortgage.

The residential mortgage market is important to most Americans because home ownership is an enduring American dream, and most home purchases will require a mortgage loan. During their heyday, savings and loan associations were the primary source of mortgage loans to finance home purchases. Today, however, the residential mortgage industry is more diverse, and nearly every financial institution participates. With two-thirds of Americans owning their homes, this segment of the mortgage market is critical to the nation's economy. It is important for borrowers and lenders to understand market procedures and be able to analyze the decisions involved.

▌ THE HOMEBUYERS' FINANCIAL CALCULUS

For the mathematically challenged, the word *calculus* is intimidating. In the present context, however, the word simply implies computations for rational financial decision making. The key decisions homebuyers must make are whether to buy instead of rent, how much of the purchase price can be financed, and how much should be financed. Other important financial decisions include the trade-off between discount points and the contract interest rate and whether to refinance an existing mortgage.

Home Ownership: An Investment or a Consumption Decision?

Purchasing a residence can be viewed as either a consumption or an investment decision or as both. Everyone must live somewhere. If one does not buy, one must rent. Other than those who live with others (usually family members) for free, everyone has to make the decision whether to rent or to buy a place to live.

When the residence choice is approached as a consumption choice, it can be analyzed as a net-cash-flow cost issue. The choice with the lowest cost is the best choice. It is a net cost decision, because home ownership provides tax deductions for mortgage interest and real estate taxes. This leads to lower income taxes for the homeowner, and the tax reduction can be treated as a cash flow back to the homeowner, thereby reducing the net costs of shelter.

It needs to be emphasized that mortgage interest and property taxes are not necessarily fully deductible from income taxes. If a homeowner does not have other itemized deductions at least equal to the standard deduction available to all taxpayers, a portion of the itemized interest and property taxes will simply make up the balance of the standard deduction. Moreover, when a taxpayer's adjusted gross income exceeds a threshold amount, the percentage of itemized deductions that offset taxable income begins to shrink. The extent to which property taxes and mortgage interest will be tax-deductible and thereby reduce the after-tax cost of ownership, therefore, differs among taxpayers.

In contrast to the cost of home ownership, the cost of renting is never tax-deductible. And the cost of renting is more than just a monthly rent check. Tenants must make deposits that may be refundable at the end of the lease but that involve forgoing the income that could have been earned by investing the deposited funds.

And tenants are usually held financially responsible for damage they inflict on the premises beyond normal wear and tear.

For the homebuyer, initial cash expenditures are usually required for closing costs and/or a down payment. Furthermore, the homeowner incurs costs of property maintenance and repairs that the renter does not. As a consumption decision, all of these costs must be considered, and they can be equated by putting them into a present value context, as explained in Appendix B. Discounting all the cash flows allows a resident to compare the total present value of the two decisions. The appropriate discount rate is the opportunity cost to the individual, the earnings forgone by not investing the funds. Because it is a consumption decision, the best decision is the one with the lowest negative present value.

Home ownership, however, is not just a consumption decision. It is also an investment decision and can be analyzed in the same way as commercial property investments. The present value of all future costs and benefits must be greater than the initial cash outlay. While most homes appreciate in value, some do not appreciate enough to cover selling expenses. This is likely to be the case when the home ownership period is short. If the rate of appreciation is low, the increased sales price may not justify the investment.

Nevertheless, the owner-occupied home is not purely an investment. It is also a product of consumption, a necessity of shelter. Therefore, the rent/buy decision must be one that combines the calculations of both consumption and investment. If a home appreciates in value during the period of ownership sufficiently to cover transaction costs when the homeowner sells, the funds expended for a down payment at the time of purchase will be recouped. If appreciation exceeds transaction costs, the seller will more than recoup the initial down payment. Under current income tax law, as much as $500,000 (for couples filing a joint return) of any gain on disposal of a home in which the owner has lived for at least two years will be free of income tax liability. When the anticipated tax-free appreciation is included in the calculation, the decision for a long-term period often favors home ownership.

HOW MUCH CAN A BUYER FINANCE?

The amount of mortgage debt homebuyers can accept depends on their financial circumstances and the requirements of the lender. Chapter 3 detailed the underwriting standards for loan qualification. Capacity or ability to repay the debt is a critical component and sets the limit for the amount of debt a lender will approve. Lenders examine their historical records to assess the amount of debt a typical borrower can handle with a given income level. Debtors' incomes are assessed in terms of the relationship between their financial responsibilities and their income. Lender guidelines establish minimum permissible ratios between income and housing expenses, and between recurring expenditures (e.g., housing expenses and payments on long-term debt). The actual ratios vary both with the type of loan and from lender to lender. The type of loan can be determined by the size, the loan-to-value (LTV) ratio, and the availability of loan insurance or guarantees. Example 10.1 illustrates how these ratios limit the amount of money a homebuyer can borrow.

EXAMPLE 10.1

Mark applies for a home mortgage loan with Airborne Credit Union and with Last State Bank. Both institutions require housing expense-to-income ratios of 28 percent, but their permissible total-debt-service-to-income ratios differ. The credit union uses 36 percent and the bank uses 34 percent. Mark's income is $3,000 per month, and his other long-term debt service obligation is $240 per month. The taxes and insurance on the home will be $140 per month. The interest rate for a 30-year, 80 percent LTV ratio mortgage loan at Airborne Credit Union is 6 percent, and the rate at the Last State Bank is 5.75 percent.

Because both lenders in Example 10.1 require the same ratio of housing expense or total mortgage payment to income, the maximum allowable housing expense will be the same.

$$\text{Payment/Income} = 0.28$$
$$\text{Payment/\$3,000} = 0.28$$
$$\text{Payment} = \$3,000 \times 0.28 = \$840 \times \$140 \text{ for taxes and insurance}$$
$$= \$700 \text{ principal and interest payment}$$

But the lenders charge different interest rates and have different requirements regarding the permissible ratios of total debt service to income. As a consequence, the amounts they will lend to Mark differ. Last State Bank will lend no more than $109,669, whereas Airborne Credit Union will lend as much as $116,754.

Last State Bank

With allowable principal and interest totaling $700 per month, and with interest on a 30-year mortgage loan at 5.75 percent, the potential loan based on the payment-to-income ratio is $119,951; that is the loan size that will result in a monthly principal and interest payment of $700. (See Appendixes B and C for the calculations.) But remember, Last State Bank requires that total debt service not exceed 34 percent of monthly income: 0.34 times $3,000 = $1,020. Of this amount, $240 will be absorbed by other long-term debt and $140 by property taxes and insurance, leaving only $640 to cover principal and interest on the mortgage loan. With interest at 5.75 percent on a fully amortizing 30-year loan, this implies a loan of no more than $109,669. Here are the numbers in summary form:

Total monthly income		$3,000
Times: Permissible long-term-obligations-to-income ratio		× 0.34
Maximum permissible long-term obligations		$1,020
Less: Payments on existing long-term debt	$240	
Property taxes and insurance	140	380
Maximum principal and interest		$640

CALCULATOR APPLICATION

PMT = 700 (enter as negative number)

n = 360 (12 months × 30 years)

i = .479167 (5.75 ÷ 12)

Solve for present value:

PV = $119,951

Airborne Credit Union

With interest on a 30-year mortgage loan at 6 percent, monthly principal and interest of $700 will service a mortgage loan of only $116,754, which compares unfavorably with the $119,951 loan limit imposed by Last State Bank's payment-to-income criterion. But in contrast to Last State Bank, Airborne Credit Union's income-to-total-debt-service requirement does not pose a restriction. Airborne stipulates that total debt service must not exceed 36 percent of income. With income of $3,000, this imposes a maximum debt service obligation of $1,080, of which $240 will be absorbed by other long-term debt and $140 by property taxes and insurance, leaving $700 to cover principal and interest on the mortgage loan. With interest at 6 percent on a fully amortizing 30-year loan, this implies a loan of $116,754, which is the limit also imposed by the credit union's maximum allowable payment-to-income ratio. Here are the summarized numbers:

Total monthly income		$3,000
Times: Permissible long-term-obligations-to-income ratio		× 0.36
Maximum permissible long-term obligations		$1,080
Less: Payments on existing long-term debt	$240	
Property taxes and insurance	140	380
Maximum principal and interest		$ 700

CALCULATOR APPLICATION

PMT = 700 (enter as negative number)

n = 360 (12 months × 30 years)

i = .5 (6 ÷ 12)

Solve for present value:

PV = $116,754

Even though Last State Bank has a lower interest rate than Airborne Credit Union, its more conservative total debt ratio results in a smaller loan for Mark. The question of whether this homebuying debtor should pay the higher interest rate to avail himself of the larger loan, however, remains open.

How Much Should a Buyer Finance?

The amount of mortgage loan buyers can finance is determined by the lender, but the buyers must decide how much of the available credit to utilize. Borrowing more rather than less has obvious advantages: With a given amount of money available for a down payment, a larger loan permits the homebuyer to purchase a more costly residence; with a given home purchase price, a larger loan permits the buyer to spend less on the down payment. Less obvious are the costs associated with larger loans: greater financial risk and higher incremental interest rates.

Financial Risk

Encumbering oneself with higher monthly payments in order to borrow a greater amount increases the risk that income will not be sufficient to service the debt and cover other living expenses. The lender's allowable maximum **expense-to-income** and **total-debt-service-to-income ratios** are designed to reduce the lender's risk exposure. But the ratios might not be optimal for the borrower. A borrower who routinely saves a large percentage of income, for example, could weather a reduction in income by reducing the savings rate rather than cutting into consumption or defaulting on the debt service obligation; this option is not available to a borrower who barely scrapes by on available income. Moreover, a borrower whose income stream is reliable and predictable would incur less risk than, say, a commissioned salesperson.

Incremental Interest Rates

Because higher LTV ratio loans are generally viewed as more risky, lenders charge higher interest rates. The rates quoted by lenders may seem to differ only modestly yet result in a drastic difference in the cost of borrowing. The quoted rate is an average applicable to the total amount borrowed. But the borrower's decision should be predicated on the incremental rate: the rate applicable to the additional amount of borrowed funds.

Example 10.1 presents an excellent illustration of this distinction. In the example, Airborne Credit Union quotes a 6 percent per annum interest rate and will lend $116,754, while Last State Bank quotes a 5.75 percent rate and will lend $109,669. Both loans are fully amortizing over 30 years. The difference in the average annual interest rate is only one-quarter of 1 percent (25 basis points), but the cost of borrowing the additional $7,085 available from Airborne Credit Union is 9.58 percent per annum, approximately two-thirds higher than the rate applicable to the $109,669. To see this, first determine the additional amount borrowed and additional monthly payment required.

	Airborne Credit Union	**Last State Bank**	**Difference**
Available loan amount	$116,754	$109,669	$7,085
Monthly principal and interest payment	$700	$640	$60

The analysis shows that borrowing from Airborne Credit Union rather than Last State Bank generates $7,085 of additional funds and requires $60 per month of additional principal and interest payments for 30 years. The additional $60 per month in payments is the incremental cost, and the $7,085 is the incremental benefit. To express the cost in terms of a rate, simply treat the incremental benefit as a loan amount, the incremental cost as the principal and interest payment, and solve for the annual (incremental) interest rate. Using a financial calculator or applying the factors from the tables in Appendix D reveals the rate to be 9.58 percent.

CALCULATOR APPLICATION
PV = 7,085
PMT = 60 (enter as negative number)
n = 360 (12 months × 30 years)

Solve for interest rate:
i = 9.58 (.7985 × 12)

The Cost of Borrowing Revisited

Our analysis of the incremental cost of the loans available to the borrowers in Example 10.1 illustrates that there is more to analyzing the cost of borrowing than simply comparing quoted interest rates. Chapter 5 introduced the problem by explaining the difference between nominal and effective interest rates; the **effective interest rate** is what borrowers actually pay for the use of borrowed money. This is the rate charged by the lender plus an additional amount to amortize any up-front borrowing costs over the period of the loan. The effective rate often differs greatly from the nominal rate quoted by the lender. Fees or points charged on a loan are the most common reasons for differences in the effective rate and the rate specified in the loan documents.

The borrower's debt service obligation is based on the face amount of the loan, but the borrower receives only the face amount minus fees and/or discount points. As a consequence, when there are fees or discount points, the effective interest rate exceeds the stated, or contract, rate on the mortgage note. Chapter 9 illustrates the calculations of these enhanced yields to lenders or holders in due course of mortgage notes. For the moment, let us concentrate on the implications for the borrower.

Should a Homebuyer Pay Points?

Borrowers can usually qualify for lower contract interest rates by paying a fee when the loan closes (that is, when final documents are signed and loan proceeds disbursed). This fee is called *discount points* or, more simply, **points** (a point equals 1 percent of the face amount of the loan). Points enhance the yield to the lender and increase the borrower's cost, because the contract interest rate (the **nominal interest rate**) is applied to the face amount of the mortgage note but the actual net proceeds disbursed by the lender are reduced by the amount of the points paid. For example, if a homebuyer signs a $200,000 note and pays three points, the net proceeds from the loan are only $194,000.

Face amount of loan (the amount on which interest is computed)	$200,000
Less: Discount points (0.03 times $200,000)	6,000
Net proceeds from borrowing	$194,000

The benefit to a borrower of paying discount points is a lower contract interest rate and, therefore, smaller monthly payments. Paying points is advantageous only if it reduces the effective cost of borrowing. The effective interest rate, discussed in more detail in Chapter 5, is the discount rate that makes the present value of debt service payments, including any lump-sum payoffs, equal to the net proceeds received from the loan. When there are no prepayment penalties and the borrower pays no front-end charges, the effective interest rate will be the same as the contract rate—the rate specified on the mortgage note. But when front-end charges such as discount points or back-end charges such as prepayment penalties apply, the effective cost of borrowing will exceed the contract rate. To see the impact on the effective rate of paying discount points, consider Example 10.2.

EXAMPLE 10.2

A homebuyer is offered a $150,000, 30-year, fully amortizing mortgage loan with two interest rate possibilities. If she pays one discount point at closing, the contract interest rate will be 6.25 percent per annum. Without the discount point, the rate will be 6.5 percent per annum.

On a before-tax basis, and assuming the loan in Example 10.2 is outstanding for the full 30-year term, the analysis is simple. First, calculate the net loan proceeds to be received by the borrower, which is the face amount of the loan minus the discount point. Then use a financial calculator or the tables in Appendix D to determine monthly principal and interest payments at 6.5 percent and 6.25 percent, respectively. Using these numbers, compute the effective rate by finding the discount rate that makes the 30-year stream of principal and interest payments have a present value equal to the net loan proceeds. The analysis reveals that paying the point to get the lower contract interest rate will lower the effective rate modestly if the loan runs full-term. The computations are summarized in Table 10.1.

TABLE 10.1 | Effective Interest Rate of Two Borrowing Alternatives When Loans Run Full-Term

	Loan Proposal	
	With Point	**Without Point**
Face Amount of Note	$150,000	$150,000
Less: Discount	1,500	0
Loan Proceeds	$148,500	$150,000
Monthly Principal and Interest Payment*	$923.58	$948.10
Effective Interest Rate	6.35%	6.50%

*Remember the borrower has to make monthly payments on the entire $150,000

CALCULATOR APPLICATION
PV = 150,000
n = 360 (12 months x 30 years)
i = .520833 (6.25 ÷ 12)

Solve for PMT:
PMT = $923.58

PV = 150,000
n = 360 (12 months x 30 years)
i = .541667 (6.5 ÷ 12)

Solve for PMT:
PMT = 948.10

CALCULATOR APPLICATION
PV = 148,500 (enter as negative number)
n = 360 (12 months x 30 years)
PMT = 923.58

Solve for i:
i = 6.35 (.5288 × 12)

PV = 150,000 (enter as negative number)
n = 360 (12 months x 30 years)
PMT = 948.10

Solve for i:
i = 6.5 (.5417 × 12)

The analysis in Table 10.1, which leads to the conclusion that paying a discount point reduces the effective interest rate for this borrower, assumes that the loan will remain outstanding over the entire 30-year loan period, and it ignores the income tax consequences of the loan. Relaxing these simplifying assumptions complicates the analysis and changes the outcome.

TABLE 10.2 | Effective Pretax Interest Rate with Two Borrowing Alternatives When Loans Are Paid Off before Maturity

	Loan Proposal	
	With Point	**Without Point**
Face Amount of Note	$150,000	$150,000
Less: Discount Points (1)	1,500	0
Net Loan Proceeds	$148,500	$150,000
Payments		
Monthly, for Six Years	$923.58	$948.10
Lump Sum, after Six Years (Rounded)	$137,606	$138,098
Effective Pretax Interest Rate	6.46%	6.50%

CALCULATOR APPLICATION

PV = 148,500 (enter as negative number)	PV = 150,000 (enter as negative number)
n = 72 (12 months x 6 years)	n = 72 (12 months x 6 years)
PMT = 923.58	PMT = 948.10
FV = 137,606	FV = 138,098
Solve for i:	*Solve for PMT:*
i = 6.46% (.53825 × 12)	i = 6.5% (.5417 × 12)

Suppose the homebuyer in Example 10.2 expects to dispose of the home after six years. To determine the most beneficial alternative on a pretax basis, the consequence of paying off the loan before maturity must be incorporated into the analysis. This requires computing the remaining balance at the end of the expected six-year holding period (balloon payment). The procedure, explained in Appendixes B and C, reveals that with the discount point, the remaining balance after six years will be $137,606, when rounded to the nearest whole dollar. Without the discount point, the balance after six years will be $138,098 when rounded to the nearest whole dollar. Computing the pretax cost of the two alternatives, as illustrated in Table 10.2, reveals that the shortened holding period increases the effective yield, but the loan with the point still is most advantageous to the debtor.

To summarize, paying discount points to get a lower contract interest rate generates a benefit in the form of lower monthly payments, but the offsetting cost is a reduction in loan proceeds, net of the discount points. The points must be amortized over the life of the loan, and the shorter the period that the loan is outstanding, the smaller will be the benefit of having paid points to lower the contract interest rate. With a sufficiently short loan period, paying points will increase the effective interest rate.

Our illustrations have ignored the income tax consequences of paying discount points. But the after-tax cost of paying points is reduced if the borrower receives a tax reduction as a consequence. Offsetting this benefit, the smaller monthly interest payments will result in reduced annual deductions for interest expense. As explained earlier, however, to get the *full benefit* of these income tax consequences, the taxpaying borrower must have sufficient itemized deductions to equal the benefit of the standard deduction *before including the mortgage interest.* Moreover, adjusted gross income must not exceed the amount above which itemized deductions are progressively reduced.

Logically, all calculations should be done on an after-tax basis. But a borrower who incorporates tax consequences in the decision to pay points must make two crucial assumptions:

1. That the rules for deductibility of home mortgage interest will not change drastically during the forecast period. In an era when major income tax legislation is almost an annual affair, this assumption borders on the audacious.

2. That gross income and itemized deductions will not fluctuate sufficiently to move the taxpayer into a different marginal income tax bracket or to alter the percentage of itemized deductions that can be used to reduce taxable income.

To see how income tax considerations might alter the decision, revisit Example 10.2 and Table 10.2, but incorporate the expected income tax consequences to estimate the after-tax cost of borrowing with and without the point, given that the loan is expected to be paid off in six years. Because the interest element in the monthly debt service will be an itemized deduction on the borrower's income tax return but the principal element will not, the payments must be divided into these two portions. Table 10.3 presents the breakdown, which is expressed in annual terms for analytical convenience.

See Appendix C for a demonstration of the use of a financial calculator in calculating a loan amortization schedule.

A workable after-tax illustration requires an assumption that the borrower gets the full benefit of itemizing deductions: that other itemized deductions equal or exceed the amount of the standard deduction and that adjusted gross income does not exceed the threshold at which itemized deductions begin to offset progressively less of adjusted gross income. With these assumptions and a further assumption that the borrower is in the 40 percent (combined state and federal) income tax bracket, Table 11.4 shows the expected after-tax reduction in the borrower's annual debt service obligation due to paying the point.

TABLE 10.3 Annualized Loan Amortizeation with and without a Discount Point (values rounded to nearest whole dollar)

Year	Without Point				With Point			
	Debt Service	Interest Paid	Principal Paid	Remaining Balance	Debt Service	Interest Paid	Principal Paid	Remaining Balance
1	$11,377	$9,700	$1,677	$148,323	$11,083	$9,326	$1,757	$148,243
2	11,377	9,588	1,789	146,536	11,083	9,212	1,871	146,372
3	11,377	9,469	1,908	144,626	11,083	9,092	1,991	144,381
4	11,377	9,340	2,037	142,589	11,083	8,964	2,119	142,262
5	11,377	9,204	2,173	140,416	11,083	8,827	2,256	140,006
6	11,377	9,059	2,318	138,098	11,083	8,683	2,400	137,606

Using information from Table 10.4, the difference in annual after-tax debt service with the point and the after-tax costs without the point can be estimated. These differences are shown in Table 10.5. The ending loan balances after six years, both with and without the point, are shown in Table 10.3. These balances are extracted from Table 10.3 and shown in Table 10.5 to compute the difference in cash disbursed to pay off the loan after six years. The differences in annual tax disbursements, monthly payments, and in the loan payoff amount must be discounted to express them in present value terms. The present value can then be compared with the cost of paying the point. Assuming the appropriate discount rate to be 9 percent (the borrower's after-tax opportunity cost of capital), the present value is shown in Table 10.5 to be approximately $977 (with all intermediate calculations rounded to the nearest dollar).

Discount points on a mortgage loan to purchase a residence are an itemized deduction on a borrower's federal income taxes when the points are typical of those charged in the market area and points are paid on a loan for home puchase. (Points paid on refinancing are only deductible over the life of the loan.) Continuing with the assumptions that the borrower is in the 40 percent combined state and federal income tax brackets and gets the full benefit of the itemized deduction, the after-tax cost of the points is $900.

Total points paid (0.01 × $150,000)	$1,500
Less: income tax deduction (0.40 × $1,500)	600
After-tax cost of paying the point	900

To determine whether paying the point will be advantageous, compare the present value of the expected after-tax benefits with the after-tax cost. Because

TABLE 10.4 | Tax Differences with and without a Discount Point (values rounded to nearest whole dollar)

	Year					
	1	**2**	**3**	**4**	**5**	**6**
Without Point:						
Annual Interest Expense	$9,700	$9,588	$9,469	$9,340	$9,204	$9,059
With Point:						
Annual Interest Expense	$9,326	$9,212	$9,092	$8,964	$8,827	$8,683
Interest Difference	($374)	($376)	($377)	($376)	($377)	($376)
Times: (Tax Rate)	0.40	0.40	0.40	0.40	0.40	0.40
Tax Differences	$150	$150	$151	$150	$150	$150

TABLE 10.5 | Present Value of Expected Future Cash Flows due to Paying a Discount Point (values rounded to nearest whole dollar)

Year	Tax Differences	Present Value at 9%
1	$150	($138)
2	150	(126)
3	151	(117)
4	150	(107)
5	151	(98)
6	151	(90)
Present Value of Taxes at 9%		($676)

Add: Present Value of Monthly Payment Savings	$24.52	$1,360
Add: Present Value of Reduced Loan Balance after Six Years		
Sixth-Year Balance without Point	$138,098	
Sixth-Year Balance with Point	137,606	
Balance Reduction with Point	492	
Present Value at 9%		$293
Present Value of Total Expected Saving from Refinancing		$977

TABLE 10.6 | Anticipated Future Cash Disbursement Changes due to Refinancing

	Financing Alternatives		Reduction Expected by Refinancing
	Existing 7% Loan	New 6% Loan	
Monthly Principal and Interest Payment	$798.36	$704.31	$94.05
Balance Owed after Three Years (Rounded)	$112,957	$112,873	$84

the after-tax cost of $900 is less than the present value of the expected after-tax benefits, the borrower will be better off paying the point. The deductibility of the point reduces the advantage of paying the higher interest rate to avoid paying the point, but without the full tax deductibility the reduction is not sufficient to offset the short amortization period.

The illustration incorporates the most straightforward of the many possible assumptions about future tax consequences. Exploring the variety of possible after-tax outcomes associated with different income tax situations is beyond the scope of this textbook. Students who anticipate advising prospective borrowers, however, are urged to invest the time and intellectual effort to become familiar with the rules and the tax planning software available to help with such pro forma calculations.

The Refinancing Decision

The question of when to refinance a mortgage that carries a contract interest rate higher than the prevailing market rate is a perennial source of confusion. A widely employed oversimplification is to refinance when interest rates drop 200 basis points (two percentage points) below the contract rate on the existing mortgage. A refinement on the basic two-point rule, sometimes called the *2 + 2 rule*, says refinancing should be undertaken if market rates drop two percentage points below the contract rate on the existing loan and the borrower does not plan to pay off the mortgage for at least two years. Borrowers who follow these rules would miss many opportunities for beneficial refinancing.

The only infallible rule is that the longer the duration of the mortgage, the more likely it is that a borrower will benefit from refinancing when current rates drop below the contract rate on the existing mortgage loan. A reliable decision-making technique is to compute the present value of the expected benefits from refinancing and compare them with the costs of the refinancing.

Refinancing costs can include prepayment penalties on existing mortgage loans (these have been outlawed on home mortgage loans in most states), charges for appraisal and credit reports, origination and underwriting fees, and closing costs.

These costs vary from lender to lender and between geographic locales, and they will often be lower when the borrower refinances with the existing lender.

Benefits of refinancing include all the changes in future cash flows as a result of the refinancing. The changes are the same ones as with payment of points because they are consequences of a reduced interest rate. They include lower monthly payments, increased equity at mortgage payoff, and increased taxes from lower interest deductions.

EXAMPLE 10.3

After paying two years of payments on a 7 percent, 30-year, $120,000 mortgage, a debtor still owes $117,473.50 and discovers that he can refinance the balance with a new 30-year mortgage loan, this one at 6 percent interest, by paying $2,000 in refinancing costs. Whether or not he refinances, the homeowner expects to sell the home in 3 years and use a portion of the sales proceeds to retire the outstanding loan.

To see how the analysis might proceed, consider the fact in Example 10.3. The monthly payment will be lower after refinancing. The repayment obligation on the new loan will continue for two years longer than that on the old, but this is not a concern for our borrower because whether or not he refinances, he expects to pay off the balance of the existing mortgage loan in three years. The remaining balances at the end of three years will also differ; it will be lower with the new loan, and that is an additional benefit to be derived from refinancing.

The analysis is similar to that employed in determining whether to pay points to get a lower contract interest rate. The first step is to determine the difference in future expenditures for principal and interest with and without refinancing. The monthly principal and interest payment on the old 7 percent mortgage is $798.36. The monthly payment on a new $117,473.50 mortgage to be amortized over 30 years with interest at 6 percent is $704.31, a reduction of $94.05 each month. The balance on the old mortgage will be further reduced over the next 3 years (if the borrower does not refinance) to $112,957 (rounded to the nearest whole dollar). If the borrower does refinance, the remaining balance on the new mortgage after three years will be $112,873 (rounded to the nearest whole dollar). Thus, refinancing will decrease the remaining loan balance after three years by approximately $84. These calculations, which are explained in Appendixes B and C, are summarized in Table 10.6. Keep in mind that the new loan balance could be higher when refinancing other examples because the new loan is starting at year 0 and the old loan may be much later in the amortization schedule.

To achieve the expected benefits from refinancing, as summarized in Table 10.6, the homeowner must pay $2,000 in refinancing costs (see Example 10.3). To decide whether the expected benefits justify the cost, the homeowner must express the anticipated future benefits in present value terms. This involves discounting, as explained in Appendixes B and C. Assuming the appropriate discount rate (the homeowner's opportunity cost of capital) to be 10 percent, the present value of the future savings in Table 10.6 is approximately $2,978. Because the present value exceeds the initial $2,000 cost, refinancing appears to be an attractive alternative. See Appendix C for an illustration of NPV calculation.

CALCULATOR APPLICATION

n = 36 (12 months × 3 years)	n = 3
i = .8333 (10 ÷ 12)	i = 10
PMT = 94.05	PMT = 0
FV = 0	FV = 84
Solve for PV:	*Solve for PV:*
PV = $2,914.73	PV = $63.11

Note that our analysis has been done on a before-tax basis. But the lower amount of interest incurred with the new mortgage results in a higher income tax obligation. A more exact analysis will involve comparing the after-tax cost of servicing the debt with the two loans. Because the interest but not the principal portion of the debt service is an itemized deduction on the borrower's income tax return, a preliminary step involves determining the portion of each year's debt service that represents payment of interest. A financial calculator's amortization function quickly reveals the monthly and annual interest and principal paid. For analytical convenience, the amounts are expressed in annual terms. These calculations, called an **amortization table**, are shown on an annualized basis in Table 10.7. See Appendix C for calculations of amortization tables.

Assuming the borrower's income tax situation is such that he gets full benefit from itemized deductions, and further assuming that he is in the 30 percent (combined state and federal) income tax bracket, the data from Table 10.7 can be used to determine the expected tax differences. Because the tax is assumed to be at 30 percent, this is accomplished in Table 10.8 by multiplying the interest expense by the tax rate (0.30), which equals 30 percent. These calculations, for both the existing 7 percent loan and the alternative 6 percent loan, are shown in Table 10.8.

TABLE 10.7 | Annualized Loan Amortization with and without Refinancing (values rounded to nearest whole dollar)

	Old (7%) Loan				New (6%) Loan			
Year	Debt Service	Interest Paid	Principal Paid	Remaining Balance	Debt Service	Interest Paid	Principal Paid	Remaining Balance
1	$9,580	$8,178	$1,402	$116,072	$8,452	$7,009	$1,443	$116,031
2	9,580	8,077	1,503	114,569	8,452	6,920	1,532	114,499
3	9,580	7,968	1,612	112,957	8,452	6,826	1,626	112,873

TABLE 10.8 | Tax Differences with and without Refinancing (values rounded to nearest whole dollar)

	Year		
	1	**2**	**3**
With Old Loan:			
Annual Interest Expense	$8,178	$8,077	$7,968
With New Loan:			
Annual Interest Expense	$7,009	$6,920	$6,826
Interest Difference	($1,169)	($1,157)	($1,142)
Times: (Tax Rate)	0.30	0.30	0.30
Tax Differences	$351	$347	$343

TABLE 10.9 | Present Value of Expected Future Cash Flows due to Refinancing (values rounded to nearest whole dollar)

Year	Tax Differences	Present Value at 9%
1	$351	($319)
2	347	(287)
3	347	(258)
Present Value of Additional Taxes		($864)

Add: Present Value of Monthly Payment Savings	$94.05	$2,915
Add: Present Value of Reduced Loan Balance after Three Years		
Third-Year Balance without Refinancing	$112,957	
Third-Year Balance with Refinancing	112,873	
Balance Reduction due to Refinancing	$84	
Present Value at 10%		63
Present Value of Total Expected Savings from Refinancing		$2,114

The information in Table 10.8 is used in Table 10.9 to determine the advisability of refinancing. The annual savings from refinancing are determined by subtracting the after-tax debt service without refinancing from the after-tax cost with refinancing. The annual savings are discounted to express them in present value terms, and the present value is compared with the cost of refinancing. Assuming the appropriate discount rate to be 9 percent (the borrower's after-tax opportunity cost of capital), the present value is shown on Table 10.9 to be $2,114. Because this exceeds the expected $2,000 cost of refinancing, the refinancing option appears attractive.

SUMMARY

Home ownership is at the same time a consumption and a financing issue, as is the home mortgage financing decision. When faced with alternatives, the rational approach is to forecast costs and benefits from viable alternatives and see which forecast generates the highest present value. Where the alternatives entail differential risk, the discount rates should be adjusted to reflect the difference in perceived risk.

The amount of debt homebuyers can finance is determined by the interaction of market interest rates, the homebuyers' individual financial circumstances, and financial ratios utilized by the lenders. Key ratios employed by lenders are the expense-to-income ratio and the total-debt-service-to-income ratio. Whether homebuyers should avail themselves of all the available home mortgage credit depends on the incremental cost of increasing the size of the mortgage loan, and upon the individual homebuyer's budget.

Homebuyers should pay points when the present value of the expected future savings from doing so is greater than the cost of paying the points. When market interest rates decline, borrowers should consider refinancing their loans if the expected cost of refinancing is less than the present value of the future savings from refinancing.

KEY TERMS

amortization table	financial risk	points
effective interest rate	incremental interest rates	total-debt-service-to-income ratio
expense-to-income ratio	nominal interest rate	

RECOMMENDED READING

Jaffee, Austin J., and C. F. Sirmans. *Real Estate Investment Decision Making.* Englewood Cliffs, N.J.: Prentice-Hall, 1982.

Kolbe, Phillip T., and Gayton E. Greer. *Investment Analysis for Real Estate Decisions,* 6th ed. Chicago: Dearborn Real Estate Education, 2006, chap. 7.

▮ INTERNET REFERENCES

For more information on loan-to-value ratio:
www.mortgageresearchcenter.com/mortgages/ltv.php

General information on residential borrowing and lending:
www.msdwhomeloans.com
http://realtytimes.com/

▮ REVIEW QUESTIONS

1. How is buying a home both a consumption and an investment decision?

2. What items should be considered when making the rent-or-buy decision?

3. What factors determine how much of the purchase price a homebuyer *can* finance?

4. What factors determine how much of the purchase price a homebuyer *should* finance?

5. What factors determine the effective cost of a home mortgage loan?

6. What cash flows should be analyzed to determine the advisability of paying discount points to get a lower contract interest rate on a mortgage loan?

7. What are key considerations when considering the advisability of refinancing an existing mortgage loan?

8. How can mortgage lenders match the maturities of their liabilities and assets?

▮ DISCUSSION QUESTIONS

1. When is renting instead of buying a residence a better decision for families?

2. In the late 1970s, homes in many parts of the country were appreciating by more than 10 percent per year, and homebuyers were often advised to borrow as much as they could to buy the most house they could afford. Was this wise advice?

3. If the government reduces income tax rates, how will key homebuying decisions be affected?

4. If a homebuyer has extra cash available, should it be used to pay discount points to get a lower contract interest rate or to increase the down payment and thereby reduce the loan amount?

5. When interest rates drop, some homebuyers refinance existing mortgage loans several times as rates continue declining. Is this wise?

▊ PROBLEMS ——

1. Steve Chef has annual income of $48,000 and a long-term debt service obligation on car and boat loans totaling $350 per month. Assuming he is considered an acceptable credit risk, how much can he borrow on a 6.75 percent, 30-year mortgage, 80 percent LTV loan if the lender's allowable housing expense-to-income ratio is 28 percent and its total-debt-service-to-income ratio is 35 percent? Steve's taxes and insurance on his new home will be $1,440 per year.

2. Instead of the 6.75 percent loan in Problem 1, should Steve pay two points to get a 6.25 percent, $170,000, monthly payment, 30-year loan? Steve's combined federal and state income tax rate is 29 percent, and his opportunity cost is 12 percent. Steve plans to sell his house in 4 years.

3. What should be Steve's decision in Problem 2 if he keeps the house for 6 years?

4. Kennedie obtained a 15-year, 7 percent, fully amortizing, monthly payment, $150,000 mortgage 1 year ago. If she can get a new 15-year mortgage at 6.5 percent with $1,500 in costs, should she refinance her old mortgage? Her combined tax rate is 26 percent, and her opportunity cost is 11 percent. She plans to keep the mortgage for 3 more years.

5. What should Kennedie do in Problem 4 if she plans to keep the mortgage for 4 more years instead of 3 more years?

Problem Loans and Foreclosures

After studying this chapter, you should understand the problems and the alternatives facing both borrower and lender when mortgagors fail to honor their obligations to mortgagees.

Real estate has a justified reputation as a front-line defense against inflation's ravages. Less justifiably, it has been touted as a way for investors of average intelligence and initiative to gain great wealth with minimal personal risk.

Whether preaching defensive investment or aggressive wealthbuilding, real estate investing advocates usually counsel maximum use of borrowed money. Late-night cable television is virtually supported by pitches for seminars and audiocassette courses on acquiring real estate without using any of one's own funds. However, an environment that glorifies financial leverage almost guarantees a steady stream of problem loans. Moreover, even conservatively financed operations occasionally stumble. When financial mishaps lead to default, lenders hasten to protect their positions. Their last-ditch defensive maneuver is foreclosure, the financial equivalent of an airplane pilot's decision to abandon the aircraft and parachute to safety.

A mortgagor's failure to fulfill *any* of the agreed-on terms in a security agreement constitutes **default**, but the most common incident involves failure to meet repayment obligations. Default is precisely the contingency against which a security agreement is intended to protect a lender. Lenders' recourse varies from state to state, but a universal element is the expense and frustration incurred by lenders trying to salvage their financial positions. Mortgages with default insurance from the Federal Housing Administration or private mortgage insurers or with a Department of Veterans Affairs guarantee will result in less loss for lenders, but they will still involve the headaches of foreclosure.

PROBLEM LOANS: ACTIONS SHORT OF FORECLOSURE

After intense personal interaction leading to the paperwork morass of loan closing, borrowers are often virtually abandoned by their lenders. Subsequent contact, typically, is limited to two annual forms: an audit report asking for verification of data on the service company's books and an escrow analysis to determine adequacy of balances held by the service company for insurance and taxes. If, for any reason, payments are not received within the established grace period, however, the situation changes dramatically. Lenders' collection policies differ, of course, but the common denominator is a close personal relationship with defaulting borrowers.

Traumatic experience has taught most lenders that successful collection programs must be based on personal contact rather than mere correspondence. Determining the precise cause of the default is an early goal of the lender's representative. Depending on the findings, lenders may agree to a rescheduling of payments or to voluntary conveyance of the ownership interest.

Knowing fully that even the best credit investigation and most stringent underwriting criteria will not preclude some defaults, lenders set the stage for this eventuality by the terms in loan documents. In the words of the late James Graaskamp, "Loan terms should provide *progressive pain* and *bailout provisions*."

Progressive Pain

Lenders insert provisions into the note that will empower them to exert selective and progressive pain when borrowers fail to honor their obligations. These include authority to impose late charges and penalties and to seize control of a property and levy management fees. Late charges are usually automatic. Typical wording is as follows:

> Borrower shall pay to the note holder a late charge of ____ percent of any monthly installment not received by the note holder within ____ days after the installment is due.
>
> Payment coupon books provided by most lenders prominently feature late charge provisions. They usually cite the regular payment "... if received by the ____ day of the month" and a higher amount (that includes the standard late charge) "if received after the ____ day of the month."

Additional penalty provisions are common. They are often progressive and are an option available to the lender. One such clause states the following:

> If any payment is more than 10 days delinquent, a late charge of two cents for each dollar of such payment shall be due. In addition, if a loan payment is not received within 20 days of the due date, a default interest rate of the regular loan rate plus 6 percent will accrue on the entire outstanding principal balance, and this interest will commence to accrue retroactively as of the next day after the due date, and will continue to accrue until the late payment and all accrued interest are received.

The ultimate turn of the screw short of foreclosure is to seize control of the property. Clauses designed with this eventuality in mind include such wording as the following:

> Upon acceleration under paragraph ____ hereof, or abandonment of the property, lender shall be entitled to enter upon, take possession of and manage the property and to collect the rents of the property, including those past due. All rents collected by lender shall be applied first to payment of the costs of management of the property and collection of rents, including, but not limited to, reasonable attorney's fees, and then to the sums secured by this mortgage.

To keep unscrupulous or unfortunate debtors from repeatedly defaulting, curing the default, and then repeating the pattern, modern mortgage loan documents almost universally include an **acceleration clause**. This permits the mortgagee to declare the entire amount of the loan due and payable immediately in the event of default. Even though the borrower might otherwise have 25 or 30 years in which to repay, the acceleration clause empowers the note holder to insist on immediate payment *in full* if the mortgagor breaches specified terms of the agreement.

Remember, the acceleration clause is merely an option for the mortgagee—it is a weapon of massive retaliation whose mere presence, the lender hopes, will preclude its ever having to be used. Whether the clause is eventually exercised will depend on the mortgagee's opinion of the mortgagor's willingness and ability to cure the default and on a prognosis of the eventual outcome of foreclosure or voluntary conveyance.

▌ALTERNATIVES TO FORECLOSURE

Lenders do not want to foreclose on a mortgage if they can salvage the situation. **Foreclosed property** held by the lender (also known as **OREO** *[Other Real Estate Owned]* or **REO** *[Real Estate Owned]* on the lender's balance sheet) is a threat to operations. The operating expenses of a property are negative cash flows for the lender, in contrast to a loan in good standing that generates positive cash flows. Regulators can actually shut down a lender that has too many OREOs. Therefore, lenders will often make attempts to avoid foreclosure. Alternatives include restructuring the loan with a lower interest rate, deferring interest, or extending maturities. The debtor can also transfer the mortgage obligation to another person, who takes the property "subject to" the existing mortgage.

Voluntary Conveyance

If all salvage efforts fail, lenders are forced to strip mortgagors of their ownership interest. Depending on the nature of the lien interest and provisions of state statutes, this is typically done by public sale pursuant to a foreclosure proceeding or by a trustee's sale of the mortgaged property. Such proceedings can be expensive and time-consuming, however, and some mortgagees will offer defaulting debtors an opportunity to voluntarily convey their equity interest in exchange for cancellation of the mortgage debt. Reflecting the hard reality of the mortgagor's limited alternatives, the procedure is sometimes referred to as *transfer* (or *deed*) *in lieu of foreclosure*, or *friendly foreclosure*; it may benefit both parties.

Voluntary conveyance enables defaulting mortgagors to avoid the embarrassment and frustration of a foreclosure suit and minimizes the negative marks on their credit ratings. It also eliminates the very real possibility that, in foreclosure, there will be residual liability for a loan balance not satisfied by proceeds of a foreclosure sale. In voluntary conveyance, lenders routinely waive the right to seek a **deficiency judgment**, a ruling from the court that permits collection of any loan balance not satisfied by proceeds from the foreclosure sale.

Voluntary conveyance can be attractive to mortgagees because they immediately acquire title for quick resale. There are potential problems, however. The conveyed property will remain subject to junior liens, if there are any, that would have been extinguished by foreclosure proceedings. Offsetting this disadvantage is that voluntary conveyance eliminates the right of redemption associated with foreclosure (discussed in the next section), which can be a serious impediment to disposing of property acquired at a foreclosure sale.

There are severe tax consequences concerning the voluntary conveyance of a home. If a lender forgives or cancels part of a mortgage debt, the amount of debt forgiven is considered taxable income. Debtors who lose their homes will face hefty tax bills. This is also true for a short sale, where a home is sold for less than the amount owed on the mortgage and the lender agrees to forgive the balance. For example, if a mortgagor owes $150,000 on his or her mortgage and the house is sold for $130,000 and the lender forgives the $20,000 of unpaid balance, that $20,000 is considered taxable income for the debtor. In the 25 percent tax bracket, the debtor would owe the government $5,000 in taxes. Congress is considering legislation that would exclude forgiven mortgage debt on a primary residence from any federal income tax.

▌ FORECLOSURE: A LENDER'S LAST RESORT

Modern foreclosure law, though embedded in state statutes, is founded on principles that evolved from early English common law. There was a time when default penalties were swift, simple, and sure: A defaulting borrower was dispossessed from the mortgaged premises and forfeited all claims. Over the years, this harsh remedy was modified by judicial decree, and there evolved through English common law many of the principles and provisions embedded in modern statutory foreclosure provisions. The history of foreclosure law is an intriguing story of political and legal contention between creditor and debtor classes. The tide of fortune flowed first toward one group, then the other, but with neither gaining a clear-cut, lasting advantage.

Mortgages and deeds of trust typically contain words of conveyance, followed by a **defeasance clause** intended to render nominal conveyance void on satisfaction of the debtor's obligation. Before modern foreclosure law evolved, default rendered the defeasance clause inoperative, and the mortgagee immediately gained good title to pledged property. That was the law of the land in England until about the eleventh century AD. The courts enforced mortgage contracts as written, and default simply extinguished a mortgagor's interest.

Defaulting debtors who felt they had been dealt an unjust blow had the right, however, to petition for redress. Such petitions were heard by the king's chancellor, who ruled on the basis of equity rather than strict adherence to law. In cases of special misfortune or unique hardship, the chancellor might order a mortgagee to accept delinquent payments and reconvey mortgaged lands to the petitioner. Our modern heritage from this practice of basing legal redress on equity is evidenced by mortgage foreclosure cases being heard in Chancery Court, which is a court of equity rather than a criminal court.

Equity of Redemption

By the early seventeenth century, relief for defaulting borrowers was granted as a routine matter. The opportunity to redeem property after default had been converted from a privilege granted under unique circumstances to a vested right. This right, which exists today in all jurisdictions in the United States, became known as the **equitable right of redemption**, or **equity of redemption**. Today, equity of redemption is firmly established, and it is a property right that can be sold, inherited, or otherwise conveyed.

Lenders that have attempted to reassert their once dominant position by inserting into mortgages a waiver of the equitable right of redemption have generally been unsuccessful. Courts routinely invalidate such attempts as contrary to the public interest. The courts base their decisions on the rather obvious fact that needy borrowers are not in a good bargaining position. Any provisions purporting to deprive a mortgagor of well-established rights are thus ruled absolutely void. A document that functions as a mortgage is generally treated as such, no matter how it might be disguised.

Equity of redemption begins when a judge enters an order (a decree) in response to a mortgagee's petition. The decree states the amount of additional time a defaulting borrower has to redeem the mortgaged property. The period of the equity of redemption differs among the states, but generally extends for several months. In other countries the period can be as long as several years.

Foreclosure Suits

During its early development, no time limit was placed on the equity of redemption. This put mortgagees in an untenable position. Their technical ownership of mortgaged property after the mortgagor's default and dispossession had little practical value, because the mortgagor could reacquire good title simply by making redemption. Thus, it became necessary for mortgagees also to petition the king's chancellor. Immediately on default they would ask the chancellor to specify a definite time limit within which the mortgagor must exercise the equity of redemption.

This is the origin of the modern foreclosure suit. In response to a successful petition, the Chancery Court enters a decree specifying an exact time period (such period having been determined by state laws) during which the equity of redemption will exist. The equitable right of redemption is thereafter forever lost.

Actual foreclosure may be accomplished by transferring title directly to the mortgagee (**strict foreclosure**), or by public sale (**foreclosure by sale**). Except under limited and rigidly prescribed circumstances, strict foreclosure exists today only in Connecticut and Vermont.

Foreclosure by sale prevents mortgagees from profiting by a mortgagor's misfortune. Sale is at public auction, with property going to the highest bidder. Sales proceeds are applied first to cover disposal costs and expenses incurred to secure possession, maintain the property, and prepare it for sale; then to satisfy balances due mortgagees. Any remaining funds are remitted to the mortgagor. If sales proceeds are insufficient to cover amounts due, mortgagees may (under most circumstances) seek a deficiency judgment, which leads to attachment and sale of the mortgagor's other assets. The general, involuntary lien of a deficiency judgment is not an option for mortgagees in states such as California, where such a judgment is forbidden by law.

Statutory Right of Redemption

Equitable rights of redemption are extinguished by a foreclosure sale. But 27 states have enacted laws that give a defaulting mortgagor one last opportunity to redeem. With minor variations, these laws permit a mortgagor, for a period of time fixed by the statute, to reclaim property by remitting the foreclosure sale price (plus expenditures incurred for maintenance, improvements, and interest) to the successful bidder. This privilege is called the **statutory right of redemption**.

Statutory redemption periods start with the foreclosure sale and run for a period of time (generally 6 to 12 months) specified in enabling legislation. In some states the statutory redemption period is longer for agricultural land than for other real estate.

In states having a statutory right of redemption, successful bidders at foreclosure sales receive certificates of sale instead of deeds. These certificates typically entitle them to receive deeds if redemption is not made during the statutory redemption period. In some states a mortgagor has full rights of possession during both the equitable and statutory redemption periods.

PRIORITY OF CREDITORS' CLAIMS

Any mortgage that results in a foreclosure sale and extinguishes all other mortgage interests is called a **senior mortgage**. Those interests subordinate to the senior mortgage are called **junior liens**. There is, of course, also an order of priority among junior liens. Lien priorities are usually clearly distinguished, but these distinctions sometimes become clouded.

Significance of Lien Priority

Lien priority becomes important if a lienholder wishes to sell the security interest in mortgaged property or to otherwise employ it in a financial transaction. Priority becomes even more significant when a mortgagor defaults on one or more underlying debt obligations.

Lien Priority and Market Value

Market value of a credit interest is determined in part by the level of risk that the underlying credit obligation will not be honored. The greater the default risk, the less the mortgage instrument's value. Should a debtor default, chances of recovering the full amount of the outstanding indebtedness are far greater for a senior lienholder than for those holding notes secured by junior liens.

Lien Priority and Mortgage Default

In most states a defaulting mortgagor's interest is foreclosed by public sale of mortgaged property. Sales proceeds are applied first to cover administrative costs, then to satisfy mortgage indebtedness. Lien priority becomes critical when sales proceeds are insufficient to satisfy all remaining liens.

Senior lienholders' entire claims are satisfied before any funds are allocated to junior lienholders. Junior lienholders' claims are then met in the order of priority of their liens, until the funds are exhausted. Thus, the probability of receiving anything from a defunct debtor declines rapidly as the number of prior claims mounts.

Lien Priority Governed by Recording Statutes

Recording laws in most states provide that the priority of mortgage liens on single parcels of real estate is established by the order in which they are recorded, rather than that in which they are executed. The time of recording, however, does not establish priority where mortgagees have actual knowledge of a previously executed mortgage or if they are parties to a written agreement to the contrary. Such an agreement is called a **subordination agreement**, and it may be executed between mortgagee and mortgagor or between two mortgagees. Mortgagees have actual notice or knowledge when they have direct information about a lien. Thus, **actual notice** is direct knowledge, while **constructive notice** is the presumption that parties have the responsibility to examine the public records.

Seniority of Purchase-Money Mortgages

Properly recorded purchase-money mortgages (mortgages taken by sellers to secure notes received in partial payment for property) generally have priority over all other liens created by a purchaser's actions. Generally, a purchase-money mortgage must be recorded simultaneously with the deed involved in the conveyance. Of course, the purchase-money mortgage is junior to any preexisting mortgage lien. Where parties so desire, the priority of the purchase-money mortgage may be reduced by appropriate wording in the mortgage. When a purchase-money mortgage is utilized for the sale of raw land, the purchase-money mortgagee often allows subordination of his or her mortgage to a development loan.

Priority of Mechanics' and Materialmen's Liens

An important exception to the general rule that lien priorities are established by the order in which they are recorded relates to claims arising from having provided building materials (**materialmen's liens**) or services (**mechanics' liens**) in connection with construction or property improvements. In most states, these liens have a priority that is established by the date that material or service is first furnished to a building site, even though several months may elapse before the lien is actually recorded. (Other liens do not require recording to be effective, but the date of recording generally establishes their priority; mechanics' and materialmen's liens must be recorded to be effective.)

Many states give claimants lien preference only on the enhanced value brought about through the material and labor they have furnished under the contract that gives rise to the claim. Other states extend the lien priority to the entire property value without regard to the contribution properly attributable to the contract.

Priority of Tax Liens

Most state statutes give property tax liens priority over all other liens on a property, without regard to the time the obligation was created or recorded. In such states, for example, even a purchase-money mortgage or a materialman's lien will be subordinate to a tax lien, which is created after both of the above have become a matter of public record.

EXAMPLE 11.1

Dudley Deadbeat has defaulted on both of his mortgages:

(1) A loan from Rust Belt Savings and Loan obtained to purchase his home three years ago and (2) a home equity mortgage from Employees Credit Union, originated last year. The indebtedness is $65,000 on the first mortgage and $15,000 on the second mortgage. Both mortgages were recorded when they were originated. Deadbeat also failed to pay for a swimming pool that was installed in his backyard four months ago, and Waterhole Company has recorded a mechanic's and materialman's lien for $8,000. Deadbeat is also delinquent on $2,000 of real property taxes on his home.

Deadbeat's house is sold in a foreclosure sale and, after paying administrative costs, the net proceeds total $80,000.

To see how all these rules interact, consider Example 11.1. The priority of liens dictates that the $80,000 of net sales proceeds be distributed as follows:

County taxes	$2,000
Rust Belt S&L	$65,000
Employees Credit Union	$13,000

Because the net proceeds from the foreclosure sale of Deadbeat's home are not sufficient to pay off all liens, and assuming that the state where Deadbeat resides permits deficiency judgments, Employees Credit Union and Waterhole Company will probably sue for the remaining indebtedness. If the sale proceeds had totaled more than the $90,000 owed, Deadbeat would receive the excess.

SUMMARY

Except for casual correspondence concerning audits and address labels to use in sending payments, plus a deluge of advertisements for mortgage insurance, borrowers are unlikely to hear from their mortgage holder unless payments are late. Then comes a series of letters and telephone calls, followed eventually by a foreclosure suit. At this point the borrower's options have narrowed, usually, to the choice of either paying off the balance of the mortgage (because the acceleration clause will have been activated) or transferring the right of redemption to a more financially stable and creditworthy party.

Lenders and defaulting debtors sometimes agree to a voluntary conveyance as an alternative to foreclosure. This saves the defaulting debtor the bother and embarrassment of a foreclosure suit and spares the lender the time and expense associated with foreclosure. Offsetting the benefit to the lender is the possible complication of intervening liens and the lost opportunity for a deficiency judgment.

The lender's last resort in default is foreclosure, a suit wherein the courts are asked to strip the defaulting mortgagor of all rights. After a redemption period, property is sold at public auction (except in two New England states, where strict foreclosure applies), with the proceeds applying first to cover the foreclosure costs, then to satisfaction of the lien. Any remaining sales proceeds are given to the defaulting borrower. If the proceeds are inadequate to satisfy the mortgage balance plus accrued interest and penalties, the lender may seek a deficiency judgment and attach other borrower assets.

In many states, borrowers have an additional opportunity to redeem their property after the foreclosure sale, a provision called the *statutory right of redemption*. If they exercise this right, they must compensate the winning bidder at the foreclosure sale by paying the amount of the winning bid plus interest at a rate specified in the statute.

Lien priority becomes vitally important when a borrower defaults, because sales proceeds are applied to satisfy lien balances in the order of their priority. Only after the first lien is fully satisfied will any cash be disbursed to the second lienholder, only then to the third, and so on. Thus, the more junior a lien, the less likely that anything can be salvaged in a foreclosure sale.

Lien priority is governed by statute. In most states, tax liens are absolutely senior to all others. Other lien priorities are generally established by the date and time of their having been recorded; first recorded, first served. Materialmen's liens and mechanics' liens are important exceptions to the general rule. In most states these date back to the time materials were delivered or work was performed.

▌ KEY TERMS

acceleration clause	foreclosed property (OREO, REO)	statutory right of redemption
actual notice	foreclosure by sale	strict foreclosure
constructive notice	junior liens	subordination agreement
default	lien priority	voluntary conveyance (friendly foreclosure, transfer/deed in lieu of foreclosure)
defeasance clause	materialman's lien	
deficiency judgment	mechanic's lien	
equitable right of redemption (equity of redemption)	senior mortgage	

▌ INTERNET REFERENCES

Information on avoiding foreclosure:
www.hud.gov/foreclosure/index.cfm

▌ REVIEW QUESTIONS

1. What constitutes default on a mortgage loan?
2. What is the most common issue in default?
3. What do acceleration clauses stipulate?
4. Why might a lender not prefer voluntary conveyance to foreclosure?
5. Why might voluntary conveyance benefit a defaulting borrower?
6. Describe the major sequence of events in a typical foreclosure action.
7. What is a defeasance clause, and what is it designed to accomplish?
8. How does the equitable right of redemption differ from the statutory right of redemption?
9. If a foreclosure sale generates more cash than is needed to cover costs and compensate the lender, what happens to the excess?
10. How is the priority of mechanics' and materialmen's liens established?
11. What is the priority of tax liens?
12. What is the priority of a properly recorded purchase money mortgage?

▌ DISCUSSION QUESTIONS

1. Why would a lender be particularly interested in gaining control of mortgaged rental property when a borrower defaults?
2. Is lender possession and control likely to be more important in the case of rental property than in the case of a borrower-occupied residence? Discuss.
3. Discuss the ethics of a sophisticated lender attempting to persuade a defaulting borrower to deliver a deed in lieu of foreclosure. Because there are likely to be vast differences in borrowers' and lenders' financial resources, experience, and legal knowledge, what special safeguards—if any—should states erect to protect borrowers?
4. Because it is difficult, and often impossible, for a lender or buyer to determine that material has been delivered or recent work accomplished on a property, is it fair for mechanic's and materialman's liens to have priority over the claims of buyers or lenders when the materialman's or mechanic's lien has not been filed at the time of the purchase or loan?
5. Discuss how lien priority might affect the market value of a mortgage loan on the secondary mortgage market.
6. Tax liens generally take priority over all other claims, regardless of the sequence of filing. Is this fair or socially desirable?

PROBLEMS

1. Given the following liens and recording dates, how would foreclosure sale proceeds of $100,000 be distributed? The administrative costs of the April 2008 foreclosure sale are $10,000.

Lien	Amount	Date Recorded
Mechanic's Lien for New Porch	$5,000	7 August 2006
Home Equity Mortgage	$10,000	18 July 2005
Materialman's Lien for Lumber	$4,000	10 September 2006
Real Estate Taxes	$3,000	Not recorded
Purchase-Money Mortgage	$78,000	1 April 1999

2. How would your answer change in Problem 1 if the foreclosure sale proceeds were $120,000?

3. How would your answer change in Problem 1 if the home equity mortgage was not recorded?

PART THREE

Construction and Commercial Financing

A market separate from the residential market involves construction and commercial financing. Development and construction loans make up a unique part of the mortgage family. The collateral is yet to be finished and value is added in the process. The risks are substantially higher than with permanent financing, and the returns are correspondingly higher, too. Commercial mortgages are also riskier than residential mortgages as they involve income-producing properties. Decision making for commercial mortgages is examined in Part Three. Furthermore, the examination is done from the viewpoint of both the borrower and the lender. The approaches examined in this part range from the simple and traditional to the complex.

CHAPTER 12

Development and Construction Financing

After studying this chapter, you should understand how mortgage financing is employed in the real estate development process, from initial land acquisition through the final construction phase.

Loans made to finance construction and development are radically different from those that finance the finished product. There are actually three levels of lending involved in the development process: *land loans*, *land development loans*, and *construction loans*. Land loans, which finance acquisition and "warehousing" of unimproved acreage, are made on the strength of an asset for which the market is volatile and unpredictable. Land development loans, which finance improvements to the land, stand somewhere between land loans and construction loans in their complexity and risk.

LAND LOANS

The chain of events leading to a real estate development project starts when someone buys, or obtains the option to buy, a tract of raw (i.e., unimproved) acreage. The land may be completely undeveloped, lacking even utilities or other basic essentials such as sewers, roads, curbs and gutters, and so forth. It is often not appropriately zoned or platted, and perhaps not yet annexed to a municipality.

Raw acreage's development potential is untested, a fact that makes lenders wary. The nature of the land (contour, topology, access, etc.) determines what can be developed on it; the market determines the pace and scope of development. The land will often be developed at different times, in different-sized parcels, and for various purposes. These facts dictate that land loans incorporate more flexible financing arrangements than those that fund other stages of the development process.

Individuals who first spot a parcel's development potential and begin the long chain of events leading to productive use often are not themselves developers. The first purchasers may merely acquire title and hold land until its potential is recognized by developers, or they may be developers themselves who are "warehousing" land to ensure its availability when needed.

Whether developer or speculator, the person who carries the land until it is ready for development will often seek long-term mortgage financing. Such loans present special underwriting problems. The market for land is highly volatile, and in times of real estate market disruptions, it can virtually disappear. Hapless lenders may become reluctant owners of large tracts that take years to liquidate. Unpleasant experiences have made many lenders unwilling to make land loans at all; those who do will seldom lend more than 50 percent to 60 percent of the land's market value.

Seller Financing

Institutional lenders' reluctance to advance funds on raw land, and their consequent imposition of low loan-to-value (LTV) ratios and short loan periods, have spawned substantial financing by sellers of land. Special benefits with **seller financing** may include lower interest rates and more extended loan periods. Front-end fees may be lower or even absent altogether.

Land sellers are usually not in the lending business, and thus have no concern with—or concept of—"cost of funds." Whereas an institutional lender is concerned with the spread between borrowing and lending rates, land sellers are inclined to view their profit as stemming from sale of the land and so are likely to be less concerned with the contract interest rate.

Because sellers who take back promissory notes are often concerned with spreading their income tax liability over an extended period by using the installment method of reporting the sale,[1] they may be willing to extend financing over a substantially longer period than an institutional lender would be. The credit approval process is likely to be more timely and informal, and far less costly. Front-end costs are reduced by avoiding commitment fees, appraisal fees, and lender's legal fees.

Partial Release Provisions

The lien of a land loan mortgage may cover several separate parcels or a single large parcel that is subsequently subdivided. Such loans are often repaid in installments, and parcels are released from the lien as they are sold or developed and refinanced. To accomplish this in an orderly fashion, the mortgage lien documents must provide for repayment in such a way that the loan balance is always adequately secured by the remaining collateral. The sequence of releases, for example, must not leave the remaining parcels landlocked or with little development potential. A mortgage covering several parcels and containing release clauses is often referred to as a **blanket mortgage**.

Developers' needs to dispose of parcels and generate additional cash often conflict with lenders' wishes to maintain sufficient collateral to secure the remaining balance of land loans. Lenders seek wording in loan documents that will give them discretion as to the location of released parcels. Such wording is particularly favorable to lenders, but it may unacceptably restrict developers' alternatives.

Purchase-Money Mortgages

A common approach to seller financing is for the seller to convey title and the buyer to simultaneously deliver a mortgage to secure the note given in part payment for the land. If such a *purchase-money mortgage* (or *take-back mortgage*) is recorded simultaneously with the deed, it becomes a lien on the property senior to any lien the buyer might create.

Purchase-money mortgages may create problems for developers unless sellers agree to subordinate the liens to financing that is to be acquired later from institutional lenders. Such agreement is accomplished by a **subordination agreement** in the mortgage itself, wherein the seller agrees that the purchase money mortgage will be subordinate to that of another lender. The clause usually spells out in considerable detail the permissible amount and nature of the senior debt and the uses to which funds may be put. Tightly drawn subordination clauses often conflict with developers' wishes and needs for flexibility in the development process and thus become subjects of extended negotiation.

Installment Land Contracts

Instead of using mortgages, seller financing of raw land is sometimes accomplished via an **installment land contract**. The seller retains title and, sometimes, possession and use of the land under this arrangement. Installment land contracts are frequently nonrecourse instruments, a provision that makes them very similar to the option arrangements that are discussed later.

At their simplest, installment land contracts require periodic payments of principal and interest to amortize the purchase price over the contract period, at which time (after all payments are made) the seller transfers ownership of the property to the buyer. Developers that enter into this arrangement will usually insist on the right to accelerate the payments or to prepay the total amount and take title to the entire parcel at any time.

Installment land contracts can become extremely complex. Purchasers may be given the right to acquire title to successive parcels in a series of transactions that might extend over many years. When coupled with the right to accelerate the rate of takedowns (i.e., acquisition of parcels) or to delay takedowns without forfeiting the continued right to make subsequent purchases, these arrangements give a developer maximum flexibility to match land purchases with the pace of development.

Options as a Financing Technique

Though options are not, strictly speaking, a financing device, they serve admirably as a substitute for the financing that would otherwise be needed to warehouse land (i.e., to hold it for future use). Options are considered a more conservative approach to securing land for future use than are outright purchases. The developer who options land has no holding costs (taxes, insurance, interest, maintenance, etc.) until the option is exercised. If the economy falters or initial judgment about the land's development potential proves faulty, the developer can simply decline to exercise the option.

While they do enhance flexibility and permit reservation of choice sites with a minimum of front-end cost, land options may be expensive. Sellers will be inclined to price land higher to compensate for the uncertainty associated with options. This tendency is particularly prevalent when the option period is long.

Option provisions range from the very simple to the extremely elaborate. The simplest is a straightforward arrangement that gives an optionee the right to buy designated land for a specific price within the option period. The price of the option is often included as a part of the purchase price if the option is exercised; otherwise, the option price is retained by the optionor. **Declining credit options** permit progressively smaller portions of the option price to be counted toward the purchase, as the option period grows. Options sometimes provide for a gradually increasing land price as the option period is extended. **Rolling options** permit the optionee to add specified new parcels to the option contract as parcels already included in it are acquired.

TABLE 12.1 | Development Stages and Financing Arrangements

Financing	Development Stage	Duration
None	Option to buy	8–26 months
	Engineering, feasibility, and market studies	2–4 months
	Rezoning	4–12 months
	Preliminary plat	2–4 months
	Final plat and engineering	4–6 month
Development	Close sale	end of option
	Develop land	6–36 months
Construction	Construct buildings	3–24 months
Permanent	Sell/lease/occupy	6–360 months

Option agreements need to be carefully drawn and can become exceedingly complex legal documents. A well-drafted agreement not only will include the option price, term, and land description but also will incorporate the entire wording of the purchase contract that will become operative if the option is exercised. If the seller is to provide financing, all the related documents (note, mortgage, etc.) should be drafted and made a part of the option agreement. This is the only way to forestall possible future conflict over contract terms.

Options and installment land contracts can accomplish essentially the same objectives when the installment land contracts are *nonrecourse* (that is, when sellers have no rights in the event of default other than to retain previous payments and keep title to parcels that have not already been transferred).

The value of the option approach to land acquisition can be seen in Table 12.1. The use of an option postpones the interest costs of financing, while essential analysis and required paperwork are completed. During the option period, the developer continually reevaluates the project's feasibility. If the analysis shows that the project will not be profitable, the developer can abandon it with minimal loss.

If land is purchased rather than optioned, the developer is burdened with interest charges during the predevelopment stage and must resell the property when the project is canceled. In contrast, only the option fee is lost if a developer concludes that development of an optioned property is not feasible. Moreover, experienced developers often insist that all or a portion of the option fee be refundable if the option is dropped early in the predevelopment stage. In exchange for the refund provision, the developer usually agrees to give the landowner copies of the studies that led to dropping the option. These studies (which frequently cost more than the refunded option fee) may assist the owner in future sales efforts.

LAND DEVELOPMENT LOANS

Land development is an intermediate step in the overall development process. This step typically includes such things as grading the land; obtaining zoning (or rezoning); installing various utilities; and constructing sewers, drains, gutters, and even streets. It is often accomplished by the same developer that also constructs the buildings and other final improvements. In other cases, it is a distinct operation by a business entity that then seeks to sell the improved parcels to subsequent entities that will construct and market buildings. This latter approach is particularly prevalent in the single-family residential home market, where a land company will subdivide large tracts and sell small packages of homesites to individual builders. It is also quite common in connection with industrial parks, where users may have special needs that that require buildings be custom-designed to their specifications.

Where a **land development loan** is negotiated separate and apart from a construction loan, lenders and borrowers alike face special problems. The end product of the development is building lots, and demand for the lots may be hard to estimate accurately. The lender's concerns are very similar to those of lenders who provide funds for construction, and need not be considered separately.

CONSTRUCTION AND DEVELOPMENT LOANS

In contrast with long-term real estate loans, construction advances are generally treated like commercial loans, secured by the credit rating of the borrower as well as by the real estate. Construction lending is one of the most complicated of all real estate loans; the documentation is very complex and voluminous, loan administration is very involved and time-consuming, and the list of things that can go wrong is long. It follows that construction lending is potentially the most profitable area of real estate finance.

Construction loans are intended to be outstanding only during the period of construction. This makes them ideal for lenders that depend on short-term sources for funds and thus must be leery of committing a substantial part of their assets for lengthy periods. Consequently, about half of these loans are made by commercial banks. Other important construction lenders are savings associations, mortgage bankers, and real estate investment trusts.

How Construction Lenders Control Risk

For the lender, construction loans are vulnerable to a wide variety of risks, not the least of which is that full value of the collateral does not exist at the time the loan is made. There are two primary concerns of construction lenders: (1) Will the borrower complete the project in accordance with the plans and specifications, on time, and at the budgeted cost? (2) Will sufficient funds be available to retire the construction loan when the project is completed?

To assure themselves that projects will proceed on schedule and as planned, lenders carefully evaluate builders' and subcontractors' experience and financial responsibility. In many cases, the builder and even the subcontractors will have to post surety bonds to guarantee their performance.

In addition to analyzing construction plans and budgets, the lender will analyze income and expense projections for the completed project and will draw conclusions about the project's feasibility; that is, the likelihood that objectives will be met. Depending on the lender's analysis of the borrower's capabilities, construction financing may not be available without a firm prior commitment from another competent lender to provide long-term financing when construction is completed. Such commitments are called **takeout**, or **end loan**, **commitments**. Some construction loans are "uncovered" (i.e., made without takeout commitments), if a lender willing to issue the commitment cannot be found. This is, obviously, more risky for the construction lender, to say nothing of the borrower.

According to the Comptroller of the Currency's *Commercial Real Estate and Construction Lending: Comptroller's Handbook,*[2] banking risk consists of the potential effects that events, expected or unexpected, may have on a bank's capital or earnings. (See the text box "Documenting Construction Loans" on the next page, for guidelines recommended for banks in the *Comptroller's Handbook* to reduce the risks associated with real estate and construction lending by thoroughly documenting the bank's loan transaction files.)

Commercial construction loan proceeds are typically disbursed in stages as construction progresses. Payments (called **draws** or **progress payments**) are usually made to the developer, either directly or indirectly through the title insurer, on completion of various stages of construction. Lenders require that applications for advances (except for the initial advance) be accompanied by an itemized listing of the work completed, along with paid receipts and **lien waivers** or releases from suppliers and subcontractors as evidence that construction costs have been paid. Laws in some states are more favorable for the subcontractor (materialmen's liens) than the lender.

Most lenders also require certification from the general contractor or the supervising architect that completed work conforms to plans and specifications and satisfies all government regulations, that the completed work justifies the amount of the requested advance or draw, and that the undisbursed loan balance will be sufficient to complete the project.

An alternative loan disbursement approach, more costly and time-consuming for the lender, is to make payments directly to suppliers, contractors, and subcontractors on receipt of invoices and payment instructions from the borrower. This approach, called the **voucher plan**, assures the lender that funds are applied directly to the project and that suppliers and subcontractors are paid. Most developers dislike the voucher plan because it deprives them of a key element of control over contractors.

Before funding the final advance, the construction lender will require evidence that all improvements have been completed in accordance with the plans and specifications and that appropriate government authorities have approved the premises for occupancy. The final advance will include a portion of construction costs that has been held back from the general contractor (usually about 10 percent, though

20 percent is not unheard of) to ensure project completion in a satisfactory manner. Thus, the lender will be reluctant to disburse this final payment until assured that all problems have been fully resolved.

DOCUMENTING CONSTRUCTION LOANS

According to the Comptroller of the Currency's *Commercial Real Estate and Construction Lending: Comptroller's Handbook,** banking risk is the potential effects that events, expected or unexpected, may have on a bank's capital or earnings. To reduce the applicable risks associated with real estate and construction lending, a bank's documentation files should include the following:

- Financial and background information on the borrower to substantiate the expertise and financial strength of the borrower to complete the project.

- The construction loan agreement that sets forth the rights and obligations of the lender and borrower, conditions for advancing funds, and events of default. In some states, the agreement must be cited in either the deed of trust or mortgage. The loan agreement should specify the performance of each party during the entire course of construction. Any changes to the borrower's plans should be approved both by the construction lender and the takeout lender because changes can increase the cost of construction without necessarily increasing the sale price of the completed project. Alternatively, lower construction costs may not indicate a true saving, but might instead indicate that lesser quality materials or workmanship are being used.

- A recorded mortgage or deed of trust that can be used to foreclose and to obtain title to the collateral.

- A title insurance binder or policy, usually issued by a recognized title insurance company or, in some states, an attorney's opinion. The policy should be updated with each advance of funds, if such additional protection is available.

- Insurance policies and proof of premium payment as evidence that the builder has adequate and enforceable coverage, including liability, fire, builder's special risks, and, where appropriate, flood insurance.

- An appropriate appraisal or evaluation showing the market value of the property on an "as is" and "as completed" basis, and when a stabilized level of occupancy is achieved.

- Project plans, feasibility study, and construction budget showing the development plans, project costs, marketing plans, and equity contributions. The documentation should include a detailed cost breakdown for the land and "hard" construction costs, as well as the indirect or "soft" costs for the project, such as administrative costs, and architectural, engineering, and legal fees. If internal expertise is not available, the bank may need to retain an independent construction expert to review these documents to assess the reasonableness and appropriateness of the construction plans and costs.

- Property surveys, easements, and soil reports.

■ The architect's certification of the plan's compliance with all applicable building codes, and with zoning, environmental protection, and other government regulations, as well as an engineer's report on compliance with building codes and standards.

■ The takeout commitment, if any, from a permanent lender and the terms of the loan. The documentation files should indicate that the bank verified the financial ability of the permanent lender to fund the takeout commitment and reviewed the takeout agreement to determine the circumstances in which it could be voided. Although documentation for a takeout commitment varies, it often includes:

  – the amount of the commitment;

  – details of the project being financed;

  – expiration date of the commitment;

  – standby fee requirement;

  – floor and ceiling rental rates and minimum occupancy requirements;

  – an assignment of rents;

  – a requirement that the construction loan is to be fully disbursed and not in any way in default at the time the settlement occurs.

■ The commitment agreement, sometimes referred to as the **buy/sell contract** or the **tri-party agreement**, signed by the borrower, the construction lender, and the permanent lender. The agreement prevents the permanent lender from withdrawing the takeout commitment because of unacceptable documentation. It also protects the construction lender against unforeseen events, such as the death of a principal, before the permanent loan documents are signed. The agreement provides the permanent lender with an assurance that the loan will be available at the stipulated time and usually eliminates the need for a standby fee. On occasion, the agreement may include an assignment of rents giving the permanent lender the right to receive lease payments and/or rents directly from the lessees.

■ A completion or performance bond written by an insurance company.

■ An owner's affidavit or a borrowing resolution, which empowers a representative of the borrower to enter into the loan agreement.

■ Evidence that property taxes have been paid to date.

■ Any environmental surveys deemed necessary, given the location and type of project.

*Adapted from U.S. Department of the Treasury, Comptroller of the Currency Administrator of National Banks, *Commercial Real Estate and Construction Lending: Comptroller's Handbook* (Washington, D.C.: Government Printing Office, 1995).

The Cost of Construction Funds

Construction loan interest is higher than that for long-term mortgage loans, reflecting the greater risk and higher administrative costs. Moreover, a borrower's actual cost is usually considerably above the interest rate stipulated in the loan documents. The effective cost is influenced by factors such as loan fees (which often include nonrefundable commitment fees) and the average principal amount outstanding over the loan period, as well as the contract interest rate.

To see this, consider a construction loan of $1 million for one year with interest at 10 percent per annum, a loan origination fee of one point, and a nonrefundable commitment fee of one-half of a point, payable when the lender agrees to grant the loan. Because the loan is disbursed in stages as construction progresses, the average loan balance will be considerably less than the $1 million maximum amount. Let's assume the actual disbursement pattern results in an average outstanding loan balance for the year of $500,000.

Total contract interest paid will be 0.10 times $500,000, or $50,000. Additionally, the borrower will have paid $5,000 for the commitment fee (0.005 times the $1 million loan commitment) and $10,000 as a loan origination fee (0.01 times the $1 million loan commitment) at the initial loan closing. Thus the cost for the loan will have been $50,000 plus $5,000 plus $10,000, for a total of $65,000, for using (on average) $500,000 for one year. The effective cost of the funds will have been $65,000/$500,000, or 13 percent. A detailed example of a (somewhat simplified) construction loan with a table of disbursements and interest accumulation through the construction period is shown in the "Construction Loan Example" at the end of the chapter.

Managing Interest Rate Risk during Construction

Lenders rarely specify fixed interest rates for construction loans. Generally, rates are indexed to some criterion such as the lender's *prime rate* (the rate charged to its most creditworthy corporate borrowers), the rate charged for overnight interbank loans (the *federal funds rate*), or the London Interbank Offered Rate (LIBOR). (There are many free Internet sites at which one may check the daily [even intradaily] quotes for various money rates. One good site is *www.banxquote.com/money.* asp.) The actual rate on the construction loan will normally be several points over the index. Such loans are often characterized as *floating rate loans*, and they can cause radical (and alarming) variations in construction loan costs.

Developers who are unwilling to bear the risk of a ruinous run-up in the cost of a floating rate construction loan might be able to negotiate an interest rate "cap": a maximum above which the floating rate loan ceases to float. However, they must expect to pay for this shifting of interest rate risk to the lender through higher initial rates or other fees. Large-scale developers may be able to avoid interest rate risk less expensively by engaging in interest rate swaps or by taking a hedge position in the interest rate futures market.

An **interest rate swap** involves agreeing to pay another party a fixed interest rate on an obligation equal in amount to the anticipated construction loan disbursement, in exchange for a promise to pay the developer's floating rate.[3] The interest obligations are netted, and there is (usually) a quarterly distribution of the net interest. The developer is protected against interest rate increases during construction but also forgoes any possibility of benefiting from interest rate declines. The objective is to ensure interest rate expense predictability at minimum cost (this is an elementary swap arrangement). Swaps can become incredibly complex, and they can be used for speculating on interest rate movements as well as for hedging against them. Developers who use interest rate swaps will generally have to guarantee their side of the obligation with a letter of credit from a commercial bank.

Alternatively, a developer might hedge by taking a position in an **interest rate futures contract**. The most widely employed of these are contracts to deliver, or to take delivery of, $1 million face value Treasury notes or Treasury bills with a specified period until maturity, at a future date stipulated in the contract. These standard contracts—the only variable is the contract price—are regularly traded on the Chicago Mercantile Exchange.

Because they are fixed-interest securities, the prices of futures contracts move inversely with interest rates: As interest rates increase, the market values of futures contracts decline. A builder wishing to hedge against interest rate increases can *sell short* (agree to acquire the securities and deliver them at a specified future date). If rates do increase, the greater construction interest cost will be partly offset by profit from buying now-less-expensive futures contracts to cover the short position. When this happens, the Exchange will offset the developer's short and long positions in a purely bookkeeping operation; no actual Treasury securities are involved in either transaction. If interest rates decline, the developer will lose money by covering the short position with now-more-costly contracts, but this will be partly offset by lowered rates on the construction loan. The net result of this hedging is a more predictable outcome for the combined construction loan and interest rate futures position. A detailed real world example to illustrate the cost of construction funds to include construction lending with up-front fees, draws, interest accruals, and final repayment with takeout is in the "Construction Loan Example" at the end of the chapter.

SUMMARY

Loans to acquire and improve land and to construct buildings are the most complicated part of the real estate lending industry. They are also potentially the most lucrative. Land loans, provided by institutional lenders to finance acquisition of raw acreage, seldom exceed 50 percent to 60 percent of the land's estimated market value. Because institutional lenders are loath to extend substantial sums on the security of raw land, sellers often extend credit to buyers. This might be accomplished via a purchase-money mortgage or by an installment land contract. In the latter arrangement, the seller retains title until the buyer fulfills the contract terms.

Whether financing is provided by lending institutions or by sellers, provision for partial release from the mortgage lien is often crucial to land buyers, who may want to develop and sell subparcels in piecemeal fashion.

Instead of outright purchase of land that they intend to develop in the future, many buyers acquire purchase options, which give them the right to buy at the specified price any time during the option period. This is considered a more conservative approach to holding land than is an outright purchase.

Land improvement loans—granted to finance improvements to make the land ready for construction—are often provided by construction lenders. Construction loans are a specialized type of financing that requires that the lender closely monitor construction progress and to ensure that all vendors and subcontractors are paid. Construction lenders may insist that borrowers secure a binding commitment from a reputable takeout lender before the construction loan commitment is issued.

Interest rates on construction loans are usually pegged to the lender's cost of short-term funds, and can prove quite volatile. To control interest rate risk during construction, developers sometimes take a position in the interest rate futures market or engage in interest rate swaps.

KEY TERMS

blanket mortgage

buy/sell contract (tri-party agreement)

construction loan

declining credit option

draws (progress payments)

installment land contract

interest rate futures contract

interest rate swap

land development loan

lien waivers

option agreements

rolling option

seller financing

subordination agreement

takeout (end loan) commitment

voucher plan

NOTES

1. Section 453 of the Internal Revenue Code permits sellers who take back a promissory note in part payment to defer recognition of the taxable gain on the sale. Instead of paying taxes in the year of the transaction, they recognize the gain on a ratable basis as they collect the principal portion of the note.

2. U.S. Department of the Treasury, Comptroller of the Currency Administrator of National Banks, *Commercial Real Estate and Construction Lending: Comptroller's Handbook* (Washington, D.C.: Government Printing Office, 1995).

3. The floating rate used in most interest rate swaps is the London Interbank Offered Rate, commonly known by the acronym LIBOR. This is the average interbank rate quoted by major banks for Eurodollar deposits in the London market. The rate is regularly quoted in the financial section of major newspapers such as the *New York Times* and the *Wall Street Journal*.

INTERNET REFERENCES

For additional information on seller financing:
www.financialservicesguide.net/seller.html

To view *Commercial Real Estate and Construction Lending: Comptroller's Handbook:*
www.occ.treas.gov/handbook/realcon.pdf

For news on land development:
www.landdevelopmenttoday.com

The Urban Land Institute provides information on current issues in land use and financing:
www.uli.org

REVIEW QUESTIONS

1. What are the three levels of lending involved in financing the preparation of land and buildings for occupancy by tenants?
2. How does "raw acreage" differ from improved land?
3. Why are sellers of raw land so often asked to provide financing?
4. What is a partial release provision, and why is it often so important to land developers?
5. Who lends on the strength of a purchase-money mortgage?
6. What is a subordination clause, and why is it important that such a clause be included in long-term land loans?
7. How do installment land contracts differ from mortgage-secured land loans?
8. Describe rolling options.
9. Describe declining credit options.
10. Why are construction and development loans more complicated and difficult to administer than are other types of real estate loans?

DISCUSSION QUESTIONS

1. Discuss the relative merits of purchase options, purchase-money mortgages, and installment land contracts from the perspective of a land seller.

2. Discuss the pros and cons of the above instruments from the perspective of a land buyer.

3. Loan commitments are not the same as actual loans, and they are virtually unused in lending except when associated with real estate. Discuss why real estate borrowers and lenders might be more interested in written commitments than are participants in other lending arenas, such as commercial lending.

Construction Loan Example

The following is a simplified example of a conventional construction loan for a self-storage (also known as a miniwarehouse) development with a table of disbursements and interest accumulation through the construction period.

Today most construction loans are made by commercial banks, and they are typically "full-recourse." (A "nonrecourse" loan is secured by only the real estate itself; that is, the lender has "no recourse" to any assets of the borrower other than the real estate in case of default. A "full-recourse" loan is the opposite. The lender has "recourse" to other assets of the borrower as collateral, not just the real estate, so that full dollar recovery can be made in case of default.) As cash flows are negative (the development is spending, not making, money) during the construction stage of most projects, construction loans generally are interest only. Interest payments may be made to the construction lender throughout the construction term or, as in the example, borrowed as part of the loan and advanced as part of the monthly draw. The results are exactly the opposite of a typical self-amortizing mortgage loan in which the principal balance decreases each month throughout the term of the loan. The balance of a construction loan increases with each draw during the construction phase by an amount equal to the construction and related expenses plus the interest accumulation.

Though it certainly has not always been the case, today's underwriting standards typically require that the borrower have a precommitted, permanent loan to takeout (replace) the construction lender. The bank also seeks to minimize its lending risk by requiring that the developer contribute 15 percent to 20 percent of the total development costs (the developer's equity contribution) before it begins disbursing funds.

Roxbury Self Storage, Ltd

#1. **Land Acquisition**—See Project Budget for breakdown. Land Acquisition Costs here are paid by the Borrower/Developer as part of his 15 percent to 20 percent equity contribution = $546,000.

#2. **Closing Costs**—See Project Budget for breakdown. Closing Costs here are paid by the Borrower/Developer as part of his 15 percent to 20 percent equity contribution = $47,631.85.

#3. **Construction**—See Construction Detail Breakdown.

#4. **Fees**—$10,475 miscellaneous construction related legal fees.

#5. **Legal**—$40,000. Here, in addition to assorted legal fees that are incurred throughout the development process, this includes some legal expense ($8,000) for zoning and entitlements, which are included as part of the Borrower/Developer's equity contribution.

#6. **Developer's Fee**—The Borrower/Developer here is able to charge the project a fee in the amount of $335,000 to compensate him for his time, risk, and out-of-pocket expenses incurred in putting the project together. Although this varies with lenders, most construction lenders are amenable to about a 10 percent development fee.

#7. **Property Taxes**—In this example, property taxes are due January 31 for the preceding year. This $12,446.75 expense (taxes on the raw land) can be expected to increase substantially next year when the development is completed.

#8. **Contingency**—The construction lender's primary concern is that the borrower has the financial capacity to complete the planned project on time and on budget. Accordingly, after thoroughly evaluating the project and assessing the borrower's professional and financial capabilities, the prudent lender will be sure to include a contingency amount, generally, 2 percent to 5 percent of the total project budget, to provide funds to cover unanticipated problems.

#9. **Operating Deficit**—This $81,529 expense is start-up expenses. It includes such preopening expenses as:

Computer and Monitor	$1,500
Laser Printer	900
Miscellaneous Software	3,000
Office Supplies	1,200
Petty Cash and Cash Drawer	1,000
Copier	550
Fax Machine	200
Telephones Expense	300
Inventory Fixtures	4,500
Retail Inventory	4,000
Office/Gate Signage, Banners, etc.	850
Cleaning Equipment and Supplies	1,200
Personnel (preopening)	4,000
Advertising	3,600
Total	26,800

Added to this are the costs associated with operating the property from the opening date through the stabilization date, which here is assumed to be 12 months and to total $54,729. As the property leases up over the first year of operations, the amount of monthly shortfall decreases until (in theory) its revenues are sufficient to cover the expenses associated with operating the property (it stabilizes).

#10. **Amount Funded by Developer**—This is the amount of the Borrower/Developer's equity that the construction lender requires be in the deal before any of the funds borrowed from the construction lender are released. Typically, this will be in the range of 15 percent to 20 percent of the expected construction loan amount. Reference #1, #2, and #5 above.

#11. **Amount Funded by Loan**—This is simply the monthly amount advanced by the construction lender after the Borrower/Developer's required equity contribution is in the deal.

#12. **Interest Rate**—In this example, the unpaid principal balance bears interest at a floating rate equal to the prime rate (as reported in The Wall Street Journal), plus 1 percent per annum. The calculation of the interest due is simply the product of the previous period's principal balance excluding interest, times this period's interest rate, times the number of days outstanding since the previous calculation, all divided by 360 days. For simplicity purposes, interest on the principal amount outstanding is adjusted monthly in this example, the rate for each month being the rate in effect at the close of business the last day of the previous month. In an actual construction loan, it would, typically, be calculated on the principal amount adjusted daily, the rate for each day being the rate in effect at the close of business on that day. It is notable that the term of this construction loan begins in December 2000 and ends in December 2002, a period during which the prime rate fell by 475 basis points, making it a particularly good period to illustrate the calculation of interest accrual over the term of a construction loan. (A basis point equals one one-hundredth of one percentage point. Thus, if the prime rate falls from 9.5 percent to 4.75 percent, it is said to have decreased by 475 basis points.) The rate on the construction loan could just as easily have gone the other way, as it did over the period from March 1994 through March 1995, when the prime rate increased by 300 basis points.

#13. **Interest Due**—Interest due in any month Y = the previous month's principal balance excluding interest, times interest rate associated with month Y, times the number of days since the last draw (which, in this example, is one month) divided by 360.

#14. **Principal Balance Excluding Interest**—The sum of the previous month's principal balance excluding interest plus the amount funded by loan during the current month.

#15. **Principal Balance Including Interest**—Simply the above plus interest due, as calculated in #14 above. The following is a simplified example of a conventional construction loan for a self-storage (also known as a miniwarehouse) development with a table of disbursements and interest accumulation through the construction period.

TABLE 12.2 | Roxbury Self Storage, LTD, Construction Loan Draw

Requisition	Date	Land Acquisition #1	Closing Costs #2	Construction #3	Fees #4	Legal #5	Developer Fee #6	Property Taxes #7	Contingency #8
Loan Closing	31-Dec-00	$546,000.00	$47,631.85						
1	31-Jan-01			$47,201.22		$8,000.00		$12,446.75	
2	28-Feb-01			1,250.84					
3	31-Mar-01			20,087.52					
4	30-Apr-01			5,515.80	$1,327.50				
5	31-May-01			5,396.25	1,196.76				
6	30-Jun-01			30,159.19	1,504.00	11,000.00	83,750.00		
7	31-Jul-01			203,343.81					
8	31-Aug-01			403,392.45	2,537.00				
9	30-Sep-01			528,327.28					
10	31-Oct-01			428,915.24	3,909.00	9,000.00	83,750.00		
11	30-Nov-01			240,850.68					
12	31-Dec-01			241,563.81		12,000.00			
13	31-Jan-02			211,777.11			83,750.00		
14	28-Feb-02			17,399.95					
15	31-Mar-02								
16	30-Apr-02								
17	31-May-02								
18	30-Jun-02						83,750.00		
19	31-Jul-02								
20	31-Aug-02								
21	30-Sep-02								
22	31-Oct-02								
23	30-Nov-02								
24	31-Dec-02								
Total		$546,000.00	$47,631.85	$2,385,181.14	$10,474.26	$40,000.00	$335,000.00	$12,446.75	$144,000.00
Budget		$546,000.00	$47,631.85	$2,384,942.12	$10,475.00	$40,000.00	$335,000.00	$12,300.00	$144,000.00

TABLE 12.2	Roxbury Self Storage, LTD, Construction Loan Draw *(continued)*

Requisition	Date	Operating Deficit #9	Amount Funded by Developer #10	Amount Funded by Loan #11	Interest Rate #12	Principal Interest Due #13	Balance Excluding Interest #14	Balance Including Interest #15
Loan Closing	31-Dec-00		$601,631.87		10.50%	-	-	-
1	31-Jan-01			$59,647.97	10.50%	-	$59,647.97	$59,647.97
2	28-Feb-01			1,250.84	9.50%	$440.73	60,898.91	61,339.54
3	31-Mar-01			20,087.52	9.50%	498.19	80,986.33	81,925.25
4	30-Apr-01			6,843.30	9.00%	607.40	87,829.63	89,375.95
5	31-May-01			6,593.01	8.50%	642.86	94,422.64	96,611.82
6	30-Jun-01			126,413.19	8.00%	629.48	220,835.83	223,654.49
7	31-Jul-01			203,343.81	7.75%	1,437.77	424,179.64	428,472.07
8	31-Aug-01			405,929.45	7.75%	2,830.81	830,109.09	837,232.33
9	30-Sep-01			528,327.28	7.50%	5,188.18	1,358,436.36	1,370,747.79
10	31-Oct-01			516,574.24	7.00%	8,188.35	1,875,010.61	1,895,510.39
11	30-Nov-01			249,850.66	6.50%	10,156.31	2,124,861.27	2,155,517.36
12	31-Dec-01	26,800.00		268,363.80	6.00%	10,978.45	2,393,225.07	2,434,859.61
13	31-Jan-02	7,500.00		231,277.11	5.75%	11,849.79	2,624,502.18	2,677,986.51
14	28-Feb-02	7,168.00		108,317.95	5.75%	11,737.36	2,732,820.13	2,798,041.81
15	31-Mar-02	6,792.00		6,792.00	5.75%	13,531.26	2,739,612.13	2,818,365.07
16	30-Apr-02	6,365.00		6,365.00	5.75%	13,127.31	2,745,977.13	2,837,857.38
17	31-May-02	5,882.00		5,882.00	5.75%	13,596.40	2,751,859.13	2,857,335.78
18	30-Jun-02	5,335.00		89,085.00	5.75%	13,185.99	2,840,944.13	2,959,606.77
19	31-Jul-02	4,715.00		4,715.00	5.75%	14,066.62	2,845,659.13	2,978,388.39
20	31-Aug-02	4,012.00		4,012.00	5.75%	14,089.97	2,849,671.13	2,996,490.15
21	30-Sep-02	3,216.00		3,216.00	5.75%	13,654.67	2,852,887.13	3,013,361.03
22	31-Oct-02	2,315.00		2,315.00	5.75%	14,125.75	2,855,202.13	3,029,801.78
23	30-Nov-02	1,293.00		1,293.00	5.75%	13,681.18	2,856,495.13	3,044,775.96
24	31-Dec-02	136.00		136.00	5.75%	14,143.62	2,856,631.13	3,059,055.58
Total		$81,529.00		$2,856,631.14		$202,424.45		$3,059,055.58
Budget		$54,729.00				$200,000.00		$3,775,077.97

TABLE 12.3 | Roxbury Self Storage, LTD, Construction Detail Breakdown

	1/31/01 Draw 1	2/28/01 Draw 2	3/31/01 Draw 3	4/30/01 Draw 4	5/31/01 Draw 5	6/30/01 Draw 6	7/31/01 Draw 7	8/31/01 Draw 8
General Conditions	$11,557.89	$1,250.84	$1,342.89	$420.00		$17,284.02	$6,603.08	$28,763.58
Site Work							182,266.38	92,415.60
Concrete								212,215.50
Masonry								
Metals								
Woods & Plastics								
Thermal & Moisture Prot.								
Doors & Windows								
Finishes								5,393.07
Specialties								
Equipment								
Security Systems								
Conveying Systems								
Mechanical								1,625.13
Electrical								23,560.20
Architectural/Engineering	31,648.33		18,744.63	2,800.80		4,825.11	1,121.18	2,716.39
Permits/Fees	3,995.00			2,295.00		6,825.00		
Overhead & Profit					5,396.25	1,225.06	13,353.16	25,849.71
Change Orders								
Signage								
Off/Apt								
Construction Supervision								10,853.27
Retainage Release								
	$47,201.22	$1,250.84	$20,087.52	$5,515.80	$5,396.25	$30,159.19	$203,343.80	$403,392.45

TABLE 12.3 | Roxbury Self Storage, LTD, Construction Detail Breakdown *(continued)*

	1/31/01 Draw 9	2/28/01 Draw 10	3/31/01 Draw 11	4/30/01 Draw 12	5/31/01 Draw 13	6/30/01 Draw Final	Total
General Conditions	$7,719.07	$14,487.19	$11,107.71	$114,737.93			$215,274.20
Site Work	75,625.47	43,327.80	38,618.77	63.90			$432,317.92
Concrete	3,680.10	2,686.50					$218,582.10
Masonry	81,032.40	990.00					$82,022.40
Metals	245,139.34	113,623.53	11,101.13				$369,864.00
Woods & Plastics	30,579.30						$30,579.30
Thermal & Moisture Prot.		4,109.40					$4,109.40
Doors & Windows	538.20	115,918.85	26,506.67	3,248.49			$146,212.21
Finishes		14,328.00	15,513.30	9,741.60			$44,975.97
Specialties			4,766.34	10,975.78			$16,642.12
Equipment	5,758.20						$5,758.20
Security Systems				31,672.82		17,399.95	$49,072.77
Conveying Systems							$0.00
Mechanical	10,239.26	18,099.27	23,643.00	18.94			$53,625.60
Electrical	20,235.60	48,355.33	14,204.62	10,636.16			$116,991.91
Architectural/Engineering	1,991.45	1,303.09	903.53	432.01	555.50		$67,042.02
Permits/Fees			21,706.54	21,706.54			$40,217.79
Overhead & Profit	32,586.65	24,991.24	13,843.20				$111,849.02
Change Orders	1,448.97		8,402.40	19,393.20			$29,244.57
Signage		4,988.50		4,993.28			$9,981.78
Off/Apt			50,533.47	13,943.16			$64,476.63
Construction Supervision	10,853.27	21,706.54	21,706.54				$65,119.62
Retainage Release					211,221.61		$211,221.61
	$528,327.28	$428,915.24	$240,850.68	$241,563.81	$211,777.11	$17,399.95	$2,385,181.14

TABLE 12.4 | Roxbury Self Storage, LTD, Project Budget

	Budgeted	"Actual"	
Land Acquisition	$546,000.00	$546,000.00	not funded
Closing Costs*	47,631.85	47,631.85	not funded
General Contractors†	2,384,942.12	2,385,181.14	
City and Permit Fees	10,475.00	10,474.26	
Legal‡	40,000.00	40,000.00	
Property Taxes	12,300.00	12,446.75	
Operating Deficit	54,729.00	81,529.00	
Interest Expense	200,000.00	202,424.45	
Developer's Fee	335,000.00	335,000.00	
Subtotal	$3,631,077.97	$3,660,687.45	
Contingency	144,000.00	144,000.00	
Total Project Costs	$3,775,077.97	$3,804,687.45	

* Includes:	
Loan Commitment Fee	12,500.00
Attorney & Document Preparation	16,985.80
Title Insurance	11,081.05
Courier/Federal Express Fees	84.00
Escrow Fee to Title Company	125.00
Government Recording and Transfer Charges	106.00
Plan Review Fee to Lender	750.00
Environmental Assessment (Phase I Report)	3,000.00
Appraisal Fee	3,000.00

† Includes all construction
‡ Includes zoning and entitlements

Check		
	$3,804,687.45	Total project costs
	3,059,055.58	Total balance including interest #15
	745,631.87	
	601,631.87	Amount funded by developer
	144,000.00	Contingency not in construction draw

Developing and Analyzing the Income Property Operating Statement

An understanding of the components of income property operating statements permits analysts to evaluate the income stream's viability. After studying this chapter, you should be able to construct an operating statement for a rental property, to compare statements with norms or with statements from comparable properties and judge the significance of variations, and to draw conclusions based on relationships among components.

Mortgage lenders and equity investors alike try to determine rental real estate's prospects for generating net cash flow. Equity investors know that economic benefit from ownership depends on a property's ability to generate cash flow; mortgage lenders understand that cash flow from a mortgaged property provides resources for paying the interest and repaying the principal of the loan and is the ultimate source of market value that provides collateral for the loan.

Investors who include real estate in their portfolios do so because they expect the ownership to generate a stream of economic benefits. Their interest in the physical property typically extends only to the extent that it affects the anticipated stream of economic benefits because real estate assets are only a means to the ultimate end of financial gain. The desirability of an equity position in investment property, therefore, is a function of the amount, the timing, and the certainty of expected cash flows from ownership or, ultimately, from disposal of the property.

Mortgage lenders are concerned about the stream of economic benefits generated by real estate that is pledged as loan collateral. They understand that, in most cases, the property's cash flow will be the principal source of funds to service the debt. Lenders want assurance, therefore, that the cash flow will be sufficient for this purpose and that it will continue over the life of the mortgage indebtedness. Lenders also understand that if a borrower defaults and it becomes necessary to foreclose, the amount, timing, and certainty of expected future cash flows from the property will determine whether a foreclosure sale generates enough money to salvage the loan principal.

A property's past operating history or the recent history of comparable properties is the starting point for forecasting future benefits. This history is incorporated into a forecast by considering how anticipated changes in the economic, social, and political environment will affect the property's ability to generate rents and how these factors will affect the cost of maintaining and operating the property. The analysis will also include a forecast of likely changes in a property's market value over the anticipated holding period. Most of the factors that affect operating performance also influence the property's market value. Additional considerations include expectations for the future and the cost of capital.

As a starting point for addressing these issues, this chapter introduces a typical real property operating statement. It demonstrates how the statement can be rendered more meaningful by analyzing the property's past operating history and using these data to estimate current operating results. The chapter concludes by illustrating how current information can be extended into the future by examining economic trends that might alter the past and present operating environment.

▍OVERVIEW OF THE OPERATING STATEMENT

Traditional income statements, as prepared by accountants, show operating revenues "when earned" and operating expenses "when incurred," whether or not these represent actual cash receipts and disbursements. Real estate investment analysts, however, are concerned with actual cash flows into and out of investors' coffers. Real estate operating statements, therefore, usually present cash inflows and outflows

TABLE 13.1 | Apartment Building Annual Operating Statement

Potential Gross Rent		$1,500,000
Less: Allowance for Vacancies and Rent Loss		90,000
		1,410,000
Plus: Other Income (parking)		9,000
Effective Gross Income		1,419,000
Less: Operating Expenses		
Management Fee	$72,750	
Utilities	126,700	
Insurance	44,400	
Supplies	19,000	
Advertising	20,000	
Maintenance	82,000	
Repairs and Replacements	53,900	
Property Tax	183,000	601,750
Net Operating Income		$817,250
Less: Debt Service		710,000
Before-Tax Cash Flow		$107,250
Less: Income Tax Liability		31,400
After-Tax Cash Flow		$ 75,850

from operations and extend the presentation to include nonoperating cash flows such as those from debt service, income taxes, and capital expenditures. A typical income property operating statement is illustrated in Table 13.1.

The **potential gross rent** shown in Table 13.1 is the amount of rental revenue the property would generate with no vacancies. Adjusting potential gross rent to reflect losses from vacancies and uncollectible accounts and to include income from sources other than rents results in **effective gross income**. On a historical basis, this is the gross revenue a building has actually produced.

Operating expenses, shown in the next section of the operating statement in Table 13.1, include all cash expenditures required to maintain and operate the property so as to generate the gross rent. **Net operating income (NOI)** is simply the difference between effective gross income and operating expenses. Were there no income taxes and no nonoperating expenditures, this would be the net cash flow to the investor.

All entries below NOI in Table 13.1 reflect cash flows stemming from property ownership but not directly attributable to its operation. **Debt service,** for example, is a consequence of using borrowed money to acquire a property. Likewise, the final cash-flow item, *income taxes,* is determined in large measure by the investor's individual income tax position rather than specifically by the operating results of property on which the report is based. The bottom line, **after-tax cash flow**, is the amount of cash remaining at the end of the reporting period after all operating expenses have been paid, all obligations to borrowers satisfied, and all income tax obligations met.

ESTIMATING CURRENT OPERATING RESULTS

The history of a property's recent operations is usually the best starting point for estimating the results of current operations. But unless prepared by a reliable and disinterested party from original source documents, the property's operating records should be viewed with suspicion. Analysts seek to verify all records by referring to the original source documents and by comparing reported operating results with known or determinable outcomes from similar properties in the same market area.

To estimate recent gross income, inspect the property's **rent roll** and leases to determine contract rental rates, vacancies, and **rent concessions** (arrangements between landlords and tenants that result in making actual rents less than those reflected on leases). Verify indicated rental rates, if possible, by conversing with the property manager and tenants. Check conclusions for reasonableness by comparing them with estimates of effective rents in comparable properties in the same market area.

As with gross income, the most appropriate starting point for estimating operating expenses is the immediate past experience of the property. If possible, reconstruct several years of operating history to detect trends. Adjust information provided by the current owner to allow for inconsistencies with data from other sources. Compare results with published averages where possible, and further investigate any seeming inconsistencies or anomalies.

Identifying Comparable Properties

Comparable properties are frequently the most valuable source of data for estimating a property's recent operating history. The challenge is to find properties that are truly comparable. If it is to be useful for estimating ability to command rents, a comparable property must function as a *close* substitute for the one you are analyzing. This means that it must not only offer approximately the same amenities but must also be similarly located. This latter criterion presents a particular challenge and frequently renders impossible the task of collecting a sizable sample of comparable observations.

Comparable properties will closely replicate the physical and locational characteristics of the property under analysis, to the extent that these characteristics affect the ability of the property to command rent.

Functional efficiency and **physical durability** are key physical characteristics affecting a property's ability to remain competitive. Functional efficiency is a measure of how well a property is designed to do the job it is intended to perform. Physical durability is a measure of the structure's remaining physical life and is determined by the soundness of design and the extent to which routine maintenance has forestalled structural deterioration.

Functional efficiency is related to specific property uses and can be evaluated only in that context. Houses are compared with design needs for modern family lifestyles; warehouse design is evaluated in terms of compatibility with modern storage and transportation technology; office buildings are judged according to modern business needs. Well-designed structures may be functionally very efficient when first put into service but may be rendered less appropriate for their tasks as alterations in lifestyles, taste, and technology alter use patterns. Less-well-designed buildings may be functionally inefficient from the outset. Loss of efficiency due to defective or dated design is called **functional obsolescence**. It reduces a building's competitive position relative to more functionally efficient structures and may eventually lead to abandonment or a change of use.

The economic specialization characteristic of modern urban life creates interdependence among sites. The impact of this interdependence can usefully be classified in terms of *key locational characteristics*. Activity at one location generates movement of people and things, the expense of which is called **transfer costs**. Relationships that create such movement are called **linkages**, and properties between which the movement occurs are said to be *linked*. Examples include movement between place of residence and work, school, or shopping; movement of goods between wholesaler and retailer; and movement of raw material to manufacturing locations and of finished goods to points of consumption. The desire to minimize transfer costs is an important factor in many location decisions. Sites that offer greater transfer cost economies have a competitive advantage that enhances their ability to command rents.

Tenants are frequently enticed to locations that actually increase their transfer costs because the desirable neighborhood factors such sites offer more than compensate. Desirable neighborhood factors are those environmental influences that increase a site's value because of their attractiveness. These include such considerations as a prestigious address or aesthetic surroundings, a desirable view, or neighbors whose activities somehow complement those of a tenant.

Using Published Data

Published sources of information on operating expenses for various types and sizes of properties are readily available. These data are generally not sufficiently precise to serve reliably as a sole source of information for re-creating a property's recent operating history because they are simply averages of a group of properties and provide no measure of dispersion about the mean. They do, however, serve as valuable benchmarks against which to compare other data for reasonableness. The most frequently used sources are as follows:

- *Income/Expense Analysis: Apartments* (Chicago: Institute of Real Estate Management), published annually

- *Income/Expense Analysis: Condominiums, Cooperatives and P.U.D.s* (Chicago: Institute of Real Estate Management), published annually

- *Income/Expense Analysis: Suburban Office Buildings* (Chicago: Institute of Real Estate Management), published annually

- *Dollars and Cents of Shopping Centers* (Washington, D.C.: The Urban Land Institute), published periodically

- *Downtown and Suburban Office Building Exchange Report* (Washington, D.C.: Building Owners and Managers Association International), published annually

- *Trends in the Hotel Industry* (London, England: PKF International), published annually

RECONSTRUCTING THE OPERATING HISTORY

To illustrate procedures for estimating the results of current operations where reliable accounting data are not readily available, consider Example 13.1, which provides data on a 50-unit apartment complex called "Noname Apartments."

EXAMPLE 13.1

Noname Apartments is a 50-unit complex consisting of 7 two-bedroom units, each having 1,000 square feet of living area; 25 one-bedroom units, each containing 750 square feet of living area; and 18 studio-type units, each with 600 square feet of living space. The selling price is $2.21 million. The owner provides a statement of the property's most recent annual operating results, presented in Table 13.2.

Estimating Effective Gross Income

Inspecting the rent role of the property in Example 13.1 reveals that some tenants are on 24-month leases, some are on 12-month leases, and some are renting on a month-to-month basis. Contract rental rates, as reported on the rent roll and verified by inspection of the leases, are deemed unreliable indicators of actual market experience because tenants report having received a number of concessions from the landlord. Some received special decorating allowances as an inducement to sign their leases. Others received substantial discounts on parking fees at a nearby garage operated by the same company that owns the apartment building. Concessions seem to be related to periods when vacancies were particularly high, but this is impossible to verify because both the owner and the management firm refuse to confirm concessions reported by tenants.

Fortunately, a number of apartment buildings in the immediate neighborhood offer similar accommodations. Services provided by these other properties are essentially the same as those of the property being analyzed. All the units chosen as sources of comparable market data offer single baths and kitchen-dining room combinations, which conforms to the profile of units in the property under analysis. The data on comparable properties are as follows:

- *Property A* contains a total of 55 units: 10 two-bedroom units with 990 square feet of living area rent for $770 per month; 30 one-bedroom units with 725 square feet rent for $645 per month; 15 studios with 590 square feet rent for $525 per month. Currently, two one-bedroom units and one studio are vacant. All the two-bedroom units are under lease.

TABLE 13.2 | Prior Owner's Operating Statement for Year Ended December 31, 20xx, Noname Apartments

Gross Revenue:
Rent Receipts		$380,000
Parking Fees		4,000
Total		$384,000

Expenses:
Management Fees	$18,100	
Salaries	32,300	
Utilities	17,300	
Insurance	9,000	
Supplies	3,400	
Advertising	4,900	
Maintenance and Repairs	35,600	
Property Taxes	30,000	150,600
Net Income for the Year		$233,400

TABLE 13.3 | Derivation of Market Rental Rates on Properties Deemed Comparable to Noname Apartments

	Comparable Property			
	A	**B**	**C**	**E**
Two-Bedroom Units				
Monthly Rental	$770	$810	$765	$775
Square Feet	990	1025	980	995
Rent per Square Foot	$0.78	$0.79	$0.78	$0.78
One-Bedroom Units				
Monthly Rental	$645	$660	$640	$655
Square Feet	725	750	730	755
Rent per Square Foot	$0.89	$0.88	$0.88	$0.87
Studio Units				
Monthly Rental	$525	$540	$525	$575
Square Feet	590	610	595	650
Rent per Square Foot	$0.89	$0.89	$0.88	$0.88

- *Property B* is a 60-unit building with 20 two-bedroom, 20 one-bedroom, and 20 studio units. Two-bedroom units have 1,025 square feet of living area and rent for $810 per month. One-bedroom units have 750 square feet of living area and rent for $660. Studios contain 610 square feet and command rents of $540. Currently, one two-bedroom, one one-bedroom, and one studio unit are vacant.

- *Property C* has 90 units, of which 20 are two-bedroom and 45 are one-bedroom apartments. The remaining 25 units are all studios. Two-bedroom units contain 980 square feet of living area and rent for $765. One-bedroom units have 730 square feet of living area and rent for $640. Studios have 595 square feet of living area and rent for $525. This complex currently has two vacant one-bedroom units and two vacant studios. All two-bedroom units are rented.

- *Property D* is a 120-unit building containing 30 two-bedroom, 66 one-bedroom, and 24 studio apartments. Two-bedroom units each have 995 square feet of living area and rent for $775. One-bedroom units have 755 square feet of living area and rent for $655. Studios rent for $575 and have 650 square feet of living area. There are five vacant one-bedroom and one vacant studio apartments.

Table 13.3 consolidates and arrays gross rental data from the sample of comparable properties. Expressing gross rents on a per-square-foot basis for each type of rental unit eliminates minor differences due to variation in the size of units and thus facilitates comparison. The data suggest the single best estimate of market rental value for two-bedroom units is 78 cents per square foot. The best estimate of rental values for both one-bedroom units and for studios appears to be 88 cents per square foot. Studio apartments renting for no more per square foot than one-bedroom units is cause for reflection, but this conclusion is reinforced by discussions with local property management specialists, who report that the market simply will not support higher rates for studios.

Vacancy data from the market sample are consolidated and arrayed in Table 13.4, along with inferences drawn about appropriate market vacancy rates. Because the data are drawn from such a small sample, there is a large probable error. Ideally, a much larger sample would be employed, perhaps permitting application of formal statistical sampling techniques, but a sample of that nature is frequently either impossible or prohibitively expensive to collect.

Because the sample is so small, an unusually high (or low) vacancy rate in one of the comparable properties would have a disproportionate impact on the average for the sample. The aberration might be caused by some temporary problem with the property, incompetent management, or some other factor that should not be attributed to the property being analyzed. For these reasons, the analyst's judgment is an important factor in drawing inferences from sample data. For the Noname Apartments, we conclude that market estimates in fact reflect most likely experience under typically competent management.

TABLE 13.4 | Derivation of Market Vacancy Factors Applicable to Noname Apartments

| | Comparable Property | | | | |
	A	B	C	E	Total
Two-Bedroom Units					
Number of Units	10	20	20	30	80
Vacancies	0	1	0	0	1
Percent Vacant	0	5.0	0	0	1.2
One-Bedroom Units					
Number of Units	30	20	45	66	161
Vacancies	2	1	2	5	10
Percent Vacant	6.7	5.0	4.4	7.6	6.2
Studio Units					
Number of Units	15	20	25	24	84
Vacancies	1	1	2	1	5
Percent Vacant	6.7	5.0	8.0	4.2	6.0

Data concerning market rental rates and most probable vacancy experience, drawn from the comparable properties and exhibited in Tables 13.3 and 13.4, are employed to arrive at estimates of potential gross rent and allowance for vacancy losses for the Noname Apartments. Final conclusions are computed in Table 13.5 and are incorporated into the first-year operating forecast, which is shown in Table 13.6.

Estimating Current Operating Expenses

Operating expenses reported by a previous or current owner will often be unreliable. The owner might not understand what items are conventionally included in expenses. An early step, therefore, is to convert the current owner's statement to a more useful format, eliminating items that are not properly included in expenses and adding items that should be there but have been excluded.

The prior owner of Noname Apartments reported the operating results shown in Table 13.2. That owner revealed that maintenance and repair charges included expenditures to replace outmoded bathroom fixtures and bragged that personally doing considerable maintenance work enabled operating expenses to be held to a low level. Comparing Noname Apartments with similar apartment buildings in the

TABLE 13.5 | Estimated Gross Revenue and Vacancy Rates for Noname Apartments

	2-bedroom	1-bedroom	Studio
Estimated Potential Gross (monthly)			
Market Value per Sq. Ft.	$0.78	$0.88	$0.88
Times: Sq. Ft. per Unit	1000	750	600
Rent per Unit	$780	$660	$528
Times: Number of Units	7	25	18
Total Potential Monthly Rent	$5,460	16,500	$9,504
Annual (Monthly × 12)	$65,520	$198,000	$114,048
Estimated Vacancy Factor			
Annual Potential Gross	$65,520	$198,000	$114,048
Times: Vacancy Factor			
(From Table 13.4)	0.012 (1.2%)	0.062 (6.2%)	0.060 (6.0%)
Vacancy Loss Estimate	$786	$12,276	$6,843

Total Annual Potential Gross Revenue (rounded to nearest $1,000) = $378,000

Total Annual Vacancy Loss Estimate (rounded to nearest $1,000) = $ 20,000

TABLE 13.6 | First-Year Operating Forecast for Noname Apartments

Potential Gross Rent		$378,000
Less: Allowance for Vacancies		20,000
		358,000
Plus: Other Income (parking)		4,000
Effective Gross Income		$362,000
Less: Operating Expenses		
Management Fee	$18,100	
Salary Expense	32,300	
Utilities	17,300	
Insurance	9,000	
Supplies	3,400	
Advertising	4,900	
Maintenance and Repairs	29,000	
Property Tax	49,000	163,000
Net Operating Income Annual		$199,000

area reveals that a maintenance and repair program, including all routine costs but excluding items properly attributable to capital expenditures, typically costs about 8 percent of effective gross rent.

The prior owner's statement shows $30,000 of property taxes, but the tax assessor indicates that property taxes for the ensuing year will be about $49,000. All other reported expense items appear reasonable for a building this size and age, based on the analyst's experience with comparable properties and on reference to published standards.

REVISED OPERATING FORECAST

Effective gross income estimated for the ensuing year, after including revised estimates of vacancy losses and parking income, is $362,000. Revised operating expenses, adjusted for expected changes during the ensuing year, total $163,000. These computations yield an estimated first-year NOI of $199,000. These revised revenue and expense estimates are presented in the operating forecast in Table 13.6. The first-year forecast, adjusted to eliminate the influence of extraordinary items, is generally incorporated in the appraiser's estimate of a property's market value. This topic is addressed in Chapter 14.

RATIO ANALYSIS

Ratios are widely employed to gauge the reasonableness of relationships between various measures of value and performance. They figure prominently in many appraisals, a topic addressed in Chapter 14, but are also useful in judging the reasonableness of reported or forecasted operating results and making preliminary property acquisition or disposition decisions. They are also useful adjuncts to other analytical steps for a lender evaluating a loan application.

Income multipliers express the relationship between market value and either gross or net income from operations. The operating ratio highlights the relationship between gross income and operating expenses. The breakeven ratio shows the percent of gross income required to meet cash expenditure requirements.

Income Multipliers

Income multiplier analysis is a simple technique whose contemporary usefulness belies its antiquity. Income multipliers express the relationship between price and either gross or net income, and it is often used as an adjunct to the direct sales comparison approach to value estimating.

Multipliers are also valuable tools for equity investors. The multipliers do not serve as ample tools of analysis in isolation, but can play a valuable role as preliminary filters. Multiplier analysis permits obviously unacceptable opportunities to be weeded out swiftly and inexpensively. More extensive (and more costly) analysis can then be concentrated on properties that show promise of meeting predetermined investor criteria.

To use multiplier analysis as a filter, first determine the relationship prevailing in the market area of interest for properties comparable to that being investigated. Automatically reject all opportunities whose multipliers exceed this benchmark figure. Opportunities that pass the preliminary screening test are subjected to further analysis.

Gross income multipliers, also often referred to as **gross rent multipliers,** reflect the relationship between a property's price and its effective gross income.

When using gross income multiplier analysis for initial evaluation of prospective property acquisitions, the analyst must decide whether to use potential or effective gross income estimates. The determining factor is likely to be the form in which data are available. Data regarding vacancy rates and credit losses will often be unreliable and difficult to verify. For this reason the most appropriate measure will most likely be potential gross income. Using data from Example 13.1 and Table 13.6, we can determine that the gross income multiplier for Noname Apartments is 5.85:

$$\text{Multiplier} = \text{Market price/Potential gross income}$$
$$= \$2,210,000/\$378,000$$
$$= 5.85$$

Net income multipliers are calculated in the same fashion. They differ only in that net income instead of potential gross income is employed as the divisor. Because substantial research may be necessary to determine the appropriate measure of NOI, gross income multiplier analysis is generally the more useful profitability measure. From Example 13.1 and Table 13.6 we can determine that the net income multiplier for Noname Apartments is 11.11:

$$\text{Net income multiplier} = \text{Market price/Net operating income}$$
$$= \$2,210,000/\$199,000$$
$$= 11.11$$

Financial Ratios

Frequently employed examples of ratio analysis include the operating ratio, the breakeven ratio, and the debt coverage ratio.

The **operating ratio** is the percentage of effective gross income consumed by operating expenses. It will be lower for relatively more efficient properties. The operating ratio, however, can be misleading because it reflects in part the efficiency of management as well as of the property itself. Some investors, in fact, look for properties with high operating ratios, intending to reduce the ratios through efficient management and thereby increase indicated property values. The operating ratio for Noname Apartments (using data from Table 13.6) is 45 percent:

$$\text{Operating ratio} = \text{Operating expenses / Effective gross income}$$
$$= \$163,000/\$362,000$$
$$= 45\%$$

Breakeven ratio analysis, as traditionally employed in real estate, tends to be less useful than its counterpart in corporate finance. Corporate financial analysts express the relationship as it exists between gross revenues and variable costs, while real estate analysts relate gross revenues to total costs. As real estate occupancy levels change, the operating ratio as traditionally expressed may be altered drastically. The ratio between gross revenue and variable expenses, in contrast, tends to remain relatively more constant and so provides a more reliable indicator.

Breakeven ratios (frequently called **default ratios**) are most useful when employed on a before-tax cash-flow basis. They indicate the relationship between cash inflows and outflows from all sources, including debt service payments ($165,615 for this property—20-year, monthly payment loan for $1,650,000 at 8 percent). The lower the breakeven cash-flow ratio, the greater the decline in gross revenue (or the increase in operating expenses) can be before investors experience negative cash flow from a project. This makes the ratio a useful measure of risk for the mortgage lender. Applying the formula to the Noname Apartment project in Example 13.1 and using data from Table 13.6 reveals that the breakeven point occurs at 90.8 percent of projected effective gross income:

$$\text{Breakeven ratio} = (\text{Operating expenses} + \text{Debt service})/\text{Effective gross income}$$
$$= (\$163,000 + \$165,615)/\$362,000$$
$$= 0.908, \text{ or } 90.8\%$$

The **debt coverage ratio** was introduced in Chapter 5. By expressing the extent to which NOI can decline before becoming insufficient to meet the debt service obligation, this ratio provides an indication of safety associated with the use of borrowed funds. The debt coverage ratio for Noname Apartments (using data from Example 13.1 and Table 13.6) is determined to be 1.20:

$$\text{Debt coverage ratio} = \text{Net operating income}/\text{Annual debt service}$$
$$= \$199,000/\$165,615$$
$$= 1.20$$

TRADITIONAL PROFITABILITY MEASURES

A shared characteristic of all traditional profitability measures is an attempt to relate cash investment to expected cash returns in some systematic fashion. They have not been equally successful in those attempts. Traditional techniques differ in the degree to which they incorporate available data into the analysis. They differ also in that some ignore the issue of risk, while others make rudimentary attempts to adjust for risk differentials.

Overall Capitalization Rate

Also known as the **free-and-clear rate of return**, the **overall capitalization rate** (or *cap rate*) expresses the first year's expected NOI as a percentage of market price. We saw earlier that a market-derived capitalization rate can be used to estimate market value. When market value has been estimated, the capitalization rate can be computed and compared with market rates to judge the reasonableness of the value estimate. The rate for Noname Apartments (using data from Example 13.1 and Table 13.6) is determined to be 9 percent:

$$\text{Rate} = \text{Net operating income/Market price}$$
$$= \$199,000/\$2,210,000$$
$$= 0.09, \text{ or } 9\%$$

Recall that the net income multiplier is market price divided by NOI. The overall capitalization rate, therefore, is simply the reciprocal of the net income multiplier. Thus, for Noname Apartments, the reciprocal of the 9 percent capitalization rate is 1/0.09, or 11.11, which is the net income multiplier for the example.

Usefulness of overall capitalization rates is limited by the nature of financing arrangements and by the approach most investors take to arrive at an acceptable sales price. In a typical negotiating session there is an acknowledged trade-off between price and financing terms. Because this trade-off is not reflected in the overall capitalization rate, comparison of rates between properties with significantly different financing arrangements can be misleading.

SUMMARY

Real estate value stems from the stream of future benefits that ownership or use bestows. Estimating the value of real estate to individual investors therefore entails forecasting the stream of benefits that will flow from the investment. The starting point for such a forecast is to reconstruct the operating history of the property. Past trends are projected into the future, with revisions to reflect perceived changes in the economic, political, and social environment that are likely to affect the property's ability to generate future benefits.

A typical operating statement starts with an expression of the gross rent the property would generate if fully rented. This amount is adjusted for vacancies and rent losses, plus revenue from sources other than rent, to arrive at effective gross revenue. Subtracting operating expenses from the effective gross revenue yields net operating income. This amount is adjusted for financing costs and income taxes to arrive at an estimate of net cash flow to the equity investor.

Sources of information regarding rental revenue and operating expenses include the past operating history of the property itself, the operating records of comparable properties, and data from published sources. The last source supplies primarily benchmark information against which to gauge the reasonableness of data from other sources.

Lenders and appraisers often rely on ratio analysis to gauge the reasonableness of various measures of value and property performance. Income multipliers show the relationship between property value and income-generating capacity. Operating ratios show the percentage of effective gross rent consumed by operating expenses and are a measure of operating efficiency. The breakeven ratio shows the occupancy level required for an income property to cover all related expenditures. Capitalization rates are the ratio of property net operating income to market value.

KEY TERMS

after-tax cash flow

breakeven ratio (default ratio)

debt coverage ratio

debt service

effective gross income

functional efficiency

functional obsolescence

gross income multiplier (gross rent multiplier)

income multiplier analysis

linkages

net income multiplier

net operating income (NOI)

operating expenses

operating ratio

overall capitalization rate (free-and-clear rate of return, cap rate)

physical durability

potential gross rent

rent concessions

rent roll

transfer costs

RECOMMENDED READING

Friedman, Jack P., and Nicholas Ordway. *Income Property Appraisal and Analysis*. Reston, Va.: Reston Publishing Company, Inc., 1981, 133–50.

Kolbe, Phillip T., and Gaylon E. Greer. *Investment Analysis for Real Estate Decisions*, 6th ed. Chicago: Dearborn Real Estate Education, 2006, chapters 4–7 and 9.

Neels, Kevin. *Revenue and Expense Accounts for Rental Properties*. Santa Monica, Calif.: Rand Corporation, 1982.

Ring, Alfred A., and James H. Boykin. *The Valuation of Real Estate,* 3rd ed. Englewood Cliffs, N.J.: Prentice-Hall, 1986, 248–82.

INTERNET REFERENCES

Operating income statement for one- to four-family investment property and two- to four-family owner-occupied property:
www.dallasappraisal.com/images/opinc.pdf

General resource for real estate valuation:
www.pwcreval.com/survey/faq.asp

For information on commercial loans:
www.c-lender.com

REVIEW QUESTIONS

1. How do income and expense statements prepared by accountants differ from operating statements used by real estate investment analysts?

2. What items should be considered when forecasting income and expenses over an investor's anticipated holding period?

3. Carefully inspect the prior owner's operating statement for Noname Apartments (Table 13.2). Do you see any problems with the owner's presentation of income and expenses?

4. Describe the process used to estimate rentals for the Noname Apartments.

5. List some of the considerations inherent in the expense items as presented by the current owner of the Noname Apartments.

6. What is the value of published data in developing an estimate of the operating history of a property?

7. Describe some of the forces affecting the ability of a property to generate rents.

8. How are income multipliers used in measuring investment worth?

9. Why might some investors search out properties with high operating ratios?

DISCUSSION QUESTIONS

1. Offering brochures for rental property frequently state that current rental rates can be raised. Comment on such claims.

2. How does our concept of gross income and operating expenses differ from those you studied in accounting? Which is the correct definition?

3. You are analyzing a new apartment complex (the only one of its kind) recently constructed on the fringe of an urban area. Because of its access to open areas and freedom from congestion, noise, and so forth, the units are in great demand. In fact, net operating income per rental unit is almost 50 percent above that of slightly older but otherwise comparable units that are clustered in an area closer to the central city. Because of the high rents and virtual zero vacancies that yield a 50 percent premium in net operating income, the owner argues that his property is worth 50 percent more than the other units. Comment on this assertion.

PROBLEMS

1. Use the following information on Maegen's Manor Apartments to develop an operating statement down to net operating income (expense data represent annual averages).

Advertising:	$ 800
Insurance:	5,000
Laundry Room Income:	600
Maintenance:	9,800
Manager Salary:	8,000
Real Estate Taxes:	25,000
Rents: 40 Studio Units at $500 per Month	
Repairs & Replacements:	7,000
Supplies:	3,000
Utilities:	10,200

Vacancy and Bad Debts: 9 percent of potential gross

2. If comparable apartments in the area have rents of $540 per unit, what would be the net operating income of Maegen's Manor Apartments (in Problem 1) after raising the rents to the same level as the comparable units, assuming no change in vacancy and bad debt losses?

3. If increasing the rents to the level suggested in Problem 2 drives the vacancy and bad debt losses for Maegen's Manor Apartments to 15 percent of potential gross, what will the net operating income be?

4. An analysis of comparable apartments and industry averages reveals the following percentages (of effective gross income) for various operating expenses for buildings like Maegen's Manor Apartments (presented in Problem 1):

Advertising:	1%
Insurance:	3
Maintenance:	5
Management:	5
Real Estate Taxes:	12
Repairs & Replacements:	4
Supplies:	1
Utilities:	5

How do the estimates for Maegen's Manor Apartments (presented in Problem 1) compare with these percentages? What might this tell you about the expense estimates for Maegen's Manor Apartments?

5. Caveat Majeure, a recently rehabilitated apartment building, is offered for sale at $3.5 million. A typical buyer can expect to borrow 70 percent of the purchase price on a first mortgage loan with interest at 8 percent and level monthly payments based on a 20-year amortization. The first-year operating forecast, which is believed to be reliable, is presented below.

Potential Gross Income	$740,000
Less: Vacancies and Uncollectable Rent	37,000
Effective Gross Income	$703,000
Less: Operating Expenses	400,000
Net Operating Income	$303,000

6. Based on the first-year forecast and assuming the property is purchased for the asking price, compute the following:

   a. Potential gross rent multiplier

   b. Effective gross rent multiplier

   c. Net income multiplier

   d. Operating ratio

   e. Breakeven (default) ratio

   f. Debt coverage ratio

   g. Overall capitalization rate

Traditional Approaches to Measuring Property Value

After studying this chapter, you should understand how appraisers use the three approaches to real estate value and reconcile them into a single opinion of value. You should be able to extract operating ratios and financial ratios from an appraisal report and use them to draw conclusions about the safety of a lender's principal.

When a lender receives an application for a mortgage loan to finance the development or acquisition of a real estate asset, the loan officer faces the problem of evaluating the degree of risk inherent in the mortgage investment. This is perhaps the most difficult, yet the most critical, challenge facing the lender.

Mortgage risk is the danger that the expected yield or the principal will be impaired. What is the likelihood that the borrower will fail to meet the terms of the contract? If he or she does, what are the lender's chances of salvaging the principal amount of the debt?

Earlier chapters have made the case that the best assurance that the repayment obligation will be honored is a reasonable likelihood that the mortgaged property will generate an income stream sufficient to meet the debt service obligation. A second level of assurance is the character of the borrower: Does the applicant have a record of honoring financial obligations even under difficult circumstances? The lender's fallback position, the recourse when all else fails, is foreclosure.

In a sense, foreclosure is an admission of failure. The lender has misjudged the borrower or the economic climate and has abandoned all hope of resuscitating the loan. Now comes the attempt to salvage the principal by a foreclosure sale of the collateral.

Anticipating the possibility of such an outcome, the analyst will be concerned with the relationship between the amount of principal at risk and the market value of the collateral—the **loan-to-value ratio**. This ratio was discussed in earlier chapters, but the collateral's value was taken as a given. The reality is that value can never be determined exactly, short of an actual sale. It can only be estimated, and that is the job of the real estate appraiser.

An early step in the analysis of mortgage risk, therefore, is an appraisal of the property. This figure is an expert opinion of the current market value; what the property would sell for as of the date of the appraisal, if it had been exposed to the market for a reasonable time prior to that date. The estimate presumes reasonably informed parties, each acting in his or her own best interest and with neither subject to undue compulsion.

The premier textbook on real estate appraising, *The Appraisal of Real Estate* (Chicago: The American Institute of Real Estate Appraisers), now in its 12th edition, contains more than 700 pages. Obviously, therefore, we can only skim the surface here. Anyone interested in an in-depth understanding should delve into the Appraisal Institute's extensive library of materials on the subject.

▌ THE ECONOMIC BASIS OF PROPERTY VALUE ───────────

The analyst usually starts by analyzing the economic environment of the property being appraised. A typical first step is observations about the relationship between the national or regional economy and that of the city or community in which the property is located. The analysis proceeds from the wider or more general to the narrow and more specific—from the general economy to the neighborhood. Although this part of an appraisal report is often skipped by the mortgage loan analysis, it should, in fact, be studied intensely. Because the property is immovable, its value is acutely influenced by favorable or unfavorable neighborhood trends.

THE LOCATIONAL BASIS OF PROPERTY VALUE

The users of a site will be concerned with convenience and accessibility. They may also be concerned about aesthetic issues such as the view from the property itself and from major access routes. All these factors will influence the relative desirability of the property and thus its market value.

Convenience and Accessibility

How much time and resources are consumed in moving people and material from and to the site? Other things being equal, users will prefer a site that minimizes the aggregate costs associated with such movement. Therefore, sites with a locational advantage will tend to command premium market prices, and those less advantageously located will suffer in comparison.

Locational elements will differ in their importance, depending on the use for which the site is intended. Residential properties will need short and convenient routes to schools and to shopping and employment centers. Retail sites will need to be advantageously located relative to their prospective customer base. Manufacturing facilities will need a location that permits convenient access to workers and raw materials and economical shipment of finished products.

Neighborhood Factors

Even when no movement of people or goods is involved, property values are influenced by location near certain points in the landscape. A prestigious address can be an important contribution to value, particularly for residential properties.

A location with a desirable view will command a premium price if used for residential or office purposes. In contrast, unfavorable exposure can detract from market value. Locations near objectionable or incompatible uses often have a depressing impact on desirability and thus, on value. Examples include noise from traffic or activity at other sites, smoke, odors, or congestion.

THE PHYSICAL BASIS OF PROPERTY VALUE

The appraisal analyst shifts from analysis of the neighborhood to the specific property and focuses on the physical structure as a foundation of value. The focus should be on the functional efficiency of the layout, the durability of the construction, and the structure's aesthetic appeal.

Functional Efficiency

A property's desirability is in large part determined by how well the design and layout accommodate the intended use: Is a residential structure appropriately designed for modern family sizes and lifestyles? Is an office building sufficiently accommodative of changing business patterns? Does a factory or warehouse layout fit the modern pattern of manufacturing or storage technology?

Some buildings incorporate faulty design and exhibit functional obsolescence even when they are new. More typically, a building will be appropriately designed for its intended use at the time of construction. But things change: lifestyles evolve, technology moves forward, business patterns alter, and so forth. A structure that was ideal for the intended use when it was new might become less competitive as it ages because it does not incorporate the innovative design characteristics of newer buildings.

Physical Durability

Value is affected not only by how well a building accommodates its intended use but also by how long it is likely to continue being productive. How resistant is the structure to wear and tear? How adaptable is it to changing its way of carrying on the intended use? These are measures of a building's remaining economic life.

Aesthetic Appeal

Visual appeal is particularly important in determining the value of dwellings, but it is a major factor in other structures as well. The criterion should not be how well the design appeals to the appraiser's or analyst's tastes, but its appeal to the market in general. How will a typical or representative buyer view the design in comparison with the design of other properties that serve the same purpose?

Good building design, appropriate positioning of buildings on the site, and tasteful landscaping are the keys. Extreme architectural styles or those that do not fit well into the general architectural framework of the neighborhood will not appeal to a wide segment of the buying population and therefore will not make as great a contribution to property value.

THE THREE APPROACHES TO VALUATION ANALYSIS

For well over half a century, real estate appraisers have estimated property value three different ways and reconciled the conclusions into a single estimate of value. These so-named *three approaches* are related in that they all rely on market phenomena as indicators of value:

- The **cost approach** involves estimating the current cost to reproduce or replace building and other improvements on and to the land and subtracting an estimate of value loss due to depreciation. To this amount the appraiser adds an estimate of the site's value.

■ In the **sales comparison approach** the appraiser uses the prices of recently sold comparable properties as an indication of what the subject property would bring if exposed to the market for a reasonable length of time.

■ The **income capitalization approach** measures the value of a property's ability to generate a stream of net operating income (NOI).

In a perfectly efficient economic system and with all supply and demand factors, both short-run and long-term, in equilibrium, the three approaches should result in identical indications of value. But, of course, we do not live in such a world. Consequently, the three approaches are expected to generate differing but closely related value indications that must be reconciled, using the appraiser's informed judgment about their relative reliability.

THE COST APPROACH

Under most circumstances, a rational and informed buyer will pay no more for a property than it would cost to produce an equally desirable substitute. The appraiser estimates the cost to construct a reproduction of or replacement for the existing buildings and site improvements, including a sufficient profit to induce an entrepreneur to undertake such a project. From this estimate, the appraiser subtracts an estimate of accrued depreciation on the buildings and site improvements being appraised. This yields an estimate of the market value of the buildings and other improvements, as they currently exist. Adding an estimate of the site value results in a value indication by the cost approach.

For most improvements, reliable reproduction or replacement cost information is easily obtainable. The information can be either collected from builders in the area or inferred from the actual costs of recently constructed buildings after adjustments for differences in size, design, and construction quality. Most commonly, appraisers rely on estimates from computerized construction cost-estimating services.

Estimating accrued depreciation is usually the most difficult part of the cost approach. The most common procedure is to rely on a computerized cost-estimating service to produce a typical depreciation estimate for a building of the type and age of the one being appraised. Adjustments are necessary for elements of depreciation that are atypical, such as an extraordinarily high level of preventive or deferred maintenance, or for design flaws or unusual neighborhood conditions.

Example 14.1 illustrates the derivation of a value indication using the cost approach.

EXAMPLE 14.1

A "mom-and-pop style" self-storage facility (not institutional quality) contains 36,619 square feet of space. Built 10 years ago, it is expected to have a useful economic life of 50 years. A comparison with recently sold vacant land in the market area results in a value estimate of $.84 per square foot for the land. Reference to a computerized cost service reveals that a typical price for self-storage units of this type (concrete slab floor;

steel frame, roll-up doors, roof, and siding) is $25.40 per square foot. The paving is part concrete (988 square feet) but mostly asphalt (47,000 square feet). The cost service reports the concrete paving to cost $3.50 per square foot and the asphalt to cost $2.25. The facility is protected with 5,250 feet of chain link fencing estimated to cost $1.50 per linear foot. Architectural fees are estimated to be 3.5 percent of total cost. For a project of this type, entrepreneurs typically expect a profit of about 25 percent of cost. Market value estimated by the cost approach is $1,155,000:

Replacement Cost New:		
Buildings (36,619 sq. ft. @ $25.40)		$930,123
Paving		
Concrete (988 sq. ft. @ $3.50)	$3,458	
Asphalt (47,000 sq. ft. @ $2.25)	105,750	109,208
Fencing (5,250 linear ft. @ $1.50)		7,875
Subtotal		$1,047,206
Add: Architectural Fee @ 3.5 percent		36,652
Total Cost to Developer		$1,083,858
Add: Entrepreneurial Profit @ 25 percent		270,964
Total Replacement Cost New		$1,354,822
Less: Depreciation (10/50 X $1,354,822)		270,964
Replacement Cost New, Less Accumulated Depreciation		$1,083,858
Add: Land Value (84,607 sq. ft. @ $0.84)		71,070
Total Value Estimate Using the Cost Approach		$1,154,928
Value Estimate, Rounded		$1,155,000

THE SALES COMPARISON APPROACH

In this approach, market value is estimated by analyzing recent sales of similar properties in the same market area. Because no two properties are exactly alike, there is no reason to expect that the property being analyzed will sell for exactly the same amount as any one of those used in the comparative analysis. By adjusting observed sales prices to reflect the influence on value of differences such as size, age, construction quality, special financing, conditions of sale, locational desirability, and market conditions, the appraiser or analyst infers the price at which the subject property would have sold as of the date of the appraisal, if it had been exposed to the market for a reasonable length of time. With a sufficient number of recently sold properties, this approach may yield a very reliable value estimate.

Elements of Comparison

To generate a reliable value estimate by reference to recently sold properties, the appraiser must consider differences between the properties being used for analysis and the property being appraised. The Appraisal Institute lists nine basic elements of comparison that, "in most cases . . . cover all the significant factors to be considered."[1]

Real Property Rights Conveyed

If a comparable property's sale conveyed greater or lesser rights than those associated with the property under appraisal, an adjustment to the observed sales price must be made to reflect the influence on value of this difference. For example, a property might be sold subject to a long-term lease with rents above or below current market rents. Or the property might be subject to an easement that limits the owner's flexibility in how the property is used or altered.

Atypical Financing

Sellers who take back a promissory note at below-market interest in part payment of the purchase price often inflate sales prices. Or the seller might have provided financing on a greater portion of the purchase price than is typical in the market area. Less frequently, a sales price might have been affected because the buyer assumed an outstanding mortgage note that carried a below-market interest rate.

Conditions of Sale

Buyers who are highly motivated will often pay more for a property than it would ordinarily command. Highly motivated sellers might cut the price to effect a quick sale.

Market Conditions

When market conditions have changed since the date of a sale, the sales price must be adjusted to show what the comparable property would have sold for if current market conditions had prevailed at the time of the sale. Market conditions might shift because of changes in available financing, revisions to income tax laws, or changes in supply and demand conditions. If market prices have increased, an upward adjustment will be made to an observed sales price; if prices in general have declined, the adjustment will be downward.

Locational Desirability

Property values may be sensitive to differences in the desirability of locations. There might be a sizable difference, for example, in the value of otherwise similar residential properties if one has a view of a park or golf course and the other overlooks a traffic artery. Similarly, there is likely to be a considerable difference in the value of retail sites if one is on a heavily traveled street and the other on a less-traveled street.

Physical Characteristics

Properties that differ in size, age, design, or physical condition will not have the same value. To make an observed sale comparable, the appraiser adjusts the price of the recently sold property to remove the influence of the physical difference.

Economic Characteristics

The value of income-producing properties is influenced by such economic characteristics as the rent-generating potential and the cost of operating the property.

If the difference is inherent in the property rather than a characteristic of current management, an adjustment to the sales price of a recently sold comparable property will be warranted.

Differences in Use

A property's highest and best use is that which results in the greatest property value. A property that has a highest and best use other than its current use might command a premium price due to the possibility of converting it to its highest and best use.

Nonrealty Components

If a transaction included items that are not generally considered realty (items such as a valuable business name, furniture and fixtures, or equipment, for example), the price will be higher than would be warranted for the real estate alone. The value contributed by these nonrealty components must be deducted to derive an indication of the value of the real estate.

The Sales Comparison Approach Illustrated

Adjustments for differences between the subject property and recently sold comparable properties might be based on absolute dollar amounts or percentages of the observed sale prices, depending on the market data available. Example 14.2 illustrates the approach by using percentage adjustments.

EXAMPLE 14.2

To further analyze the property introduced in Example 14.1, the appraiser gathered information on eight self-storage facilities that were recently sold in the market area. To adjust for differences in storage area, the sales prices were converted to a price per square foot of building area. The buildings on all of the recently sold properties were constructed of masonry; the property being appraised was constructed of steel. Computerized cost services indicated steel construction costs about 10 percent less than masonry. Comparisons between properties indicated adjustments needed to be made for differences in physical appearance, desirability of location, and in one case, inadequate land area. The adjusted values per square foot of building area yield a value estimate of $1,045,000 using the direct sales comparison approach.

ADJUSTMENT GRID OF COMPARABLE SALES

Sale No.	Price	Masonry Construct	Appearance	Location	Land Ratio	Adjusted Price
1	$41.45	Less 10%	Less 5%	Less 20%	Plus 5%	$29.02
2	38.08	Less 10%	Less 5%	Less 10%	-0-	28.56
3	32.48	Less 10%	-0-	-0-	-0-	29.23
4	36.97	Less 10%	Less 5%	Less 10%	-0-	27.73
5	27.07	Less 10%	Less 5%	Plus 15%	-0-	27.07

Sale No.	Price	Masonry Construct	Appearance	Location	Land Ratio	Adjusted Price
6	35.35	Less 10%	Less 5%	-0-	-0-	30.05
7	40.51	Less 10%	Less 5%	Less 15%	-0-	28.36
8	35.00	Less 10%	Less 5%	Less 5%	-0-	28.00

Subject Property	$28.50
Value Indication (36,619 sq. ft. @ $28.50)	$1,043,642
Value Indication, Rounded	$1,045,000

THE INCOME CAPITALIZATION APPROACH

Investors who build or buy income-producing properties focus primarily on the property's NOI; physical and locational characteristics are important only to the extent that they contribute to or detract from the amount or duration of the income. Informed investors will not pay more for a property than they would have to pay to acquire a substitute property that generates a comparable income stream. The income capitalization approach involves estimating the NOI a property can generate and the value of such an income stream in the marketplace. NOI is the income remaining after subtracting all expenses involved in operating the property but not the cost of financing or an allowance for depreciation.

The most common and most straightforward approach to capitalizing the NOI is called *direct capitalization*. It involves converting a single NOI—usually the income anticipated for the following year—into an indication of value by dividing the income by a capitalization rate. The rate might best be thought of as a market-derived ratio between income and value. If the capitalization rate is derived by reference to recently sold income properties, the resulting value indication is often quite reliable. The approach is illustrated in Example 14.3.

EXAMPLE 14.3

Self-storage facilities similar to the property described in Example 14.1 have recently sold at prices varying around eight times their NOI, indicating a market capitalization rate of 1/8, or 12.5 percent. The property described in Example 14.1 has a reasonable expectation of generating $120,000 of net operating income next year. Applying the income capitalization approach, this implies a value of $960,000:

$$\text{Value} = \text{Income/Rate}$$
$$= \$120,000/0.125$$
$$= \$960,000$$

Rounded, the indicated value is $960,000.

RECONCILING THE THREE APPROACHES

The *Uniform Standards of Professional Appraisal Practice (USPAP)* requires that appraisers use all three of the standard approaches if they are applicable and explain the omission of any approach. If properly applied, the approaches should generate reasonably similar value indications. The appraiser's final task is to reconcile the value indications of the approaches used and arrive at a final conclusion of value. This involves applying judgment concerning the reliability of data used in each approach and deciding on the degree of confidence that should be placed in each indicator. The appraiser should explain the judgmental factors used and the logic involved in arriving at a final conclusion.

The final conclusion of value should be viewed as the midpoint of a probability distribution of possible outcomes if the property were exposed to the market for a reasonable period of time and with neither buyer nor seller acting under undue stimulus. Example 14.4 uses information from Examples 14.1 through 14.3 to arrive at a final conclusion of value for the property described in Example 14.1.

EXAMPLE 14.4

The value indications generated by applying the three approaches examined in Examples 14.1 through 14.3 are summarized below:

Cost Approach (from Example 14.1)	$1,155,000
Sales Comparison Approach (from Example 14.2)	$1,045,000
Income Capitalization Approach (from Example 14.3)	$960,000

The appraiser concludes, after a careful review of the data used in each approach, that the income capitalization approach is as reliable as the other two approaches combined, and that the cost approach is three times as reliable as the sales comparison approach. Weighting each of the value indications accordingly generates the following indication of value:

Approach	Value Indication	Weight	Weighted Indication
Cost	$1,155,000	0.375	$433,125
Sales Comparison	1,045,000	0.125	130,625
Income Capitalization	960,000	0.500	480,000
Weighted Indication		1.00	$1,043,750
Final Conclusion (Rounded)			$1,044,000

SUMMARY

Mortgage lenders rely on real estate appraisers to tell them the value of real estate pledged as security for a loan. Appraisers recognize that a property's desirability stems from its economic and locational variables as well as from the size, nature, and condition of the property itself. Because the property is fixed in location, particular attention is paid to the desirability of the location. The appraiser also seeks to estimate the contributions to value made by the physical durability and aesthetic appeal of improvements on and to the land.

Appraisers have traditionally relied on the so-called three approaches to estimate market value: the cost approach, the sales comparison approach, and the income capitalization approach. They derive a value indication from each approach and reconcile them into a single opinion of value.

KEY TERMS

aesthetic appeal

cost approach

functional efficiency

income capitalization
approach

loan-to-value ratio

sales comparison
approach

NOTE

1. Appraisal Institute, *The Appraisal of Real Estate,* 12th ed. (Chicago: Appraisal
Institute, 2001), 426.

RECOMMENDED READING

American Institute of Real Estate Appraisers. *The Appraisal of Real Estate,* 12th ed. Chicago: The American Institute of Real Estate Appraisers, 2001, 469–95.

Brigham, Eugene F., and Joel F. Houston. *Fundamentals of Financial Management,* 10th ed.
Mason, Ohio: Thompson/South Western, 2004.

Kolbe, Phillip T., and Gaylon E. Greer. *Investment Analysis for Real Estate Decisions,* 6th
ed. Chicago: Dearborn Real Estate Education, 2006.

Pyhrr, Stephen A., James R. Cooper, Larry E. Wofford, Steven D. Kapplin, and Paul D.
Lapides. *Real Estate Investment Strategy, Analysis, Decisions,* 2nd ed. Boston: Wiley,
1989, 309–16.

INTERNET REFERENCES

FHA information on the cost approach:
www.fhalibrary.com/fha_appraisals/fha_appraisal_process/cost_approach.asp

FHA information on the sales comparison approach:
*www.fhalibrary.com/fha_appraisals/fha_appraisal_process/sales_
comparison.asp*

For Data Documentation and Appraisal Reporting Standards:
www.usdoj.gov/enrd/land-ack

REVIEW QUESTIONS

1. Briefly state the procedure involved in applying each of the so-called three
approaches to real estate valuation.
2. Why is it inappropriate in reconciling the three approaches to simply take a
mathematical average of the three value indications?
3. List several major factors governing the relative attractiveness of a real
estate investment.

DISCUSSION QUESTIONS

1. How useful would an appraiser's opinion of value be if the appraisal were performed prior to loan closing and a foreclosure sale were required due to borrower default five years later?

2. If the three approaches to appraising property value are expected to yield roughly similar value indications, why not cut the cost of the appraiser by having the appraiser use only the most reliable of the three?

PROBLEMS

1. Based on the following data relating to recently sold, comparable properties, estimate the value of the subject property using the direct sales comparison method. The only adjustments that appear warranted are for changes in the market (comparable land and buildings have been increasing in value at about 6 percent per annum in recent years) and differences in building size.

Property	Sales Price	Date of Sale	Building Size (sq. ft.)	Current Land Value
A	$750,000	6 months ago	5,000	$150,000
B	980,000	4 months ago	6,500	190,000
C	1,080,000	1 week ago	7,000	220,000
Subject			6,000	195,000

2. *Current* net operating incomes for the properties presented in Problem 1 are as follows:

Property	NOI
A	$62,000
B	80,000
C	86,500
Subject	75,000

Based on this information, estimate the subject property's current market value using the income capitalization approach and applying a direct capitalization rate.

3. Current construction costs for properties such as the subject and the comparable properties in Problem 2 are approximately $140 per square foot. The subject and all the comparables are approximately eight years old and all have been equally well maintained. None have experienced functional or economic obsolescence. If market-derived depreciation estimates reflect straight-line (constant percentage) rates of depreciation, what does this suggest about the useful economic lives of the buildings?

Complex Property Valuation Problems

After studying this chapter, you should understand the limitations of a traditional appraisal report as a measure of risk associated with a loan. Based on multiple-year operating projections, you should be able to judge the extent to which the risk of default, as well as loss of principal in the event of a foreclosure sale, changes through time. You should be able to compute the present value of sums to be received in the future.

Chapter 14 introduced real estate valuation and explained how appraisers arrive at an estimate of real estate market value. Emphasis was placed on the so-called three approaches that the *Uniform Standards of Professional Appraisal Practice* require that appraisers apply whenever possible. Chapter 14 observed that several variations of the income capitalization approach are used but stated that the most common application is to use an overall capitalization rate to express the relationship between a property's income-generating potential and its market value.

Even though the overall capitalization rate applied to the forecast income or a typical year's income is the most widely used income capitalization technique, it is inadequate for rational mortgage lending. The same shortcoming exists with the other two of the traditional three approaches. They are designed to estimate what the property would have sold for as of the date of the appraisal, assuming the property had been exposed to the market for a reasonable period of time. But the date of the appraisal is generally a month or so earlier than the date of the loan closing. A dynamic market can move up or down substantially in that time. Moreover, the mortgage lender should be concerned about market value over a substantial number of years, not just the value at the time the loan is initiated.

▌ THE LIMITATIONS OF TRADITIONAL APPRAISAL TECHNIQUES

Chapter 14 made the argument that a mortgaged property's market value is the lender's assurance that if all else fails, the loan balance can be paid out of the proceeds of a foreclosure sale. The chapter summarized the three approaches that have traditionally been used to estimate market value.

FIGURE 15.1 | The Characteristic Mortgage Default Pattern over Time

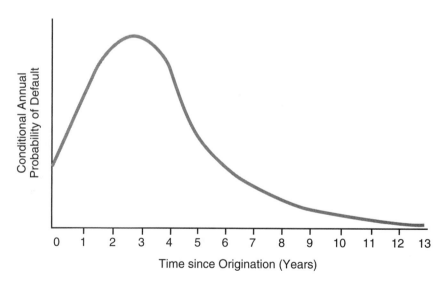

FIGURE 15.2 | Relationship between Property Income and Market Value

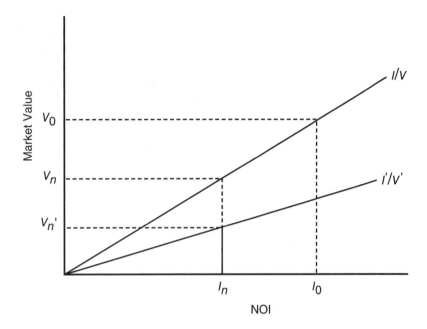

Mortgage lenders, however, need something more. Borrowers seldom default during the first year of a long-term loan. Figure 15.1 illustrates a representative pattern of default and indicates that the probability of default actually increases for several years and then drops off sharply. But the probability persists throughout the term of the loan.

If a property's market value drops faster than the loan is amortized, the lender's risk exposure actually grows through time. This is not an improbable occurrence, because rental projects become less competitive as they age. They may suffer from higher-than-average vacancy rates and command below-average rent. We saw in Chapter 14 that net operating income (NOI) is capitalized to estimate market value. It follows that as income earning potential drops, market value will decline. Moreover, as a project ages the income stream is typically capitalized at a higher rate. This translates into a lower market value per dollar of NOI.

These relationships are illustrated in Figure 15.2, which shows how the relationship between NOI and property value is determined by the capitalization rate. The line in Figure 15.2 labeled I/V is the relationship between income and value at the time the loan is originated. The income is estimated to be I_0 and the value to be V_0. But if the actual income falls below the estimated amount of I_0, say to I_n, at the market determined capitalization rate expressed by I/V, the market-value will decline to V_n.

As the property ages, however, or if market conditions deteriorate, the market-derived capitalization rate might rise. If the rate shifts to the relationship depicted in Figure 15.2 by the line I'/V', the drop in the property's income-earning potential will cause market value to drop to V_n'. The drop in value has two components: from V_0 to V_n as a consequence of the declining NOI; from V_n to V_n' due to the higher capitalization rate.

For these reasons, lenders need a market forecast over the entire period of the loan. Chapter 13 explained how to analyze market data and develop a forecast of the future income stream. Chapter 14 explained how to express the income forecast as an estimate of market value. The estimate can be developed for every year of the loan amortization period. Because most defaults occur within the first ten years, the forecast should at least cover that period.

Real estate appraisal, as traditionally practiced, has been compared to driving a car by looking in the rear-view mirror. Curves, grades, and straightaways visible in the mirror present a history of recent driving experience and give a hint about what might be encountered in the near future. But it does nothing to help the driver negotiate specific road hazards.

In like manner, traditional appraisals tell the lender what the relationship between a loan and the collateral's market value would have been had the loan closed as of the date of the appraisal, but they reveal little about the future. In a reasonably stable market environment, the market value might change little, if at all, between the date of the appraisal and the loan closing date, but there is still the problem of managing risk over the loan repayment period.

As explained in Chapter 14, the benefit of the appraisal is that it tells the lender what a property might reasonably bring in a foreclosure sale as of the date of the appraisal. It is a measure of the risk of loss of principal in the event of foreclosure, *assuming market value remains unchanged.*

That assumption is precisely the problem. Should foreclosure become necessary, it will happen at some date after the loan closes. The most likely time of foreclosure, the period of greatest risk, typically lies in the second through about the fifth year of the loan. Thereafter, the likelihood of default declines drastically and, by the tenth year, is very low.

Because the likelihood of mortgage default tends to grow for a period after loan origination, as illustrated by Figure 15.1, lenders need to procure market forecasts that cover the entire periods of their loans, with emphasis on the first ten years of the repayment periods. The forecast has two valuable dimensions: (1) It estimates the operating results from the property over the forecast period and thereby tells the lender whether the property is likely to generate enough cash flow to service the loan. (2) It estimates the market value on a year-by-year basis, as an indication of the risk of principal loss in the event default is resolved by foreclosure.

The first step in developing a multiple-year perspective is to generate a year-by-year operating forecast. Based on these long-range projections, the lender can estimate a property's future market value by applying anticipated capitalization rates or by employing the discounted cash-flow technique.

▌ DEVELOPING A MULTIPLE-YEAR OPERATING FORECAST ─────

Chapter 13 explained how to reconstruct a property's recent operating history and extend the analysis into a near-term forecast of operating results. A multiple-year forecast simply extends the one-year forecast.

Data from the past are employed to develop a forecast for every year in the forecast period. Without systematic forecasting procedures, uncertainty about future eventualities will overwhelm the analyst and encourage reliance on "rules of thumb" as substitutes for hard analysis. This can lead to disastrous outcomes by blinding analysts and decision makers to significant trends that careful investigation might reveal.

Forecasting Gross Revenue

Forecasting effective gross revenue over a projection period requires anticipating changes in major factors that affect a property's ability to command rents. These may conveniently be categorized as *physical* and *locational* characteristics and must be compared with anticipated changes in the same characteristics affecting the properties with which the subject property will compete for tenants. Revenue forecasting is largely an exercise in estimating how these factors will change over the forecasting period and how the changes will affect a property's ability to command rent.

If the operating history of a property has been reconstructed for several years, the task of forecasting for additional years is greatly simplified. If the operating history cannot be reconstructed with a degree of accuracy but a single year of operating results is reliably available, the trend can be imputed by the trends shown in the published data sources referenced in Chapter 13. Those sources generally show a five-year history, by property category. Extract the history for a category that is deemed a peer group for the property under analysis, and note the year-to-year rate of change in rental rates per unit of measure, such as per square foot or per rental unit. It is reasonable to expect the recent trend to continue unless political, economic, or social change alters it over the forecast period.

Anticipating trend-altering changes requires an understanding of the interaction of politics, economics, and social change. Relevant changes might occur at the national, state, or metropolitan level. For example, a shift in Federal Reserve monetary policy or government fiscal policy will affect future inflation rates and, thus, changes in general rental rates as well as in the cost of operating a property. Changing neighborhood trends or alterations in the rate and direction of urban growth will influence demand for rental space and, thus, the ability of a property to command rents. Building patterns will influence the supply of competing properties. Many of these trends are relatively long-term and telegraph themselves months or even years before the major impact is felt.

Forecasting Operating Expenses

As buildings age, they become more expensive to maintain. And as they become less competitive because of new buildings designed for the same tenant category, it becomes necessary to spend more to market the space. Operating expenses, therefore, both in absolute terms and as a percentage of gross income, tend to grow over time, even as, in many cases, gross rental income decreases.

A useful way to estimate the trend of operating expenses as a property ages is to study the published data sources presented in Chapter 13. Most of the listed sources offer data grouped by building type and by building age. By comparing the actual results during a single time period for groups of buildings of different ages in the same use category as the property under analysis, one can estimate the rate of change in operating expenses attributable to building age without having the data distorted by changes in the general price level.

Forecasting Changes in Market Value

Developing a multiple-year forecast of operating revenue and expenses, as explained above, completes a major portion of the task of estimating future market value. Chapter 14 developed the concept of an overall capitalization rate, which is the ratio of a property's NOI to its market value. Recall that the relationship is

$$\text{Rate} = \text{NOI/Value},$$

where *rate* is the overall capitalization rate, *NOI* is the property net operating income, and *value* is the property's market value. It follows that

$$\text{Value} = \text{NOI/Rate},$$

and applying an appropriate capitalization rate to each year's forecasted NOI will yield a multiple-year forecast of market values. Coupling these with the calculated remaining balance of the mortgage loan for each year will generate a trend of loan-to-value (LTV) ratios. If the trend is to lower ratios (because market value is expected to drop faster than the remaining loan balance), the lender is alerted to possible increased risk exposure in future years.

Capitalization rates change with the cost of capital and with investors' perceptions of future cash flows from investment. Therefore, just as it is necessary to develop a forecast of property revenues and expenses, it is necessary to generate a forecast of capitalization rates. Fortunately, changes in capitalization rates tend to occur gradually and to be modest on a year-to-year basis. Table 15.1 illustrates these trends over a 12-year period for one category of rental property.

Instead of trying to forecast the capitalization rate trend over the long term, an analyst might develop a short-term forecast that incorporates the tendency for rates to revert to their mean values. Note, for example, that the 12-year arithmetic average in Table 15.1 is 9.04. The trend climbed above that level in 1991, but in 1994, it began regressing toward the mean. It dipped below the mean in 1996 and might reasonably be expected to start climbing back toward the mean. In the early years of

| **TABLE 15.1** | Capitalization Rates for Class A Apartment Buildings, 1989–2000 |

Year	Rate
1989	8.7
1990	8.8
1991	9.2
1992	9.6
1993	9.6
1994	9.4
1995	9.2
1996	9.0
1997	8.8
1998	8.9
1999	8.8
2000*	8.5

*Cap rates dropped to abnormally low levels in 2001 and therefore are not displayed.

Printed with permission from C. B. Richard Ellis.

| **TABLE 15.2** | First-Year Operating Forecast for Noname Apartments |

Potential Gross Rent		$378,000
Less: Allowance for Vacancies		20,000
		$358,000
Plus: Other Income (Parking)		4,000
Effective Gross Income		$362,000
Less: Operating Expenses		
Management Fee	$18,100	
Salary Expense	32,300	
Utilities	17,300	
Insurance	9,000	
Supplies	3,400	
Advertising	4,900	
Maintenance and Repairs	29,000	
Property Tax	49,000	163,000
Net Operating Income Annual		$199,000

the new millennium cap rates dropped to abnormally low levels, but long-term averages remain similar. A forecast for a property of this class, therefore, might involve a capitalization rate that increases each year until it gets back to 9 percent, then level off at 9 percent for the remaining years of the forecast.

Note, however, that as properties age, they typically fall out of their original classification and into a different category. Thus, a Class A apartment building might eventually become a Class B building. Market forces then result in a generally higher capitalization rate, reflecting poorer prospects for sustained income growth.

To see how a multiple-year forecast might look, consider again the Noname Apartments from Chapter 13. Table 13.6 presented a one-year forecast of operating results. That forecast is reproduced here as Table 15.2.

Let us revisit Chapter 13, where the Noname Apartments are offered at $2.21 million. Assume that the prospective buyer applies for a $1,650,000 loan at 8 percent, payable in equal monthly payments over 20 years. The payments will be $13,801.26 and the annual debt service obligation will be 12 times this amount, or $165,615. The first-year debt coverage ratio (NOI/Debt Service, as explained in Chapter 13) is expected to be $199,000/$165,615, or 1.20.

CALCULATOR APPLICATION

n = 240
i = .66667 (8 ÷ 12)
PV = 1,650,000

Solve for PMT:
PMT = $13,801.26

Let us suppose an analyst has concluded that the market value is approximately the same as the $2.21 million offering price. To assess the adequacy of the debt coverage ratio and the LTV ratio over the first six years of the loan period, the analyst develops a six-year operating forecast. The property is in the path of rapid urban growth, and, after considering available market data, the analyst concludes that effective gross income and operating expenses will grow at about 6 percent per annum over the forecast period. This conclusion is incorporated into the six-year NOI projection shown in Table 15.3.

With the forecast, it is possible to project debt coverage ratios for each year of the six-year period. This is shown near the bottom of Table 15.3. Because the NOI is expected to grow each year and the loan carries a fixed interest rate, the debt coverage ratio is expected to increase from the first-year level of 1.20 to a sixth-year level of 1.61.

The implied capitalization rate (NOI/Value) of Noname Apartments is $199,000/$2,210,000, or 9 percent. Applying the appropriate rate to the following year's anticipated NOI each year will yield annual market value estimates. In

TABLE 15.3 | Multiple-Year Forecast for Noname Apartments

	Year					
	1	2	3	4	5	6
Effective Gross Income*	$362,000	$384,000	$407,000	$431,000	$457,000	$484,000
Less: Operating Expenses*	163,000	173,000	183,000	194,000	206,000	218,000
Net Operating Income	$199,000	$211,000	$224,000	$237,000	$251,000	$266,000
Less: Debt Service	165,615	165,615	165,615	165,615	165,615	165,615
Before-Tax Cash Flow	$33,385	$45,385	$58,385	$71,385	$85,385	$100,385
Debt Coverage Ratio	1.20	1.27	1.35	1.43	1.52	1.61
Ending Loan Balance	$1,615,124	$1,577,354	$1,536,449	$1,492,149	$1,444,172	$1,392,213
Capitalization Rate	9.0	9.0	9.0	9.0	9.0	9.0
Market Value $ (millions)†	2.21	2.34	2.49	2.63	2.79	2.96
Loan-to-Value Ratio	0.73	0.67	0.62	0.57	0.52	0.47

*Rounded to the nearest $1,000.

†Next year's anticipated NOI divided by current year capitalization rate. Value rounded to nearest $10,000.

Table 15.1 we saw that the property's current 9 percent ratio is very close to the 12-year average for Class A apartments. Over future years the applicable capitalization rate will fluctuate, but there is likely to be a tendency to reverse directions and return to the mean value of about 9 percent. Our analyst concludes that the most likely rate is 9 for each year in the forecast. The resulting annual market value estimates are also shown near the bottom of Table 15.3.

Based on the anticipated annual market values, the analyst can calculate an expected LTV ratio at the end of each year. With market value growing and the loan balance decreasing, the ratio is expected to decline steadily. This is shown in the bottom row of Table 15.3.

DISCOUNTED CASH FLOW APPROACH

Although capitalization rates have been characterized as a ratio of income to market value, their potential informational content is much greater. The ratio can also be viewed as a discount rate that expresses the present value of a perpetual income stream. If the never-ending income stream is constant in amount, the capitalization rate is simply the yield rate one can expect to earn if one pays the present value for the right to the income stream. For example, the present value of the right to receive $100 per annum forever, when discounted at, say, 10 percent, is $1,000. To determine this, we set up an algebraic equation expressing the relationship:

$$I = PV \times r,$$

where I is the annual income that goes on forever, PV is the present value, and r is the annual interest or yield rate. When structured this way, the equation is straightforward: If one earns 10 percent per year on $1,000, the annual income is 0.1 times $1,000, or $100. Because only the annual earnings are included in the income stream, the principal remains untouched and so lasts forever.

A shift from determining the annual income from a known principal amount to solving for the principal (the present value of the income stream) when the earnings are known requires only a restructuring of the equation:

$$PV = I/r,$$

where the terms have the same meanings as before. If I is $100 and r is 10 percent, it follows that PV must be $100/0.1, or $1,000. Change the discount rate to, say, 12 percent and the present value becomes $100/0.12, or $833.33.

Note that this equation is the same as the one we used when capitalizing a single year's income, except that in the capitalization equation we used NOI (the property's net operating income) instead of the symbol I for the annual income and the symbol R instead of r. NOI is simply the income I from a rental property. The relationship between R, the overall capitalization rate, and r, the yield rate, is subtler.

Of what use, though, is a formula that presupposes an eternal stream of income, when no one reasonably expects a real property to generate income forever? The mathematics of a perpetual annuity is explored at length in Appendix B. The annuity table in Appendix D reveals that the present value of a level annuity for a specified period converges with that for a perpetual annuity as the specified period lengthens. Consider an annuity capitalized at 10 percent, for example. Reading down the 10 percent column of the annuity table, we see that as the number of years grows, the annuity factor gets ever closer to 10, the factor for a perpetual annuity. For a cash flow stream that is expected to last more than 40 or 50 years, there is little difference between using the annuity factor and simply capitalizing the first year's cash flow at 10 percent. For this reason, we can often approximate the market value of an income property by using an overall capitalization rate.

Moreover, when the overall capitalization rate is used to express the present value of future income from a property, there is no implication that the annual income will remain stable. There is, rather, the implication that the income will change at a reasonably constant rate. This is an application of a financial model known as the *Gordon Growth Model*, and the capitalization rate R is actually the rate of return on the investment minus the rate of growth (or plus the rate of decline) in the annual income. For example, if the first year's income is $100, the target rate of return is 12 percent, and the income is expected to grow at 2 percent per annum, the present value would be $1,000:

$$PV = R_1/(r - g),$$

where R is the first year's expected income, r is the target rate of return, and g is the expected growth rate of the income. Substituting the numbers gives us

$$PV = \$100/(0.12 - 0.02)$$
$$= \$100/0.10$$
$$= \$1,000$$

This formulation works reasonably well, even though income is not expected to change at a precisely constant rate. All that is needed is that there be no abrupt shifts in the income level; that it grow or decline at a reasonably constant annual rate. The further the expected rate of change in NOI deviates from a constant rate, the less reliable the overall capitalization rate technique becomes.

How, then, does one place a value on a property if a significant shift in income is expected at some future date? To solve such a valuation problem, one must resort to discounting discrete cash flows.

Discounting expresses anticipated future cash flows as a present-value equivalent. At the point in time where the anticipated future cash flows are expected to begin changing at a reasonably constant rate over the long term, the market value for that point can be estimated by applying an overall capitalization rate. That future market value can then be discounted to express it in present-value terms. The sum of the present values of the interim cash flows and the present value of the capitalized future amount gives an indication of the price the property is likely to command today if exposed to the market for a reasonable length of time.

Suppose, for example, a property is expected to generate $100,000 the first year, $150,000 the second year, and $300,000 the third year, and to be worth $4 million at the end of the third year. (The $4 million estimate is reached by capitalizing the fourth year's expected income; a possibility because the rate of change in income is expected to settle down at that point.) If the appropriate discount rate is 12 percent, the present value of the expected income (and therefore the value indicated by the income capitalization approach) can be determined by using discount factors taken from the 12 percent column of Table D.1 in Appendix D. Appendix C explains how the tables are derived, explains how they are used, and shows how problems of this type can be solved with a financial calculator. Here is the solution using factors from the table.

Year	Discount Factor at 12%	Net Cash Flow	Present Value
1	0.892857	$100,000	$89,286
2	0.797194	150,000	119,579
3	0.711780	300,000	213,534
3	0.711780	4,000,000	2,847,121

Value Indicated by the Income Capitalization Approach = $3,269,520

Value Indication, Rounded $3,270,000

If a property's income is expected to change at a fairly constant rate, using the overall capitalization rate technique or the discounted cash flow technique should yield about the same indication of value. Some appraisers, in fact, use discounted cash flow as a crosscheck on the overall capitalization rate technique. To illustrate, consider the Noname Apartments, for which a six-year cash-flow forecast was developed in Table 15.3. Note that the forecast anticipates growth in the NOI of about 6 percent per annum. If the appropriate discount rate is 15 percent and if the NOI is expected to continue growing at 6 percent, the appropriate capitalization rate at the end of the sixth year will be 15 percent minus 6 percent, or 9 percent.

Market value at the end of the six-year operating forecast, therefore, is expected to be the seventh year's income forecast capitalized at 9 percent. With a 6 percent growth rate, the NOI for Year 7 will be 1.06 times that of Year 6. Rounded to the nearest $1,000, this is $282,000:

$$
\begin{aligned}
NOI_7 &= NOI_6 \times 1.06 \\
&= \$266,000 \times 1.06 \\
&= \$281,960 \\
&= \$282,000 \text{ rounded}
\end{aligned}
$$

Market value at the end of Year 6, therefore, is expected to be $3.13 million. When rounded to the nearest $10,000:

$$
\begin{aligned}
Value_6 &= NOI_7/Rate \\
&= \$282,000/0.09 \\
&= \$3,133,333 \\
&= \$3,130,000 \text{ rounded}
\end{aligned}
$$

TABLE 15.4 | Present Value of Expected Future Benefits from Noname Apartments

Year	Projected NOI	PV Factor @ 15%	Present Value
1	$199,000	0.869565	$173,043
2	211,000	0.756144	159,546
3	224,000	0.657516	147,284
4	237,000	0.571753	135,505
5	251,000	0.497177	124,791
6	266,000	0.432328	114,999
Present value of first six years' expected NOI			$855,168
Add PV of sixth-year market value, discounted			
($3,130,000 × 0.432328)			1,353,187
Present value of all anticipated benefits			$2,208,355
Present value, rounded			$2,210,000

Discounting each of the first six years' estimated NOI and the sixth-year market value projection (appraisers call this latter value a **reversion**) yields the present value of all anticipated cash flows from the property. Using a 15 percent discount rate, we should arrive at a present value close to the value derived by capitalizing the first year's projected income at 9 percent. Table 15.4 shows the result of the discounting operation. After rounding, the overall present value is the same as the market value derived by capitalizing the first year's income: $2.21 million.

SUMMARY

Traditional real estate appraisal gives mortgage lenders an opinion of a property's market value as of the date of the appraisal, usually a matter of days or weeks before a loan closes. But lenders need a tool for assessing the risk of default over the period of the loan and of the likelihood of principal loss in the event of a foreclosure sale. This requires a multiple-year forecast of operating results.

The starting point for a multiple-year operating forecast is the single-year forecast, usually incorporated into an appraisal. To extend this over a number of years, the analyst notes current trends in each major operating category and judges how the trends might be altered over the forecast period. Based on the multiple-year operating forecast and incorporating a forecast of overall capitalization rates, the lender can estimate what the property's value is likely to be during each year of the forecast.

When the operating forecast indicates a discontinuity in the rate of change in a property's operating results, capitalization rates become useful only when coupled with discounted cash flow. The forecast of operating results beyond the point of discontinuity can be capitalized to estimate what the market value will be at that point. The future market value can be discounted to express it as a current value. Discounting the expected operating results prior to the discontinuity and summing them along with the present value of the future capitalized value yields an estimate of current market value.

KEY TERMS

discounted cash flow approach	forecasting operating expenses	reversion
forecasting gross revenue	forecasting changes in market value	

RECOMMENDED READING

Brigham, Eugene F., and Joel F. Houston. *Fundamentals of Financial Management*, 10th ed. Mason, Ohio: Thompson/South Western, 2004.

Epley, Donald R., and James H. Boykin. *Basic Income Property Appraisal*. Reading, Mass.: Addison-Wesley, 1983, 140–57.

Friedman, Jack P., and Nicholas Ordway. *Income Property Appraisal and Analysis*. Reston, Va.: Prentice-Hall, 1989.

Kolbe, Phillip T., and Gaylon E. Greer. *Investment Analysis for Real Estate Decisions*, 6th ed. Chicago: Dearborn Real Estate Education, 2006.

Pyhrr, Stephen A., James R. Cooper, Larry E. Wofford, Steven D. Kapplin, and Paul D. Lapides. *Real Estate Investment Strategy, Analysis, Decisions*, 2nd ed. Boston: Wiley, 1989, 284–316.

▌ INTERNET REFERENCES

For a wealth of information on real property valuation and other real estate topics:
http://realdataexchange.com

▌ REVIEW QUESTIONS

1. Why is a traditional appraisal report inadequate as a measure of risk associated with a foreclosure sale?

2. Why might the risk of principal loss in a foreclosure sale increase through time?

3. What advantage does a multiple-year operating forecast offer a mortgage lender that a traditional appraisal report does not?

4. What are some circumstances that might alter operating trends?

5. What is the relationship between a discount rate and a capitalization rate?

6. What are the factors in the equation for the Gordon Growth Model?

7. Under what circumstances might an overall capitalization rate, used without recourse to discounted cash-flow analysis, give an unreliable estimate of market value?

8. Under what circumstances will the present value of an annuity for a specified period be very close to the value of a perpetual annuity?

▌ DISCUSSION QUESTIONS

1. Chapter 15 discusses problems with the overall capitalization technique when there is likely to be a discontinuity in the rate of change in a property's operating results. What are some examples of when such a discontinuity might be encountered?

2. What effect, if any, might an increase in the rate of return prospects in the stock or bond markets have on market-derived real estate capitalization rates?

3. Can you think of circumstances that might cause a property's market value to decline faster than the reduction in the remaining balance of a fully amortizing mortgage?

▍ PROBLEMS ────────────────────────────────────

1. Refer to the six-year operating forecast for Noname Apartments presented in Table 15.3.

   a. Reconstruct the table, assuming that effective gross income grows at 3 percent per annum and operating expenses grow at 6 percent per annum. Would you expect the reduced prospect for growth in NOI to have an impact on the market-derived overall capitalization rate?

   b. Based on the reconstructed table, what would be the LTV ratio at the end of the sixth year if the market-derived overall capitalization rate dropped to 8.5 percent?

2. Reconstruct Table 15.3 and estimate the current market value of Noname Apartments using the discounted cash-flow technique. In this reconstruction, assume that NOI in years two and three will be 50 percent below that forecast for year one (while the property's access road is undergoing improvements), but that the fourth year's NOI will be the same as that in year one and NOI will grow thereafter at 6 percent per year for the foreseeable future. Capitalize the sixth year's NOI at 9 percent, and discount the cash flows at 15 percent.

Real Estate Value from the Borrower's Perspective

After studying this chapter, you should understand the difference between market value and the value of a property to an individual investor. Starting with a multiple-year operating forecast, you should be able to compute the present value of anticipated cash flows to the equity position and the internal rate of return to an equity investor.

Chapter 15 introduced discounted cash-flow analysis and explained how a lender can use the concept to measure the degree of risk exposure associated with a loan. The concept of present value of future benefits is also a useful tool for equity investors. Using that technique, real estate equity investors can estimate the relationship between costs and benefits of prospective portfolio adjustments such as purchases, sales, or refinancing.

The equity investor's perspective is somewhat different from that of the lenders, however. Lenders are concerned with the relationship between net operating income (NOI) and debt service on the one hand and between market value and the loan balance on the other; equity investors focus on the portion of NOI that remains after satisfying claims of the lender and the tax collector and on the value of the real estate as an asset in the investment portfolio.

Figure 16.1 illustrates the distinction by starting with the NOI and showing that the equity investor's entitlement is a residual after the prior claims of the mortgage lender and the Internal Revenue Service have been satisfied. Holders of mortgage-secured debt have a senior claim on the NOI. Their portion—annual debt service— flows down the left-hand side of Figure 16.1. The balance of the NOI accrues to the equity investors, but part of it is siphoned off as income taxes. The residual is the after-tax cash flow to the equity investors, as shown on the right-hand side of Figure 16.1. The bottom of the diagram illustrates the transformation of these expected cash flows into lump-sum equivalents via discounting.

The present value of the debt position is the amount of the mortgage loan (or, in the case of a preexisting loan, its remaining balance). The present value of the equity position is the value today of anticipated after-tax cash flows during the ownership period and of the after-tax cash flow from disposal at the end of the period.

▌ REVIEW OF PRESENT VALUE

Present value is the value now of benefits that are expected to accrue in the future. A present value in excess of the initial cost means a project is expected to yield a rate of return in excess of the discount rate employed. If the discount rate is the target rate of return, this implies that the project is worthy of further consideration. A present value totaling less than the required initial equity expenditure results in automatic rejection.

To use this approach for real estate analysis, discount all anticipated future cash flows to the equity investor at the minimum acceptable rate of return. The result is the present value of the equity position:

$$PV = CF_1/(1 + i) + CF_2/(1 + i)^2 + CF_3/(1 + i)3 + \cdots + CF_n/(1 + i)^n,$$

where i is the minimum acceptable rate of return; n is the number of years in the projection period; and CF_1 is the cash flow expected in the first year, CF_2 that for the second year, and so on.

FIGURE 16.1 | Cash-Flow Distribution and Value Relationships

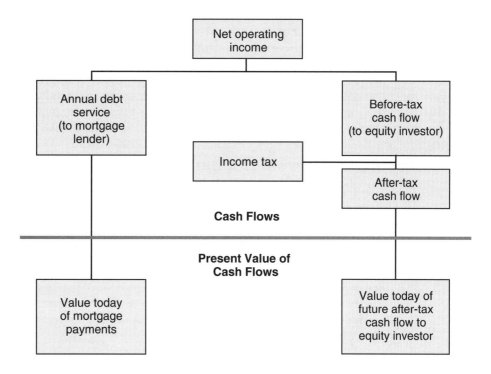

EXAMPLE 16.1

An investment proposal is expected to generate $15,000 of after-tax cash flow each year for eight years and $40,000 of after-tax cash flow from disposal at the end of the eighth year. The required equity cash outlay to acquire the asset is $90,000. The investor's minimum acceptable rate of return is 10 percent.

The present value of anticipated cash flows from the investment opportunity described in Example 16.1 is $98,684, when discounted at 10 percent. Because this exceeds the required initial equity expenditure of $90,000, the expected rate of return exceeds the minimum acceptable rate of 10 percent, and the project merits further consideration.

Subtracting the required initial equity expenditure from the present value yields **net present value (NPV)**. A zero or a positive net present value means a project is expected to yield a rate of return equal to or greater than the acceptable rate and therefore merits further consideration. A net present value of less than zero means the project is expected to yield a rate of return less than the minimum acceptable rate and therefore should be rejected.

The concept can be applied to the Noname Apartment project described in Chapter 13. Recall from that chapter that the apartment complex can be acquired for $2.21 million and there is available a $1.65 million mortgage loan at 8 percent, amortized over 20 years. Equity investors will supply the $560,000 balance of the purchase price. A prospective equity investor might develop a forecast of after-tax cash flows and discount at the minimum acceptable rate of return. If the present value exceeds the $560,000 required equity investment, the project merits further consideration. If the present value is less than the required down payment, the proposal is rejected.

An example of NPV calculation using a financial calculator may be found in Appendix C and on the CD-ROM.

FORECASTING THE AFTER-TAX CASH FLOWS FROM OPERATIONS

The starting point for estimating the after-tax cash flows to an equity investor is the multiple-year operating forecast presented in Table 15.3. Assuming the anticipated holding period for the investment is, in fact, six years, the forecast in Table 15.3 can be used to illustrate the procedure. The first three rows of the table (Effective Gross Income, Operating Expenses, and Net Operating Income) are repeated in Table 16.1. The items generally included as operating expenses will be deductible for income tax purposes. To determine the taxable income from the property, we need only extend the analysis to include tax-deductible items that are not considered operating expenses. The most common examples are *interest expense* and *depreciation allowance*.

Interest Expense

Recall from Chapter 13 that the $1.65 million mortgage loan available in connection with this investment proposal carries an 8 percent interest rate and will be amortized over 20 years with level monthly payments of $13,801.26. Each payment will include tax-deductible interest for one month, calculated on the remaining balance at the beginning of the month. The remainder of the monthly payment will be applied to reduce the principal balance and is not deductible.

In this manner, one could develop an amortization table on a month-by-month basis. The procedure would be needlessly time-consuming, however, because inexpensive financial calculators are programmed to show the interest and principal portions of payments. Using such a calculator, we developed the partial amortization table presented here as Table 16.2.

This annual interest expense is not an operating expense item, because it relates to the decision to use financial leverage rather than to the operation of the property. It is tax deductible, however, and must be subtracted from NOI to arrive at taxable income. The annual interest expense (assuming the property is acquired at the beginning of the year and sold at the end) is shown on line 4 of Table 16.1.

TABLE 16.1 | Forecast of After-Tax Cash Flow from Operations, Noname Apartments

	Year					
	1	**2**	**3**	**4**	**5**	**6**
1. Effective Gross Income*	$362,000	$384,000	$407,000	$431,000	$457,000	$484,000
2. *Less:* Operating Expenses*	163,000	173,000	183,000	194,000	206,000	218,000
3. Net Operating Income	$199,000	$211,000	$224,000	$237,000	$251,000	$266,000
4. *Less:* Interest Expense	130,739	127,845	124,710	121,315	117,638	113,656
5. Depreciation	61,612	64,291	64,291	64,291	64,291	61,612
6. Taxable Income (Loss)	$6,649	$18,864	$34,999	$51,394	$69,071	$90,732
7. *Times:* Tax Rate	0.28	0.28	0.28	0.28	0.28	0.28
8. Income Tax (Savings)	$ 1,862	$ 5,282	$ 9,800	$ 14,390	$ 19,340	$ 25,405
9. Net Operating Income	$199,000	$211,000	$224,000	$237,000	$251,000	$266,000
10. *Less:* Debt Service	165,615	165,615	165,615	165,615	165,615	165,615
11. Income Tax	1,862	5,282	9,800	14,390	19,340	25,405
12. After-Tax Cash Flow	$31,523	$40,103	$48,585	$56,995	$66,045	$74,980

*Rounded to the nearest $1,000.

Depreciation Allowance

Annual deductions for depreciation permit an investor to recover the cost of buildings and other improvements on and to the land over a period specified by law. No **depreciation allowance** is permitted for recovery of the cost of land, so the investor must allocate the acquisition cost between land and improvements in accordance with their relative market values. We will assume that, based on an appraisal, the purchaser of Noname Apartments can appropriately allocate 80 percent of the $2.21 million value to the improvements. The amount to be recovered via depreciation deductions, therefore, is 0.80 times $2.21 million, or $1,768,000.

From time to time, revisions to the Internal Revenue Code alter the allowable recovery period and recovery method. Currently, the recovery period for residential rental property is 27.5 years. The allowance is taken in equal monthly increments:

$$\text{Monthly allowance} = \$1,768,000/(12 \times 27.5)$$
$$= \$5,357.58$$

The annual allowance (other than during the year of acquisition and the year of disposal) is simply 12 times the monthly allowance, or $64,290.96. During the year of acquisition and the year of disposal, the allowance is computed based on the actual number of months of ownership, including half a month's allowance during the initial month and again during the final month. Depreciation deductions for the purchaser of Noname Apartments (assuming a purchase in the first month of the tax year and sale in the final month of the sixth year) are shown on line 5 of Table 16.1.

TABLE 16.2 | Loan Amortization for a $1,650,000 Loan with Interest at 8 Percent

Year	Annual Debt Service	Interest	Principal	Remaining Balance
1	$165,615.12	$130,739.49	$34,875.63	$1,615,124.37
2	165,615.12	127,844.98	37,770.14	1,577,354.23
3	165,615.12	124,710.08	40,905.04	1,536,449.19
4	165,615.12	121,314.98	44,300.14	1,492,149.05
5	165,615.12	117,638.09	47,977.03	1,444,172.02
6	165,615.12	113,656.02	51,959.10	1,392,212.92

See Appendix C for demonstration of the use of a financial calculator to produce an amortization table.

Income Taxes

Subtracting tax-deductible items that are not considered operating expenses from NOI yields taxable income, shown on line 6 of Table 16.1. The income taxes attributable to any investment will be the difference in tax liability with and without the investment. Unless the investment moves the taxpayer between income tax brackets, the taxes can be determined by multiplying the taxable income or tax-deductible loss by the incremental income tax bracket. Assuming our investor to be in the 28 percent income tax bracket (combined federal and state taxes), either with or without investing in Noname Apartments, the expected annual income tax consequences of ownership are shown on line 8 of Table 16.1.

After-Tax Cash Flow from Operations

To determine the expected **after-tax cash flow** from the investment, we start again with NOI, from line 3 of Table 16.1. This amount is brought down to line 9, and nonoperating cash disbursements are subtracted. For Noname Apartments, the nonoperating disbursements are debt service and income taxes. Debt service, taken from Table 16.2, is shown on line 10 of Table 16.1. Income taxes are brought down from line 8 and entered on line 11. Net of these items, the expected after-tax cash flow is shown on line 12. Before proceeding with an analysis of the after-tax cash flows, prudence dictates a detour to introduce two possible tax complications not addressed in the example. They are *passive activity loss provisions* and the *alternative minimum tax*.

The Passive Activity Loss Problem

Section 469 of the Internal Revenue Code defines income and losses from certain activities as *passive* and, with limited exceptions, does not permit **passive activity losses (PALs)** to be offset against other income. PALs not offset against current passive activity income must be carried forward and offset against passive activity income in future years. When a passive activity asset is sold, any PAL carryovers attributable to it become deductible.

Code Section 469 includes real estate held for rental purposes in its catalog of passive activities, but the section includes important exceptions:

- Real estate rental income or losses are not considered passive if the taxpayer is actively engaged in a real property trade or business such as brokerage, development, or management. This requires that the taxpayer (or the taxpayer's spouse if they file a joint return) have at least a 5 percent ownership interest (*Note:* income and losses from limited partnership interests are *always* passive) in the activity and that more than 50 percent of the taxpayer's working hours (and at least 750 hours during the tax year) be devoted to the activity.

- Rental income that is incidental to the primary business activity or where substantial personal service is involved (such as hotels, motels, and resorts) is not considered to be passive.

- An exception for small-scale operators permits up to $25,000 of PAL each year to be offset against other income, provided the taxpayer's adjusted gross income (before subtracting the PAL) does not exceed $100,000. This exception is phased out ratably as the taxpayer's adjusted gross income moves from $100,000 to $150,000.

The Alternative Minimum Tax Trap

In addition to computing income tax liability using the regular computation procedure, taxpayers are required to compute an **alternative minimum tax**. The taxpayer is liable for the greater of the regular tax or the alternative minimum tax. Expenditures that are deductible in the regular computation may not be deductible in the alternative computation. As a consequence, some of the anticipated income tax advantages of real estate investing might prove unavailable to taxpayers who become liable for the alternative minimum tax. These complex issues are beyond the scope of this text, but rational investors must consider them.

▌ AFTER-TAX CASH FLOW FROM DISPOSAL

The final step in the cash-flow projection is to estimate the after-tax cash flow that will be generated when the investor disposes of the property at the end of the project period. In Chapter 15 the expected market value of the Noname Apartments after six years was determined to be $3.13 million (see Table 15.3). From this selling

TABLE 16.3 | Expected Income Tax Consequences of Disposal for Noname Apartments

Expected Taxable Gain:		
Selling Price		$3,130,000
Less: Adjusted Tax Basis:		
Initial Tax Basis	$2,210,000	
Less: Cumulative Depreciation	380,388	
	$1,829,612	
Add: Selling Costs (.06 × $3,130.000)	187,800	
Adjusted Basis		2,017,412
Taxable Gain		$1,112,588
Expected Income Taxes:		
Tax Due to Recovery of Depreciation (.25 × $380,388)		$95,097
On Long-Term Capital Gain (.20 × $732,200)		146,440
Total		$241,537

price the investor will pay selling costs, such as brokerage and legal fees; pay the remaining balance of the mortgage loan; and pay income taxes on the gain. What remains is the after-tax cash flow from the sale.

Estimating the Taxable Gain

The difference between an income property's selling price and the taxpayer's adjusted tax basis in the property is either a taxable gain or a tax-deductible loss. The adjusted tax basis is the purchase price, including any costs associated with getting good title, minus all depreciation deductions, plus selling costs.

Assuming our investor's selling costs will equal 6 percent of the sales price, the expected taxable gain on disposal of the Noname Apartments is $1,112,588. Table 16.3 shows the calculations.

Estimating the Income Tax

Current income tax law establishes a two-tier tax rate on the sale of property that has been subject to depreciation deductions computed on a straight-line basis (that is, equal annual depreciation deductions). The gain that results from reducing the tax

TABLE 16.4 | Forecasted After-Tax Cash Flow from Disposal for Noname Apartments

Sales Price		$3,130,000
Less: Selling costs (.06 × $3,130,000):	$187,800	
Income Taxes (from Table 16.3)	241,537	
Mortgage Balance (from Table 16.2)	1,392,213	1,821,550
After-Tax Cash Flow		$1,308,450

TABLE 16.5 | Present Value of Anticipated Future Equity Cash Flows for Noname Apartments

Year	After-Tax Cash Flow	PV Factor@ 15%	Present Value
1	$31,523	.8695652	$27,411
2	40,103	.7561437	30,324
3	48,585	.6575162	31,945
4	56,995	.57175325	32,587
5	66,045	.49717674	32,836
6	74,980	.43232760	32,416
From Disposal	$1,308,450	.43232760	565,679
Total: Present Value of Expected After-Tax Cash Flows			753,198
Less: Initial Equity Investment			560,000
Net Present Value			$193,198

basis by claiming depreciation deductions is taxed at a 25 percent rate. The balance of the long-term gain is taxed at a 20 percent rate. Because the total gain on sale of Noname Apartments is expected to exceed the cumulative depreciation deductions ($380,388, the sum of the deductions shown on line 5 of Table 16.1), this amount of the gain will be taxed at the 25 percent rate. The remaining $732,200 of the gain will be taxed at the 20 percent rate. The total anticipated tax on disposal is $241,537. The calculations are shown at the bottom of Table 16.3.

After-Tax Cash Flow

The expected after-tax cash flow from selling the apartment complex is the expected selling price minus all related cash disbursements. The calculations are shown in Table 16.4.

PRESENT VALUE AND NET PRESENT VALUE

To compute the **present value** of the investment opportunity, simply discount all anticipated cash flows at the target rate of return. Net present value is the present value of anticipated future cash flow minus the initial cash outlay. For Noname Apartments, with a 15 percent target rate of return the present value of expected future after-tax cash flows to the equity investor is $753,198. Because this exceeds the required equity investment of $560,000 (the purchase price minus the mortgage loan), the investor expects to earn more than the 15 percent target rate of return. These numbers are shown in Table 16.5.

An alternative way to show the expected outcome is to use net present value. This is merely the present value of future cash flows minus the initial cash outlay. We have seen that the present value exceeds the down payment; therefore, it follows that the net present value will be greater than zero. When net present value exceeds zero, the prospective investment merits further consideration. The net present value calculation for Noname Apartments is shown at the bottom of Table 16.5.

Investment opportunities that meet the initial criterion of having an expected present value in excess of the required equity investment or having a net present value in excess of zero must be compared and ranked in terms of their expected benefits and related risk. One ranking procedure that permits comparing investments that require different equity cash outlays is to express the present value in terms of *present value per dollar of initial cash outlay*. Another approach is to compare the expected internal rates of return. This latter technique is explained in the following section.

INTERNAL RATE OF RETURN

An alternative approach to evaluating the after-tax cash flows to the equity investor is to determine the discount rate that will make the present value of the future cash flows equal the amount of the initial equity investment. This rate, called the **internal rate of return**, or **IRR**, is then compared with the minimum acceptable rate to determine whether the investment proposition merits further consideration. The equation for the internal rate of return is

$$0 = \Sigma_{t=0-n} \ [CF_t / (1 + k)^t]$$

where CF_t is the cash flow projected for year t, and k is the IRR. All the terms in the equation are taken as known except k, for which the appropriate value is determined to satisfy the equation.

Consider the after-tax cash flow expectations from Noname Apartments, presented in column two of Table 16.5. The internal rate of return is simply the discount rate that makes the present value of the cash flows exactly equal to the $560,000 required equity cash outlay.

If the internal rate of return is equal to or greater than an investor's required rate of return, a project is considered further. If the internal rate of return is less than the minimum acceptable rate of return, the project is rejected.

Because discounting at a 15 percent target rate of return yields a positive net present value, it follows that the internal rate of return will be greater than 15 percent. To find the exact number, one can experiment with different rates, using successive approximations until the net present value approaches zero. Many inexpensive hand-held calculators are programmed to do the successive approximation calculations and solve for the internal rate of return. Using such a calculator reveals that the internal rate of return for the after-tax cash flows in Table 16.5 is approximately 21.6 percent.

Having calculated the internal rate of return based on expected cash flows in Table 16.5, the investor compares the result with the required rate of return. Because the internal rate of return exceeds the required rate (21.6 percent versus 15 percent), the project is considered further. Ultimate acceptance or rejection depends on estimates of relative riskiness and on the relative attractiveness of alternative investment opportunities.

The major distinction between the internal rate of return approach and the present value approach is that the latter requires that a predetermined discount rate be introduced early in the analysis. This difference, however, is more illusory than substantive as an argument for one method over the other. Those who use the internal rate of return technique must specify some minimal **threshold rate** against which the internal rate of return is measured to determine its acceptability. Internal rate of return users, therefore, delay but do not escape the obligation to determine an investor's required rate of return.

The internal rate of return has little substantive advantage over alternative methods of applying discount rates to projected cash flows, and it has serious weaknesses not found in the alternatives. Under special circumstances it can generate conflicting decision signals when compared with other discounted cash-flow techniques. Potential dissonance stems from peculiarities of the internal rate of return equation, which can mathematically yield more than one solution, and from problems associated with the reinvestment assumption inherent in choices among alternative investments that exhibit different patterns of anticipated after-tax cash flows. See Appendix C for a demonstration of the use of a financial calculator to calculate IRR.

COMPARING NET PRESENT VALUE WITH THE INTERNAL RATE OF RETURN

Under most circumstances, the internal rate of return and net present value approaches will give the same decision signals. When this occurs, there is little significance in the choice of one over the other. The rules are as follows:

- *When using internal rate of return*, reject all projects whose internal rate of return is less than the minimum required rate. Projects with an internal rate of return equal to or greater than the minimum acceptable rate (the *hurdle rate*) are considered further.

- *When using net present value*, discount at the minimum acceptable rate of return and reject all projects with a net present value of less than zero. Projects with a net present value of zero or greater are considered further.

The essential similarity of these decision criteria is reflected in their mathematical formulation. The only structural difference is the discount rate. Remember that the discount rate employed in the internal rate of return is the effective yield; the net present value will be exactly zero when the internal rate of return equals the minimum required rate of return.

There are, however, some conditions under which contradictory signals emerge. The two techniques may, for example, rank alternatives in different order. Because investors must often choose among alternative proposals rather than make a simple choice to accept or reject one investment, this can be a serious problem. Limited equity funds frequently dictate choice from among several opportunities, all of which may meet minimum acceptance criteria. Inconsistent rank ordering can occur where projects differ in the size of the initial investment or in the timing of cash receipts and disbursements.

SUMMARY

Equity investors view operating forecasts from a different perspective than do lenders. The lender's primary interest is the relationship between net operating income and the annual debt service obligation. The equity investor is concerned with the amount of cash flow remaining after satisfying the claims of mortgage lenders and the Internal Revenue Service.

To move from a forecast of net operating income to an estimate of after-tax cash flow to the equity investor, the income tax consequences of operations must be determined. Generally, effective gross revenue is taxable and operating expenses are tax deductible. Additionally, investors may deduct interest expense and an allowance for depreciation.

Forecasting after-tax cash flow from property disposal involves deducting from the expected selling price an estimate of (1) selling costs, (2) income taxes on the gain, and (3) the remaining mortgage loan balance. Capital gain taxes are levied on a two-tier basis: one rate for gains attributable to having claimed depreciation allowances and a lower rate for gains attributable to increases in property value over the holding period.

Modern investment evaluation techniques generally involve some variation of a discounted cash-flow model expressing the present value of all anticipated future cash flows. Most common are the internal rate of return and the present value/net present value models.

KEY TERMS

after-tax cash flow
alternative minimum tax
depreciation allowance

internal rate of return (IRR)
net present value (NPV)

passive activity losses (PALs)
present value
threshold rate (hurdle rate)

RECOMMENDED READING

Brigham, Eugene F., and Joel F. Houston. *Fundamentals of Financial Management*, 10th ed. Mason, Ohio: Thompson/South Western, 2004.

Epley, Donald R., and James H. Boykin. *Basic Income Property Appraisal*. Reading, Mass.: Addison-Wesley, 1983, 140–57.

Friedman, Jack P., and Nicholas Ordway. *Income Property Appraisal and Analysis*. Reston, Va.: 1981, 37–116.

Kolbe, Phillip T., and Gaylon E. Greer. *Investment Analysis for Real Estate Decisions*, 6th ed. Chicago: Dearborn Real Estate Education, 2006.

Pyhrr, Stephen A., James R. Cooper, Larry E. Wofford, Steven D. Kapplin, and Paul D. Lapides. *Real Estate Investment Strategy, Analysis, Decisions,* 2nd ed. Boston: Wiley, 1989, 284–316.

▌ INTERNET REFERENCES

For further information on interest expense:
www.treasurydirect.gov/govt/reports/ir/ir_expense.htm

IRS homepage:
www.irs.gov

Guide to the Alternative Minimum Tax:
www.fairmark.com/amt

▌ REVIEW QUESTIONS

1. Under what conditions will a project be rejected when using present value in investment decision making?

2. Describe the internal rate of return.

3. What is the major difference between the internal rate of return approach and the present value approach?

4. What is the importance of the discount rate chosen when evaluating investment opportunities?

5. What effect do the amount and cost of mortgage financing have on the present value of the after-tax cash flows to the equity investor?

▌ DISCUSSION QUESTIONS

1. If you were assessing the extent to which a financial consultant exercised due diligence in evaluating an investment proposal, would you be influenced by the consultant's choice between internal rate of return and present value as an evaluation methodology?

2. Because cash-flow projections and cost of capital estimates are, at best, inexact, in most cases does it really make a practical difference whether an analyst uses present value or internal rate of return as a decision criterion?

PROBLEMS

1. Reconstruct Tables 16.1 through 16.5, with the following altered assumptions:

   ■ The interest rate on the $1.65 million loan is 7 percent per annum instead of the 8 percent incorporated on the tables.

   ■ Of the initial $2.21 million tax basis, 75 percent is attributable to the building and thereby can be recovered via the depreciation allowance.

   ■ The taxpayer's marginal income tax rate (combined federal and state) is 40 percent.

   ■ The taxpayer's target rate of return (the hurdle rate) is 16 percent.

2. Compute the expected internal rate of return on the Noname Apartments investment, based on the reconstructed tables in Problem 1.

Case Study

Drs. Grass and Pasteur have formed a general partnership for investments in real estate. They own 16 apartment complexes throughout the city and are requesting a $2 million, nonrecourse, permanent mortgage to purchase another apartment complex, a 60-unit complex called Ginny Gardens. The doctors have submitted all necessary information, including the loan application and the nonrefundable $8,000 application fee. They have provided the financial statements for the past five years of operations for Ginny Gardens, as well as those of all their other complexes. The property statements provide enough information to determine that all the complexes have positive cash flows.

The sales price in the contract is $2.5 million. Purchase expenses are $20,000. The apartment complex has 60 two-bedroom units, which rent for $695 per month (the average in that part of town). The vacancy rate last year was 7 percent, and the other income from laundry and recreation rooms totaled $4,000 last year. The operating expenses last year were $212,000. The financial statements for the earlier years are consistent with last year's figures. The property has been inspected by the lender's real estate analyst, and he has concluded that it is well maintained. The analyst and the appraiser also noted that the area vacancy rate (8 percent) is, on average, slightly higher than that of Ginny Gardens. The appraiser agreed that all other past-year numbers represent normalized cash flows. A Phase I environmental audit was performed and revealed no problems.

The tenants at Ginny Gardens are employed at a variety of local firms, with the largest number (12 percent) at a nearby tire manufacturer. The complex is located near the center of town, one mile from the interchange for the Interstate. The property is nine years old and has no deferred maintenance required. It is in compliance with the Americans with Disabilities Act and contains no lead paint or asbestos. The complex's vacancy rate has been consistent over the past four years, varying no more than 1 percent. The immediate neighborhood has seven other apartment complexes, one newer than Ginny Gardens, two the same age, and the rest older. The financial numbers for Ginny Gardens appear in line with those of the competition. No new complexes are currently under construction in the area.

The 16 other complexes owned by Drs. Grass and Pasteur have a total of 900 units, and in the 11 years that they have owned them, only one has had a vacancy rate above 10 percent–Dent the Tenants Apartments had a 14 percent vacancy rate last year. Their portfolio has stabilized occupancy and their cash flows are reliable.

The doctors are requesting a $2 million, monthly payment loan to be amortized over 20 years with a 10-year stop. The lender's quoted rate is 7.625 percent. In addition to the $8,000 application fee, the lender is requiring one and one-half points to be paid at closing.

Calculate the loan payment, debt service, gross income multiplier, net income multiplier, loan-to-value ratio, debt coverage ratio, operating expense ratio, and cap rate for the proposed purchase.

If the lender's standard credit parameters are 75 percent LTV ratio, 1.20 DCR, 45 percent OER, and 10.75 percent cap rate, do you think the lender should approve the loan. Why or why not? Are there any changes to the loan you would recommend?

If the lender grants the loan, calculate its yield.

Mathematics of Compounding and Discounting

Because real estate decisions generate benefits and costs that are spread differentially through time, it is necessary to adjust for timing differences to make them directly comparable. This appendix explains how such adjustments are made under a variety of circumstances.

Economic rationale for time adjustments is the first topic. The appendix then addresses how to measure growth of money through the compounding of interest income. Present value of a future sum is closely related to how a present amount grows and is logically the next topic of exploration. The text then moves a step further in complexity by considering the present value of a series of future amounts. Because payments to retire a loan are reciprocal to the present value of a series of future receipts, these topics are presented back to back. A final topic addressed is techniques for extending the usefulness of compound interest and discount tables.

▌ CONCEPTUAL BASIS FOR COMPOUNDING AND DISCOUNTING

Compound interest and *discount* are based on two fundamental propositions: More is better than less, and sooner is better than later. From these propositions it follows that people will insist on being compensated for waiting and that there will be a trade-off between the amount received and timeliness of receipt.

That more of a good thing is better than less is not a matter for serious dispute. Economists have considered this a self-evident proposition since the dawn of their discipline. If one bottle of champagne is gratifying, two will be even more so; three are even more desirable than two; and so forth. Fundamental to this concept (and certainly to our example) is that one need not consume the greater quantity if one does not wish to do so. Increased gratification stems from certain knowledge that more is

FIGURE B.1 | Time Preference for Money

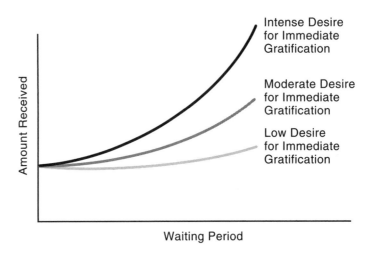

readily available if desired. Two bottles thus provide the same option as one, plus the intoxicating choice of still more refreshment.

A preference for present over future receipt is only a small step farther into abstraction. Who would not (other things being equal) prefer $500 today to the certain promise of $500 next month? Choosing the promise of future receipt reduces one's option for present consumption without offering anything in return. Current receipt, in contrast, provides the option of consumption now, next month, or at any time in the distant future. Clearly, the want-satisfying power of a good is generally enhanced by current receipt.

The more intense the desire for immediate gratification, the greater will be the rate of trade-off, as illustrated in Figure B.1. This relationship is sometimes called *time preference for money*, or the *time value of money*. The topmost line in Figure B.1 represents an individual who has a very high time preference. The individual's strong preference for immediate receipt indicates that he or she will insist on handsome compensation for waiting. The lower line in the figure represents the trade-off function of someone who has relatively low time preference and can therefore be induced to wait with very little compensation. The middle line represents the trade-off function of one with only a moderate time preference.

Growth in the amount available for consumption, as a consequence of waiting, is called *compound interest*. Reducing the amount available, as a consequence of opting for more immediate receipt, is called *discounting*. The greater the rate of compound interest or discount, the steeper will be the slope of the trade-off functions in Figure B.1.

▌ HOW MONEY PLACED ON DEPOSIT WILL GROW ─────────────

If $1,000 placed on deposit for one year earns 7 percent interest, the amount of interest will be .07 times $1,000, or $70. The amount on deposit at the end of the year (assuming no withdrawals of either principal or interest) will be $1,000 plus $70, or $1,070. This simple example incorporates all the elements of compound interest. The general relationship can be expressed as

Final Amount = Original Amount + Interest Earned

CALCULATOR APPLICATION

$n = 1$

$i = 7$ (not $7 \div 12$ because only 1 year)

$PV = 1,000$ (enter as a negative number)

Solve for FV:

$FV = \$1,070$

Because annual interest is usually expressed as a rate or percentage of the amount on deposit (the principal), the same relationship can be expressed as

Final Amount = Original Amount + (Original Amount × Interest Rate)

Rearranging terms on the right-hand side of the equation yields

Final Amount = Original Amount × $(1 + i)$

where i is the interest rate. In the illustration of $1,000 placed on deposit for one year at 7 percent interest, this becomes

$$\$1,070 = \$1,000 \times 1.07$$

Suppose now that the $1,000 principal amount is left on deposit for three years, with interest at 7 percent per year compounding annually. Annual compounding means that accumulated interest itself earns interest in all subsequent periods. Table B.1 illustrates how compound interest accumulates so that the final amount after three years (hereafter called the *compound value*) totals $1,225.04. Expressed in terms of the preceding equation, the compound value at the end of three years is

After 1 year: $1,000 × 1.07

After 2 years: ($1,000 × 1.07)(1.07)

After 3 years: ($1,000 × 1.07)(1.07)(1.07)

$$= (\$1,000)\,(1.07)^3$$
$$= \$1,000 \times 1.22504$$
$$= \$1,225.04$$

TABLE B.1 | How a Debt Accumulates at Compound Interest

Year	Amount Owed at Start of Current Year	Plus Interest at 7%	Amount Owed at Year End
1	$1,000.00	0.07 × $1,000.00	$1,070.00
2	$1,070.00	0.07 × $1,070.00	$1,144.90
3	$1,144.90	0.07 × $1,144.90	$1,225.04

CALCULATOR APPLICATION

n = 3
i = 7
PV = 1,000 (enter as negative number)

Solve for FV:
FV= $1,225.04

This relationship among principal, compound interest, and time is summarized in more general fashion as

$$V_n = PV (1 + i)^n$$

where V_n is the compound value, PV is the initial amount deposited (or borrowed), i is the interest rate, and n is the number of time periods involved.

The only laborious arithmetic in the formula is raising $(1 + i)$ to the nth power. For the problem illustrated, there are only three periods over which to calculate the compound value. But suppose there had been 75 periods! In the absence of a good calculator or a set of tables, the calculation of $(1 + i)^n$ would be tedious in the extreme.

Fortunately, inexpensive financial calculators will quickly handle the computational chores. Also, tables are readily available that give solutions to $(1 + i)^n$ for various values of both i and n. An excerpt from such a table, showing representative values of i and n, is reproduced here as Table B.2. A more complete table appears in Appendix D as Table D.2. Time periods in the table are expressed as years, but they could just as well be days, months, quarters, or any other period appropriate to the problems being considered.

The solution shown in Table B.1 can be derived quickly by referring to Table B.2. Simply extract the value for $(1 + i)^n$ by reading down the column in Table B.2 under the 7 percent rate and across the row indicating value after three years. That factor

TABLE B.2 | How a Debt Accumulates at Compound Interest

Year	6%	7%	8%	9%	10%	12%	14%
1	1.0600	1.0700	1.0800	1.0900	1.1000	1.1200	1.1400
2	1.1236	1.1449	1.1664	1.1881	1.2100	1.2544	1.2996
3	1.1910	1.2250	1.2597	1.2950	1.3310	1.4049	1.4815
4	1.2625	1.3108	1.3605	1.4116	1.4641	1.5735	1.6890
5	1.3382	1.4026	1.4693	1.5386	1.6105	1.7623	1.9254
6	1.4185	1.5007	1.5869	1.6771	1.7716	1.9738	2.1950
7	1.5036	1.6058	1.7138	1.8280	1.9487	2.2107	2.5023
8	1.5938	1.7182	1.8509	1.9926	2.1436	2.4760	2.8526
9	1.6895	1.8385	1.9990	2.1719	2.3579	2.7731	3.2519
10	1.7908	1.9672	2.1589	2.3674	2.5937	3.1058	3.7072
15	2.3966	2.7590	3.1722	3.6425	4.1772	5.4736	7.1379
20	3.2071	3.8697	4.6610	5.6044	6.7275	9.6463	13.7435
25	4.2919	5.4274	6.8485	8.6231	10.8347	17.0001	26.4619

(1.2250) is the compound amount of $1 left on deposit for three years at 7 percent. Multiplying this factor by the $1,000 initial payment yields the value for V.

Now consider a real estate application of compound interest. Suppose a vacant residential building lot, currently worth $5,000, is expected to increase in value at a compound annual rate of 10 percent for at least the next six years. The lot's expected value after six years is expressed by the following equation:

$$V_6 = PV \times (1.10)^6$$
$$= \$5,000 \times 1.7716$$
$$= \$8,858$$

where V_6 is the expected value at the end of the sixth year. The factor (1.7716) can be derived by solving for $(1.10)^6$, or it can be taken from a table such as Table B.2. Multiplying the factor by the initial $5,000 market value of the property gives its expected value of $8,858.

PRESENT VALUE OF A FUTURE AMOUNT

The equation for the future value of an initial amount can easily be altered to solve for the present value of a known future amount. The restructured equation is

$$PV = \frac{V^n}{(1+i)^n}$$

where the symbols have the same meaning as before, but the initial amount PV is the unknown. In this form, the equation is used to solve problems involving the present value of known or estimated future amounts or the interest (discount) rate required to equate known present values with known or estimated future amounts.

EXAMPLE B.1

A parcel of land is expected to be worth $1,500 per acre when water mains are extended five years hence. How much can an investor pay for the land today and still expect to earn 12 percent per annum on his investment before considering transaction costs and income taxes, assuming carrying costs (the cost to maintain the land) exactly equal rental revenue from the property?

Example B.1 illustrates. To solve the problem, first express it as

$$PV = \frac{V^n}{(1+i)^n}$$
$$= \$1,500/(1.12)^5$$
$$= \$1,500/1.7623$$
$$= \$851$$

With simple algebraic sleight of hand we can reconfigure $PV = V_n/(1 + i)^n$ to read $PV = V_n \times 1/(1 + i)^n$. Note that performing the multiplication in our restructured equation (that is, multiplying V_n by 1) takes us right back to the original formulation. With this restructured format we are able to consistently multiply by factors in compound interest or discount tables. Table D.1 in Appendix D provides values for $1/(1 + i)^n$, which we use when solving for present values of single sums due in the future. Table B.3 is an excerpt from Table D.1.

To employ Table B.3 to answer the question posed in Example B.1, we restate the equation as

$$PV = V_5 \times \frac{1}{(1+i)^n}$$

The value of $1/(1 + i)^n$ can be solved with a calculator or taken from a table such as Table B.3. To use the table, read down the 12 percent column and across the five-year row. The factor at the intersection of the column and row is .5674. Multiplying this factor by the \$1,500 expected future value of the land gives the present value per acre (rounded to the nearest dollar) of \$851 when the future value is discounted at 12 percent.

Note the distinction between Tables B.2 and B.3. The first gives values for $(1 + i)^n$, while the latter gives values for $1/(1 + i)^n$. Because these are reciprocals of each other, separate tables are not really needed. All the values for either table can be derived by dividing the corresponding values from the other table into 1. This reciprocal relationship is illustrated in Figure B.2, with reference to Example B.1. The future value of the land (\$1,500) is the compound amount of \$851 growing at 12 percent per annum for five years. Conversely, the value to the investor (\$851) is the present value of \$1,500 to be received in five years, when discounted at 12 percent per annum.

A by-product of the convenience of separate tables for present and future values is the problem of determining which to use. One way to keep this straight is to remember that the solution to factors on the future-value table is always greater than that for the percent value at the same interest rate (so long as the rate is greater than zero). This reflects the basic idea that an amount received in the present is always more valuable than the promise of receiving the same amount at a future date. The future amount must be larger to induce one to wait.

HOW A SERIES OF DEPOSITS WILL GROW

Our discussion so far has focused on the present and the future value of a single sum: how a deposit grows or the present value of a single amount due in the future. But suppose a series of amounts is to be left on deposit or the present value of a series of payments or receipts must be determined.

Consider first the case of a series of fixed payments left on deposit. Any series of equal periodic amounts is called an *annuity*. Conventionally, annuity payments are assumed to be made at the end of each period, though this is not a necessary assumption. Tables can be designed with any desired assumption about the timing of periodic cash flows. As a matter of convention, however, most annuity tables are

TABLE B.3 | Present Value of $1 Due at a Future Date $[1/(1 + i)^n]$

	Annual Discount Rate						
Year	6%	7%	8%	9%	10%	12%	14%
1	0.9434	0.9346	0.9259	0.9174	0.9091	0.8929	0.8772
2	0.8900	0.8734	0.8573	0.8417	0.8264	0.7972	0.7695
3	0.8396	0.8163	0.7938	0.7722	0.7513	0.7118	0.6750
4	0.7921	0.7629	0.7350	0.7084	0.6830	0.6355	0.5921
5	0.7473	0.7130	0.6806	0.6499	0.6209	0.5674	0.5194
6	0.7050	0.6663	0.6302	0.5963	0.5645	0.5066	0.4556
7	0.6651	0.6227	0.5835	0.5470	0.5132	0.4523	0.3996
8	0.6274	0.5820	0.5403	0.5019	0.4665	0.4039	0.3506
9	0.5919	0.5439	0.5002	0.4604	0.4241	0.3606	0.3075
10	0.5584	0.5083	0.4632	0.4224	0.3855	0.3220	0.2697
15	0.4173	0.3624	0.3152	0.2745	0.2394	0.1827	0.1401
20	0.3118	0.2584	0.2145	0.1784	0.1486	0.1037	0.0728
25	0.2330	0.1842	0.1460	0.1160	0.0923	0.0588	0.0378

FIGURE B.2 | Relationship between Present Value and Future Value When Compounding and Discounting at 12 Percent

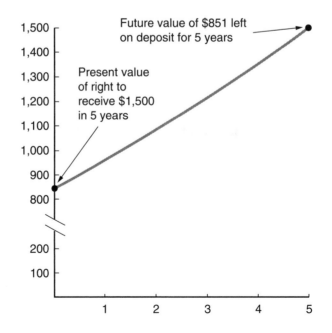

designed with the assumption that all cash flow occurs instantaneously at the end of each period. For example, payments of $500 per annum made at the end of each year for five years constitute a five-year annuity. If these payments were deposited into an account paying 7 percent per annum, how much would be in the account at the time the last payment is made?

The first payment draws interest for four years, the second for three years, the third for two years, and the fourth for one year; the final payment draws no interest at all. If the compound values of all these payments are summed, the total is the compound value of the annuity. The problem is expressed algebraically as

$$S = R_1 (1 + i)^{n-1} + R_2 (1 + i)^{n-2} + R_3 (1 + i)^{n-3} + \ldots + R_{n-1} (1 + i) + R_n$$
$$= R_k[(1 + i)^{n-1} + (1 + i)^{n-2} + (1 + i)^{n-2} + \ldots + (1 + i) + 1]$$

where S is the compound value of the series of payments, R is the amount of the level annual payment, i is the compound annual interest rate, n is the number of payments to be made, and k indicates that R is a constant. For convenience, the above expression is frequently condensed as follows:

$$S = R_k \left[\sum_{t=1}^{n-1} (1+i)^t + 1 \right]$$

where $\sum_{t=1}^{n-1}$ simply means add together the value of $(1 + i)^t$ for n minus one periods, and t indicates the time periods from one through n minus one.

Substituting $500 for R_k, 7 percent for i, and five years for n, we solve for the compound value of $100 per year for five years:

$$S = \$500 \left[\sum_{t=1}^{4} (1.07)^t + 1 \right]$$

$$= \$500 \, [(1.07) + (1.07)^2 + (1.07)^3 + (1.07)^4 + 1]$$
$$= \$500 \times 5.75074$$
$$= \$2,875.37$$

CALCULATOR APPLICATION

n = 1
i = 6
FV = 1,000

Solve for PV:
PV = $943.40

The solution can be reached much more conveniently by referring to tables that give the value of the bracketed term in the preceding equation. Values for the bracketed term can be derived with a financial calculator or extracted from a table such as Table D.5 of Appendix D and in the excerpt from that table presented here as Table B.4. Read across the top of the table to the 7 percent column and down the left margin to the five-year row. The value found at the intersection of the column and row is 5.75074. Substituting this value for the bracketed term in the preceding equation, we determine the compound amount to be $500 × 5.75074 = $2,875.37. This solution is diagrammed in Figure B.3.

PRESENT VALUE OF AN ANNUITY

We have seen that any series of periodic payments received or paid at regular intervals may be called an *annuity*. Examples include pension checks from a retirement fund or payments on a fully amortized installment note. While all such regular periodic streams of cash technically qualify as annuities, not all are popularly known as such.

TABLE B.4 | How $1 Deposited at the End of Each Year Will Grow

$$\left[\sum_{t=1}^{n-1} (1+i)^t + 1 \right]$$

	Annual Discount Rate						
Year	6%	7%	8%	9%	10%	12%	14%
1	1.00000	1.00000	1.00000	1.00000	1.00000	1.00000	1.00000
2	2.06000	2.07000	2.08000	2.09000	2.10000	2.12000	2.14000
3	3.18360	3.21490	3.24640	3.27810	3.31000	3.37440	3.43960
4	4.37462	4.43994	4.50611	4.57313	4.64100	4.77933	4.92114
5	5.63709	5.75074	5.86660	5.98471	6.10510	6.35285	6.61010
6	6.97532	7.15329	7.33593	7.52333	7.71561	8.11519	8.53552
7	8.39384	8.65402	8.92280	9.20043	9.48717	10.08901	10.73049
8	9.89747	10.25980	10.63663	11.02847	11.43589	12.29969	13.23276
9	11.49132	11.97799	12.48756	13.02104	13.57948	14.77566	16.08535
10	13.18079	13.81645	14.48656	15.19293	15.93742	17.54874	19.33730
15	23.27597	25.12902	27.15211	29.36092	31.77248	37.27971	43.84241
20	36.78559	40.99549	45.76196	51.16012	57.27500	72.05244	91.02493
25	54.86451	63.24904	73.10594	84.70090	98.34706	133.33387	181.87083

FIGURE B.3 | How $500 Deposited at the End of Each Year for Five Years Will Grow

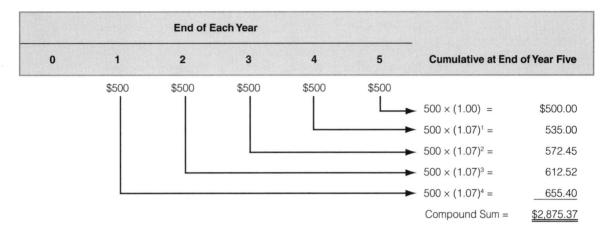

The present value of an annuity is best thought of as the amount that, if invested today at a given interest rate, will provide the known periodic payments for the prescribed period.

To illustrate, suppose funds are to be placed on deposit with interest at 6 percent per annum, sufficient to permit withdrawals in $1,000 increments at the end of each year for three years. To determine the amount of the required initial deposit (assuming there is to be a balance of exactly zero after the third annual withdrawal), the problem might be broken into three separate subquestions:

■ *Subquestion 1*: How much must be deposited today to accumulate $1,000 in one year? To solve this question, first restructure the basic equation to solve for the present value of a single future amount:

$$PV = R_1 \times 1/(1 + i)$$

CALCULATOR APPLICATION

n = 3
i = 6
FV = 1,000

Solve for PV:
PV = $839.62

---

where R_1 is the first periodic withdrawal, i is the interest rate, and there is just one compounding period. The $1/(1 + i)$ is taken from Table B.3

or derived with a calculator. Substituting the appropriate numerical values into the equation, we have

$$PV = \$1,000 \times 1/(1.06)$$
$$= \$1,000 \times .9434$$

■ *Subquestion 2*: How much must be deposited today to accumulate $1,000 in two years? Again, substituting the appropriate numbers into the basic equation, we have

$$PV = \$1,000 \times .1/(1.06)^2$$
$$= \$1,000 \times .8900$$

CALCULATOR APPLICATION

n = 2
i = 6
FV = 1,000

Solve for PV:
PV = $890.00

■ *Subquestion 3*: How much must be deposited today to provide $1,000 in three years? Numerical substitution results in the following equation:

$$PV = \$1,000 \times 1/(1.06)^3$$
$$= \$1,000 \times .8396$$

CALCULATOR APPLICATION

n = 3
i = 6
FV = 1,000

Solve for PV:
PV = $839.62

The total amount to be deposited to provide for the three annual withdrawals is the sum of the three values just calculated. Therefore, the total present value *PV*, the amount to be placed on deposit, is

$$PV = [\$1,000 \times 1/(1.06)] + [\$1,000 \times 1/(1.06)^2] + [\$1,000 \times 1/(1.06)^3]$$
$$= \$1,000 \,[1/(1.06) + 1/(1.06)^2 + 1/(1.06)^3]$$

TABLE B.5 | Present Value of an Annuity of $1 per Year

$$\left[\sum_{t=1}^{n-1}\frac{1}{(1+i)^t}\right]$$

	Annual Discount Rate						
Year	6%	7%	8%	9%	10%	12%	14%
1	0.9434	0.9346	0.9259	0.9174	0.9091	0.8929	0.8772
2	1.8334	1.8080	1.7833	1.7591	1.7355	1.6901	1.6467
3	2.6730	2.6243	2.5771	2.5313	2.4869	2.4018	2.3216
4	3.4651	3.3872	3.3121	3.2397	3.1699	3.0373	2.9137
5	4.2124	4.1002	3.9927	3.8897	3.7908	3.6048	3.4331
6	4.9173	4.7665	4.6229	4.4859	4.3553	4.1114	3.8887
7	5.5824	5.3893	5.2064	5.0330	4.8684	4.5638	4.2883
8	6.2098	5.9713	5.7466	5.5348	5.3349	4.9676	4.6389
9	6.8017	6.5152	6.2469	5.9952	5.7590	5.3282	4.9464
10	7.3601	7.0236	6.7101	6.4177	6.1446	5.6502	5.2161
15	9.7122	9.1079	8.5595	8.0607	7.6061	6.8109	6.1422
20	11.4699	10.5940	9.8181	9.1285	8.5136	7.4694	6.6231
25	12.7834	11.6536	10.6748	9.8226	9.0770	7.8431	6.8729
30	13.7648	12.4090	11.2578	10.2737	9.4269	8.0552	7.0027

Values for $(1/1.06)^t$, where t ranges from one through three, were derived in subquestions one through three. Summing these three values, we get

$$PV = \$1,000 \times (.9434 + .8900 + .8396)$$
$$= \$1,000 \times 2.6730$$
$$= \$2,673$$

The general form of the preceding computation can be expressed as

$$PV = R_k \times [1/(1 + i) + 1/(1 + i)^2 + \ldots + 1/(1 + i)^n]$$

where R_k is the amount of a level periodic receipt, PV is the initial deposit, and i is the discount (interest) rate.

Alternatively, the same concept can be expressed as

$$PV = R_k \left[\sum_{t=1}^{n} \frac{1}{(1+i)^t} \right]$$

The practical problem in solving these calculations is the time required to do the computations when the number of compounding periods and thus the number of values to be summed is very large. Precomputed tables for the cumulative values simplify the problem, as does the availability of a financial calculator (procedures using a financial calculator are explained in Appendix C). These cumulative values are presented in Table D.3 in Appendix D. An excerpt is presented here as Table B.5.

Returning to the problem of a three-year annuity of $1,000 per year with a 6 percent per annum discount (interest) rate, determining the present value (that is, the required initial deposit) involves finding the annuity factor in Table B.5, which lies at the intersection of the 6 percent column and the three-year row. This factor (2.6730) multiplied by the $1,000 annual annuity payment equals the amount of the initial deposit ($2,673):

$$PV = R_k \left[\sum_{t=1}^{3} \frac{1}{(1.06)^t} \right]$$

$$= \$1,000 \times 2.6730$$
$$= \$2,673$$

PRESENT VALUE OF A PERPETUAL ANNUITY

A *perpetuity* is a never-ending stream of payments or receipts. For such a cash-flow pattern to exist, it must necessarily be the case that each installment represents only accrued interest. If some principal were retired with each payment, then the principal would eventually be exhausted and the stream would end; there would not be a perpetual flow. This being the case, it follows that each payment is simply the interest rate per period multiplied by the principal amount of the annuity:

$$R_k = PV \times i$$

where R_k is the periodic payment or receipt, PV is the present value (principal amount) of the annuity, and i is the rate of interest per period. To solve for the present value, simply transpose the symbols in the equation:

$$PV = R_k / i$$

To illustrate, consider a perpetual annuity of $10,000 per annum, with interest at 8 percent per annum. The present value of the perpetuity is

$$PV = R_k / i$$
$$= \$10,000/.08$$
$$= \$125,000$$

Suppose the appropriate discount rate associated with the above annuity moves to, say, 10 percent per annum. This reduces the present value of the perpetuity to $100,000:

$$PV = R_k/i$$
$$= \$10,000/.10$$
$$= \$100,000$$

This result leads to the generalized observation that there is an inverse relationship between the discount rate and the present value of any future series of payments or receipts.

▌ PAYMENTS TO AMORTIZE A LOAN

Suppose you were to receive a lump-sum educational grant of $10,000 to be spent during four years of university study. How much could you withdraw at the end of each year, in four equal installments, to exactly exhaust the fund with the last annual withdrawal if the balance in the fund draws interest at 6 percent? This is an annuity problem not unlike those investigated earlier. Recall the general expression for a level annuity, which is

$$PV = R_k \left[\sum_{t=1}^{n} \frac{1}{(1+i)^t} \right]$$

The essential difference here is that the initial payment PV is known and the periodic receipt R_k is the unknown quantity. The problem can be solved with a financial calculator or by using factors from Table B.5. To use the table, find the value for the summation of $1/(1 + i)^t$, where the interest rate, i, is 6 percent and the time periods range from one through four years. The factor is 3.4651. The problem can thus be expressed as

$$PV = R_k \left[\sum_{t=1}^{4} \frac{1}{(1.06)^t} \right]$$

$$= R_k \times 3.4651$$

and, as the value of PV is known to be $10,000,

$$\$10,000 = R_k \times 3.4651$$

Solving for R_k yields

$$R_k = \$10,000/3.4651$$
$$= \$2,885.92$$

Note that the final solution involves dividing by an annuity factor. Recall that division is the same as multiplying by a reciprocal (that is, $a/b = a \times 1/b$). Tables can easily be generated that incorporate reciprocals of values from an annuity table. Such a table (incorporating monthly, rather than annual, payments) is included here as Table B.6. A more complete table appears as Table D.4 in Appendix D.

CALCULATOR APPLICATION
n = 4
i = 6
PV = 10,000

Solve for PMT:
PMT = $2,885.91

The factors in Table B.6 are often called *loan-amortization factors*, or *debt constants*. The table itself is then referred to as an *amortization table*. It gives the equal periodic payment necessary to repay a $1 loan, with interest, over a specified number of payment periods. (A table showing the distribution of a specific payment schedule between principal and interest is frequently called an *amortization schedule*.) Because Table B.6 gives repayment factors based on monthly payments, it is not reciprocal to Table B.5. A table of annual payments, however, would be.

TABLE B.6 | Monthly Payment to Amortize a $1 Debt

Year	Interest Discount Rate						
	6%	**7%**	**8%**	**9%**	**10%**	**12%**	**14%**
1	0.086066	0.086527	0.086988	0.087451	0.087916	0.088849	0.089787
2	0.044321	0.044773	0.045227	0.045685	0.046145	0.047073	0.048013
3	0.030422	0.030877	0.031336	0.031800	0.032267	0.033214	0.034178
4	0.023485	0.023946	0.024413	0.024885	0.025363	0.026334	0.027326
5	0.019333	0.019801	0.020276	0.020758	0.021247	0.022244	0.023268
6	0.016573	0.017049	0.017533	0.018026	0.018526	0.019550	0.020606
7	0.014609	0.015093	0.015586	0.016089	0.016601	0.017653	0.018740
8	0.013141	0.013634	0.014137	0.014650	0.015174	0.016253	0.017372
9	0.012006	0.012506	0.013019	0.013543	0.014079	0.015184	0.016334
10	0.011102	0.011611	0.012133	0.012668	0.013215	0.014347	0.015527
15	0.008439	0.008988	0.009557	0.010143	0.010746	0.012002	0.013317
20	0.007164	0.007753	0.008364	0.008997	0.009650	0.011011	0.012435
25	0.006443	0.007068	0.007718	0.008392	0.009087	0.010532	0.012038
30	0.005996	0.006653	0.007338	0.008046	0.008776	0.010286	0.011849

To see how an amortization table works, consider a $100,000 loan that calls for interest at 8 percent per annum on the unpaid balance. If the loan is to be repaid in equal monthly installments (including both interest and principal) over, say, five years, monthly payment obligations can be determined by multiplying the $100,000 face amount by the amortization factor from Table B.6, which lies at the intersection of the 8 percent column and the five-year row. The product, $2,027.60, is the amount the lender must receive each month for five years to recover the initial $100,000 outlay and receive 8 percent per annum interest on the outstanding balance of the loan.

CALCULATOR APPLICATION

n = 60 (12 months x 5 years)

i = .6667 (8 ÷ 12)

PV = 100,000

Solve for PMT:

PMT = $2,027.64

Had the $100,000 loan in the preceding example called for annual payments, Table B.6 would not have been usable. No table of annual amortization payments is given, because loans seldom provide for this repayment pattern. But an amortization factor can be derived easily by calculating the reciprocal of the factor for an 8 percent, five-year annuity. Divide the annuity factor, 3.9927, from Table B.5, into one. The quotient, 0.25046, is the annual payment to retire a five-year, 8 percent loan of $1, with annual payments. Multiplying this factor by a $100,000 loan amount gives the annual payment necessary to retire the loan in five years: $25,046. The problem also can be solved without reference to tables. With annual payments, the equation is

$$\text{Payment} = \text{Loan Amount} \times \left[\frac{i}{\left(1 - \left[\frac{1}{(1+i)^n} \right] \right)} \right]$$

If payments are made monthly, the equation is revised accordingly:

$$\text{Payment} = \text{Loan Amount} \times \left[\frac{\dfrac{i}{12}}{\left(1 - \left[\dfrac{1}{(1+\dfrac{i}{12})} \right]^{12n} \right)} \right]$$

Note that an annual payment is somewhat more than the sum of 12 monthly payments on a loan of the same size with the same amortization period and interest rate

($25,046 vs. $24,331.20 in the preceding example). This is because interest on the outstanding balance is greater for the annual payment note as a result of the balance not having been "paid down" at monthly intervals during the year. In general, the more frequently payments are made, the less the total interest obligation will be and thus the less the total debt service payment.

EXTENDING THE USEFULNESS OF FINANCIAL TABLES

Even though they are rapidly being rendered superfluous by inexpensive financial calculators, tables can be used to solve a wide variety of real estate investment and financial problems. Several applications are illustrated here to provide additional exercise in using the tables, as well as to demonstrate their versatility. These extended uses are by no means exhaustive. They are intended rather to demonstrate the flexibility of compound interest and discount concept, the total usefulness of which is limited only by imagination and inventiveness.

Finding Values Not in the Tables

Interest and discount tables give factors for values at intervals over a wide range. Sometimes, however, the rate under consideration falls at an intermediate point between those in a table. When this happens, estimate the actual value by *interpolating* between table values most nearly approximating the rate being sought.

Interpolation involves assuming a linear relationship between tabular values. This introduces a degree of error, because the actual relationship is quadratic rather than linear. The convenient assumption greatly simplifies calculations, however, and the error will generally be insignificant if interpolation is between those tabular values closest to the unknown factor.

FIGURE B.4 | Interpolating between Known Present Value Factors

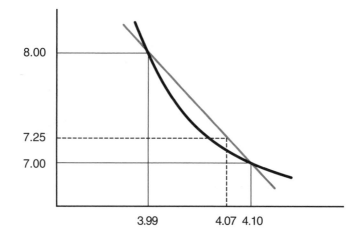

FIGURE B.5 | Interpolating to Find Values Not on the Tables

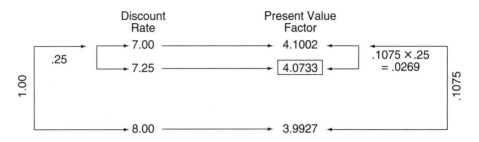

The problem is illustrated in Figure B.4. The curved line shows the relationship between values from Table B.5 for discount rates of 7 and 8 percent and for all intermediate discount rates. Interpolation results in estimates of values not in the table, as indicated by the straight line in the illustration. Distance between the curved (actual) function and the straight (estimated) line represents error introduced by interpolation. Obviously, the wider apart the known values from which an unknown factor is estimated, the greater the error introduced by the assumption of linearity.

Figure B.4 depicts the consequence of using straight-line interpolation to estimate the appropriate present value factor for a five-year annuity when the discount rate is 7.25 percent. Table B.5 gives annuity present value factors for discount rates of 7 and 8 percent but for no intermediate rates. Because 7.25 percent falls one-fourth of the way between these given factors, approximate an appropriate factor by moving one-fourth of the distance between the factor for 7 percent and that for 8 percent. The 7 percent factor is 4.1002, and that for 8 percent is 3.9927. Multiply the difference by 0.25 and subtract this amount from the factor of 7 percent. The result is a factor of 4.0733, determined as follows:

$$4.1002 - .25 (4.1002 - 3.9927) = 4.0733$$

Figure B.5 diagrams the preceding calculations. The total number of percentage points between 7 and 8 percent is 8 minus 7, or one point. The distance between discount rates of 7 and 7.25 percent is 7.25 minus 7, or 0.25 point. Because 0.25 point is 25 percent of one point, the "target" discount rate lies 25 percent of the distance between the known values. Assume a linear relationship and estimate the discount factor for the 7.25 percent rate by moving 25 percent of the distance between the discount factor for 7 percent and that for 8 percent.

The total distance between the factor for 7 percent, 4.1002, and that for 8 percent, 3.9927, is 0.1075. Twenty-five percent of this distance is 0.25×0.1075, or 0.0269. Moving this far from the 4.1002 value associated with the 7 percent discount rate results in an estimate of 4.0733 for the factor associated with a discount rate of 7.25 percent.

Remaining Balance of a Note

Understanding the reciprocity of annuity tables and amortization tables (with the same time period between payments) sets the stage for easily determining the remaining balance on a fully amortizing note. The face amount of a note can be thought of as the present value of an annuity whose periodic receipts are the debt service payments. But amortization tables are used because the present value is known and the future payments are unknown, whereas with conventional annuity problems, the known factors are the future payments and the present value is unknown.

To see this relationship clearly, consider a $100,000 loan calling for level monthly payments to fully amortize the loan over 25 years, with interest at 9 percent. Referring to the amortization table (Table B.6), multiply the factor found at the intersection of the 9 percent column and the 25-year row by the $100,000 face amount of the loan. The monthly payment is found to be $839.20. The same answer results from solving the equation, as discussed earlier, or using a financial calculator.

CALCULATOR APPLICATION

n = 300 (12 months × 25 years)
i = .75 (9 ÷ 12)
PV = 100,000

Solve for PMT:
PMT = $839.20

Now, remembering the reciprocal relationship between annuity and amortization factors, treat the remaining payments as a level monthly annuity and discount (the annuity period will be the number of monthly payments remaining, and the discount rate will be one-twelfth the contract rate of interest). You can also use the amortization table to determine the present value of a monthly annuity of $839.20 that extends for 25 years, when discounted at 9 percent. To derive the present value factor for the monthly annuity using the table, go back to the intersection of the 9 percent column and 25-year row of the amortization table and divide the factor into one. The result ($1/.008392 = 119.16$), when multiplied by the monthly payment, yields the remaining balance of $100,000. We, of course, already knew this to be the present value, because that is the amount of the original loan. The approach, however, can be used to determine the remaining balance at any future date by simply substituting the remaining number of payments for the period.

CALCULATOR APPLICATION

n = 300 (12 months × 25 years)
i = .75 (9 ÷ 12)
PMT = 839.20

Solve for PV:
PV = $100,000

EXAMPLE B.2

Determine the present value, when discounting at 6 percent per annum, of a five-year annuity of $1,000 per annum (paid at the end of each year), with the first annuity payment due four years hence.

Present Value of a Deferred Annuity

To find the present value of an annuity that does not start until some time in the future, find the value of the annuity at the beginning of the first year of payments or receipts and then discount this amount to the present as a single sum. Alternatively, solve for an annuity that extends over both the annuity payment period and the period of the deferral and subtract the present value of the annuity for the period of the deferral; the remainder is the present value of the deferred annuity.

Example B.2 illustrates the problem. The first annuity payment or receipt is due in four years. Because payments are made at the end of each year, the annuity period actually starts at the beginning of the year in which the first payment is made. There is, therefore, a three-year lapse before the annuity period starts.

Solution Alternative A

The first step is to solve for the value of the annuity at the beginning of the annuity period (three years hence). At that point there is a straightforward five-year annuity of $1,000 per annum. The value at that point (which we will call V_3) is $4,212.40, determined as follows:

$$V_3 = R_k \left[\sum_{t=1}^{5} \frac{1}{(1.06)^t} \right]$$

$$= \$1,000 \times 4.2124$$
$$= \$4,212.40$$

The second step is to discount V_3 as a single sum due three years hence. The present value is $3,537. Here is the calculation:

$$PV = V_3 \times 1/(1.06)^3$$
$$= \$4,212.40 \times .8396$$
$$= \$3,536.73$$

These two steps can, of course, be combined into a single mathematical operation, with the same results. Here is the combined computation:

$$PV = R_k \left[\sum_{t=1}^{5} \frac{1}{(1.06)^t} \right] \times \left[\frac{1}{(1.06)^3} \right]$$

$$= \$1,000 \, (4.2124 \times .8396)$$
$$= \$1,000 \times 3.53673$$
$$= \$3,536.73$$

CALCULATOR APPLICATION

n = 5	n = 35
i = 6	i = 6
PMT = 1,000 (enter as negative number)	FV = 4,212.36
Solve for PV:	*Solve for PV:*
PV = $4,212.36	PV = $43,536.78

Solution Alternative B

Determine what the present value would be if the annuity extended over both the deferral period and the payment period (three years + five years = eight years). From this value subtract the value of the annuity for the first three years (the period of the deferral). The remainder is the present value of the annuity for the period in which it is actually to be received.

For the annuity in Example B.2, the present value would be $6,209.80 if payments extended over the entire eight-year period:

$$PV = R_k \left[\sum_{t=1}^{8} \frac{1}{(1.06)^t} \right]$$

$$= \$1,000 \times 6.2098$$
$$= \$6,209.80$$

CALCULATOR APPLICATION

n = 8
i = 6
PMT = 1,000 (enter as negative number)

Solve for PV:
PV = $6,209.79

From this amount subtract the value of the annuity for the period of the deferral. This is three years, and the value to be subtracted is $2,673, determined as follows:

$$PV = R_k \left[\sum_{t=1}^{3} \frac{1}{(1.06)^t} \right]$$

$$= \$1,000 \times 2.6730$$
$$= \$2,673$$

CALCULATOR APPLICATION

n = 3

i = 6

PMT = 1,000 (enter as negative number)

Solve for PV:

PV = $2,673.01

The present value of the five-year annuity that will be received, starting after three years, is simply the present value of the last five years of the eight-year annuity. To find this amount, subtract the present value of the three-year annuity (the portion of the eight-year annuity that will not be received) from the present value of the eight-year annuity. The computation yields the same solution as before, except for a small rounding error. Here are the numbers:

$$PV = \$6,209.80 - \$2,673$$
$$= \$3,536.80$$

These computations can also be consolidated into a single equation, with the same results:

$$PV = R_k \left[\sum_{t=1}^{8} \frac{1}{(1.06)^t} \right] - \left[\sum_{t=1}^{3} \frac{1}{(1.06)^t} \right]$$

$$= \$1,000 \, (6.2098 - 2.6730)$$
$$= \$1,000 \times 3.5368$$
$$= \$3,536.80$$

Annuities in Advance

Our earlier statement that annuity payments or receipts are treated as if the transaction occurred at the end of each period needs further elaboration. This is not a necessary assumption for using discounting and compounding; it is merely a convention adopted when constructing annuity tables. A table incorporating the assumption that cash flow occurs at the beginning of each period, or at any intermediate point within the periods, could easily be developed.

Such tables are not frequently available. Existing tables must therefore be modified when working with cash flows that occur at the beginning of each period. Annuities with this sort of schedule are conventionally called *annuities in advance*.

To find the present value of annuities in advance, simply multiply the annual amount by

$$\sum_{t=1}^{n} \frac{1}{(1+i)^t}$$

and add one more payment. Example B.3 illustrates.

EXAMPLE B.3

Determine the present value of an annuity of $1,000 per annum for five years when the appropriate discount rate is 6 percent per annum and when the annuity payment is made at the beginning of each year. (Values are rounded to the nearest whole dollar.)

$$PV = R_k \left[\sum_{t=1}^{4} \frac{1}{(1.06)^t} \right] + R$$
$$= (\$1,000 \times 3.4651) + \$1,000$$
$$= \$3,465 + \$1,000$$
$$= \$4,465$$

CALCULATOR APPLICATION

	or in Begin mode
n = 4	
i = 6	n = 5
PMT = 1,000 (enter as negative number)	i = 6
	PMT = 1,000

Solve for PV: *Solve for PV:*
PV = $3,465.11 + $1,000 = $4,465.11   PV = $4,465.11

To solve this type of problem you must specify whether payments are made at the beginning or end of the compounding period. Most modern financial calculators default to payment at the end of each period but easily can be reset to calculate payment at the beginning of each period.

To find the compound value of an annuity when payments are made at the beginning rather than the end of each period, multiply the amount of the annual annuity payment by

$$\sum_{t=1}^{n+1} \frac{1}{(1+i)^t}$$

where n is the actual number of payments, and subtract the amount of one payment. Example B.4 demonstrates these calculations.

EXAMPLE B.4

Determine the compound (future) value of an annuity of $1,000 per annum for five years when the compound interest rate is 6 percent per annum and when payments are made at the beginning of each year. (All amounts are rounded to the nearest whole dollar.)

$$S = R_k \left[\sum_{t=1}^{6} \frac{1}{(1.06)^t} \right] - R$$

$$= \$1,000 \ (6.9753) - \$1,000$$
$$= \$6,975 - \$1,000$$
$$= \$5,975$$

CALCULATOR APPLICATION

n = 6
i = 6
PMT = 1,000

Solve for FV:
FV = $6,975.32 − 1,000.00 = $5,975.32

or in Begin mode

n = 5
i = 6
PMT = 1,000

Solve for FV:
FV = $5,975.32

Compounding and Discounting with Financial Calculators

Financial tables such as those discussed in Appendix B and presented in Appendix D have for many years been a major labor-saving device for analysts by greatly simplifying computational chores. The tables themselves are well on their way to being outmoded, however, by the ready availability of low-cost electronic calculators programmed to do financial computations. Many of these calculators are not much larger than a standard business card (some are even incorporated into wristwatches), and many of them cost less than a book of financial tables.

This appendix is intended to demonstrate the use of financial calculators to solve problems such as those explained in Appendix B. To show comparability of calculator solutions with those derived from tables, each example demonstrates how table values themselves may be derived by using calculators. Illustrations then show how calculators can be utilized to find other values that are not found in the tables.

▌ FUTURE VALUE OF A DOLLAR

The future value interest factor (Table D.2 of Appendix D) is used to calculate how a sum left on deposit at a compound rate of interest will grow. The compound interest formula is

$$FV = PV\,(1 + i)^n$$

where

FV = Future Value
PV = Present Value (amount invested today)
$\;\,i$ = Rate
$\;\,n$ = Number of Periods

EXAMPLE C.1

The future value interest factor for three years at 8 percent (shown in Table D.2 in Appendix D) is calculated as follows:

$$FV = (1 + .08)^3$$
$$= 1.2597$$

The future value interest factor in Example C.1 can be determined by using a calculator with the keys *n, i*, *PV*, *PMT*, and *FV* by entering *n* = 3, *i* = 8, *PV* = 1, and solving for *FV*. To calculate the factors for Example C.1 and all following examples in this appendix, use the following substitutions:

1. *Monthly Factors*

    n = Number of Months

    i = Annual Rate/12

2. *Quarterly Factors*

    n = Number of Quarters

    i = Annual Rate/4

3. *Semiannual Factors*

    n = Number of Half Years

    i = Annual Rate/2

EXAMPLE C.2

1. *FV* of $1 for three years at 8 percent per annum, compounded monthly.

    $$FV = (1 + .006667)^{36}$$
    $$= 1.270237$$

    Calculator solution:

    n = 36   *i* = 8/12

    PV = 1   *FV* = ?

2. *FV* of $1 for three years at 8 percent, compounded quarterly.

    $$FV = (1 + .02)^{12}$$
    $$= 1.268242$$

    Calculator solution:

    n = 12   *i* = 8/4

    PV = 1   *FV* = ?

3. *FV* of $1 for three years at 8 percent, compounded semiannually.

    $$FV = (1 + .04)^6$$
    $$= 1.26532$$

    Calculator solution:

    n = 6   *i* = 8/2

    PV = 1   *FV* = ?

COMPOUND VALUE OF AN ANNUITY

The compound value of an annuity equation is used to calculate how much an amount invested periodically will be worth at some future date if it earns interest at a compound rate. The compound value formula is

$$FV = PMT \times ([(1 + i)^n - 1]/i)$$

where

FV = Future Value
PMT = Payment (amount invested periodically)
i = Rate
n = Number of Periods

EXAMPLE C.3

The future worth of an annuity factor for three years at 8 percent is calculated as follows:

$$FV = ([(1 + .08)^3 - 1]/.08)$$
$$= 3.2464$$

The factor in Example C.3 can be determined with a financial calculator by entering **_n_** = 3, **_i_** = 8, **_PMT_** = 1, and solving for **_FV_**.

EXAMPLE C.4

1. *FV* of $1 per month for three years at 8 percent per annum, compounded monthly.

$$FV = \$1 \times ([(1 + .00667)^{36} - 1]/.00667)$$
$$= \$40.54$$

   Calculator solution:
   _n_ = 36   **_i_** = 8/12
   PMT = 1   **_FV_** = ?

2. FV of $1 per quarter for three years at 8 percent per annum, compounded quarterly.

$$FV = \$1 \times ([(1 + .02)^{12} - 1]/.02)$$
$$= \$13.41$$

   Calculator solution:
   _n_ = 12   **_i_** = 8/4
   PMT = 1   **_FV_** = ?

3. *FV* of $1 semiannually for three years at 8 percent per annum, compounded semiannually.

$$FV = \$1 \times ([(1 + .04)^6 - 1]/.04)$$
$$= \$6.63$$

   Calculator solution:
   _n_ = 6   **_i_** = 8/2
   PMT = 1   **_FV_** = ?

█ PRESENT VALUE OF A DOLLAR

The present value of a dollar formula is used to calculate how much some amount to be received in the future is worth today considering compound interest. The formula is

$$PV = FV \times 1/(1 + i)^n$$

where

PV = Present Value
FV = Future Value
  i = Rate
  n = Number of Periods

EXAMPLE C.5

The present value interest factor for three years at 8 percent (found in Table D.1 in Appendix D) is calculated as follows:

$$PV = (1 + .08)^3$$
$$PV = .7938$$

The present value interest factor in Example C.5 can be determined using a calculator by entering **n** = 3, **i** = 8, **FV** = 1, and solving for **PV**.

EXAMPLE C.6

1. *PV* of $1 at the end of three years at 8 percent per annum, compounded monthly.
$$PV = 1/(1 + .00667)^{36}$$
$$= .7873$$

    Calculator solution:
    n = 36   **i** = 8/12
    FV = 1   **PV** = ?

2. *PV* of $1 at the end of three years at 8 percent per annum, compounded quarterly.
$$PV = 1/(1 + .02)^{12}$$
$$= .7885$$

    Calculator solution:
    n = 12   **i** = 8/4
    FV = 1   **PV** = ?

3. *PV* of $1 at the end of three years at 8 percent per annum, compounded semiannually.
$$PV = 1/(1 + .04)^6$$
$$= .7903$$

    Calculator solution:
    n = 6   **i** = 8/2
    FV = 1   **PV** = ?

▮ PRESENT VALUE OF A LEVEL ANNUITY

The present value annuity formula is used to calculate how much an amount to be received periodically in the future is worth today, for a given rate of interest or discount. The formula is

$$PV = PMT \times [(1 - [1/(1 + i)^n])/i]$$

where
  PV = Present Value
  PMT = Payment per Period
  i = Rate
  n = Number of Periods

EXAMPLE C.7

The present value interest factor of an annuity for three years at 8 percent (found in Table D.3 in Appendix D) is calculated as follows:
$$PV = [(1 - [1/(1 + .08)^3])/.08]$$
$$= 2.5771$$

Example C.7 can be solved using a calculator by entering $n = 3$, $i = 8$, $PMT = 1$, and solving for PV.

EXAMPLE C.8

1. PV of $1 per month for three years at 8 percent per annum.
$$PV = 1 \times [(1 - [1/(1 + .0066667)^{36}])/.0066667]$$
$$= 31.9118$$

    Calculator solution:
    $n = 36$ $i = 8/12$
    $PMT = 1$ $PV = ?$

2. PV of $1 per quarter for three years at 8 percent per annum.
$$PV = 1 \times [(1 - [1/(1 + .02)^{12}])/.02]$$
$$= 10.5753$$

    Calculator solution:
    $n = 12$ $i = 8/4$
    $PMT = 1$ $PV = ?$

3. PV of $1 per period semiannually for three years at 8 percent per annum.
$$PV = 1 \times [(1 - [1/(1 + .04)^6])/.04]$$
$$= 5.2421$$

    Calculator solution:
    $n = 6$ $i = 8/2$
    $PMT = 1$ $PV = ?$

▌ AMOUNT TO AMORTIZE $1 (MORTGAGE CONSTANT)

The *mortgage constant* is used to calculate the payment on a fully amortizing loan. It is the percentage of the original loan that must be paid periodically in order to fully repay principal and interest over the term of the loan. The formula is

$$MC = i/(1 - [1/(1 + i)^n])$$

where

MC = Mortgage Constant
i = Rate
n = Number of Periods

EXAMPLE C.9

The mortgage constant for a three-year loan at 8 percent interest, with annual payments, is calculated as follows:

$$MC = (.08)/(1 - [1/(1 + .08)^3])$$
$$= .3880$$

The constant in Example C.9 can be derived using a financial calculator by entering n = 3, i = 8, PV = 1, and solving for **PMT**.

EXAMPLE C.10

1. Payment (*PMT*) per period to amortize $1 over three years at 8 percent per annum, with monthly payments.
    $$PMT = .006667/(1 - [1/(1 + .006667)^{36}])$$
    $$= .0313$$

    Calculator solution:

    n = 36 i = 8/12
    PV = 1 PMT = ?

2. Payment (PMT) per period to amortize $1 over three years at 8 percent per annum, with quarterly payments.
    $$PMT = .02/(1 - [1/(1 + .02)^{12}])$$
    $$= .0946$$

    Calculator solution:

    n = 12 i = 8/4
    PV = 1 PMT = ?

3. Payment (PMT) per period to amortize $1 over three years at 8 percent per annum, with semiannual payments.
    $$PMT = .04/(1 - [1/(1 + .04)^6])$$
    $$= .1908$$

    Calculator solution:

    n = 6 1 i = 8/2
    PV = 1 PMT = ?

CALCULATOR APPLICATION

AMORTIZATION SCHEDULE EXAMPLES FOR HEWLETT-PACKARD 12C AND HP12BII

Term = 30 years
Loan = $100,000
Interest Rate = 10%
Monthly Payment = $877.57

HP-12C	**HP-17BII**
10 ENTER 12 ÷ i	FIN
100,000 PV	TVM
30 ENTER 12 × n	10 I%YR
PMT = $877.57	100,000 PV
g END	360 n
12 f AMORT (is the n key)	PMT = $877.57
$9,974.98 is the portion of the 1st year's payments applied to interest.	OTHER
x ⋛ y	12 P/YR END AMORT
555.88 is the portion of the 1st year's payments applied to principal.	12 #P
RCL PV	INT
$99,444.12 is the balance remaining after one year.	*$9,974.98 is the portion of the 1st year's payments applied to interest.*
	PRIN
12 f AMORT	*555.86 is the portion of the 1st year's payments applied to principal.*
$9,916.77 is the portion of the 2nd year's payments applied to interest.	BAL
x ⋛ y	*$99,444.14 is the balance remaining after one year.*
614.09 is the portion of the 2nd year's payments applied to principal.	NEXT
RCL PV	INT
$98,830.04 is the balance remaining after two years.	*$9,916.77 is the portion of the 2nd year's payments applied to interest.*
	PRIN
	614.07 is the portion of the 2nd year's payments applied to principal.
	BAL
	$98,830.07 is the balance remaining after two years.

CALCULATOR APPLICATION

NET PRESENT VALUE AND IRR EXAMPLES FOR HEWLETT-PACKARD 12C AND HP17BII:

See **Table 16.5**: Present Value of Expected Future Benefits for Noname Apartments

HP-12C

560,000 [CHS] [g] [CFO] (is [PV] key)

31,523 [g] [CFj] (is [PMT] key)

40,103 [g] [CFj]

48,585 [g] [CFj]

56,995 [g] [CFj]

66,045 [g] [CFj]

74,980 [ENTER] 1,180,610 [+] [g] [CFj]

15 [i]

[f] [NPV] (is [PV] key)

NPV = 137,929.68

IRR = 19.87

Note: To calculate the IRR, enter the cash flows using the same method described above but do not input any value for [i] and do not press [f] [NPV] rather, press [f] [IRR] (the [FV] key). The 12C may take several seconds to produce an answer for IRR. The 17BII is considerably faster.

HP-17BII

[FIN]

[CFLO]

[____] (gold shift key) clear data (is [INPUT] key)

[YES]

560,000 [+/−] [INPUT]

Stores initial investment in FLOW (0)

31,523 [INPUT] [INPUT]

Stores 1st cash flow in FLOW (1) and prompts for # times (1) = 1

40,103 [INPUT] [INPUT]

Stores 2nd cash flow in FLOW (2) and prompts for # times (2) = 1

48,585 [INPUT] [INPUT]

Stores 3rd cash flow in FLOW (3) and prompts for # times (3) = 1

56,995 [INPUT] [INPUT]

Stores 4th cash flow in FLOW (4) and prompts for # times (4) = 1

66,045 [INPUT] [INPUT]

Stores 4th cash flow in FLOW (5) and prompts for # times (5) = 1

74,980 + 1,180,610 = 1,255,590

[INPUT] [INPUT]

Stores 4th cash flow in FLOW (5) and prompts for # times (5) = 1

[EXIT]

[CALC]

15 [I%]

[NPV] = 137,929.68

[IRR%] = 19.87

Note: While this may seem more cumbersom than the 12C it actually is much faster, very powerful, and easy to use, after you have solved for NPV (or before) you can calculate, among other things, the IRR by simply pressing [IRR%]

CALCULATOR APPLICATION

CALCULATE THE FINAL PAYMENT OF THE UNPAID BALANCE OF A PARTIALLY AMORTIZED LOAN
(i.e. the **Balloon Payment**): Two methods computing the balloon payments
below for both the Hewlett-Packard 12C and HP17B11

The monthly payments on a $100,000 loan at 9.0% interest are $804.62 based
on a full 30 year amortization period. If the loan balance is paid in full at the end
of year 10 what is the balloon payment?

HP-12C

20 [ENTER] 12 [×] because 20
            years remain
9 [ENTER] 12 [÷] [i]
804.62 [CHS] [PMT]
[PV] = $89,429.15

or

10 [ENTER] 12 [×] because 10
            years have past
9 [ENTER] 12 [÷] [i]
100,000 [PV]

804.62 [CHS] [PMT]
[FV] = $89,430.25*

minor differences due to rounding

HP-17BII

[FIN] [TVM]

Make sure payments are set to 12
periods per year; [END MODE].

240 [n]
9 [I%YR]
804.62 [+/-] [PMT]
[PV] = 89,429.45

or

120 [n]
9 [I%YR]
100,000 [PV]
804.62 [+/-] [PMT]
[FV] $89,430.25*

RECOMMENDED READING

Steiner, Bob. *Mastering Financial Calculations: A Step-by-Step Guide to the Mathematics
   of Financial Market Instruments,* 2nd ed. Upper Saddle River, N.J.: Financial Times
   Prentice Hall, 2007.

White, Mark A. "Financial Problem-Solving with an Electronic Calculator." *Financial Practice and Education* (Fall 1991): 73–88.

Financial Tables

TABLE D.1 | Present Value of $1
PVIF $(r,n) = 1 + r)^{-n}$

Period	1%	2%	3%	4%	5%	6%	7%	8%	9%	10%
1	.9901	.9804	.9709	.9615	.9524	.9434	.9346	.9259	.9174	.9091
2	.9803	.9612	.9426	.9246	.9070	.8900	.8734	.8573	.8417	.8264
3	.9706	.9423	.9151	.8890	.8638	.8396	.8163	.7938	.7722	.7513
4	.9610	.9238	.8885	.8548	.8227	.7921	.7629	.7350	.7084	.6830
5	.9515	.9057	.8626	.8219	.7835	.7473	.7130	.6806	.6499	.6209
6	.9420	.8880	.8375	.7903	.7462	.7050	.6663	.6302	.5963	.5645
7	.9327	.8706	.8131	.7599	.7107	.6651	.6227	.5835	.5470	.5132
8	.9235	.8535	.7894	.7307	.6768	.6274	.5820	.5403	.5019	.4665
9	.9143	.8368	.7664	.7026	.6446	.5919	.5439	.5002	.4604	.4241
10	.9053	.8203	.7441	.6756	.6139	.5584	.5083	.4632	.4224	.3855
11	.8963	.8043	.7224	.6496	.5847	.5268	.4751	.4289	.3875	.3505
12	.8874	.7885	.7014	.6246	.5568	.4970	.4440	.3971	.3555	.3186
13	.8787	.7730	.6810	.6006	.5303	.4688	.4150	.3677	.3262	.2897
14	.8700	.7579	.6611	.5775	.5051	.4423	.3878	.3405	.2992	.2633
15	.8613	.7430	.6419	.5553	.4810	.4173	.3624	.3152	.2745	.2394
16	.8528	.7284	.6232	.5339	.4581	.3936	.3387	.2919	.2519	.2176
17	.8444	.7142	.6050	.5134	.4363	.3714	.3166	.2703	.2311	.1978
18	.8360	.7002	.5874	.4936	.4155	.3503	.2959	.2502	.2120	.1799
19	.8277	.6864	.5703	.4746	.3957	.3305	.2765	.2317	.1945	.1635
20	.8195	.6730	.5537	.4564	.3769	.3118	.2584	.2145	.1784	.1486
25	.7798	.6095	.4776	.3751	.2953	.2330	.1842	.1460	.1160	.0923
30	.7419	.5521	.4120	.3083	.2314	.1741	.1314	.0994	.0754	.0573
40	.6717	.4529	.3066	.2083	.1420	.0972	.0668	.0460	.0318	.0221
50	.6080	.3715	.2281	.1407	.0872	.0543	.0339	.0213	.0134	.0085
60	.5504	.3048	.1697	.0951	.0535	.0303	.0173	.0099	.0057	.0033

Period	12%	14%	15%	16%	18%	20%	24%	28%	32%	36%
1	.8929	.8772	.8696	.8621	.8475	.8333	.8065	.7813	.7576	.7353
2	.7972	.7695	.7561	.7432	.7182	.6944	.6504	.6104	.5739	.5407
3	.7118	.6750	.6575	.6407	.6086	.5787	.5245	.4768	.4348	.3975
4	.6355	.5921	.5718	.5523	.5158	.4823	.4230	.3725	.3294	.2923
5	.5674	.5194	.4972	.4761	.4371	.4019	.3411	.2910	.2495	.2149
6	.5066	.4556	.4323	.4104	.3704	.3349	.2751	.2274	.1890	.1580
7	.4523	.3996	.3759	.3538	.3139	.2791	.2218	.1776	.1432	.1162
8	.4039	.3506	.3269	.3050	.2660	.2326	.1789	.1388	.1085	.0854
9	.3606	.3075	.2843	.2630	.2255	.1938	.1443	.1084	.0822	.0628
10	.3220	.2697	.2472	.2267	.1911	.1615	.1164	.0847	.0623	.0462
11	.2875	.2366	.2149	.1954	.1619	.1346	.0938	.0662	.0472	.0340
12	.2567	.2076	.1869	.1685	.1372	.1122	.0757	.0517	.0357	.0250
13	.2292	.1821	.1625	.1452	.1163	.0935	.0610	.0404	.0271	.0184
14	.2046	.1597	.1413	.1252	.0985	.0779	.0492	.0316	.0205	.0135
15	.1827	.1401	.1229	.1079	.0835	.0649	.0397	.0247	.0155	.0099
16	.1631	.1229	.1069	.0930	.0708	.0541	.0320	.0193	.0118	.0073
17	.1456	.1078	.0929	.0802	.0600	.0451	.0258	.0150	.0089	.0054
18	.1300	.0946	.0808	.0691	.0508	.0376	.0208	.0118	.0068	.0039
19	.1161	.0829	.0703	.0596	.0431	.0313	.0168	.0092	.0051	.0029
20	.1037	.0728	.0611	.0514	.0365	.0261	.0135	.0072	.0039	.0021
25	.0588	.0378	.0304	.0245	.0160	.0105	.0046	.0021	.0010	.0005
30	.0334	.0196	.0151	.0116	.0070	.0042	.0016	.0006	.0002	.0001
40	.0107	.0053	.0037	.0026	.0013	.0007	.0002	.0001	*	*
50	.0035	.0014	.0009	.0006	.0003	.0001	*	*	*	*
60	.0011	.0004	.0002	.0001	*	*	*	*	*	*

*The factor is zero to four decimal places.

TABLE D.2 | Future Value of $1 at the End of n Periods
$FVIF^{k,n} = (1 + k)^n$

Period	1%	2%	3%	4%	5%	6%	7%	8%	9%	10%
1	1.0100	1.0200	1.0300	1.0400	1.0500	1.0600	1.0700	1.0800	1.0900	1.1000
2	1.0201	1.0404	1.0609	1.0816	1.1025	1.1236	1.1449	1.1664	1.1881	1.2100
3	1.0303	1.0612	1.0927	1.1249	1.1576	1.1910	1.2250	1.2597	1.2950	1.3310
4	1.0406	1.0824	1.1255	1.1699	1.2155	1.2625	1.3108	1.3605	1.4116	1.4641
5	1.0510	1.1041	1.1593	1.2167	1.2763	1.3382	1.4026	1.4693	1.5386	1.6105
6	1.0615	1.1262	1.1941	1.2653	1.3401	1.4185	1.5007	1.5869	1.6771	1.7716
7	1.0721	1.1487	1.2299	1.3159	1.4071	1.5036	1.6058	1.7138	1.8280	1.9487
8	1.0829	1.1717	1.2668	1.3686	1.4775	1.5938	1.7182	1.8509	1.9926	2.1436
9	1.0937	1.1951	1.3048	1.4233	1.5513	1.6895	1.8385	1.9990	2.1719	2.3579
10	1.1046	1.2190	1.3439	1.4802	1.6289	1.7908	1.9672	2.1589	2.3674	2.5937
11	1.1157	1.2434	1.3842	1.5395	1.7103	1.8983	2.1049	2.3316	2.5804	2.8531
12	1.1268	1.2682	1.4258	1.6010	1.7959	2.0122	2.2522	2.5182	2.8127	3.1384
13	1.1381	1.2936	1.4685	1.6651	1.8856	2.1329	2.4098	2.7196	3.0658	3.4523
14	1.1495	1.3195	1.5126	1.7317	1.9799	2.2609	2.5785	2.9372	3.3417	3.7975
15	1.1610	1.3459	1.5580	1.8009	2.0789	2.3966	2.7590	3.1722	3.6425	4.1772
16	1.1726	1.3728	1.6047	1.8730	2.1829	2.5404	2.9522	3.4259	3.9703	4.5950
17	1.1843	1.4002	1.6528	1.9479	2.2920	2.6928	3.1588	3.7000	4.3276	5.0545
18	1.1961	1.4282	1.7024	2.0258	2.4066	2.8543	3.3799	3.9960	4.7171	5.5599
19	1.2081	1.4568	1.7535	2.1068	2.5270	3.0256	3.6165	4.3157	5.1417	6.1159
20	1.2202	1.4859	1.8061	2.1911	2.6533	3.2071	3.8697	4.6610	5.6044	6.7275
21	1.2324	1.5157	1.8603	2.2788	2.7860	3.3996	4.1406	5.0338	6.1088	7.4002
22	1.2447	1.5460	1.9161	2.3699	2.9253	3.6035	4.4304	5.4365	6.6586	8.1403
23	1.2572	1.5769	1.9736	2.4647	3.0715	3.8197	4.7405	5.8715	7.2579	8.9543
24	1.2697	1.6084	2.0328	2.5633	3.2251	4.0489	5.0724	6.3412	7.9111	9.8497
25	1.2824	1.6406	2.0938	2.6658	3.3864	4.2919	5.4274	6.8485	8.6231	10.835
26	1.2953	1.6734	2.1566	2.7725	3.5557	4.5494	5.8074	7.3964	9.3992	11.918
27	1.3082	1.7069	2.2213	2.8834	3.7335	4.8223	6.2139	7.9881	10.245	13.110
28	1.3213	1.7410	2.2879	2.9987	3.9201	5.1117	6.6488	8.6271	11.167	14.421
29	1.3345	1.7758	2.3566	3.1187	4.1161	5.4184	7.1143	9.3173	12.172	15.863
30	1.3478	1.8114	2.4273	3.2434	4.3219	5.7435	7.6123	10.063	13.268	17.449
40	1.4889	2.2080	3.2620	4.8010	7.0400	10.286	14.975	21.725	31.409	45.259
50	1.6446	2.6916	4.3839	7.1067	11.467	18.420	29.457	46.902	74.358	117.39
60	1.8167	3.2810	5.8916	10.5196	18.679	32.988	57.946	101.26	176.03	304.48

*FVIF > 99,999

Period	12%	14%	15%	16%	18%	20%	24%	28%	32%	36%
1	1.1200	1.1400	1.1500	1.1600	1.1800	1.2000	1.2400	1.2800	1.3200	1.3600
2	1.2544	1.2996	1.3225	1.3456	1.3924	1.4400	1.5376	1.6384	1.7424	1.8496
3	1.4049	1.4815	1.5209	1.5609	1.6430	1.7280	1.9066	2.0972	2.3000	2.5155
4	1.5735	1.6890	1.7490	1.8106	1.9388	2.0736	2.3642	2.6844	3.0360	3.4210
5	1.7623	1.9254	2.0114	2.1003	2.2878	2.4883	2.9316	3.4360	4.0075	4.6526
6	1.9738	2.1950	2.3131	2.4364	2.6996	2.9860	3.6352	4.3980	5.2899	6.3275
7	2.2107	2.5023	2.6600	2.8262	3.1855	3.5832	4.5077	5.6295	6.9826	8.6054
8	2.4760	2.8526	3.0590	3.2784	3.7589	4.2998	5.5895	7.2058	9.2170	11.703
9	2.7731	3.2519	3.5179	3.8030	4.4355	5.1598	6.9310	9.2234	12.166	15.917
10	3.1058	3.7072	4.0456	4.4114	5.2338	6.1917	8.5944	11.806	16.060	21.647
11	3.4785	4.2262	4.6524	5.1173	6.1759	7.4301	10.657	15.112	21.199	29.439
12	3.8960	4.8179	5.3503	5.9360	7.2876	8.9161	13.215	19.343	27.983	40.037
13	4.3635	5.4924	6.1528	6.8858	8.5994	10.699	16.386	24.759	36.937	54.451
14	4.8871	6.2613	7.0757	7.9875	10.147	12.839	20.319	31.691	48.757	74.053
15	5.4736	7.1379	8.1371	9.2655	11.974	15.407	25.196	40.565	64.359	100.71
16	6.1304	8.1372	9.3576	10.748	14.129	18.488	31.243	51.923	84.954	136.97
17	6.8660	9.2765	10.761	12.468	16.672	22.186	38.741	66.461	112.14	186.28
18	7.6900	10.575	12.375	14.463	19.673	26.623	48.039	85.071	148.02	253.34
19	8.6128	12.056	14.232	16.777	23.214	31.948	59.568	108.89	195.39	344.54
20	9.6463	13.743	16.367	19.461	27.393	38.338	73.864	139.38	257.92	468.57
21	10.804	15.668	18.822	22.574	32.324	46.005	91.592	178.41	340.45	637.26
22	12.100	17.861	21.645	26.186	38.142	55.206	113.57	228.36	449.39	866.67
23	13.552	20.362	24.891	30.376	45.008	66.247	140.83	292.30	594.20	1178.7
24	15.179	23.212	28.625	35.236	53.109	79.497	174.63	374.14	783.02	1603.0
25	17.000	26.462	32.919	40.874	62.669	95.396	216.54	478.90	1033.6	2180.1
26	19.040	30.167	37.857	47.414	73.949	114.48	268.51	613.00	1364.3	2964.9
27	21.325	34.390	43.535	55.000	87.260	137.37	332.95	784.64	1800.9	4032.3
28	23.884	39.204	50.066	63.800	102.97	164.84	412.86	1004.3	2377.2	5483.9
29	26.750	44.693	57.575	74.009	121.50	197.81	511.95	1285.6	3137.9	7458.1
30	29.960	50.950	66.212	85.850	143.37	237.38	634.82	1645.5	4142.1	10143.
40	93.051	188.88	267.86	378.72	750.38	1469.8	5455.9	19427.	66521.	*
50	289.00	700.23	1083.7	1670.7	3927.4	9100.4	46890.	*	*	*
60	897.60	2595.9	4384.0	7370.2	20555.	56348.	*	*	*	*

TABLE D.3 | Present Value of an Annuity of $1 per Period for n Periods

$$PVIFa(r,f) = \sum_{i=1}^{n} \frac{1}{(1+r)^t} = \frac{\left[1 - \dfrac{1}{(1+r)^n}\right]}{r}$$

Number of Payments	1%	2%	3%	4%	5%	6%	7%	8%	9%
1	0.9901	0.9804	0.9709	0.9615	0.9524	0.9434	0.9346	0.9259	0.9174
2	1.9704	1.9416	1.9135	1.8861	1.8594	1.8334	1.8080	1.7833	1.7591
3	2.9410	2.8839	2.8286	2.7751	2.7232	2.6730	2.6243	2.5771	2.5313
4	3.9020	3.8077	3.7171	3.6299	3.5460	3.4651	3.3872	3.3121	3.2397
5	4.8534	4.7135	4.5797	4.4518	4.3295	4.2124	4.1002	3.9927	3.8897
6	5.7955	5.6014	5.4172	5.2421	5.0757	4.9173	4.7665	4.6229	4.4859
7	6.7282	6.4720	6.2303	6.0021	5.7864	5.5824	5.3893	5.2064	5.0330
8	7.6517	7.3255	7.0197	6.7327	6.4632	6.2098	5.9713	5.7466	5.5348
9	8.5660	8.1622	7.7861	7.4353	7.1078	6.8017	6.5152	6.2469	5.9952
10	9.4713	8.9826	8.5302	8.1109	7.7217	7.3601	7.0236	6.7101	6.4177
11	10.3676	9.7868	9.2526	8.7605	8.3064	7.8869	7.4987	7.1390	6.8052
12	11.2551	10.5753	9.9540	9.3851	8.8633	8.3838	7.9427	7.5361	7.1607
13	12.1337	11.3484	10.6350	9.9856	9.3936	8.8527	8.3577	7.9038	7.4869
14	13.0037	12.1062	11.2961	10.5631	9.8986	9.2950	8.7455	8.2442	7.7862
15	13.8651	12.8493	11.9379	11.1184	10.3797	9.7122	9.1079	8.5595	8.0607
16	14.7179	13.5777	12.5611	11.6523	10.8378	10.1059	9.4466	8.8514	8.3126
17	15.5623	14.2919	13.1661	12.1657	11.2741	10.4773	9.7632	9.1216	8.5436
18	16.3983	14.9920	13.7535	12.6593	11.6896	10.8276	10.0591	9.3719	8.7556
19	17.2260	15.6785	14.3238	13.1339	12.0853	11.1581	10.3356	9.6036	8.9501
20	18.0456	16.3514	14.8775	13.5903	12.4622	11.4699	10.5940	9.8181	9.1285
25	22.0232	19.5235	17.4131	15.6221	14.0393	12.7834	11.6536	10.6748	9.8226
30	25.8077	22.3965	19.6004	17.2920	15.3725	13.7648	12.4090	11.2578	10.2737
40	32.8347	27.3555	23.1148	19.7928	17.1591	15.0463	13.3317	11.9246	10.7574
50	39.1961	31.4236	25.7298	21.4822	18.2559	15.7619	13.8007	12.2335	10.9617
60	44.9550	34.7609	27.6756	22.6235	18.9293	16.1614	14.0392	12.3766	11.0480

Number of Payments	10%	12%	14%	15%	16%	18%	20%	24%	28%	32%
1	0.9091	0.8929	0.8772	0.8696	0.8621	0.8475	0.8333	0.8065	0.7813	0.7576
2	1.7355	1.6901	1.6467	1.6257	1.6052	1.5656	1.5278	1.4568	1.3916	1.3315
3	2.4869	2.4018	2.3216	2.2832	2.2459	2.1743	2.1065	1.9813	1.8684	1.7663
4	3.1699	3.0373	2.9137	2.8550	2.7982	2.6901	2.5887	2.4043	2.2410	2.0957
5	3.7908	3.6048	3.4331	3.3522	3.2743	3.1272	2.9906	2.7454	2.5320	2.3452
6	4.3553	4.1114	3.8887	3.7845	3.6847	3.4976	3.3255	3.0205	2.7594	2.5342
7	4.8684	4.5638	4.2883	4.1604	4.0386	3.8115	3.6046	3.2423	2.9370	2.6775
8	5.3349	4.9676	4.6389	4.4873	4.3436	4.0776	3.8372	3.4212	3.0758	2.7860
9	5.7590	5.3282	4.9464	4.7716	4.6065	4.3030	4.0310	3.5655	3.1842	2.8681
10	6.1446	5.6502	5.2161	5.0188	4.8332	4.4941	4.1925	3.6819	3.2689	2.9304
11	6.4951	5.9377	5.4527	5.2337	5.0286	4.6560	4.3271	3.7757	3.3351	2.9776
12	6.8137	6.1944	5.6603	5.4206	5.1971	4.7932	4.4392	3.8514	3.3868	3.0133
13	7.1034	6.4235	5.8424	5.5831	5.3423	4.9095	4.5327	3.9124	3.4272	3.0404
14	7.3667	6.6282	6.0021	5.7245	5.4675	5.0081	4.6106	3.9616	3.4587	3.0609
15	7.6061	6.8109	6.1422	5.8474	5.5755	5.0916	4.6755	4.0013	3.4834	3.0764
16	7.8237	6.9740	6.2651	5.9542	5.6685	5.1624	4.7296	4.0333	3.5026	3.0882
17	8.0216	7.1196	6.3729	6.0472	5.7487	5.2223	4.7746	4.0591	3.5177	3.0971
18	8.2014	7.2497	6.4674	6.1280	5.8178	5.2732	4.8122	4.0799	3.5294	3.1039
19	8.3649	7.3658	6.5504	6.1982	5.8775	5.3162	4.8435	4.0967	3.5386	3.1090
20	8.5136	7.4694	6.6231	6.2593	5.9288	5.3527	4.8696	4.1103	3.5458	3.1129
25	9.0770	7.8431	6.8729	6.4641	6.0971	5.4669	4.9476	4.1474	3.5640	3.1220
30	9.4269	8.0552	7.0027	6.5660	6.1772	5.5168	4.9789	4.1601	3.5693	3.1242
40	9.7791	8.2438	7.1050	6.6418	6.2335	5.5482	4.9966	4.1659	3.5712	3.1250
50	9.9148	8.3045	7.1327	6.6605	6.2463	5.5541	4.9995	4.1666	3.5714	3.1250
60	9.9672	8.3240	7.1401	6.6651	6.2492	5.5553	4.9999	4.1667	3.5714	3.1250

TABLE D.4 | Monthly Installment to Amortize a $1 Loan

$$PMT = \frac{\dfrac{i}{12}}{1 - \left(\left[1 + \dfrac{i}{12} \right]^{12n} \right)}$$

Years	6.0%	6.5%	7.0%	7.5%	8.0%	8.5%	9.0%	9.5%	10.0%
1	.086066	.086296	.086527	.086757	.086988	.087220	.087451	.087684	.087916
2	.044321	.044546	.044773	.045000	.045227	.045456	.045685	.045914	.046145
3	.030422	.030649	.030887	.031106	.031336	.031568	.031800	.032033	.032267
4	.023485	.023715	.023946	.024179	.024413	.024648	.024885	.025123	.025363
5	.019333	.019566	.019801	.020038	.020276	.020517	.020758	.021002	.021247
6	.016573	.016810	.017049	.017290	.017533	.017778	.018026	.018275	.018526
7	.014609	.014849	.015093	.015338	.015586	.015836	.016089	.016344	.016601
8	.013141	.013386	.013634	.013884	.014137	.014392	.014650	.014911	.015174
9	.012006	.012255	.012506	.012761	.013019	.013279	.013543	.013809	.014079
10	.011102	.011355	.011611	.011870	.012133	.012399	.012668	.012940	.013215
11	.010367	.010624	.010884	.011148	.011415	.011686	.011961	.012239	.012520
12	.009759	.010019	.010284	.010552	.010825	.011101	.011380	.011644	.011951
13	.009247	.009512	.009781	.010054	.010331	.010612	.010897	.011186	.011478
14	.008812	.009081	.009354	.009631	.009913	.010199	.010489	.010784	.011082
15	.008439	.008711	.008988	.009270	.009557	.009847	.010143	.010442	.010746
16	.008114	.008391	.008672	.008958	.009249	.009545	.009845	.010150	.010459
17	.007831	.008111	.008397	.008687	.008983	.009283	.009588	.009898	.010212
18	.007582	.007866	.008155	.008450	.008750	.009055	.009364	.009679	.009998
19	.007361	.007649	.007942	.008241	.008545	.008854	.009169	.009488	.009813
20	.007164	.007456	.007753	.008056	.008364	.008678	.008997	.009321	.009650
21	.006989	.007284	.007585	.007892	.008204	.008522	.008846	.009174	.009508
22	.006831	.007129	.007434	.007745	.008062	.008384	.008712	.009045	.009382
23	.006688	.006991	.007299	.007614	.007935	.008261	.008593	.008930	.009272
24	.006560	.006865	.007178	.007496	.007821	.008151	.008487	.008828	.009174
25	.006443	.006752	.007068	.007390	.007718	.008052	.008392	.008737	.009087
26	.006337	.006649	.006968	.007294	.007626	.007964	.008307	.008656	.009010
27	.006240	.006556	.006878	.007207	.007543	.007884	.008231	.008584	.008941
28	.006151	.006470	.006796	.007129	.007468	.007812	.008163	.008519	.008880
29	.006070	.006392	.006721	.007057	.007399	.007748	.008102	.008461	.008825
30	.005996	.006321	.006653	.006992	.007338	.007689	.008046	.008409	.008776

Years	10.5%	11.0%	11.5%	12.0%	13.0%	14.0%	15.0%	16.0%	17.0%
1	.088149	.088382	.088615	.088849	.089317	.089787	.090258	.090731	.091205
2	.046376	.046608	.046840	.047073	.047542	.048013	.048487	.048963	.049442
3	.032502	.032739	.032976	.033214	.033694	.034178	.034665	.035157	.035653
4	.025603	.025846	.026089	.026334	.026827	.027326	.027831	.028340	.028855
5	.021494	.021742	.021993	.022244	.022753	.023268	.023790	.024318	.024853
6	.018779	.019034	.019291	.019550	.020074	.020606	.021145	.021692	.022246
7	.016861	.017122	.017386	.017653	.018192	.018740	.019297	.019862	.020436
8	.015440	.015708	.015979	.016253	.016807	.017372	.017945	.018529	.019121
9	.014351	.014626	.014904	.015184	.015754	.016334	.016924	.017525	.018136
10	.013494	.013775	.014060	.014347	.014931	.015527	.016133	.016751	.017380
11	.012804	.013092	.013384	.013678	.014276	.014887	.015509	.016143	.016788
12	.012241	.012536	.012833	.013134	.013746	.014371	.015009	.015658	.016319
13	.011775	.012075	.012379	.012687	.013312	.013951	.014603	.015267	.015943
14	.011384	.011691	.012001	.012314	.012953	.013605	.014270	.014948	.015638
15	.011054	.011366	.011682	.012002	.012652	.013317	.013996	.014687	.015390
16	.010772	.011090	.011412	.011737	.012400	.013077	.013768	.014471	.015186
17	.010531	.010854	.011181	.011512	.012186	.012875	.013577	.014292	.015018
18	.010322	.010650	.010983	.011320	.012004	.012704	.013417	.014142	.014879
19	.010141	.010475	.010812	.011154	.011849	.012559	.013282	.014017	.014764
20	.009984	.010322	.010664	.011011	.011716	.012435	.013168	.013913	.014668
21	.009846	.010189	.010536	.010887	.011601	.012330	.013071	.013824	.014588
22	.009725	.010072	.010424	.010779	.011502	.012239	.012989	.013750	.014521
23	.009619	.009970	.010326	.010686	.011417	.012162	.012919	.013687	.014465
24	.009525	.009880	.010240	.010604	.011343	.012095	.012859	.013634	.014418
25	.009442	.009801	.010165	.010532	.011278	.012038	.012808	.013589	.014378
26	.009368	.009731	.010098	.010470	.011222	.011988	.012765	.013551	.014345
27	.009303	.009670	.010040	.010414	.011174	.011945	.012727	.013518	.014317
28	.009245	.009615	.009989	.010366	.011131	.011908	.012695	.013491	.014293
29	.009193	.009566	.009943	.010324	.011094	.011876	.012668	.013467	.014273
30	.009147	.009523	.009903	.010286	.011062	.011849	.012644	.013448	.014257

TABLE D.5 How $1 Deposited at the End of Each Year Will Grow (CFIFa)

$$CFIFa = \frac{(1+i)^n - 1}{1}$$

Years	1%	2%	3%	4%	5%	6%	7%	8%	9%
1	1.00000	1.00000	1.00000	1.00000	1.00000	1.00000	1.00000	1.00000	1.00000
2	2.01000	2.02000	2.03000	2.04000	2.05000	2.06000	2.07000	2.08000	2.09000
3	3.03010	3.06040	3.09090	3.12160	3.15250	3.18360	3.21490	3.24640	3.27810
4	4.06040	4.12161	4.18363	4.24646	4.31013	4.37462	4.43994	4.50611	4.57313
5	5.10101	5.20404	5.30914	5.41632	5.52563	5.63709	5.75074	5.86660	5.98471
6	6.15202	6.30812	6.46841	6.63298	6.80191	6.97532	7.15329	7.33593	7.52334
7	7.21354	7.43428	7.66246	7.89829	8.14201	8.39384	8.65402	8.92280	9.20044
8	8.28567	8.58297	8.89234	9.21423	9.54911	9.89747	10.25980	10.63663	11.02847
9	9.36853	9.75463	10.15911	10.58280	11.02656	11.49132	11.97799	12.48756	13.02104
10	10.46221	10.94972	11.46388	12.00611	12.57789	13.18079	13.81645	14.48656	15.19293
11	11.56683	12.16872	12.80780	13.48635	14.20679	14.97164	15.78360	16.64549	17.56029
12	12.68250	13.41209	14.19203	15.02581	15.91713	16.86994	17.88845	18.97713	20.14072
13	13.80933	14.68033	15.61779	16.62684	17.71298	18.88214	20.14064	21.49530	22.95338
14	14.94742	15.97394	17.08632	18.29191	19.59863	21.01507	22.55049	24.21492	26.01919
15	16.09690	17.29342	18.59891	20.02359	21.57856	23.27597	25.12902	27.15211	29.36092
16	17.25786	18.63929	20.15688	21.82453	23.65749	25.67253	27.88805	30.32428	33.00340
17	18.43044	20.01207	21.76159	23.69751	25.84037	28.21288	30.84022	33.75023	36.97370
18	19.61475	21.41231	23.41444	25.64541	28.13238	30.90565	33.99903	37.45024	41.30134
19	20.81090	22.84056	25.11687	27.67123	30.53900	33.75999	37.37896	41.44626	46.01846
20	22.01900	24.29737	26.87037	29.77808	33.06595	36.78559	40.99549	45.76196	51.16012
21	23.23919	25.78332	28.67649	31.96920	35.71925	39.99273	44.86518	50.42292	56.76453
22	24.47159	27.29898	30.53678	34.24797	38.50521	43.39229	49.00574	55.45676	62.87334
23	25.71630	28.84496	32.45288	36.61789	41.43048	46.99583	53.43614	60.89330	69.53194
24	26.97346	30.42186	34.42647	39.08260	44.50200	50.81558	58.17667	66.76476	76.78981
25	28.24320	32.03030	36.45926	41.64591	47.72710	54.86451	63.24904	73.10594	84.70090
26	29.52563	33.67091	38.55304	44.31174	51.11345	59.15638	68.67647	79.95442	93.32398
27	30.82089	35.34432	40.70963	47.08421	54.66913	63.70577	74.48382	87.35077	102.72310
28	32.12910	37.05121	42.93092	49.96758	58.40258	68.52811	80.69769	95.33883	112.96820
29	33.45039	38.79223	45.21885	52.96629	62.32271	73.63980	87.34653	103.96590	124.13540
30	34.78489	40.56808	47.57542	56.08494	66.43885	79.05819	94.46079	113.28320	136.30750

Years	10%	12%	14%	16%	18%	20%	22%	24%	26%
1	1.00000	1.00000	1.00000	1.00000	1.00000	1.00000	1.00000	1.00000	1.00000
2	2.10000	2.12000	2.14000	2.16000	2.18000	2.20000	2.22000	2.24000	2.26000
3	3.31000	3.37440	3.43960	3.50560	3.57240	3.64000	3.70840	3.77760	3.84760
4	4.64100	4.77933	4.92114	5.06650	5.21543	5.36800	5.52425	5.68422	5.84798
5	6.10510	6.35285	6.61010	6.87714	7.15421	7.44160	7.73958	8.04844	8.36845
6	7.71561	8.11519	8.53552	8.97748	9.44197	9.92992	10.44229	10.98006	11.54425
7	9.48717	10.08901	10.73049	11.41387	12.14152	12.91590	13.73959	14.61528	15.54575
8	11.43589	12.29969	13.23276	14.24009	15.32700	16.49908	17.76231	19.12294	20.58765
9	13.57948	14.77566	16.08535	17.51851	19.08585	20.79890	22.67001	24.71245	26.94043
10	15.93742	17.54874	19.33730	21.32147	23.52131	25.95868	28.65742	31.64344	34.94495
11	18.53117	20.65458	23.04452	25.73290	28.75514	32.15042	35.96205	40.23787	45.03063
12	21.38428	24.13313	27.27075	30.85017	34.93107	39.58050	44.87370	50.89495	57.73860
13	24.52271	28.02911	32.08865	36.78620	42.21866	48.49660	55.74591	64.10974	73.75063
14	27.97498	32.39260	37.58107	43.67199	50.81802	59.19592	69.01001	80.49608	93.92580
15	31.77248	37.27971	43.84241	51.65951	60.96527	72.03511	85.19221	100.81510	119.34650
16	35.94973	42.75328	50.98035	60.92503	72.93901	87.44213	104.93450	126.01080	151.37660
17	40.54470	48.88367	59.11760	71.67303	87.06804	105.93060	129.02010	157.25340	191.73450
18	45.59917	55.74971	68.39407	84.14072	103.74030	128.11670	158.40450	195.99420	242.58550
19	51.15909	63.43968	78.96923	98.60323	123.41350	154.74000	194.25350	244.03280	306.65770
20	57.27500	72.05244	91.02493	115.37970	146.62800	186.68800	237.98930	303.60060	387.38870
21	64.00250	81.69874	104.76840	134.84050	174.02100	225.02560	291.34690	377.46480	489.10980
22	71.40275	92.50258	120.43600	157.41500	206.34480	271.03070	356.44320	469.05630	617.27830
23	79.54302	104.60290	138.29700	183.60140	244.48680	326.23690	435.86070	582.62980	778.77070
24	88.49733	118.15520	158.65860	213.97760	289.49450	392.48420	532.75010	723.46100	982.25110
25	98.34706	133.33390	181.87080	249.21400	342.60350	471.98110	650.95510	898.09160	1238.63600
26	109.18180	150.33390	208.33270	290.08830	405.27210	567.37730	795.16530	1114.63400	1561.68200
27	121.09990	169.37400	238.49930	337.50240	476.22110	681.85280	971.10160	1383.14600	1968.71900
28	134.20990	190.69890	272.88920	392.50280	566.48090	819.22330	1185.74400	1716.10100	2481.58600
29	148.63090	214.58280	312.09370	456.30320	669.44750	984.06800	1447.60800	2128.96500	3127.79800
30	164.49400	241.33270	356.78680	530.31170	790.94800	1181.88200	1767.08100	2640.91600	3942.02600

A

absolute monopoly. A market that has only one supplier of a good or service for which there are no reasonably acceptable substitutes.

absorption rates. Rates at which the market will "absorb" a product; the rate at which units will be purchased.

abstract and opinion. A summary of the chain of past title transfers for real property and an attorney's written opinion that the title contains no defects.

abstract of title. A brief summary of each recorded document pertaining to title to a specified parcel of land.

accelerated method. A method of computing depreciation or cost recovery allowances whereby large annual allowances are claimed in the early years of ownership, offset by smaller allowances in later years.

acceleration clause. A clause that permits the mortgagee to declare the full amount of a debt due and payable if the mortgagor defaults on any of the agreed-on terms.

acceptance. The act of a party to whom a thing is offered by another, whereby he or she receives the thing with the intention of retaining it.

accredited purchasers. Investors who either (1) are sufficiently wealthy so that a contemplated securities purchase (of $150,000 or more) will not exceed 20 percent of their net worth, (2) have a net worth in excess of $1 million, or (3) have a two-year earnings record of more than $200,000 per annum and expect their current earnings to exceed $200,000.

accretion. A gradual increase in land area adjacent to a body of water because of soil deposited by wave and current action.

accrued depreciation. A loss in value due to physical deterioration, functional obsolescence, and economic or locational disadvantages.

acknowledgment. Certification by a notary public or other appropriate public official that the grantor has stated before the official that he or she executed the acknowledged document.

ad valorem. A Latin term used to describe the taxing of property according to value.

adjusted basis. The amount paid for property, plus all subsequent capital expenditures made to improve it, minus all tax deductions for depreciation or cost recovery allowances.

adjusted gross income. Gross taxable income minus a set of specific deductions spelled out in the Internal Revenue Code.

adjusted rate of return. Modified version of the internal rate of return, designed to eliminate problems associated with negative cash flows.

adverse possession. Wrongful occupancy of real estate in a manner and for a time period described in state statutes. Title then vests in the adverse possessor by operation of law and is independent of any previously recorded title to the property.

affirmative covenant. A mutual promise between neighbors that a property will be used in some specified manner.

after-tax cash flow.   Cash flow generated from a property after accounting for all operating expenses, all debt service obligations, and all income tax consequences for the current period.

agglomeration economies.   An amorphous term referring to cost reductions ascribed to proximity.

all-inclusive mortgage.   *See* wraparound mortgage.

alternative minimum tax.   A provision that specifies the minimum amount of federal income tax for which all taxpayers are liable. After computing tax liability the regular way, taxpayers must perform the alternative computation. They are required to pay the greater of the regular or the alternative minimum tax.

alternative minimum taxable income.   The income on which liability for the alternative minimum tax is computed.

amortization table.   A schedule of equal periodic payments necessary to repay a $1 loan, with interest, over a specified number of payment periods.

amortize.   To claim an expenditure, which is incurred at the beginning of the period, as an annual expense or income tax deduction over an extended period of years.

anchor tenants.   Tenants who are expected to attract customers to a shopping center and thereby generate business for other merchants in the center.

annual compounding.   Accumulated interest that in and of itself earns interest in all subsequent periods.

annual mortgage constant.   The percentage of the original principal amount that must be paid annually in order to fully repay interest and principal over the term of the loan.

annuity.   Any series of periodic payments received or paid at regular intervals.

annuity table.   A schedule providing factors used to calculate the present value of a compound level annuity.

articles of agreement.   *See* installment sales contract.

asset liquidity.   *See* liquidity.

assignment.   Transfer of contractual rights from one contracting party (the assignor) to another person (the assignee) who is not a party to the contract.

assumption clause.   A clause whereby mortgagors agree not to sell mortgaged property subject to the mortgage or to have a buyer assume an existing mortgage without prior approval of the mortgagee.

assumption fee.   A fee charged by a lender as a condition for permitting assumption of mortgage indebtedness by a party other than the original mortgagor. This permits mortgagees to adjust their rates of return to the current market when interest rates have risen.

atomistic markets.   A market in which no one person or group can measurably affect market prices. Market participants are simply price takers, in that they have a choice of accepting prevailing prices or of not participating in the market at all.

avulsion.   A sudden and perceptible shift in land boundaries due to floods or sudden alterations in the course of rivers or streams.

B

back-door approach.   A type of preliminary financial feasibility study that involves estimating the maximum amount of equity financing that investors can commit to a project, given their minimum acceptable current yield.

band of investment technique.   A technique used to calculate the weighted average cost of capital for a property. The cost of each source of funds is weighted by a factor equal to the proportion of total funds that will be derived from that source.

base lines.   A set of imaginary lines running east and west employed by surveyors for reference in locating and describing land under the government survey method of property description.

basic rate.   The sum of the weighted average cost of capital and the equity buildup factor used in order to determine the appropriate overall capitalization rate.

basis point.   A financing term frequently used to measure small changes in or differences between interest rates. One hundred basis points equals one percent. If two securities are quoted at 5.65 percent and 5.15 percent, there is a spread of 50 basis points.

bid-rent curve. A functional relationship that depicts the absolute maximum rent a firm with a specific profit profile can pay and still find remaining in business a worthwhile endeavor.

blanket mortgage. The pledge of two or more parcels of property as security for a single loan.

blind pool syndication. A form of limited partnership in which the promoter assembles a group of investors with the purpose of acquiring an undesignated asset of a specific type.

book value. The value at which assets are recorded on a firm's books of account (that is, its accounting records); usually cost minus accumulated depreciation or cost recovery allowances.

boot. Assets received as consideration in what would otherwise be an exchange of entirely like-kind assets. Receipt of boot may trigger tax liability in what would otherwise be a tax-deferred transaction. *See also* like-kind exchange.

breakeven ratio. The relationship between cash expenditure requirements and gross revenue from an investment project. Sometimes called a *default ratio*.

broker's rate of return. A rate-of-return measure that adjusts the cash-on-cash return to include equity buildup from debt amortization and thereby shows a slightly more favorable return than does the cash-on-cash measure.

building codes. The set of laws that establishes minimum standards for constructing new buildings or altering existing structures. Building codes are intended to ensure minimum protection against fire damage and to safeguard against faulty design in construction.

business risk. Risk stemming from the possibility of making inappropriate business decisions or of misjudging the economic consequences of actions.

C

capital assets. All assets held by a taxpayer (whether or not connected with the person's trade or business) except those specifically enumerated by the Commissioner of Internal Revenue. Generally, assets of a fixed or permanent nature or those employed in carrying on a business or trade.

capital expenditure. An expenditure of funds that extends the useful life of a capital asset or adds to its value.

capital formation. The raising of debt or equity funds for real estate projects.

capital goods. Products destined to be employed in the production of other goods or services.

capitalization rate. The relationship between net income from a real estate investment and the value of the investment. This relationship is usually expressed as a percentage.

capitalize. To add an amount to the tax basis of a property.

capital recovery. The portion of an overall capitalization rate comprised of recovery of the owner's capital outlay.

cash-on-cash rate of return. The first year's expected after-tax cash flow, divided by the initial cash outlay required to acquire the investment.

central business district. The focal point of urban places where goods and services are exchanged.

central place theory. The postulate that if the surrounding countryside were a flat, undifferentiated plane, central places would be located so as to minimize the distance from all points in the tributary area. It states further that the larger the city, the larger its tributary area must be.

certainty equivalents. Substitute cash flows determined by the certainty-equivalent technique.

certainty-equivalent technique. A procedure that seeks to establish substitute cash flows that leave an investor indifferent between absolutely certain receipt of the substitute amounts and the expectation of receiving the point estimates, along with attendant risk.

certificate of limited partnership. A document that must be filed with the appropriate state agency to create a limited partnership.

certified historic structure. Any structure that is either listed in the National Registry of Historic Places or located in a registered historic district and certified as being of historic significance to the district. *See also* registered historic district.

ceteris paribus. A Latin term used by economists to mean that demand schedules are applicable only so long as all factors other than price that influence buyer behavior do not change.

city planning. A procedure for formulating land use schemes, employed by municipalities in their efforts to reach specified goals in the utilization of land within the municipality.

coefficient of correlation. A measure of the extent to which the values of variables in a sample or a population are interdependent.

coefficient of determination. A measure of the percent of variation in the dependent variable associated with variation in the value of the independent variable. In regression analysis, designated by the term *r-square* (r^2).

coefficient of multiple correlation. A measure of the percentage of variance in the dependent variable that is "explained" by variation in the independent variables.

coefficient of serial correlation. A measure of the degree to which outcomes in subsequent periods are related. Possible coefficients range from zero to plus-or-minus one.

coefficient of variation. Standard deviation of the distribution of possible outcomes, divided by the expected outcome.

collective goods. *See* public goods.

commercial mortgage backed security (CMBS). Securities such as bonds or other debt instruments that are backed by loans on commercial real estate. Net yield on the mortgages is passed through to the investors in the CMBS.

commitment letter. A letter to a prospective borrower, wherein a lender states terms and conditions under which it will provide the requested funds. A precise period is usually specified during which the commitment remains effective. Commitment letters generally state conditions under which the lender may revoke the commitment and set forth any further provisions on which the commitment is contingent.

community shopping center. A shopping center that typically draws most of its customers from an area extending from 10 to 15 minutes in driving time. Community shopping centers usually feature a food store and a junior department store or a discount store as anchor tenants. Size may range from 50,000 to 100,000 square feet of retail space.

comparative advantage. An economic principle developed by the economist David Ricardo that provides an explanation of why some areas tend to concentrate on producing a limited number of goods and seek much of what they consume from other areas.

comparative sales approach. An appraisal procedure that analyzes recent sales data from similar properties and draws inferences about the value of the property being appraised.

comparative unit method. A valuation approach that estimates costs by comparison with similar buildings whose construction costs are known. To render buildings of slightly different size more directly comparable, costs are expressed on the basis of some standardized unit of measure such as per square foot or per cubic foot.

complements. Goods or services whose consumption occurs in tandem with that of the item in question. A change in the price of one good or service can cause a shift in the demand curves for its complements.

compound amount. The summation of principal and compounded interest over a specified holding period.

compound interest. Interest income attributable to previously accrued interest that has been left on deposit.

concentric zone model. An urban economic model developed by Earnest W. Burgess in the 1920s. The concentric zone model was designed to explain urban development through the use of transitional zones.

concessions. *See* rent concessions.

condemnation proceeding. The consequence of a property owner's refusal to voluntarily convey title at a price offered by a governmental agency seeking to convert the property to public use.

condominium. An ownership arrangement whereby title to specified portions of a property vests in individual users, and title to common area vests in all users jointly.

condominium association. An association, composed of all those owning interest in a condominium, that serves as a governing and managing body, usually through an elected board of directors.

condominium declaration. The enabling document that creates a condominium. The declaration desires both individual and common areas of the premises and provides for assessment of owners for costs of maintaining and insuring common areas.

conduit. *See* tax conduit.

consideration. Under contract law, the impelling reason to enter into a contract. Something of value given in exchange for a promise.

constructive notice. A legal doctrine under which notice may be attribute even though a party may be completely ignorant of the facts. Recording statutes provide that recording a document in the public record constitutes constructive notice to the world.

consumer good. The end product of the production process.

consumer price index. An index of changes in the price of a representative "market basket" of consumer goods, relating the current price to that in designated base year.

contract for deed. See installment sales contract.

contract price. Total selling price minus any preexisting mortgage to which a property will remain subject when sold under conditions permitting the transaction to be reported for tax computation purposes under the installment sales method. If the pre-existing mortgage exceeds the seller's adjusted basis in the property, the excess of the mortgage over the seller's basis must be added to the contract price.

cooperative. An apartment the tenant purchases by buying stock in the corporation that owns the building rather than simply buying the apartment.

corporations. Artificial entities, created under state laws, that are empowered to own property and transact business in their own names. They may buy, sell, and otherwise enter into contracts. As legal entities, corporations have an identity separate and distinct from that of their owners.

cost approach. An appraisal technique whereby an estimate of land value is added to the estimated cost of reproducing existing improvements on the land (net of accrued depreciation) to derive a value estimate for the entire property.

cost recovery allowance. An income tax rule that provides for recovery of capital expenditures on property having a finite useful life, acquired on or after January 1, 1981, and used in a trade or business or for production of income.

cost recovery assets. Assets on which tax-deductible cost recovery allowances may be claimed.

cotenancy. Real property title held in the name of two or more owners.

counseling. Providing competent, unbiased advice on diversified problems in the broad field of real estate involving any or all segments of the business, such as merchandising, leasing, management, planning, financing, appraising, court testimony, and other similar services.

covenant against removal. A restriction imposed by the mortgagee prohibiting the mortgagor from removing or demolishing any part of the building without the lender's consent.

covenant against waste. A restriction imposed by a mortgagee prohibiting the mortgagor from allowing the building to deteriorate during the period of the mortgage.

covenant of insurance. A mortgage clause in which the mortgagor promises to maintain adequate insurance coverage against fire and other specified hazards.

covenant of seizin. A mortgage clause whereby the mortgagor warrants that he or she is the lawful owner of the property being mortgaged. *See also* seizin.

covenant of title. A promise or assurance made by the grantor in connection with title transfer.

covenants. Promises that property will, or will not, be used in some specified manner.

covenant to pay taxes. A common mortgage clause in which the mortgagor promises to pay all property taxes and assessments levied against the property during the period of the mortgage.

cross-sectional surveys. Surveys involving one-time sampling from a population of research interest. All elements are measured at a single point in time. Cross-sectional surveys provide a "snap-shot" of the variables under observation as of the time of the survey.

curtesy. A husband's interest in his wife's property.

custom construction. a construction project that takes place on land owned by the ultimate purchaser, involving a structure built to the exact specifications of the purchaser-user.

D

dealer. In real estate, one who is in the business of buying and selling property interests for one's own account. Gains on dealers' sales are reported as ordinary income rather than as capital gains.

debentures. Bonds secured by the borrower's income stream.

debt amortization. The process of gradually extinguishing a debt by a series of periodic payments to the creditor.

debt constant. The percentage of the original principal amount that must be paid annually in order to fully repay interest and principal over the term of the loan. The constant can be expressed as an annual percentage or monthly percentage. Sometimes called a *debt service constant*.

debt coverage ratio. The relationship between a project's annual net operating income and the obligation to make principal and interest payments on borrowed funds.

Debt coverage ratios are often employed to evaluate a lender's margin of safety regarding mortgage loans.

debt service. Payments to a lender. Debt service obligations may involve payment of interest only or both principal and interest so as to fully or partially amortize a debt over a specified term.

debt service constant. *See* debt constant.

debt-to-equity ratio. The ratio between borrowed funds and equity funds.

decision model. A systematic process for identifying opportunities that show promise of contributing adequately to predetermined investment goals.

declining balance method. A method of computing annual depreciation or cost recovery allowances that provides the greatest allowance in the first year of ownership and progressively smaller allowances for each successive year.

decree. The judgment of a court of equity, ordering execution of the provisions of that judgment.

deed. A legal document that conveys title in real property from one party to another. The document must be signed, witnessed, delivered, and accepted.

deed of trust. A deed passing title to property from an owner to a trustee, who holds that property as collateral for a mortgage loan advanced by another. Also called a *trust deed* or *trust indenture*.

default. A mortgagor's failure to fulfill any of the agreed-on terms in a security agreement.

default ratio. *See* breakeven ratio.

defeasance clause. Mortgage provisions intended to render nominal conveyance void on satisfaction of the mortgagor's obligation.

deficiency judgment. A judgment against a debtor's personal assets beyond those assets owned on a defaulted debt instrument.

delivery. The legal act of transferring ownership of real estate.

demand. An economic term that refers to the entire range of relationships between price and quantity.

demand curve.   A graphic illustration of the relationship between price and the quantity of a good or service buyers will take off the market. Also called a *demand function.*

demand function.   *See* demand curve.

demand schedule.   A table that relates quantity demanded to a good's or service's price, at all relevant prices.

demand to purchase.   Desired increase in a market participant's inventory of a product, at a specific price.

dependency exemption.   An amount of adjusted gross income that taxpayers may exempt from taxable income for each person dependent on them for financial support.

dependent variable.   In regression or correlation analysis, a variable whose value is thought to be affected by the value of other variables (independent variables) included in the analysis.

deposit insurance.   An insurance program that protects depositors from loss due to bank failures.

depreciable asset.   *See* depreciable property.

depreciable property.   Property on which a tax-deductible depreciation allowance may be claimed.

depreciation.   Decline in an asset's value or useful life, due to wear, tear, action of the elements, or obsolescence.

depreciation allowance.   A tax-deductible allowance to account for the decline in value or useful life of an asset due to wear, tear, obsolescence, or action of the elements.

derived demand.   Demand for a good or service that stems from the use of that good or service in the production of something else.

descriptive statistics.   A statistical application that employs quantitative expressions to describe characteristics of a sample or an underlying population.

development.   A real estate activity that involves adding improvements such as buildings.

differentiated product.   Products that are sufficiently different from competitive products to reduce the degree of substitutability. Producers of differentiated products have some degree of control over price.

diminishing marginal utility.   The economic principle that as additional units of a good are possessed or consumer per unit of time, the additional (marginal) utility of each successive unit is less than that of the preceding unit.

discounted cash-flow approach.   An investment evaluation technique that incorporates adjustments for both volume and timing of anticipated future cash flows and is generally accepted as the most desirable approach to evaluating opportunities.

discounting.   Expressing anticipated future cash flows as present-worth equivalents.

discount points.   A reduction in net loan proceeds to make the effective interest rate equal the current market rate.

discount rate.   A rate that measures return on investment after the recovery of invested capital.

discrete probability distribution.   A probability distribution in which possible outcomes are limited in number.

disintermediation.   The situation where people, seeking better yields, withdraw their savings from major institutional lenders and participate directly in financial markets.

diversification.   The reduction in total risk through holding a variety of property types and spreading ownership over a wide geographic area.

dominant tenement.   Land that reaps the benefit of an easement.

dower.   A wife's interest in her husband's property.

dram shop insurance.   Insurance against liability arising from incidents related to liquor consumption.

due process.   Proceedings in accordance with legal precedent, statutes, and constitutional provisions, designed to protect the rights of all parties to a dispute.

E

earnest money.   Money paid as evidence of good faith or actual intent to complete a transaction, usually forfeited by willful failure to complete the transaction.

earnest money deposit.   A good-faith deposit into an escrow account (or into a broker's trust account), typically accompanied by a purchase offer.

easement.   Nonpossessory interest that permits limited use of someone else's land. Conveys only a right to use the land.

easement appurtenant.   An easement created on one parcel of land (the servient tenement) for the benefit of an adjacent parcel (the dominant tenement).

easement by expressed grant.   Easement created by a specific agreement between the affected parties.

easement by implication.   An easement created as a consequence of a landowner selling property to which access requires crossing other property that the landowner also owns. Easements by implication are created when reasonably necessary, when the need is apparent at the time property is conveyed, and when the need appears to be permanent in nature.

easement by prescription.   An easement acquired through the open, continuous, adverse use of real property for a specified period of time.

easement in gross.   An easement that constitutes personal property, independent of any related land interest.

economic base analysis.   A study that divides economic activity into domestic and export sectors and seeks to determine the degree to which activity in the domestic sector is dependent on the level of activity in the export sector.

economic base theory.   An explanation of urban growth that postulates that total economic activity in an urban area is a function of the level of activity in its export sector.

economic obsolescence.   Loss in value due to inappropriate location.

Economic Recovery Tax Act of 1981.   A major revision of the Internal Revenue Code, enacted into law in 1981.

economic rent.   Profit generated by a good or service in excess of the profit necessary to induce firms to produce the good or service. Sometimes referred to as *pure profit*.

effective gross income.   Potential gross rental revenue, minus losses for vacancies and uncollectible accounts, plus income from related sources.

effective interest rates.   Rates actually paid for the use of borrowed funds. Effective rates are a function of the amount borrowed and the amount and timing of the required repayment.

efficient markets.   Markets in which all relevant information is immediately and fully reflected in market prices. Participants in efficient markets are unable to consistently achieve above-average market yields. The hypothesis that a market is completely efficient is referred to as the *strong form* of the efficiency hypothesis.

eminent domain.   Authority vested in both federal and state governments allowing them to take private property for public use without the owner's consent.

encumbrances.   A lien, charge, or claim against real property that diminishes the value of the property but does not prevent the passing of title.

end loan.   A loan secured by a mortgage on a completed building, terminating a chain of loans to finance land acquisition and construction. Also called a *permanent loan* or a *takeout loan*.

end-loan commitment.   An agreement by a lender to provide an end loan on satisfaction of all contingencies specified by the lender.

equilibrium.   In economics, a stable, balanced, or unchanging system. A situation in which there is no tendency for anything to change.

equilibrium price.   The price at which there will be sufficient quantity of a product to satisfy the desires of all consumers at that price but with no surplus remaining on the market; the market clearing price.

equitable right of redemption.   The legal right of a borrower, or the borrower's heirs or assigns to redeem mortgaged property for a limited period of time after default. Also called *equity of redemption*.

equity.   The concept of fairness and justice applied to the portion of common law relating to the rights and duties of individuals. Also the money value of what is owned, arrived at by subtracting all that is owed from the value of the ownership to arrive at a net ownership value figure.

equity buildup.   The accumulation and growth of the money value of what is owned. That is, an increase in the net financial interest in a specific property.

equity dividend rate.   Before-tax cash flow expressed as a percentage of the required initial equity cash outlay.

equity of redemption. *See* equitable right of redemption.

equity REIT.   A type of real estate investment trust that concentrates its resources on equity interests in real property.

equity yield rate.   Interest earned on recovered capital.

escalator clause.   Lease clause that requires tenants to pay all operating expenses above amounts specified in the lease.

escheat.   The legal principle that property title reverts to the state when an intestate owner (one with no will) dies with no heirs.

escrow.   The holding by a third party of something of value that is the subject of a contract between two other parties until the contract has been consummated.

escrow agent.   A disinterested third party who acts as agent for parties to an escrow agreement.

escrow agreement.   A contract between parties to a transaction and a third party who functions as an escrow agent. The agreement contains written escrow instructions, which govern the agent's action in performance of his or her escrow duties.

estate for years.   A leasehold interest that extends for an exactly specified period, after which the interest automatically expires.

estate subject to a condition precedent.   An estate created (rather than terminated) on the happening of some specified contingency.

excess accumulated earnings tax.   A penalty tax levied on corporations that accumulate earnings in excess of corporate needs.

excess cost recovery allowance.   Cost recovery allowance actually claimed, minus what would have been claimed had the taxpayer used the straight-line cost recovery method from the beginning.

executory.   A contract that lacks some necessary performance by one of its parties and is therefore not yet completed.

expected value.   The midpoint of a symmetric probability distribution; the most likely outcome.

explicit transfer costs.   Costs measurable in dollars; specifically, cost per mile of chosen transportation mode, plus the dollar value of the time spent en route. *See also* implicit transfer costs.

external costs.   Costs incurred by the public from the act or nonact of a private party. *See also* external diseconomies.

external diseconomies.   External costs where benefits accrue to the decision maker while costs are borne by others.

external economies.   A good side effect of production or consumption, for which no payment is received or made. *See also* externality.

externality.   A good or bad side effect of production or consumption, for which no payment is received or made.

F

facilities management.   Overseeing the physical upkeep of properties as well as keeping records of income and expenses associated with their operation.

factor of production.   Goods or services that are themselves intended to be utilized in producing other goods or services.

feasibility analysis.   An analysis of the likelihood of success of a specific proposed course of action.

feasibility study.   A study of the costs and benefits of a proposed course of action, to determine the likelihood of achieving project goals within the context of specified constraints and available resources. A proposal that has a reasonable probability of satisfying explicit objectives is considered feasible. A financial feasibility study addresses the question whether the proposed course of action will meet financial objectives.

Federal Deposit Insurance Corporation (FDIC). An independent federal agency that insures deposits up to a certain amount in all national banks and in all state banks that have been accepted as FDIC members.

fee simple absolute. The greatest real property interest recognized by law. This term expresses the idea that the interest is held with no preconditions or qualifications.

fee simple defeasible. A qualified fee estate that may be subject to a condition subsequent or determinable, depending on the nature of the qualification. Some states also permit creation of fees subject to conditions precedent.

fee simple estate. Any real property interest.

fee splitting. Analogous to life estates and remainders whereby title passes to or reverts on the occurrence of some event.

fee subject to a condition subsequent. A fee that extends only until the happening of some specified act or event.

fee tail. A carryover from the feudal system, requiring that title pass to lineal descendants of the property owner.

fiduciary. One who is in a position of trust or confidence with respect to another person.

financial assets. Asset such as promissory notes, bonds, and commercial paper that represent financial claims rather than ownership of physical assets.

financial intermediaries. Institutions such as commercial banks, savings and loan associations, credit unions, and so on, that act as go-betweens from savers to user-borrowers.

financial leverage. The impact of borrowed money on investment return. That is, the use of borrowed money to amplify consequences to equity investors.

financial management rate of return. A modification of the internal rate of return, designed to eliminate problems encountered when negative cash flows are included in the forecast.

financial risk. Risk that cash flow from a project will be insufficient to meet the investor's debt service obligation.

fiscal policy. Exercise of influence on the economy by controlling government spending and taxation.

footloose industries. Industries in which firms are not restricted geographically by transportation cost considerations. Such firms frequently seek locations with a ready supply of labor or minimal labor costs.

forecasting. Predicting a future value from known, related data.

foreclosure by sale. Sale of mortgaged property at public auction as a consequence of default by the mortgagor. Foreclosure by sale extinguishes the equitable right of redemption.

foreclosure decree. A court order specifying an exact time period (a period determined by state laws) during which the equity of redemption will exist.

free and clear rate of return. *See* overall capitalization rate.

freehold. An estate in real property that, unless assigned or otherwise conveyed, remains in perpetuity, or for life.

front-door approach. A type of preliminary financial feasibility study that involves estimating the minimum gross rent required to meet investors' threshold investment acceptability criteria.

fully amortized. The ultimate retirement of a mortgage debt through installment payments that include both interest and principal over the term of the loan.

functional efficiency. A measure of how well a property performs its intended function.

functional obsolescence. The loss of functional efficiency due to defective or dated design. This reduces a building's competitive position relative to more functionally efficient structures and may eventually lead to abandonment or succession of use.

fundamental analysis. An investment analysis technique that emphasizes investigation of the underlying business activity being undertaken by the firm whose securities are being considered.

G

gap financing. *See* standby financing.

general contractor. A contractor who takes full responsibility for construction of a project by formal agreement with the owner or developer and hires others as subcontractors to perform specific tasks.

general partner. *See* limited partnership.

general partnership. An entity in which all partners have equal rights to management and conduct of the firm; each partner is, in effect, an agent for the partnership.

gentrification. Reclamation of residential areas containing physically deteriorated buildings and restoration of a deteriorated neighborhood for the use of predominantly middle-class residents.

goods or services. Items offered for sale in the marketplace. *See also* product.

graduated-payment mortgage (GPM). A mortgage that allows a borrower, in effect, to borrow additional money during the early years of the mortgage to reduce the monthly mortgage payment obligation during those early years. This additional loan is added to the mortgage and is repaid by increased debt service obligations in the later years.

grantee. A person to whom a grant is made; the purchaser.

grantor. A person who conveys real estate by deed; the seller.

gross income. For income tax computation purposes, all revenue generated from any source, unless specifically excluded by provisions of the Internal Revenue Code.

gross income multiplier. Evaluation technique that describes the relationship between most probable sales price and gross revenue. Sometimes called a *gross rent multiplier*. *See also* income multiplier analysis *and* net income multiplier.

gross rent multiplier. *See* gross income multiplier.

H

health and safety codes. Rules and regulations designed to promote public health and safety in the construction and/or demolition of improvements to real property.

hedging. Taking an investment position that will pay off if the investor's primary investment does not. Hedging reduces aggregate investor risk.

historic structure. *See* certified historic structure.

holdover tenant. A tenant who remains in possession of real estate after the expiration of the lease.

housing codes. Laws specifying minimum building standards, with the objective of promoting public health, safety, or welfare.

hurdle rate. The minimum acceptable yield on investment funds. Projects that are not expected to yield at least the investor's hurdle rate are rejected.

hybrid REIT. A real estate investment trust that mixes mortgage and equity instruments in its portfolio.

I

implicit transfer costs. Indirect costs of moving goods or people between linked sites. Although they are often more difficult to identify than are explicit transfer costs, they may also be larger. *See also* explicit transfer costs.

income. For purposes of determining federal income tax liability, all revenue generated from any source unless specifically excluded by provisions of the Internal Revenue Code.

income multiplier analysis. A technique for expressing the relationship between price and either gross or net income. *See also* gross income multiplier *and* net income multiplier.

incubator buildings. Relatively small, multitenant structures in which new or small but growing firms rent space on an interim basis until growth generates a need for larger quarters.

independent variable. In regression or correlation analysis, a variable whose value is thought to be determined by factors other than those under analysis, but which is thought to affect the value of one or more other variables (the dependent variables) in the analysis.

indifference curve. A graphic presentation of combinations of values for two variables, representing the preferences of an individual who will be indifferent among the various combinations.

inferential statistics. The drawing of conclusions from evidence contained in statistical data.

inferior goods. Consumer goods for which demand decreases as purchasing power rises.

information search costs. The cost of generating relevant market information. High information search costs tend to reduce market efficiency.

initial tax basis. The tax basis of a property at the time of acquisition. Usually, cost plus any additional outlays required to ensure good and defensible title.

installment land contract. Contract that sets forth terms and conditions under which a seller is obligated to render deeds of conveyance to the buyer at some future date. Also called a *land contract*, *contract for deed*, *articles of agreement*, or *installment sales contract*.

installment method gain. The difference between gain on disposal of an asset that qualifies for installment method reporting and the recapture of accumulated depreciation or cost recovery allowances. Only this portion of the gain may be reported using the installment method. The remainder must be recognized in the taxable year of the transaction.

installment sales method. A method for reporting sales to the Internal Revenue Service whereby a portion of the resulting income tax liability may be deferred when some of the proceeds from the sale are not collected during the current taxable year.

insurable risk. Risk of loss from natural hazards such as fire, flood, storm, and so forth, that can be transferred to an insurance company.

interim financing. Financing used during the construction phase, to be superseded by takeout financing after construction is completed.

intermediate goods. Goods combined with other goods to create consumer products.

internal rate of return. A financial analysis technique that involves setting net present value at zero and finding a discount rate to satisfy the equality condition; that is, the discount rate that makes present value exactly equal to required initial cash outlay.

Internal Revenue Code. Public Law 591-Chapter 736. This law (as subsequently revised) constitutes the statutory authority for income, employment, estate, and gift taxes levied by the Internal Revenue Service. Generally referred to by tax practitioners more simply as *the Code*.

interpolation. A procedure for estimating values that fall between tabular amounts.

intrastate offering. A security issue offered for sale solely within one state by an issuer resident in or a corporation incorporated and doing business in that state. A qualifying intrastate offering is exempt from requirements for federal registration.

investment. Commitment of money or other assets in expectation of financial gain.

investment income. *See* portfolio income.

investment interest limitation. Provision of the Internal Revenue Code that places a dollar limit on the amount of investment interest that can be deducted in any one taxable year on loans used to finance investments.

investment tax credit. A credit against income tax liability, earned as a consequence of investing in qualifying assets.

investment value. The summation of the present value of the equity position plus the present value of the debt position. The present value of the equity position is calculated on an after-tax basis and considers the tax consequences to a specific investor.

investor. Any person or entity who takes an equity position in real estate for use in a trade or business or for production of income.

itemized deductions. Taxpayer expenditures, listed in Sections 161 through 195 of the Internal Revenue Code, that may be deducted from adjusted gross income to arrive at taxable income.

J

joint probabilities. The probability of joint occurrence of two or more events. The probability that both event A and event B will occur equals the probability that A will occur times the probability that B will occur, given that A occurs. This relationship is sometimes referred to as the *multiplicative law of probability*.

joint tenancy. An estate held jointly by two or more persons under the same title in which each has the same degree of interest and the same right of possession. Joint tenancy usually entails the right of the surviving tenant(s) to take title to a decedent's interest (right of survivorship). *See also* right of survivorship.

joint tenants. Parties who hold equal and undivided interests under joint tenancy.

judgment samples. A sampling technique that regards individual observations, with respect to certain characteristics, as typical of the underlying universe.

judicial partition. A court proceeding to terminate a cotenancy arrangement when the co-owners are unable to agree on terms for sale or physical division of jointly owned real estate.

junior mortgage. A mortgage that is legally subordinate to another (senior) mortgage.

L

land contract. *See* installment sales contract.

land development. The business activity of acquiring large tracts of land, subdividing, and selling off individual smaller tracts. Also frequently called *subdivision*.

land-use controls. Publicly imposed controls on land usage aimed at assuring orderly development.

lease. Legal document conveying limited right to use a property. Document generally specifies all terms of lease a well as permitted use.

leasehold. Right of a tenant in leased property.

leasehold estate. Estate of a tenant in a leased property.

leasehold interest. Interest of a tenant in a leased property.

lessee. The holder of a leasehold interest in a property. Generally referred to as a *tenant*.

lessor. A property owner who transfers certain rights for a limited period to a tenant. Generally referred to as a *landlord*.

license. Privilege to enter onto the land of a licenser in order to do certain things that would otherwise be considered trespassing.

lien. Claim against a property that allows the proceeds from a forced sale of the property to be used to satisfy the debt.

life estate. Grants a life tenant full property rights for the remainder of his or her life.

life tenant. Individual possessing full property rights in a specific property for the remainder of his or her life.

like-kind exchange. Exchanges of assets deemed under Internal Revenue Code Section 1031 to be of like kind. Gains or losses on exchanges that involve only like-kind assets must be deferred until the newly acquired (substitute) asset is disposed of. Transactions that are only partially like-kind may result in total or partial recognition of gains or losses. Also frequently called *tax-free exchanges* or *Section 1031 exchanges*.

limited partner. *See* limited partnership.

limited partnership. An ownership arrangement involving one or more general partners and one or more limited partners. General partners assume full liability for debts of the partnership and exercise control over operations, while a limited partner's liability is limited to the extent of actual capital contribution to the partnership or additional liability voluntarily assumed.

linkages. Relationships requiring the movement of goods or people from one location to another.

linked sites. Sites that are interrelated by linkages; that is, related by the need to move goods or people from one site to the other.

liquidation damages. Monetary award specified in a contract to be awarded to the damaged party in the event of a breach by either party.

liquidity. Ability to convert an asset to cash without incurring loss.

loanable funds. Monies hold by financial intermediaries in excess of required reserves; monies available to borrowers.

loan broker. Individual who places loans with primary lenders for a fee.

loan commitment. Obligation of a lender to provide specific funds at some future date. Terms may be specified, or they may be those prevailing on the date funds are advanced.

loan origination fee. A charge by a lender, assessed at the time a loan commitment is made or at the time funds are advanced.

loan proceeds. The face amount of a loan minus amounts deducted by the lender for items such as loan origination fees or discount points.

loan-to-value ratio. Relationship of debt funds to total project value, stated as a percentage.

locational advantages. Advantages, garnered by an occupant, due solely to the locational desirability of a site.

locational benefits. The benefits derived from the use of real estate that are properly attributable to the desirability of the site location.

longitudinal studies. Studies of relationships among variables, measuring changes in the variables through time. They involve repeated measures of the same phenomena to record any variation through time. Also called *time series studies*.

long run. Economic term used to describe the length of time necessary for the operation of market forces to produce equilibrium.

long-term capital gains. Term used in tax accounting to refer to gains realized on disposal of assets held for more than six months.

M

marginal benefits. Economic term used to describe the benefits derived from an additional unit of production.

In a financial sense, it might be used to describe the financial rewards of additional investment.

marginal cost. Economic term used to describe the cost associated with production of each additional unit of a good or service.

marginal cost of capital. The cost of an additional dollar of new capital funds.

marginal cost of production. The cost of adding one more unit per period to one's rate of production.

marginal revenue. Economic term used to describe revenue derived from an additional unit of a good or service sold.

marginal utility. Satisfaction derived from the consumption of an additional unit of some economic good or service.

market. Institutional arrangement that facilitates the exchange of good and/or services.

market data approach. One of the three traditional appraisal approaches. Produces an indication of value through the analysis of recent sales of similar properties.

market demand curve. Curve showing the amount of an economic good or service that will be demanded at various price levels. Demand curves are typically downward sloping, indicating that as price increases, demand decreases.

market price. *See* transaction price.

market rent. The rent a property would command on the open market if it were currently vacant and available.

market research. Activity undertaken to determine consumer attitudes; attempts to determine what consumers want, where they want it, and how much they are willing to pay for it.

market simulation. An attempt to replicate the actions of buyers and sellers in the marketplace. In real estate, it would be an attempt to estimate the outcome of a transaction involving real property by simulating the actions of "most probable" buyers and sellers.

market value. The price at which a property can be acquired on the open market in an arm's-length transaction under all conditions requisite to a fair sale. The generally accepted definition presumes that both buyer and seller act prudently and knowledgeably and that the price is not affected by undue stimulus experienced by either party.

materialmen. Suppliers of materials in connection with construction or improvements of real property.

materialman's lien. Claim arising from having supplied materials in connection with construction or improvement of real property.

mean. In statistics, the arithmetic average.

mechanic's lien. Lien securing a claim that stems from having provided services in connection with construction or improvement of a property.

metes and bounds. A method of delineating real property boundaries by references to enduring landmarks.

microeconomic theory. Theory of small economic units. Generally referred to as the *theory of the firm.*

modified internal rate of return. A variant of the internal rate of return, intended to eliminate the multiple root problem by discounting all negative cash flows back to the time an investment commitment must be made and by compounding all positive cash flows forward to the end of the final year of the investment holding period. The modified internal rate of return is the discount rate that equates the present value of all negative cash flows with the future value of all positive cash flows.

modified pass-throughs. Ginnie Mae security backed by a pool of insured mortgage loans. A pro-rata share of the repayment of interest and principal is "passed through" to holders of the pass-through securities.

Modified Uniform Limited Partnership Act. A modified version of the Uniform Limited Partnership Act, which carefully specifies actions limited partners can take without endangering their limited liability.

monetary policy. Use of control over the money supply to stimulate or dampen economic growth.

monopolistic competition. A market arrangement where any number of competitors sell goods or services sufficiently differentiated that buyers will not be entirely indifferent among them, so that selection will be affected by elements other than price alone.

monopoly elements. A characteristic of a good or service that differentiates it from other goods or services and thereby makes the others less acceptable as substitutes.

monthly constant. The monthly debt service obligation expressed as a percentage of the amount borrowed.

mortgage. A document that pledges real estate as collateral for a loan.

mortgage-backed securities. Securities backed by real estate mortgages as collateral.

mortgage bankers. Individuals or firms that originate real estate loans. They may either hold such loans in their own investment portfolios or sell them in the secondary market.

mortgage commitment. Obligation on the part of a lender to provide funds at some future date. Loan terms may be either fixed or those that prevail at the time the funds are to be advanced.

mortgage correspondents. Individual mortgage bankers or brokers representing an institutional lender in a specified geographic location.

mortgagee. Party to whom real estate is pledged under the terms of a mortgage. Typically the lender in a real estate transaction.

mortgage participation certificates. A bond backed by real estate as collateral. Bondholders participate in the proceeds of a group of mortgages that back the certificates.

mortgage REIT. A real estate investment trust that invests primarily in real estate loans secured by first mortgages.

mortgage warehousing. The process of inventorying real estate loans. Mortgage bankers or brokers sometimes inventory loans while assembling pools of loans for subsequent transfer to larger institutional real estate lenders.

mortgagor. Party pledging real estate under the terms of a mortgage. Borrower who pledges real estate as collateral for a loan.

most fitting use. Real estate use that optimally reconciles all public and private interests.

most probable selling price. A probabilistic estimate of the price at which a future property transaction will occur; a prediction of the transaction price that will emerge if a property is offered for sale under current market conditions for a reasonable length of time at terms of sale currently predominant for such properties.

most probable use. Use to which a property is most likely to be put. Recognizes that use is not certain. Most probable use is that use having the highest probability of occurrence. Recognizes the possibility of other uses while assigning lower probabilities to them.

multiple nuclei. The theory that once a metropolitan area's major central business district is completely developed, a series of miniature central business districts will spring up throughout the metropolitan area.

multiple regression. Statistical technique used to measure the association between a dependent variable and multiple independent variables.

multiplicative law of probability. *See* joint probabilities.

N

natural price. Adam Smith's concept of long-run, market-determined price. Smith held that the price of all goods and services will, over the long run, equal the cost of production.

neighborhood. Sometimes referred to as a grouping of similar buildings, residents, or business enterprises.

neighborhood influences. Factors influencing the desirability of a neighborhood. These include physical, economic, and locational characteristics.

neighborhood shopping centers. Shopping centers that serve a trade area from which customers can commute by automobile within roughly five to ten minutes. Anchor tenants are usually food stores and drugstores, which may occupy a combined total area between 35,000 and 50,000 square feet.

net cash flow. Net monetary benefits an individual or group of individuals receive as a reward for committing funds to an enterprise. Net cash flow before taxes ignores the tax effect of investments, and net cash flow after taxes accounts for the tax effects of investment.

net income multiplier. Property market value expressed as a multiple of its net operating income. *See also* gross income multiplier *and* income multiplier analysis.

net lease. Lease arrangement under which tenants are required to pay all property operating costs.

net operating expenses. Total expenses associated with the operations of a real estate project.

net operating income. Effective gross revenue minus operating expenses.

net present value. Current capital value of all the benefits of an investment, minus the required initial cash outlay.

nominal interest rates. Quoted cost of borrowing. Actual or effective interest rates may be substantially higher due to charges such as loan origination fees and the cost of maintaining required compensating balances.

normalized expenses. An appraisal term for the operating expenses of a property as they would occur in a typical year.

normalized net operating income. The net income figure that results when a typical year's operating expenses are subtracted from a typical year's effective gross income.

O

obligee. Individual who makes a promise to pay a specified sum under the terms of a promissory note. Typically a borrower.

obligor. Individual to whom a promise is made to pay a specified sum under the terms of a promissory note. Typically a lender.

offering memorandum. A document intended to fully disclose the nature of a private offering of a security.

oligopoly. A market arrangement characterized by few producers, into which entry by new producers is extremely difficult.

operating expense ratio. Operating expenses expressed as a percentage of effective gross income.

operating expenses. Cash expenditures required to maintain property in sufficient condition to generate effective gross revenue.

operating ratio. *See* operating expense ratio.

operative words of conveyance. Words used to indicate the intention to transfer title to real property.

opportunity cost of capital. Forgone opportunity to earn interest on funds committed to other investments.

option agreement. An agreement giving one party the right to buy or sell an asset within a specified time period at a fixed or determinable price.

overall capitalization rate. Net operating income divided by a property's market value. Also called the *free and clear rate of return.*

P

partial release. A mortgage clause providing for segments of a property to be released after specified lump-sum payments on the loan. Typically used in subdivision and development financing.

partnership. An association of two or more people who join together to carry on a business for profit.

partnership agreement. Document that specifies the rights and responsibilities of individuals who join together to carry on a business for profit. May be oral, but is usually written.

party wall. An exterior wall common to two contiguous structures, each under different ownership.

passive activity. Any trade or business is a passive activity for a taxpayer who is not actively involved in operations on a "regular, continuous, and substantial (year-round) basis."

passive activity income. Income from passive trade or business activities. Income from passive activities can be used to offset losses from other passive activities. Any passive activity income not offset by losses is merged with taxable income from other sources. *See also* passive activity.

passive activity losses. Losses from passive trade or business activities. Passive activity losses can generally be offset against only passive activity income. Any remaining passive activity losses, with certain important exceptions, must be carried over and applied against future years' passive activity income, even though a taxpayer may have substantial taxable income from nonpassive sources during the year of the loss. *See also* passive activity.

pass-through certificates. Certificates backed by a pool of insured mortgages. Interest and principal collected are used to pay interest on the certificates as well as retire them.

payback period. The amount of time required for an investor to recover the capital committed to a venture.

payee. Individual to whom a promise has been made to repay a specified sum at some future date under the provisions of a promissory note.

percentage clause. Lease provision that specifies rental based on some base rate, plus a percentage of the tenant's gross sales.

percentage lease. Lease that provides for rental payments based on the tenant's gross sales.

permanent loan. *See* end loan.

perpetuity. A never-ending stream of payments or receipts.

personal consumption expenditures. Economic term used to describe individual spending on such items as food, shelter, and clothing.

personal property. Ownership interests in all properties other than real property. Examples include securities, partnership interest in a business, and ownership of an automobile. Also called *personalty.*

personalty. *See* personal property.

physical deterioration. Term used by appraisers to describe any loss in value due to physical wear.

physical durability. Ability of a building to withstand physical wear and tear.

plat. Diagram of a proposed subdivision, showing the location of all streets, sites, and easements.

police power. Power of a municipality to enforce laws designed to promote health, safety, morals, and general welfare. Building codes, planning objectives, and zoning ordinances are all enforced through the exercise of police power.

population. In statistics, the entire universe of data from which samples are drawn.

portfolio income. Income from interest, dividends, rents, royalties, gain from disposition of investment property, passive activity income that is treated as portfolio income under the phase-in rules of the Tax Reform Act of 1986, and income from a trade or business in which the taxpayer does not materially participate (unless the activity is a "passive activity" under the passive loss rules).

portfolio risk. Overall risk associated with ownership of a group of assets. Risks associated with one investment may decline when combined with another investment having offsetting risk patterns.

possibility of a reverter. Residual interest in a property that becomes effective when a life estate terminates.

potential gross income. The maximum amount of revenue a property would produce if fully rented at market rates.

potential gross rent. The amount of rental revenue a property would generate if there were no vacancies.

preliminary prospectus. Memorandum providing full disclosure of all items pertinent to a public security offering. A preliminary prospectus must be submitted to and approved by the Securities and Exchange Commission prior to any advertising of the offering.

prepaid interest. Interest paid prior to the date on which it is due. In real estate loans, prepaid interest is often deducted from the loan amount when funds are advanced.

prepayment clause. Typically a clause in a mortgage specifying penalties to be paid by the borrower in the event a loan is prepaid.

present value. The value today of anticipated future receipts or disbursements.

present value approach. Technique used to express anticipated future cash flows in terms of their current worth by adjusting for the opportunity cost of capital.

present value of an annuity. Present worth of a series of level payments received at even intervals. Current value reflects the compounded opportunity cost of capital.

price elasticity. A measure of the responsiveness of supply (price elasticity of supply) or demand (price elasticity of demand) to changes in price of a product or service.

price inelastic. A market condition in which price reductions cause a decline in total revenue and price increases result in increased total revenue. *See also* price elasticity.

price makers. Economic units operating on a large enough scale to have some control over the price of their goods or services in the marketplace.

price searchers. Economic units that recognize that they cannot completely control the price at which goods are exchanged, but also understand that they do affect market prices. Price searchers must be constantly aware of the impact their pricing decisions will have on the decisions of competitors.

price takers. Economic units operating on such a small scale that they have no control over the price of their goods or services in the marketplace.

primary data. Data gathered by researchers specifically for the problem with which they are currently grappling.

primary mortgage markets. Markets in which real estate loans originate.

principal. In finance, the amount on which interest liability is computed.

principal meridians. Imaginary lines extending north and south between the Earth's poles, used as reference lines in property surveys.

principle of substitution. Valuation principle stating that a person is not justified in paying more for a property than the cost to construct or acquire a substitute property.

private goods. Economic goods where consumption by one individual reduces the amount available for consumption by others.

private grants. Voluntary transfer of title to real property. These include transfer for consideration, gifts, and bequests.

private offering. *See* private placement.

private placement. Sale of a securities offering to a small group as opposed to a public offering, where sale is advertised to the general public. Sometimes called a *private offering*.

private placement memorandum. Prospectus for a private placement. Does not have to be submitted for SEC approval, but must provide full disclosure.

probability. A measure of the chance of occurrence associated with any possible outcome.

probability distribution. An array of all possible outcomes and their related probabilities of occurrence.

probability of acceptance error. The probability that accepting a proposed investment will prove to have been a mistake.

processing costs. The cost of converting unfinished goods to finished goods.

product. (*See also* goods and services.) The end result of the production process.

productivity. The ability of a property to generate utility or want-satisfying power. A property's ability to command rent is a measure of its productivity.

profitability index. Measure of present value per dollar of cash outlay, calculated by dividing the present value of expected future cash flows by the initial cash outlay.

promissory note. Agreement containing promise to pay a specified sum at some specific future date.

property management. Overseeing the operations of real property for others. Includes renting space, collecting rentals, supervising maintenance, budgeting, etc.

prospectus. A document that fully discloses the nature of a securities offering.

public goods. Economic goods or services for which consumption by one individual does not reduce the amount available for consumption by others. Also called *collective goods*.

public infrastructure. In real estate, the systems used to deliver public services to a site. Includes streets, sidewalks, sewer pipes, water pipes, etc.

public issue. Securities issue offered for sale to the general public. Such an issue requires registration of a prospectus with the Securities and Exchange Commission. Also referred to as a *public offering*.

public offering. *See* public issue.

purchase-money mortgage. Mortgage given by a buyer to a seller to secure part payment of the purchase price. A purchase-money mortgage is typically recorded when deed is passed, establishing its precedence over all other claims.

purchase option. The right to purchase a property within a specified time and at a predetermined price.

pure profit. *See* economic rent.

Q

quantity demanded. Amount of an economic good or service purchasers will buy per period of time at a specific price.

quantity survey method. A technique used to estimate the cost of new real property improvements. Costs are estimated in the same way an architect or builder figures construction costs.

quarter sections. Squares resulting from the intersection of guide meridians and standard parallels are divided into 36 sections, each containing 640 acres. Sections are then divisible into four quarter sections containing 160 acres each.

quiet title suit. Suit filed by an adverse possessor to gain title to property by adverse possession.

quitclaim deed. A deed that purports to convey only those rights in a property that are possessed by the person making the conveyance, with no warrants that any such rights in fact exist.

R

radial/axial development. Theory of urban development based on the idea that businesses locate along major arterial streets, creating a radial or axial pattern of growth outward from the central business district.

real assets. Physical things with economic value, such as land, buildings, machinery, gold, antiques, and so forth. In contrast with financial assets such as promissory notes, bonds, and commercial paper, real assets tend to hold their value during periods of price inflation.

real estate investment. Acquiring an ownership or a leasehold interest in real property, with a profit motive.

real estate investment trusts (REITs). Untaxed corporate entities organized to pool the resources of individual investors for investment in real estate. Some REITs invest in mortgages while others take ownership positions.

real estate service. Benefits of use of real property. Real estate provides shelter and location for users.

Real Property Administrator (RPA). Professional designation conferred on property managers by the Building Owners and Managers Association International. Designation is a sign of professional achievement for those who completely fulfill prescribed educational and experiential requirements.

recording statutes. Statutory provisions for permanent records of all transactions involving real property.

recovery property. Property subject to the cost recovery allowance provisions first introduced into the tax system by the 1981 revision of the Internal Revenue Code.

rectangular survey system. Use of a grid-type arrangement to identify land in a branch area by reference to a single geographic point.

redevelopment. Process of clearing older structures in an area and replacing them with new buildings.

red herring. Term sometimes used for a preliminary securities prospectus, which must be submitted to and approved by the Securities and Exchanger Commission before any advertising is undertaken for a public issue.

redlining. Term used to describe the unwillingness of certain financial institutions to provide real property financing in certain areas; derived from the practice of delineating areas with red lines on city maps.

regional planning. Setting standards for the overall development of large geographical areas. Standards apply to land use, transportation systems, infrastructure, etc.

regional shopping center. A shopping center that draws the majority of its customers from a trade area extending from 15 to 30 minutes in driving time from the center. It may encompass 200,000 to 400,000 square feet of retail space and usually features one or two major department stores as anchor tenants.

registered historic district. Any area listed in the National Registry of Historic Places. Also includes any area so designated by appropriate state or local statute, provided that the Secretary of the Interior certifies that the statute will substantially achieve its purpose of preservation and rehabilitation and that the district meets substantially all the requirements for listing in the National Registry.

regression analysis. Statistical technique used to measure the association among two or more variables.

Regulation B. Implementing regulation of the Federal Reserve to enforce provisions of the Equal Credit Opportunity Act enacted in 1974.

Regulation Z. Implementing regulation of the Federal Reserve to enforce provisions of the Truth-in-Lending Act enacted in 1969.

rehabilitation. Process of refurbishing older or physically deteriorated buildings for current use.

reliction. Recession of the water line of a lake or river resulting in the exposure of additional dry land.

remainderman. Individual possessing a remainder interest in real property. Remainder interest becomes operative on expiration of a life estate.

remainders. Residual interests that become effective when the life estate of another ends. *See also* reversion.

renegotiable rate mortgage. Mortgage with an interest rate subject to redetermination at fixed intervals, as specified in the body of the mortgage or the accompanying promissory note.

rent concessions. Agreements between landlord and tenant that reduce actual rental payments or receipts below those specified in a lease. A landlord might, for example, give one month's free occupancy, thereby reducing the effective rental rate over the entire occupancy period. Also simply called *concessions*.

rent escalator clauses. Lease provisions that require tenants to pay all operating expenses above amounts specified in their leases.

rent roll. A record of all tenants, showing the rent paid by each.

replacement cost. Appraisal term used to describe the cost of building a structure similar in utility to the one for which value is being estimated. Replacement cost assumes construction at current standards.

reproduction cost. Appraisal term used to describe the cost of building a structure identical to the one for which value is being estimated.

reservation. Clause used in a deed to withhold some portion of the grantor's property rights.

reserve for repairs and replacements. Appraisal adjustment used in the normalization of operating expenses to account for repairs or replacements that do not occur on an annual basis.

residential member (RM). Professional designation conferred by the American Institute of Real Estate Appraisers on individuals specializing in residential valuation. Designation signifies satisfaction of prescribed educational and experiential requirements.

residential specialists. Real estate brokers who concentrate on the sale of single-family detached dwellings, townhouses, condominiums, or cooperatives.

residual capitalization. Appraisal technique that splits income between land and building. If building value is known, remaining income is capitalized to estimate land value, and if land value is known, remaining income is capitalized to estimate building value.

restrictive covenant. Promise to refrain from using land or buildings for purposes specified in the clause creating the covenant.

revenue bonds. Securities used to finance revenue-generating projects where the income produced by the undertaking will be used for interest payments and retirement of securities.

reversion. Term used to describe the interest of one who will receive title if a conditional fee is extinguished.

right of survivorship. A right unique to joint tenancy. Should one joint tenant die, his or her interest passes to the remaining joint tenants. *See also* joint tenancy.

right to rescind. Right of an individual to terminate an agreement, returning all parties to the legal position or relationship existing prior to the agreement.

riparian lands. Lands abutting waterways or lakes. Title may extend to the water's edge or to the center of the water, depending on whether the waterway is navigable.

risk. Measurable likelihood of variance from an expected outcome. Risk is generally measured as variance or standard deviation.

risk-adjusted discount rate. A discount rate that includes the minimum acceptable yield on a riskless investment, plus a premium to compensate the investor for perceived risk associated with the venture under consideration.

risk averters. Refers to the economic concept that individuals prefer less risk to more at a given level of return. Most individuals avoid risk and will assume additional risk only if it is accompanied by expectations of additional return.

risk-free discount rate. Opportunity cost of capital based on riskless alternative investments.

risk premium. Incremental return necessary to induce investors to assume additional risk.

risk-reward indifference curve. A graphic representation of the relationship between perceived risk and acceptable rates of expected return where the investor will be equally satisfied by all risk-reward combinations.

r-square (r^2). *See* coefficient of determination.

S

S corporation.   *See* tax option corporation.

sample.   A group of observations drawn from a larger body of data (called a *population* or *universe*) and thought to be representative of the larger body.

secondary data.   Data employed in a research project that were previously gathered for some other purpose.

secondary financial markets.   Markets comprising arrangements for buying and selling existing financial instruments.

secondary mortgage market.   A market in which existing mortgage notes are traded.

Section 1031 exchange.   *See* like-kind exchange.

sector theory.   A theory developed by Homer Hoyt and based on the observation that successive waves of residential development within a given socioeconomic class tend to continue outward from the urban center in a wedge-shaped pattern.

seizin.   A covenant found in a warranty deed whereby the grantor warrants that he or she does in fact possess the rights or interest being transferred.

senior mortgage.   A mortgage that takes priority over all other mortgages.

Senior Real Estate Analyst (SREA).   A professional designation awarded by the Society of Real Estate Appraisers.

Senior Real Property Appraiser (SRPA).   A professional designation awarded by the Society of Real Estate Appraisers. The SRPA designation is awarded to commercial and industrial appraisers.

Senior Residential Appraiser (SRA).   A professional designation awarded by the Society of Real Estate Appraisers.

sensitivity analysis.   Financial analysis in which all variables but one are held constant and the result of a change in the remaining variable on the outcome is analyzed.

serial bonds.   Secured debt instruments that are retired in the sequence of their individual serial numbers.

serial correlation.   A measure of the extent to which causal factors influence outcomes over two or more time periods.

servient tenement.   Land bearing the burden of an easement appurtenant.

shift in demand.   The result of a shift in the relationship between price and quantity.

short-term capital gains.   Taxable gains on the sale of capital assets that have been owned for six months or less.

simple linear regression.   A statistical technique used to measure the association between two variables.

simulation.   The construction of a model intended as a simplified representation of realty, within which the impact of various factors can be isolated and quantified.

sinking fund payments.   Payments drawn from a fund set aside from the income of property that, with accrued interest, will eventually pay for replacement of the improvements.

sinking fund recapture technique.   A recapture computation that involves computing the recapture rate such that the sum of recovered capital and compound interest thereon will, over the useful life of the wasting asset, accumulate an amount equal to its cost.

space-time.   A four-dimensional concept combining the three dimensions of space with a fourth dimension of time. Real estate services are typically sold in space-time units.

special agent.   One whose authority to act is limited to a particular job or a specific task. Typically, a real estate broker acts in the capacity of a special agent.

special assessment.   A legal charge against real estate by a public authority to pay the cost of public improvements such as streetlights, sidewalks, and other street improvements.

special warranty deed.   A deed in which the grantor warrants or guarantees title only against defects arising during his or her ownership of the property and not against preexisting defects.

specific asset syndication. A type of syndication where the promoter gains control of a property and then assembles a group of investors.

speculation. Assumption of business risk in hope of gain; purchase or sale of assets in hope of benefiting from market fluctuations.

speculative construction. A business strategy where a developer/builder starts construction before any homes are sold, in anticipation of sufficient market demand to render the project profitable.

spread. The difference between interest earned on mortgage loans and interest paid to depositors by financial intermediaries.

standard deviation. A measure of dispersion about the mean of a probability distribution, frequently employed as an indication of risk associated with an investment venture. The square root of the variance.

standard error of the forecast. The degree of confidence to be placed in a forecast value for a dependent variable. Conceptually similar to the same measure as calculated in simple linear regression.

standard metropolitan statistical area. A federally designated geographically described urban area with cohesive patterns of trade, communication, employment, and transportation.

standard parallels. Imaginary lines running parallel with base lines (east-west lines) at 24-mile intervals, used as reference points in surveys employing the rectangular survey method.

standby financing. An arrangement where a lender agrees to keep a certain amount of money available to a prospective borrower for a specified period of time.

standby forward commitment. An agreement for future purchase of mortgage notes at yield rates specified in advance. These commitments are sold by and binding on Fannie Mae but are optional for holders of the commitments.

standby loan commitment. A binding option sold for a nonreturnable standby fee by a lender to a borrower, providing that the lender will loan a specific amount on stated terms to a borrower at any time within a stated future period. The borrower may or may not exercise the option.

statistical induction. Drawing conclusions about an underlying population from data contained in a sample.

statistical inference. Drawing conclusions about the future from a measured record of the past.

statutory exemption. The portion of income that is exempt from the alternative minimum tax.

statutory right of redemption. A statutory right granting a defaulting mortgagor an additional opportunity to recover foreclosed property. Limited in time by state statute.

straight-line method. A method of computing depreciation or cost recovery allowances whereby the allowance is claimed in equal annual increments.

strict foreclosure. Foreclosure accomplished by transferring a defaulting mortgagor's title directly to the mortgagee.

strong form efficiency hypothesis. *See* efficient markets.

subagent. One appointed by an agent to perform some duty, in whole or in part relating to the agency.

subcontractor. A person who contracts to do work for someone who has a larger contract to do the job. For example, electrical work on a new house might be done on a subcontract for the contractor who has overall responsibility for building the house.

subdivider. One who buys undeveloped acreage wholesale, segments it into smaller parcels, and sells it retail.

subdivision. *See* land development.

subdivision controls. Regulations imposed by various levels of government to regulate or control subdivision operations.

subjective value. The value of an asset to the present owner or to a prospective purchaser. Similar to the economic concept of value in use.

subordination agreement. A clause in a mortgage or lease stating that the right of the holder shall be secondary or subordinate to a subsequent encumbrance.

subscription agreement. A document that specifies the relationship between limited partners and the sponsoring general partner in a limited partnership arrangement.

substitute basis. The initial tax basis of property acquired in a like-kind exchange. The substitute basis reflects any deferred gain or loss on the property tendered in the exchange.

summation technique. A method used for developing capitalization rates, based on the idea that investors must be compensated to induce them to invest their wealth and that additional compensation is required for risk bearing and for illiquidity.

superregional shopping center. A shopping center that draws customers from an extremely wide geographic area and supports very large concentrations of retail facilities. Superregional centers frequently feature as much as 500,000 to 750,000 square feet of retail space. They may have as many as four major department stores as anchor tenants.

supply. The relationship between price and the quantity of a product suppliers place on the market during a specified time period, for all possible prices.

supply to sell. Desired decrease in a market participant's inventory of a product, at a specific price.

symmetric probability distribution. A probability distribution in which each side is a mirror image of the other.

syndicate. A group of two or more people united for the purpose of making and operating an investment. A syndicate may operate as a corporation, a general partnership, or a limited partnership.

T

table of residuals. A listing of differences between actual values for a variable and those values predicted by a regression equation.

takeout loan. *See* end loan.

tax auction. A procedure for selling tax-delinquent land or real property where verbal or written offers are taken and the property is sold to the highest bidder.

tax basis. *See* initial tax basis.

tax conduit. A partnership characteristic whereby tax-deductible losses "pass through" the partnership "conduit" and are reported by each partner in accordance with his or her individual ownership interest in the partnership.

tax credits. Direct offsets against a taxpayer's income tax liability, provided as tax incentives to induce action thought to be in the best interests of the nation.

tax deductions. Reductions in taxable income. *See also* itemized deductions.

tax deed. A deed to property taken by government for nonpayment of taxes and resold at auction pursuant to law.

tax-deferred exchange. *See* like-kind exchange.

tax-free exchange. *See* like-kind exchange.

tax lien. A lien placed on a taxpayer's property by government for nonpayment of taxes.

tax option corporation. A qualifying corporation whose shareholders have elected to be taxed directly for their shares of corporate income, rather than having the corporation itself incur income tax liability. Provisions are found in Subchapter S of the Internal Revenue Code. Sometimes called an *S corporation*.

tax preference item. Tax deductions or exemptions that are added back to adjusted gross income for purposes of computing the alternative minimum tax liability.

tax schedule income. The amount of taxable income used as a reference for computing income tax liability when employing tax rate schedules provided by the Internal Revenue Service.

tax stops. Lease provisions that require tenants to pay all property taxes beyond some specified level.

technical analysis. Attempting to estimate future changes in market values by investigating the past market behavior.

tenancy at sufferance. Wrongful occupancy, which can be terminated by a property owner at any time.

tenancy at will. A tenancy stating no fixed period and that either landlord or tenant may terminate at any time, or in the time specified by statute, usually 30 days.

tenancy by the entirety. A type of joint tenancy that can exist only between spouses, in which wife and husband take conveyance of the tenancy interest in common, with that interest being treated as a single, indivisible unit and with the survivor continuing to hold the tenancy as a matter of right.

tenancy from period to period. A tenancy by one who holds a leasehold interest for an unstated period and pays rent each period, each payment serving as renewal for an additional period. This often results from the holding over of a previous specified-term tenancy on which rental was paid each period.

tenancy in common. Tenancy by two or more parties holding an interest in the same property, that interest being undivided, although not necessarily equal in each holder.

theorems. Fundamental mathematical rules from which various mathematical operations are derived.

time preference for money. Preference for more immediate rather than delayed receipt of funds, so that investment benefits are more valued the sooner they are received.

time series surveys. *See* longitudinal studies.

time value of money. *See* time preference for money.

title closing. The meeting of parties to a sales contract at a designated place and time for the purpose of executing the contract.

title defect. A possible legal difficulty that may limit the marketability of the title.

title insurance. Insurance against losses resulting from the passage of legally invalid title, issued by a title insurance company after a title search by that company has established that legally valid title exists in the seller, who then is able to pass that title to the insured.

title insurance policy. A contract wherein the title insurer agrees to indemnify the insured against losses resulting from imperfect title.

title search. A circumspect review of all documents and records in the recorder's office pertaining to a property to determine if the seller has good title to the property.

title transfer. To convey or relinquish title to another party.

Torrens system. A system of registering title to real property that accurately determines the ownership of land and every lien and claim on it. Under this system, land title is registered in much the same way as is title to an automobile.

township. A six-mile-square area containing 36 sections, each one mile square, used in the rectangular survey system of land description.

trade area. The geographic area from which a store or shopping center draws the majority of its patronage.

transaction costs. Items such as brokerage fees, recording fees, transfer taxes, and attorney fees incurred in connection with a real estate transaction.

transaction price. The price at which a transaction actually occurred; the outcome of a bargaining process between buyer and seller. Sometimes called *market price*.

transaction range. The range of prices at which a transaction can occur between an owner and a prospective purchaser. The owner's subjective value determines the lower level of the transactions range; the prospective buyer's subjective value determines the upper level.

transactions balances. The quantity of money required to finance general business operations and satisfy day-to-day demands of householders.

transfer costs. Costs of transportation between linked sites. *See also* implicit transfer costs *and* explicit transfer costs.

transport breakpoints. Points along major transportation routes where the mode of transport must change.

trust account. A bank account separate and apart and physically segregated from a broker's own funds, in which a broker is required by state law to deposit all monies collected for clients. Similar to an escrow or special account.

trust agreement. A document that sets forth terms of security arrangements and instructs the trustee in the event of default.

trust deed. *See* deed of trust.

trustee. The person in a trust relationship who holds property for the benefit of another person (the beneficiary).

trust indenture. *See* deed of trust.

Truth-in-Lending Act. One of a series of modern consumer protection acts, requiring lenders to fully disclose the rates of interest, other charges, and all terms and conditions of each loan, in writing and clearly stated.

U

uncertainty. An environment holding an unknown number of possible outcomes, where there is no significant information about the relative chance of occurrence of each.

unfavorable financial leverage. Use of borrowed funds when their cost exceeds the rate of return on assets being financed.

Uniform Limited Partnership Act. A model law to govern creation and operation of limited partnership entities that has been enacted (in some cases, in substantially revised form) by every state except Louisiana.

unit-in-place method. A means of assessing replacement costs, in which an appraiser estimates the cost of building components separately, developing a unit cost for each component, and including overhead and profit allocation estimates as well as direct labor and materials cost, and then adds all costs together to reach total cost and thereby replacement cost.

universal agents. Agents who are empowered to perform all legal acts for their principals.

universe. In statistics, the entire population of data from which samples are drawn.

urban growth. An increase in the intensity of use of land resources. This may or may not entail an increase in population of an urban land area. It usually includes higher capital investment per unit of land employed and increased productivity associated with urban economic processes.

useful life. The period over which a property will benefit the owner's trade or business.

utility. An economic term for the want-satisfying power embodied in a good or service.

V

value in exchange. The value an asset can command in the marketplace.

value in use. The value of an asset to its owner or to a prospective owner.

variable-rate mortgage. A financing instrument that permits the lender to alter the interest rate, with a certain period of advanced notice, based on a specific base index.

variance. A measure of dispersion of possible values about the midpoint of a probability distribution of possible outcomes, frequently employed as a measure of risk. The square of the standard deviation.

vendee. The purchaser of real estate under articles of agreement or a contract for deed.

vendor. The seller of real estate under articles of agreement or a contract for deed.

void. To have no force or effect; that which is unenforceable.

voidable. That which is capable of being adjudged void but is not void unless action is taken to make it so.

voluntary conveyance. Voluntary transfer by a defaulting mortgagor of the mortgaged property to the mortgagee, to avoid a foreclosure suit and a possible deficiency judgment.

W

warranty deed. A deed that contains a clause warranting that title to real property is clear and the property is unencumbered.

weighted average cost of capital. Capital cost computed by weighting the cost of each component in accordance with the proportion of total capital it comprises.

wholesale price index.   An index of changes in the wholesale price of a representative "basket" of goods, referenced to a specified base period.

worker's compensation insurance.   Insurance against claims for injuries sustained by employees.

wraparound lender.   Assumes responsibility for meeting debt service obligations on the mortgage note that has been "wrapped." *See also* wraparound mortgage.

wraparound mortgage.   A mortgage subordinate to, but still including, the balance due on a preexisting mortgage note, in addition to any amount to be disbursed on the new note. Also called an *all-inclusive mortgage*.

Z

zoning ordinance.   The fixing by government of geographic areas in which specified kinds of buildings and businesses may be developed.

zoning regulations.   *See* zoning ordinance.

INDEX